Dr Ernst Doblhofer was born and educated in Austria. He has written a previous book, on Byzantine historiographers, and has translated into German the works of many leading American and British writers. In his capacity as philologist, he took part in Anatolian excavations, in charge of the epigraphic work to be done there in the field of the classical languages.

Ernst Doblhofer

Voices in Stone

The Decipherment of
Ancient Scripts and Writings

Translated by Mervyn Savill

PALADIN
GRANADA PUBLISHING
London Toronto Sydney New York

Published by Granada Publishing Limited
in Paladin Books 1973
Reprinted 1979

ISBN 0 586 08119 4

First published in Great Britain by
Souvenir Press Ltd 1961

Granada Publishing Limited
Frogmore, St Albans, Herts AL2 2NF
and
3 Upper James Street, London W1R 4BP
1221 Avenue of the Americas, New York, NY 10020, USA
117 York Street, Sydney, NSW 2000, Australia
100 Skyway Avenue, Toronto, Ontario, Canada M9W 3A6
Trio City Coventry Street, Johannesburg 2001, South Africa
CML Centre, Queen & Wyndham, Auckland 1, New Zealand

Printed in Great Britain by
Fletcher & Son Ltd, Norwich
Set in Monotype Baskerville

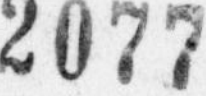

CONTENTS

Foreword ix

I. An introduction to writing 13

II. The riddle of the Sphinx: the decipherment of Egyptian writing 38

III. Ahura Mazda came to my aid: the decipherment of Old Persian cuneiform 85

IV. In cuneiform on six bricks: the decipherment of Mesopotamian cuneiform 121

V. Wedge and symbol of the land of Hatti: the interpretation of Hittite cuneiform and the decipherment of Hittite hieroglyphs 149

VI. "Cape Fennel" at "White Harbour" and Gubla the "city of paper": the decipherment of Ugaritic and Gublitic 203

VII. Of gods and princes of commerce: the decipherment of the Cypriote syllabary 227

VIII. War chariots and beakers: the decipherment of Creto-Mycenaean Linear B 238

IX. Prince Kül-Tigin, Bilge-Kagan and the wise Tonjukuk: the decipherment of the Old Turkish runic script 271

X. Decipherments of tomorrow: Etruscan, the scripts of the Indus Valley and of Easter Island . .

Notes 294

Bibliography 318

Index 323

PHOTOGRAPHS

Cuneiform script

Karnak. Obelisk of Queen Hatshepsut

Darius I

Behistun. The Darius bas-relief

Royal Hittite family at a banquet

Hittite hieroglyphic inscription from Hama

Jean François Champollion

Ignace J. Gelb

John Chadwick

Charles Virolleaud

The back of an Etruscan mirror

The two sides of the Phaistos Disc

Seals of the Indus Valley culture

Easter Island Statue of Hoa-haka-nana-ea

Ganj-i-Nameh

Cretan seal: hunting scene, labyrinth

Temple of Byblos

Naksh-i-Rustam

Inscription of King Araras from Jerablus-Carchemish

Akhnaton and Nefertiti

Page from an Egyptian Book of the Dead

SOURCES OF THE FIGURES IN THE TEXT

From F. Babinger: *Eine neuentdeckte ungarische Kerbschrift aus Konstantinopel vom Jahre 1515*, in Ungarische Rundschau für Historische und Soziale Wissenschaften, 3 Jahrgang, 1914: 88. After Th. Bartel: 94. H. Th. Bossert, *Archiv Orientalni*, XVIII and H. Th. Bossert, *Jahrbuch für kleinasiatische Forschung, I*: 61. D. Diringer *The alphabet*: 6, 71, 83, 91, 92, 93. From G. R. Driver, *Semitic Writing*: 64, 65, 66. Dunand, *Byblia Grammata*: 66, 68. After A. Erman, *Die Hieroglyphen*: 9, 21, 23, 25, 26, 31. A. J. Evans, *Scripta Minoa I*: 72, 74, 82, 83. From J. Friedrich, *Entzifferung verschollener Schriften und Sprachen*: 8, 43, 44, 45, 49, 53, 54, 55, 56, 57, 60, 63. J. Friedrich, *Entzifferungschichte der hethitischen Hieroglyphenschrift*: 62. E. Hering, *Schrieb Noah schon?*: 13. From S. Huber, *Im Reich der Inca*: 1. H. D. Jensen, *Die Schrift*: 2, 3, 4, 5, 10, 11, 12, 18, 19, 20, 22, 24, 27, 28, 29, 30, 32, 33, 34, 35, 40, 41, 46, 47, 48, 50, 51, 52, 73, 74, 87, 89. A. Jirku, *Wortschatz und Grammatik der gubliti-schen Inschriften*: 67. From *The Journal of Hellenic Studies LXXIII*: 79. R. H. Lang, *Transactions of the Society of Biblical Archaeology*: 69. W. Merlingen, *Die kretische Schrift entziffert*: 80. Messerschmidt, *Die Entzifferung der Keilschrift*: 37, 38, 39, 42. From Pallottino, *The Etruscans*: 90. Thumb, *Handbuch der griechischen Dialekte*: 70. Ullstein Photo Service, Berlin: 85, 86. M. Ventris and J. Chadwick, *Documents in Mycenaean Greek*: 75, 76, 78, 81, 84. From Weisser, *Bilderatlas zur Weltgeschichte* 14, 17. *Weltstimmen*, Part 8: 7.

FOREWORD

This book was inspired by a love of languages and scripts, and of the secrets their magic world still hold. It has a double intention. Firstly to show the procedure followed in the decipherment of several important scripts and the interpretation of languages, presented in an intelligible manner, by following the course of the investigators step by step; secondly to tell the story of the men who deciphered them, whose names are often confined to learned works and journals, to give the lay reader an insight into their working methods and to show their successes and failures.

Anyone who follows the activities of research and research workers will discover a very modern trend: international collaboration, a powerful and harmonious understanding extending beyond all man-made frontiers. "We who pursue our studies at Oxford University send you this gift, convinced that no frontier can separate those who serve science, and because we believe that by this token of our friendship we can restore peace and goodwill among nations." This can be read in the dedication—written in Latin, the international language—which Oxford University sent with all its gifts of books after the Second World War.

Another very gratifying prospect rewards the reader who is interested in decipherments: he will discover that all branches of international activity, such as trade and economic missions and diplomacy, play their part within the harmonious framework of scientific collaboration. Even the knowledge acquired during the ordéals of war is used at this high level, with a view to the general good.

I have taken the greatest pains to see that there is nothing in this work to offend the specialist critics. Many scholars have been of great assistance to me in my labours. To the investigators referred to in this work and all the experts who have given me the benefits of their advice, I express my heartfelt gratitude. Not only have they helped me in my book, but their support has been of great moral value in this very complicated and difficult subject.

I must take this opportunity of expressing my warmest thanks to all those who have placed at my disposal autobiographical and biographical material, articles, extracts, notes, photographs and illustrations, to those who have revised for me entire chapters and have given me their advice and support in a host of ways, either by correspondence or in personal interviews:

Professor Dr. Helmuth Theodor Bossert, Istanbul; Professor Dr. Wilhelm Brandis, Graz; Mr. John Chadwick, Lecturer in Classical Philology, Cambridge; Professor Edouard Dhorme, Paris; Professor Dr. Otto Eissfeldt, Halle; Father Superior Ernest-Marie, O.C.D. Baghdad; Dr. Margaret Falkner, Graz; Professor Sir Alan H. Gardiner, Oxford; Professor Dr. Ignace J. Gelb, Chicago; Professor Dr. Maria Hoffner, Tübingen; Professor Dr. Hans Jensen, Rostock; Professor Dr. Anton Jirku, Bonn; Professor Dr. Heinz Kronasser, Vienna; Professor Dr. Michel Lejeune, Paris; Professor Dr. Enno Littmann, Tübingen; Professor Dr. Manfred Mayrhofer, Würzburg; Professor Dr. Piero Meriggi, Pavia; State Librarian Dr. Weriand Merlingen, Vienna; Dr. Hugo Mühlestein, Basle; Father C-M. Tunmer, O.P. Mosul; Professor Charles Virolleaud, Paris; Professor Dr. Ernst Weidner, Graz.

This foreword would not be complete without a little personal anecdote.

Many years ago a candidate for his Doctor's thesis sat before his examiner. The conversation was going well and both parties seemed satisfied. It was an hour of undiluted pleasure until . . .

Yes, until the Professor brought the conversation round to the language of the Picenian inscriptions, a number of texts in a legible but incomprehensible script from classical Picenum, on the Adriatic coast located between the modern towns of Ancona and Pescara. The student, according to directives given by his teacher, should have studied the subject, at least superficially. He had referred to the columns devoted to this subject in the *Realenzyklopädie*. But seeing that the article was lengthy and complicated in the extreme, he had not read it to the end. He had, on the other hand, examined the inscriptions on one of the monuments—the famous Novilara Stele—and began to show off the meagre extent of his knowledge. The Professor listened attentively.

This obvious interest encouraged the student to display a certain self-assurance, and he ended his explanations with the following remark: "I studied the article on this subject in the

Realenzyklopädie but found that the author had reached no positive conclusion and did not really know what he wanted to prove."

Silence. The examiner shook his head thoughtfully and merely replied: "Hmm! Possibly!" The pleasant game of questions and answers continued.

The student acquitted himself honourably and the Professor was the first to congratulate him. Nothing more of interest happened that day. But what is the point of the story? the reader will ask. Well, this was only revealed much later. The story has an ending.

A year later the young doctor was once more reading the volume of *Realenzyklopädie* containing the article on the Picenian inscriptions. Remembering his oral, he ran down the columns and feasted his eyes on the archaic alphabet. But this time he read the text to the end. He gave a start. Impossible! There in smaller print, at the foot of the column, lost among the sources and bibliography, stood the name of the author, who was, of course, none other than his examiner.

The student became the author of this book. He has retained his love of ancient scripts and unknown languages, and this love, as he has already said, is one of the grounds for writing this book. But there was a second motive: the profound esteem in which he holds the investigator, the scholar and the man. The good-natured way in which his former teacher ignored the attack against his own authority opened his eyes, sharpened his wits and roused his sympathy for all those who at the peak of their scholarship have remained essentially human. May this book reflect a little of the true joy which is to be found in studying writings and languages and in meeting the great specialists.

ERNST DOBLHOFER

Graz, October 1957

CHAPTER I

AN INTRODUCTION TO WRITING

"*Blessed be he who invented writing.*"—Jean Paul, from a pious saying of the ancient Indians.

"In the beginning was the Word, the divine spark of coherent speech which raised man above all other creatures on this earth. It allowed him to communicate his thoughts and secret feelings to his fellow men; it created the human community. But the Word, even though it could be transmitted in the shape of a message over vast distances and in the form of laws to future generations, remained, in the last analysis, confined within the narrow limits of space and time. For both the message and the law were subject to the will of the man who transmitted them, and nothing could guarantee the faithful preservation of the originally uttered word. This goal was reached with the invention of writing." [1]

Writing cannot by any means be numbered among the most ancient inventions, but it is one of the most revolutionary that man ever introduced into his cultural evolution. It will survive, even if in the eyes of the superficial observer the film, the television, the tape recorder and the radio seem to have superseded it; and that the modern tendency to move away from the written word, from conception and intellectual assimilation in favour of an accumulation of acoustic and optical charms, risks wresting from writing its primordial and millennial role, until one day it is completely ousted.

Writing allows the thinking man to reflect upon himself. It alone allows him collective speculation as to his origin, his essence and the meaning of his existence. It alone has made possible the greatest cultures and philosophies, the great religions of the human race; it has been the mortar used by the founders and builders of empires; on it is based history as a science; it alone gave a powerful impetus to other branches of human knowledge, particularly to physics and natural science; not to forget the other countless benefits of civilisation which all humanity share and which would never have existed without writing.

As the famous historian, Arnold Toynbee, stresses in his latest work:[2]

> "Man has lived the greater part of his existence on earth, which today is estimated as having lasted between 600,000 and 1 million years, as a 'savage'. It was only in the comparatively recent blossoming of civilisations in the last 6,000 years that the various procedures of dictating and preserving graphic annotations were invented—the art which made man for the first time aware of the 'philosophical contemporaneity' of all human evolutions. Thanks to writing, he realised that there was nothing new under the sun, but that he could also descend into the depths of 'unhappy, far-off things', appreciate the most noble flights of the human imagination and exploit the treasures which countless generations had amassed, guarded and preserved down the ages to grasp at last, enriched by these spiritual and inalienable moral beacons the image of man in all his ephemeral grandeur, to assess what Pascal calls 'the splendours and miseries of man'."

Realisation of the great importance of writing was singularly alive in prehistoric times, and was expressed by the oriental races in a series of myths proclaiming its divine origin. The Babylonian Nebo, and the Egyptian, Thoth, were "scribe gods" and at the same time masters of human destinies which they recorded with the "stylus of Fate". The Jews considered the text of the first Tables of the Law given to Moses (Exodus xxxi, 18) as "divine writing", as opposed to "human writing" mentioned by Isaiah (viii, 1). Islam teaches that Allah himself created the letters and communicated them to Adam, but refused them to the angels. The Christian churches, too, have their saints who invented writing: thus Saint Mesrop and the Katholikos Sahak invented the Armenian alphabet, a new script, immediately sanctified in a translation of the New Testament. Better known are the alphabetic creations of Saints Cyril and Methodius and of Wulfila.

The Ancient Greeks, on the other hand, held a diametrically opposed view, reflecting the contrast between East and West; if in their tradition they celebrate a number of inventors of writing, these glorious creators are almost exclusively human; we hardly find a god among them—except the ingenious and talented Hermes, who is credited with many inventions but not primarily with that of inventing writing.

Until quite recently it was believed that all writing without exception originated from a pictorial representation of concepts subsequently evolving, as was the case in the East, "from the image to the letter". Today we are inclined to believe that the letter existed from the very outset and that the principal creators of "Western" writings (Anatolian, Alpine and possibly Old Iberian) had already discovered the isolated sound by the time the Greeks adopted and adapted the Phoenician alphabet, bringing about a reciprocal fusion and fecundation of the image and the letter, a meeting of East and West, of vital importance to world history.[3]

Today we know about four hundred writings without counting the so-called "forerunners" and minor variants of one and the same script. The European by and large knows the Greek characters. Cuneiform signs which most people do not know or cannot decipher, may at least recall the story of the White Whale of Ascalon—where the troop of servants present the guest with his bill in cuneiform on six clay tablets. Hebrew letters can be seen in churches and synagogues. The Western European may perhaps be familiar with the Cyrillic script of the Slavs; the philatelist remembers the Arabic characters which appear on so many stamps and Japanese and Chinese signs are familiar from the captions of oriental paintings and prints. Still more recently there has been an attempt in the German-speaking countries to arouse an interest in runes, without actually favouring the study of them. That the Old Germans, the Scandinavians and the Anglo-Saxons as well as the Ancient Turks and Hungarians used runes (certain scholars have added the Slavs to this list); that many races wrote their language not in letters but in pictures, in ideographic or syllabic signs or even in an admixture of ideographic, syllabic and phonetic signs; that there exist today languages which are legible but as yet incomprehensible, despite long and exhaustive studies, and others which cannot even be deciphered—these are less well known facts. We mention them here merely to give the reader some idea of the field to be covered if he wishes to understand the decipherment of individual scripts.

Let us now lay down a few useful general rules. Writing in the true sense of the word falls into two categories: when there is a design in its widest sense (painted or incised signs, notches, etc.), and when the writer attempts to communicate with others or with himself (mnemonic aids).

When apart from any design communication is achieved by other means, the specialist speaks of mnemotechnic writing, the first step towards actual writing. Let us quote for example the famous "tallies" used in all ages by the most disparate races, which usually give only numerical indications. Tallies are used above all as calendars showing the number of days, weeks, etc., but we also find notched sticks for the recognition of debts, details of which can be read according to how much a certain person has "on his slate"; these documents have an incontestable value when the tally on which the number of units of the sum owed is engraved is cut in two so that the creditor retains one half, "the original", and the debtor keeps "the copy". The confrontation of the two halves would soon outwit a cheat and convince the sceptic.

Another example of this mnemotechnic writing is the "messenger's baton" used in Europe until quite recently, but mainly in Australia and ancient China. Entrusted to the messengers as their name indicates, they were engraved with various signs. The best-perfected batons were adorned with groups of signs and notches capable of giving a very precise message.

One of the best known and most characteristic examples of this mnemotechnic writing are knotted cords such as the quipus of the Incas, the former rulers of Peru.

Although we have chosen the quipus as a simple example of knot-writing, it does not mean that it existed solely among the Incas. The Chinese sage, Lao-tze, refers to the role played by knot-writing in Ancient China and Darius, the Persian king, presented the Ionians with a calendar made from a strap with sixty knots (Herodotus, IV, 98). The Catholic rosary, technically speaking, is a cord, and even today we still find similar memory aids and cords among certain tribes of Hainan and Bengal, in the Riu-kiu Islands in the southern Japanese archipelago and also in Polynesia, Equatorial West Africa, California and southern Peru. Cords with knots and buckles still serve for the transmission of news in the Solomon Islands, the Carolines and Marquesas.

In spite of all the information we possess concerning the quipus, it cannot be maintained with certainty that they served only for various numerical indications. This opinion long prevailed and appeared feasible in view of the material and its capacity for expression. A quipu is composed of a rather thick main cord to which are attached a number of far finer threads.

Fig. 1.—The Inca Tupac Yupangui listens to one of his officials reading a report from a quipu.

The meaning of the knot-writing depends on the colour of the threads, the form and number of the knots as well as their distance from the main cord, the order of the threads and the way in which they are intertwined. The possibilities for expression in these quipus are amazing; some very heavy specimens have been found—generally in tombs—one of them weighing almost 10 lb. It is easy to envisage that the position, the method of attachment and the colour of the threads would allow a whole series of combinations, but it is difficult to see how they could have been translated into abstract and complicated ideas. This clearly limited the scope of such writing and is the reason why for a long time it was believed, as we have already mentioned, that the function of the quipus was in the main numerical. In support of this opinion we can cite the historian, Garcilaso de la Vega, son of a Spanish captain and a princess of Inca blood. He says expressly in his *Historia general del Peru* published at Cordova in 1617 that the Peruvians confined themselves to reading from their quipus the number of combats, missions and royal decrees without being able to

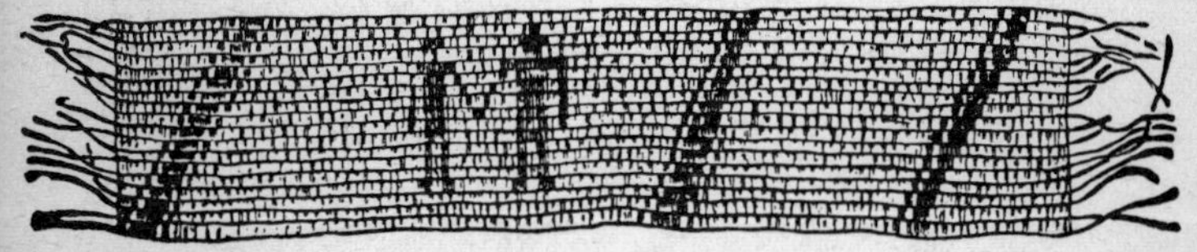

FIG. 2.—Penn Wampum belt of the Leni-Lenape.

express by means of the threads either the tenor or the text of the message. Eminent modern scholars are inclined to think—their premise has not yet been confuted—that the quipus contained not only stastistical indications but also magic formulae based on astronomical numbers (i.e. connected with astronomy), designed to ensure their dead a peaceful repose in eternity. The two interpretations are not incompatible, and the second, far from weakening the theory of the statistical character of the quipus, only confirms it in principle. The Swiss traveller and investigator, Tschudi, doubtless exaggerates when he maintains that the quipus were not only a repository of the laws and chronicles but also of poems.

Lesser-known specimens of mnemotechnic writing are the wampums of the North American Indians—belts composed of a weft of four or more adjacent cords into which are strung small pierced oval discs made from the bright-coloured shells which the Iroquois called wampums. A particular significance was given to the colour of the shells (black or violet indicated danger and hostility, red war, white happiness and peace), and the tribes could send messages to each other by means of these belts. Fig. 2 shows a classic example of this type, the famous Penn-Wampum, today in the possession of the Pensylvanian Historical Society. It was presented in 1682 by the Leni-Lenape Indians to the famous founder of Pennsylvania, William Penn. The belt is white; in the centre can be distinguished two black figures: an Indian on the left holding out a hand to an European (recognisable by his hat). This belt commemorated the peace treaty concluded in 1682 between Penn and the Delaware Indians.

A final type of mnemotechnic writing: the pictographic messages found down to modern times among certain West African negro tribes. Fig. 3 shows one of these messages, an

FIG. 3.—"Aroko" of the Yebus (North of Lagos, Nigeria).

"aroko" of the Yebus which H. Jensen refers to and explains after K. Weule: "This," he says, "is a message sent by a very sick man to his parents and friends who will read it in the following manner: 'The sickness has taken an unfavourable course and grows worse day by day. Our hope now resides in God.'"[4] Unfortunately neither of these two scholars gives any explanation as to how he arrived at this reading.

As can be seen from a study of Fig. 3, it can be interpreted in various ways and is a totally inadequate means of communication. This inadequacy was recognised by the people who wrote these messages and caused them to take a new step forward the interest and importance of which will be explained in greater detail when we deal with the particular writings in question. They lent in fact to certain of these letters the character of a phonetic rebus. H. Jensen on this subject quotes certain typical examples, this time quoting Gollmer:

> "Among the Yoruba (also in Nigeria) six cowrie shells primarily signify the number 'six' = *efa*. But *efa* also means

'attracted' (from *fa*, to draw); a string of six cowries, therefore, sent by a boy to a girl will mean: 'I am attracted to you, I love you.' Eight cowrie shells signify 'eight' = *ejo*. This same word also means 'agreement' (from *jo*, to be in agreement, to equal); a string of eight shells sent by the girl to her suitor can therefore be interpreted in the following way: 'I feel the same as you, I am in agreement.'"[5]

To avoid giving the impression that such pictographic messages are confined to Africa and to modern times, let us refer to an exciting and instructive passage in Herodotus, dealing with the campaign of the Persian King Darius I against the Scythians. This is the second time we meet Herodotus and Darius—it is in fact surprising how closely these two names are linked with the history of writing and how much knowledge we have acquired in this field from these two illustrious figures—the great Greek traveller and the Persian conqueror and restorer of the Empire. Herodotus in the passage quoted (IV, 131–3) has recorded the first pictographic message known to the Western world:

"When this had happened several times, at last Darius was in a great strait, and the kings of the Scythians, having ascertained this, sent a herald, bearing as gifts to Darius, a bird, a mouse, a frog, and five arrows. The Persians asked the bearer of the gifts the meaning of this present; but he answered, that he had no other orders than to deliver them and return immediately; and he advised the Persians, if they were wise, to discover what the gifts meant. The Persians, having heard this, consulted together. Darius's opinion was that the Scythians meant to give themselves up to him, as well as earth and water; forming his conjecture thus: since a mouse is bred in the earth, and subsists on the same food as man; a frog lives in the water; a bird is very like a horse; and the arrows they deliver up as their whole strength. This was the opinion given by Darius. But the opinion of Gobryas, one of the seven who had deposed the magus, did not coincide with his; he conjectured that the presents intimated: 'Unless, O Persians, ye become birds and fly into the air, or become mice and hide yourselves beneath the earth, or become frogs and leap into the lakes, ye shall never return home again, but be stricken by these arrows.'"[6]

Gobryas was right, as the Great King was to discover in due course.

This affords ample proof of the weakness of such "documents" and of their ambiguity (this example being chosen expressly). Darius' letter calls to mind the ancient oracles ("If Croesus crosses the Halys he will destroy a vast empire!") which only became clear after the catastrophe.

Real progress from these first stages of evolution only occur when the two previously mentioned characteristics are combined, i.e. when the drawing (in the widest sense) is designed to transmit a communication or to serve as a memory aid. The

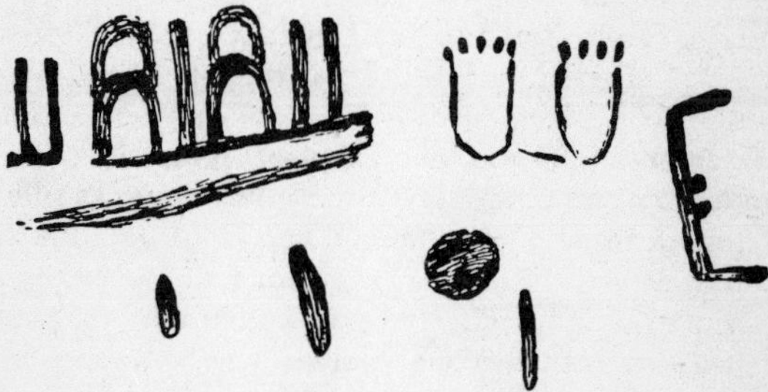

FIG. 4.—Pasiega cave drawing.

first examples of these drawings, paintings, epigraphs, petroglyphs, notches, etc., belong in the field of art history. Certain cave drawings date from the dawn of time and to some we can attribute a graphic character, such as the design above in Fig. 4, discovered in 1911 in Pasiega cave in northern Spain. This is the interpretation given by the graphologist, Hans Jensen: To the left above, the halls of the cave seem to be depicted, the footprints to the right probably signify the idea of walking towards the cave and the strange sign on the extreme right may be considered either an interdiction or an encouragement to carry out this movement.[7]

Writings of this nature were once lumped together under the general term "pictorial writing". But since this term was too general and to some extent misleading, we distinguish today between pictorial writing in the restricted sense (pictography) and "writing of ideas" (ideography or synthetic writing), which is considered to be an advance on pictorial writing. Pictography applies when an image represents nothing more than the object it portrays; if, for example, we draw a circle surrounded by rays to express the idea of the sun, this circle with its rays is a simple pictorial sign or pictogram. But this pictogram becomes an ideogram when, by some general convention, it no longer represents the concrete object depicted, but an idea associated with the object; when the circle surrounded by rays no longer signifies the "sun", but "heat", "warmth", or "warm".

Pictorial writing in its restricted sense is incredibly ancient. We can "read", for example, with Jan Tschichold, into the life-size reclining bison on the roof of the Altamira cave in northern Spain (neo-palaeolithic, about 20,000 years before our era) the emotion aroused by the killing of the animal, the commemoration of a fruitful hunt, and see in it a kind of "precursor of writing".[8] This holds good for all these primitive attempts at writing. As we have already said, an image or a sketch in pictography stands for the concrete object represented; a circle surrounded by rays is the sun, a wavy line water, a silhouette with a head, arms and legs a human being. Ideography, on the other hand, depicts the idea of "age", for example by the image of an old man leaning on a stick; the verbal idea "to walk" by a pair of legs, the quality of "coolness" by a receptacle from which water flows. *The general mark of all pictorial writing*, whether pictographic or ideographic, resides in the fact that it reveals *no connection between the graphic image and the phonetic value, the sound of the spoken language*. A series of images can possibly be "read" accurately by any spectator, irrespective of his language, and there is no relationship between the signs and the sounds. The graphic signs do not represent articulate sounds but rather cycles of thought, symbolised "ideas"; they are unconnected with any determined form of linguistic expression.

A far more modern example of this nature is the pictorial chronicle on bison skin of the Crow Indians, who belong chronologically to the modern European age, but historically to the Stone Age.

The circular central figure shows a shield, adorned with eagle feathers, on which a number of tents are arranged in the form of a crown. Around it we can see combat scenes between Indian tribes or Indians versus Whites. The heads of the slain enemies have been carefully recorded in the upper right-hand corner; away to the left traces of hoofmarks and footprints indicate the number of warriors, mounted or on foot, who have been killed. The two right angles (centre left and lower right) are strips of red cloth to which the scalps are still hanging. The whole chronicle is painted in dark brown, red and green.

Another very fine example of the same type, also on buffalo skin, is the "winter count of Lone Dog", a Dakota Indian. This "calendar" (the Dakotas count the winters as we in poetry count the springs or summers), which extends from the winter of 1800/1 to the winter of 1870/1 is in the form of a spiral starting from the centre, and each year is represented by an incident of importance to the tribe.

1800–1: Thirty Dakotas killed by Cornel Indians

1824–5: All the horses of a chief of the tribe were killed

1801–2: Epidemic of smallpox

1853–4: Introduction of Spanish blankets

1813–14: Epidemic of whooping cough

1869–70: Eclipse of the sun

FIG. 5.—From "Lone Dog's winter count".

It would obviously be wrong to suppose that the Indians, who, above all, practised this pictorial writing, used it only for their personal ends. As we have already seen, the property of this type of writing is precisely to remain independent of the language of the reader. Thus it is admirably suited to international relations. The Leni-Lenape Indians sealed their treaty with William Penn by means of a wampum belt, but this is how seven other North American tribes (among the other blessings of civilisation they discovered bureaucracy) solicited from Congress fishing rights in certain lakes: they found their own particular way through the chaos of legal paragraphs and joined together to address to Congress the petition illustrated below: a charming document.

The seven animals represent the seven tribes; ahead of them walks the crane (right), the totem of the Oshcawabis. The lines joining the eyes and hearts of the animals signify that these seven tribes are inspired by the same intention and the same desire. The line which leaves one of the crane's eyes and runs above the other animals to the four lakes (below left) indicates their common wish to obtain fishing rights in these lakes; a second line leaving the crane's other eye runs to the right ahead, signifying that they are looking with confidence to Congress for a favourable reply to their petition.

The use of ideographic writing in this form is naturally not confined to the Indians. We find it among the Eskimos, also in Africa and Oceania, and in the love-letters cut with a knife on strips of bark by Yukagirian girls in the north-east of Siberia

FIG. 6.—Petition addressed to U.S. Congress by seven North American Indian tribes, requesting fishing rights in certain lakes.

which may be quoted as little masterpieces of their kind. Fig. 7 shows a remarkable specimen which has frequently been reproduced after Krahmer published it for the first time in 1896. Since the Yukagirian tribe consisted in 1926 of no more than 2,000 souls, only 400 of whom spoke the traditional language, we can presume that by now it has been completely absorbed by its neighbours; all the more reason to present here this document, which is of the greatest ethnological interest.

The authors of these letters were exclusively young girls whose strong moral code forbade them to confess their love in words, this right being reserved to the young men. A few rare dances gave the girls an opportunity of producing these little gems and of handing them to their sweethearts.

The letter reads:

"You are going away. You love a Russian woman who bars my way to you. You will have children and they will bring you joy. But I am sad and think only of you, even if another man should come along and love me."

The frame A–B is a house; this is the home of the lovestruck girl, C suggesting the fan-shaped Yukagirian skirt and the pig-tail (dotted line). In the house are two sheaves of crossed lines signifying grief. To the left of the first house is a second, the

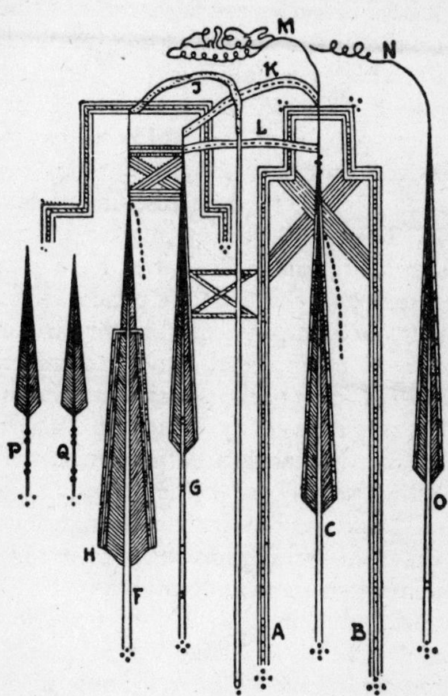

FIG. 7.—Yukagirian love-letter.

frame of which is not prolonged downwards, meaning to say that the owners, F. and G., are absent. F. is the Russian woman as can be seen by her skirt flaired at the bottom H. She is closely bound in love to her husband (lines crossed between F. and G.). The line J. extends from the Russian woman F. and cuts the lines K. and L. The latter represent the unrequited love of the Yukagirian girl for the man. The angled line M. shows that the girl still thinks of her beloved despite the line of separation, J. O. is a Yukagirian boy whose love, N., is directed on the girl. P. and Q. are the children of the couple, F. and G.

There is no space in this book to give further examples of this type of writing—many of which possess an undeniable charm.

Let us, however, mention an interesting fact in the history of culture: we still currently use pictorial writing, particularly in our cities. The commonest examples are certain road signs such as "major road ahead", "danger", "S bends", "level crossing", etc. These are genuine pictograms. One-way-street signs banning cars, trucks or cycles are ideograms. Other examples will be found on the nearest bill hoarding, particularly among advertisements of articles in daily use.

And this is not all. The dearest aspiration of our age, which aims at uniting the peoples of the world and has made several attempts to devise a universal language, today reverts to the far-distant past to find the modern instrument *par excellence*: a universal script. The Dutch journalist, Karel Janson, and the German Professor, Dr. André Eckhardt, have played leading parts in these attempts. Both used a pictographic system because at first sight pictography seems particularly suited to become an instrument of universal understanding, since, as we have said, it is independent of the phonic character of languages. In "Picto"—the name given by Janson to his writing—*Haus*, house, *maison* or *casa* will always be written in the same way: , as a well-known weekly magazine recently announced.[9]

Specimens of "Picto" at the first casual glance certainly give the impression that this writing has achieved its object, and that its creator has invented signs and combinations to meet every imaginable contingency in the field of possible expressions. Thus in "Picto" "I" *I*, |+ "have", "house". "in", "town", and the phrase "I have a house in town" is perfectly clear. But the weakness of this system (the same inconveniences apply to the symbolical writing of Professor Eckhardt) soon become apparent on closer inspection. Unconsciously the inventor has borrowed all the modes of expression foreseen in a language or languages of which he knew the syntax and the possibilities: but a single individual would possess only a rudimentary knowledge of a small part of the number of languages spoken throughout the globe. That is why such a system—comparative philology proves this—cannot be applied *a priori* to all languages. On the other hand, this pictorial writing composed of pictograms and ideograms can only express concrete representations and a few very simple abstract ideas. Let us endeavour to translate into Picto the opening of the preface to Kant's *Critique of Pure Reason:*

> "Certain kinds of knowledge leave the field of all possible experience, and seem to enlarge the sphere of our judgments beyond the limits of experience by means of concepts to which experience can never supply any corresponding objects."

The result will obviously be a host of obscurities and ambiguities making a clear and comprehensible translation for all readers virtually impossible. We have put our finger here on the limitations of all pictorial or synthetic writing: it would be useless as an organ of international science, inadequate as an instrument for the exchange of involved abstract ideas and unthinkable as a means of expressing the poetry inherent in words. This helps us to understand (this was the object of these remarks on Picto, Safo and similar systems) why, among all peoples who possessed a script, the purely pictorial or synthetic soon became outmoded, as an imperfect means of expression, and caused an inner need for further development.

Again: if in pictorial writing ⌂ can signify *maison*, house, *Haus*, *casa*, etc., on the other hand the series of letters h-o-u-s-e can only signify the English word house. Between these two elements the sign ⌂ or any similar sign with the same significance and the group of signs h-o-u-s-e on the other hand, lies the whole history of the external and internal evolution of writing (to be more exact, of one of the paths followed by this evolution—the "oriental" path—leading from the image to the letter of which we originally spoke); the external evolution, i.e. the apparent modifications which transformed the image into stylised, simplified signs or signs used as units; and the internal evolution, i.e. the variations of meanings undergone by the graphic signs.

If as a start we study the external evolution of writing, we shall see that to the extent it developed and adapted itself progressively to the needs of everyday life the need for a fixed and determined form became more and more urgent. As long as anyone remained free to draw for "house" ⌂, ⌂, ⌂, or ⌂, or to vary the size, the door remained open to ambiguity and to the most varied hypotheses: palace or cottage, tower or hayloft—every interpretation was possible. The first step towards a writing subject to norms was therefore as regards form

—the simplification and determination of the graphic signs, a process easy to follow and to decipher along the path taken by the Old Sumerian characters "from the image to the cuneiform sign".

We have chosen this example for another reason: it allows us to recognise quite clearly the influence on the graphic form of the material used, an extraordinarily important factor in the external development of writing. The material here is the clay

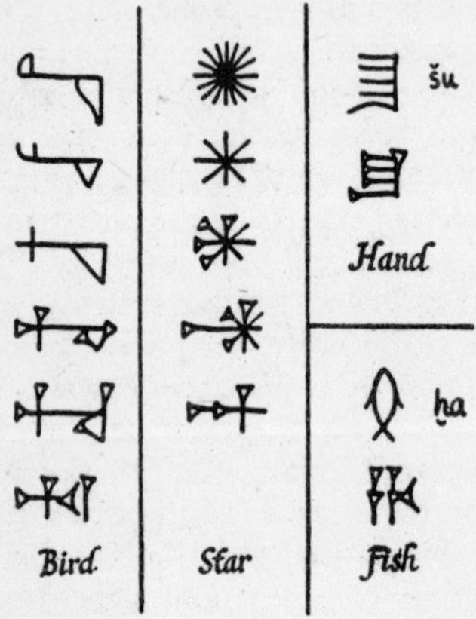

Fig. 8.—Old Sumerian pictograms and their evolution to cuneiform.

tablet on which the characters are cut with a wooden stylus or pointed reed; whence the "cuneiform" lines.

The same normalising tendency becomes manifest in the significance of the signs, and one can envisage a point (theoretical) in evolution beyond which can no longer signify "house", "palace" or "hayloft", but only one of these three words—to be precise "house". At this stage a fixed conventional sign therefore corresponds to a clear and precise meaning. Such a writing can, as the most primitive pictorial writings already did, not only translate objects and concrete actions, but also abstract ideas with the aid of symbolical signs; but it has the great advantage over both pictography and ideography of being unequivocal. We could define this as analytical pictorial writing. We say "could" because nowhere has it appeared in such a marked fashion unless, with Jensen, we take into account Nsibidi writing discovered in 1905 in southern Nigeria among the Ibo and Efik tribes. Let us take from among the signs a very eloquent one denoting a conjugal quarrel; it is written thus: ≍ (a pillow separates the married couple who are turning their backs on each other).

These two marked tendencies—one towards the fixation and precise definitions of meaning, the other towards the simplification and normalisation of the external forms of the graphic signs—continued to manifest themselves beyond the stage of pure analytical pictorial writing. In the history of civilisation, the knowledge and use of writing have not ceased to expand beyond the circle of those who guarded and perpetuated it, and to penetrate the masses, while at the same time the need for an ever greater simplification of the graphic form increased; people wanted to write ever more rapidly and with greater ease, and the fragility of the material used also contributed to the simplification of the signs. On this issue let us consider in the field of Egyptian writing the comparison made by Johannes Friedrich between the text of the Ebers papyrus in late hieratic (the script used by the priests) and the same text in hieroglyphs (Fig. 9).

If the hieroglyphs ("sacred signs") were primarily a monumental script, hieratic shows in the most striking manner how the fact of writing on papyrus refines and renders more subtle the engraved characters, so that to the eye of the novice their new aspect bears practically no resemblance to their original form.

A decisive consequence, as Fig. 9 shows: the graphic sign departs so greatly from the object it formerly so clearly represented, that the relationship between its evolved form and the original image finally disappears completely and only the word in the phonetic rendering of the original image remains bound to the graphic sign. *The latter becomes the expression of a specific sound or group of sounds.* Scholars call this process *the phonetisation of the writing.*

This was a very vital step forward. A single sign could now be used—as it frequently was—for several words of different meaning, but of the same pronunciation, whereas formerly it corresponded to a single one of them—that of the original image. The same phenomenon would be produced if in English one suddenly decided to use the sign for "pain" for the homophone of this word "pane".

The way was open to a no less significant step forward—to a second more important and incomparably more widespread

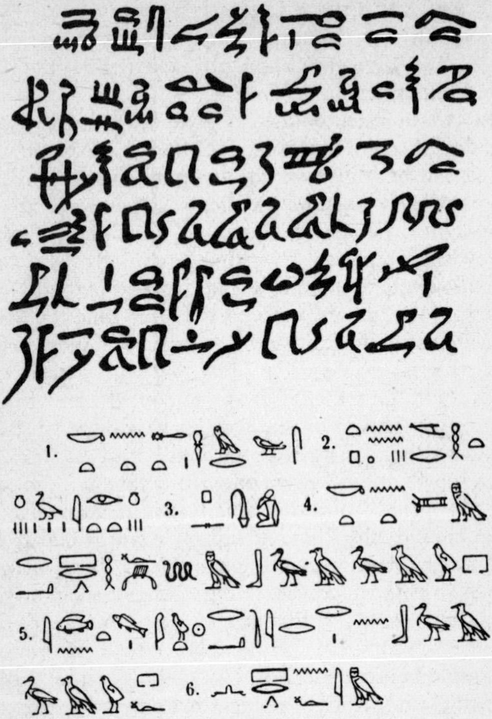

(1) *k.t n.t ẖ.t mr.ś* (2) *tpnn mrḥ.t sꜣ.w jrt.t* (3) *ps swr* (4) *k.t n.t tm rdj pr ḥfꜣw m bꜣbꜣw* (5) *jnr.t św.t rdj.tj r rꜣ n bꜣbꜣw.f* (6) *n pr.n.f jm*

(1) Another (recipe) for the stomach ache; (2) Aniseed, goose fat, milk; (3) cook, drink; (4) Another to prevent a snake leaving its hole; (5) A dried fish laid at the entrance to its hole; (6) (then) it will not come out.

Fig. 9.—Hieratic script of the Ebers papyrus with transcription in hieroglyphs.

type of writing: phonetic writing. Now numerous abstract ideas could be expressed with the aid of graphic signs relative to the origin of concrete objects provided both concrete object and abstract idea were homophones; to illustrate this in English, writing with the same sign the word "bough" and "bow", or in German the sign which had originally signified (die)

Ahnen (ancestors) or (die) *Vorfahren* (forefathers) and doubtless developed from the drawing of two old men, as the two verbal ideas with the very different meanings, "ahnen" (to suspect) and "vorfahren" (to drive).

But the new possibilities were even greater. Phonetic writing also allows us to compose new abstract ideas from the original images on the rebus principle (already applied in mnemotechnic writing); again in English we could juxtapose the images of a pan, a toe and a mime to express the word "pantomime" or to express the verbal idea "to curtail" by pictograms of a dog and a tail.

Let us, however, guard against thinking things were as easy as we have represented them. Like all means of human expression, languages and writings are alive and in perpetual evolution. There has never actually been a pure phonetic writing (how much easier would decipherment have been had this been the case!); all scripts are a combination of pictorial and phonetic writings, to which must be added certain elements of pictography or pure phonetics. The result is a remarkably illogical, fascinating and vivid mixture and yet at the same time a distinct whole, rich in meaning. It was into this labyrinth that alone, in groups or down several generations, the great decipherers penetrated to unravel its secrets.

The next stage in development flows quite naturally from phonetic writing. If the language reproduced by this writing possesses numerous monosyllabic words, or when its polysyllabic words are of simple and regular structure, phonetic writing will become syllabic. A certain number of scripts exist in which this transition can clearly be distinguished; but true syllabic languages are comparatively rare. One of the best known is the Japanese Katakana syllabary derived from Chinese characters. Fig. 10 shows how it took its signs from normal Chinese (K'ai-shu) and its phonetics.

Such a syllabic writing at first sight seems to be extraordinarily simple and useful in structure; one might be tempted to conclude that it is more practical than our European alphabetic writings, which have to use far more sounds. But this attractive supposition will not stand up to closer inspection. For a syllabic writing to be practical, the language must not possess too many syllables, because too many signs would be difficult to read at one glance. Now, as we have mentioned, there are very few languages which possess a relatively weak number of syllables involving a minimum of phonetic combinations. In this respect Japanese (at least in its old pro-

k'ai-shu	kata-kana	Phonetic value	k'ai-shu	kata-kana	Phonetic value	k'ai-shu	kata-kana	Phonetic value
阿	ア	*a*	千	チ	*ti* (*chi*)	牟	ム	*mu*
伊	イ	*i*	門 津	ツ	*tu* (*tsu*)	女	メ	*me*
宇	ウ	*u*	天	テ	*te*	毛	モ	*mo*
江	エ	*e*	土	ト	*to*	也	ヤ	*ya*
扵	オ	*o*	奈	ナ	*na*	勇 油	ユ	*yu*
加	カ	*ka*	仁 二	ニ	*ni*	與	ヨ	*yo*
幾	キ	*ki*	奴	ヌ	*nu*	良	ラ	*ra*
久	ク	*ku*	子	子	*ne*	利	リ	*ri*
个 計	ケ	*ke*	乃	ノ	*no*	流	ル	*ru*
己	コ	*ko*	八	ハ	*fa* (*ha*)	礼	レ	*re*
草 散 左	サ	*sa*	比	ヒ	*fi* (*hi*)	呂	ロ	*ro*
之	シ	*si* (*shi*)	不	フ	*fu*	曰	ワ	*wa*
須	ス	*su*	皿 邊	ヘ	*fe* (*he*)	慧	ヱ	*we*
世	セ	*se*	保	ホ	*fo* (*ho*)	伊	井	*wi*
曾	ソ	*so*	末	マ	*ma*	乎	ヲ	*wo*
多	タ	*ta*	三 美	ミ ミ	*mi*	—	—	—

FIG. 10.—The Japanese Katakana syllabary and its development from normal Chinese writing.

nunciation) represents an ideal instance; it has only open syllables (consonant + vowel) or single vowels.

But if, as occurs in nearly all languages with which we are familiar, the phonetic structure is more complicated, and there is often a succession of consonants, the inadequacy of syllabic writing becomes self-evident and its evolution will inexorably be directed towards the final stage, the alphabetic writing which, at least in principle, uses a sign for each sound.

It is surprising that this ultimate stage in evolution, so familiar today, was only achieved at very few spots on the globe. The races whose writing followed this complete evolution took two different paths. One is illustrated by the history of Egyptian writing, which, among its other signs, possesses a series of uniconsonantal signs. These are graphic signs which originally indicated words or syllables of the type consonant + vowel (such as *ka*, *ro*, etc.). As a result of abandoning the vowel (a process we can hardly envisage, but which is based on the character of the Egyptian language), these signs became simple letters representing consonants: k, r, etc.

The second path was followed by the Ancient Semites. They removed the initial sound from the word and wrote the whole sign as the phonetic value of this initial sound. Thus the old pictogram 𐤁 bēt for "house" (which probably derives from the Egyptian hieroglyphs 𓉐, ▭ and probably to a Sinaitic intermediary sign ⊓ became the letter b, with whose ancient name we are familiar in the Greek designation β. This principle, of writing the initial sound of the sign at one with the primitive sign, thus making this primitive sign a phonetic value, is known as acrophony. Should the word have an unusual sound we know the answer. How many times have we spelt out our name on the telephone? Carter . . . C for Charlie, A for apple, R for Robert, T for Tommy, E for Edward, R for Robert. . . . This is simple everyday acrophony.

One cannot contemplate the Ancient Semitic signs in Fig. 11, the forbears of our own alphabet, without a certain feeling of respect. But a closer look will throw some light on the weakness of this venerable alphabet; it contains no vowels! To the Ancient Semites (as incidentally to the Ancient Egyptians) this caused no particular worry, since the vowels played a far less important part in their languages than they do in ours. It was left to the Indo-Europeans and the Indo-Germans to give alphabetic writing its crown of purity and perfect non-ambiguity. The Ancient Persians, whose cuneiform writing was already incomplete in vowels (this greatly increased the difficulties of decipherment), took a first step in this direction, an innovation of major importance in the history of writing. But the glory of the total and definitive vocalisation of the Semitic alphabet goes to the Greeks. They transformed certain of the Semitic consonants which they did not need into vowel signs,

	Phonetic value	Old Semitic		Phonetic value	Old Semitic
1	ʼ	𐤀	12	*l*	𐤋
2	*b*	𐤁	13	*m*	𐤌
3	*g*	𐤂	14	*n*	𐤍
4	*d*	𐤃	15	*s*	𐤎
5	*h*	𐤄	16	ʻ	𐤏
6	*w*	𐤅	17	*p*	𐤐
7	*z*	𐤆	18	*ṣ*	𐤑
8	*ḥ*	𐤇	19	*q*	𐤒
9	*ṭ*	𐤈	20	*r*	𐤓
10	*j*	𐤉	21	*š*	𐤔
11	*k*	𐤊	22	*t*	𐤕

FIG. 11.—The Old Semitic alphabet.

indispensable to their language. The process of this transformation is shown clearly in the table on the following page (Fig. 12).

One would be tempted to conclude that alphabetic writing constitutes the final stage of development and that any future progress is impossible. This is untrue. All modern alphabetic writings suffer from two evils. One appears clearly in international relationships. Our letters represent, in fact, in various languages and often in a single language sounds which have long since been subject to change. Let us think in particular of English and its complicated pronunciation and also of German with its "s" in *Geist*, in *Stein* or in *sprechen*, of the "h" in *hören* and in *Wählen*, of the "n" in *nennen* and in *singen*. Examples are infinite.

Phoenician		Archaic (Thera, Melos)		Eastern Alphabets				Western Alphabets				Classical Alphabet	
Symbol	Phonetic value	Symbol	Phonetic value	Old Athenian	Milesian Alphabet	Corinth	Phonetic value	Boeotia	Laconia	Arcadia	Phonetic value	Symbol	Phonetic value
𐤀	ʾ	ΔΔ	*a*	ΔA	ΔA	ΔΔ	*a*	AAΠ	ΔA	ΔA	*a*	A	*a*
𐤁	*b*	ƘƘƘ	*b*	BB		ᒍᒉ	*b*	BB	B		*b*	B	*b*
𐤂	*g*	⅂ΓΛ	*g*	ΛΛ	Γ	CI	*g*	ΛΓ	Λ	‹C	*g*	Γ	*g*
𐤃	*d*	Δ	*d*	ΔD	Δ	ΔD	*d*	DΔD	ΔD	DΔD	*d*	Δ	*d*
𐤄	*h*	ᖷE	*e*	ᖷᖷ	ᖷE	ᖷBᙖ	*e*	FEE	ᖷF	ᖷE		E	*ē*
𐤅	*w*					ᖷF	*v*	FC	ᖷ	F	*v*		
𐤆	*z*	≢	*z*	I	I	Ξ	*z*	I			*z*	Z	*z, dz*
HB	*ḥ*	BH	*h, ē*	B	BH	B	*h(ē)*	BH	B	B		H	*ē*
⊕	*ṭ*	⊕⊗⊙	*th*	⊕	⊗⊕	⊗⊕	*th*	⊕⊞⊖	⊗⊕	⊕	*th*	Θ	*th*
𐤉	*j*	ϟϟϟI	*i*	I	I	ϟƐ	*i*	I	I	I	*i*	I	*i*
𐤊	*k*	KKK	*k*	K	KK	K	*k*	K	K	K	*k*	K	*k*
CL	*l*	ΓΛΛ	*l*	ᒪL	ΛΛ	ΓΛ	*l*	ᒪ	Λ	ΛΛ	*l*	Λ	*l*
𐤌	*m*	MM	*m*	M	M	M	*m*	MM	M	M	*m*	M	*m*
𐤍	*n*	NNN	*n*	N	NN	N	*n*	NN	NN	N	*n*	N	*n*
≢	*s*				≢Ξ	Ξ	*ks*	+	X	+	*ks*	Ξ	*ks*
O	ʿ	OC	*o*	O	O	O	*o*	O□◇	O	O	*o*	O	*ŏ*
𐤐	*p*	ΓΓ	*p*	Γ	ΓΠ	ΓΓ	*p*	Γ⊃Π	(ΓΠ	ΓΠ	*p*	Π	*p*
𐤑	*ṣ*	M	*s*			M	*s*						
Ϙ	*q*	ϘϘ	*q*	Ϙ	(Ϙ)	Ϙ	*q*			Ϙ	*q*		
𐤓	*r*	PPR	*r*	PR	PPD	P	*r*	PPRR	PPR	RR	*r*	P	*r*
W	*š*		*s*	ϟ≷	ƐƐ		*s*	ϟϟƐ	ϟϟƐƐ	ϟΣ	*s*	Σ	*s*
X+	*t*	TY	*t*	T	T	T	*t*	TT	T	T	*t*	T	*t*
ϤY	*w*	VYY	*u*	V	V	VYY	*u, ü*	VYY	YYV	V	*u*	Y	*ü*
		↓	*ks*	ΦΦ	⊘	ΦΦ	*ph*	ΦΦ	Φ		*ph*	Φ	*ph*
				X+	X	X+	*kh*	ΨΨ	ΨY	Ψ	*kh*	X	*kh*
					ΨY	Ψ	*ps*			ЖЖ	*ps*	Ψ	*ps*
		⊙O	*ō*		Ω		*ō*					Ω	*ō*

FIG. 12.—The Greek alphabets and their evolution from Phoenician signs.

A second great disadvantage: it takes a considerable time to write our letters, particularly if we wish them to be clear and beautiful. Various systems of shorthand have attempted and are attempting to remedy this defect, but each of them suffers by being limited to its own characters and to the needs of a single language. Abridged and useful writings have been invented in the same form for several languages, without ever having been enforced. The main obstacle, the lack of exactitude in the reconstruction of the sounds of different languages, has been successfully overcome for a long time in the limited field of philology, with its affiliated sciences, phonetics and teaching of language. This is achieved through different systems of scientific phonetics. It is fairly safe to say that the phonetic language of the International Phonetic Association will become more widely known and have a lasting success. This writing is based on two fundamental principles: (1) the use of a single sign for each sound of the human voice, and (2) the constant use of the same sign for the same sound. The path lies open for the creation of a bold combination: an international shorthand based on an international phonetic writing.

As a general introduction to the subject, "writing and scripts", this chapter would be incomplete without two important observations. One is a reference to the major role played by writing material in the constitution of the outward graphic form. In order to study and understand the history of decipherment it is essential to bear in mind with what instrument and on what material the text was written. We shall often have occasion to revert to this subject. Let us be content to say for the moment that men have used, and still use, a great variety of materials and instruments. Not only the stone of monuments and paper, but also textiles of all kinds: leather (vellum), wood, glass, synthetic materials, metals, wax and, above all, clay have served as a basis for writing and contributed to the evolution of its outward form. It is not so long since slates and slate pencils were banished from our schools. The bark of trees and their fibres, the leaves of plants and bones have been, and are still, used today to some extent for writing. Before the introduction of the goose's quill and the calamus, before men used the brush or manipulated the stylus, the spatula and the chisel, men, as we know today, used their forefingers as children do when playing in the sand.

A knowledge of these various materials helps us to understand another aspect of the history of writing. It explains in fact why certain languages and writings have vanished without trace, or have survived in a few meagre examples, whereas others, protected against the ravages of time and the weather, favoured by the climate and entrusted to an almost indestructible material, have remained intact and become available to us in this modern age.

At the start of this chapter we remarked that about 400 writings exist, and we have endeavoured to trace the broad outline of the development of writing. A general graph could not demonstrate how this took place in detail, nor how writings are related to or dependent on each other. We offer here a modest fragment of this extraordinary ensemble, the family tree of our Roman alphabet (according to E. Hering). The panorama is by no means complete and exaggerates somewhat in its over-simplification (particularly in the Phoenician–Etruscan–Greek line). It offers, however, a clear picture of connections which to some readers might appear new and surprising.

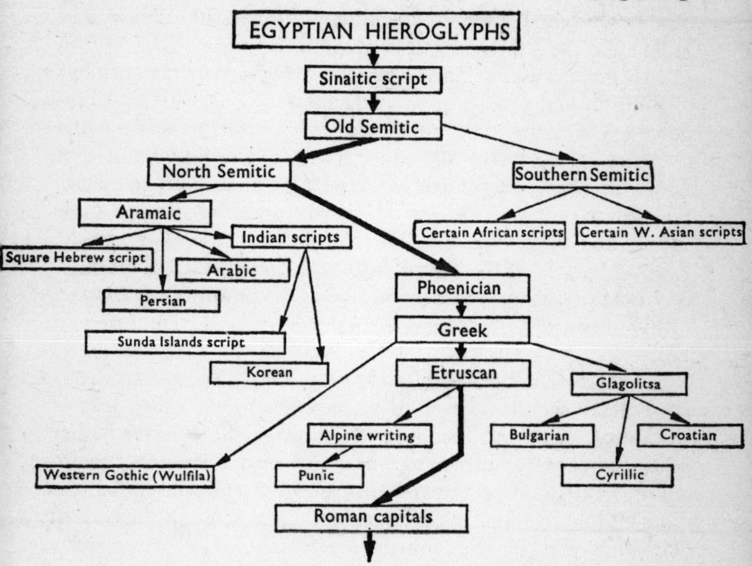

Fig. 13.—Family tree of the alphabets from Egyptian hieroglyphs to Roman capitals.

CHAPTER II

THE RIDDLE OF THE SPHINX

THE DECIPHERMENT OF EGYPTIAN WRITING

"*Hope has long been abandoned of deciphering hieroglyphs.*"—
David Åkerblad, 1802.

"*Je tiens l'affaire.*"—Jean François Champollion, 1822.

"On the pyramid of Cheops is shown an inscription in Egyptian characters and how much was expended in radishes, onions and garlic, for the workmen; which the interpreter, as I well remember, reading the inscription, told me amounted to one thousand, six hundred talents of silver. And if this be really the case, how much more was probably expended in iron tools, in bread, and in clothes for the labourers, since they occupied in building the works the time which I mentioned, and no short time besides, as I think, in cutting and drawing the stones, and in forming the subterranean excavation."[10]

This great traveller and chronicler for whom the inscriptions of the pyramid of Cheops were translated is once more Herodotus. A keen observer and an able story-teller, he was the first to make known to the West the writing of the Egyptians. But while he described the country and the inhabitants in detail, he confined himself, alas, with regard to their writing to a few simple and brief allusions. He does not mention expressly the "sacred letters" of the Egyptians, but in general terms his comments are sparing, and do not give even an approximate idea of the outward form of this writing, still less of its structure and nature.

If the brief notices of Herodotus at least did no harm, one cannot say the same thing of his successors in the literature of antiquity. Diodorus Siculus and Plutarch, the Church Father Clement of Alexandria (to whom we owe the word "hieroglyph", i.e. incised engraved character), Porphyrius and Eusebius all touched lightly on the subject, and some of them dealt with it at some length. But the material available was already a very late deformation of the 4,000-year-old Egyptian script, the so-called "enigmatic" writing of the priests, a kind of rebus, and the explanations of Diodorus, Plutarch and Eusebius refer precisely to this bastardised form, and not to the golden age of Egyptian writing. The real guide along these false routes and the main source of all later errors was a certain Horapollo of Nilopolis.

This man with the characteristic Graeco-Egyptian name (Horus-Apollon) about A.D. 300 wrote two books in Coptic on hieroglyphs, books which were translated into Greek in the 15th century and greeted by the scholars of the Renaissance with the uncritical respect they showed to all the writers of antiquity. Horapollo studied in detail the "enigmatic" script of the priests, and although recognising its decadent form, irresponsibly applied it to the genuine hieroglyphs, "letting himself go", as the Egyptologist, Erman, says, "in the wildest lucubrations". Thus, according to him, the sign depicting a vulture signified "the mother" because there are only female vultures! The sign depicting a goose meant "the son" because the goose displays more maternal affection to her young than does any other animal. Again he maintained: "the front paws of a lion depicted 'strength' because they represent the beast's most powerful limbs; 'a dirty man' is portrayed by a pig on account of that animal's notorious uncleanliness." At the time such interpretations seemed plausible, but they were none the less false.

Horapollo considered the hieroglyphs as a purely pictorial writing in which each sign represented on its own a specific idea and, which we find difficult today to credit, his conception remained an article of faith until the beginning of the 19th century. It needed a unique co-operation of intelligence and intuition to dispel the fatal obscurity into which Horapollo had plunged hieroglyphs and to lift the veil laid by this Epigone over the face of the Sphinx.

But we must not anticipate. Egypt, once the heart of ancient civilisations, bound by a thousand ties to the West, detached herself comparatively early from the Christian Church and the Roman Empire. Already under the Eastern Emperor Justinian (A.D. 527–65) the Coptic-speaking Egyptian Christians seceded *en masse* from the "Malchitic" Western Church in favour of monophysitism, the doctrine which did not recognise the divine nature of Christ and regarded His human nature as a mere outward shell. With this the strongest tie with the West had been broken. It is not surprising, therefore, that the Moslem Arabs under Amru, Caliph Omar's general, who invaded Egypt in A.D. 638 and conquered it for the Arab Empire and for Islam, were able without difficulty to reduce this country, torn by partisan factions, still bleeding from the wars against the Persians and long since a stranger to the Roman West. After Syria and Mesopotamia they had only to pluck it like a ripe fruit; and when in Ancient Alexandria, the seat of a high culture, the remains of a library once famous throughout the entire world was reduced to ashes; when the city was taken by assault, it was as though an impenetrable veil had descended between the West and the East. All the later scientific research—very meagre at the start—the expeditions, the copying of inscriptions, etc., collapsed before the threat of mob violence.

Although the epigraphs on the monuments intrigued the Arabs, their attempts at interpretation were merely imaginative rubbish. Christian pilgrims travelled the East in search of evidence for biblical history. They discovered in the Pyramids Joseph's granaries, recognised at Heliopolis the sycamore beneath which the Holy Family rested during their flight into Egypt, and saw in the bones scattered along the shores of the Red Sea the remains of Pharaoh and his host drowned in their pursuit of Moses. They paid no heed, however, to the inscriptions which did not speak to them of biblical history.

No darkness remains so dense in the long run that it cannot be penetrated. But there was a lapse of nearly a thousand years before antiquity enjoyed a Renaissance in Italy—that marvellous upsurge and fresh breeze which dispelled the shadows in which the Pyramids, the Sphinx, the obelisks and the hieroglyphs still lay.

Rome, among the testimonies of her own glorious past as an empire, had preserved numerous trophies, and the treasures towards which the humanists and archaeologists now turned their attention included several obelisks decorated with curious ciphers brought from Egypt. These inspired the first tentative investigations: but a number of works written at the time on the Roman obelisks and hieroglyphs, having arrived at no scientific result, have today justifiably been forgotten. Their authors' only merit was to have focused the attention of future archaeologists upon Egypt. One of them, however, produced a work of lasting value: the unjustly maligned Jesuit Father

Athanasius Kircher, who laid the foundation stone of modern Egyptology.

Anyone familiar with the history of the Jesuits and their pioneering achievements in science will not be surprised to find one of their community, a true son of the age, active in this field. The 17th century was in fact an epoch of violent contrasts, of constant experiment and bold changes. Its dawn had produced Bacon, Kepler and Galileo, its apogee Descartes and Pascal and its end was illuminated by the bright stars of Leibniz and Newton. If we accept the judgment of one of these luminaries,

FIG. 14.—Father Athanasius Kircher, S.J.

Athanasius Kircher deserves to be numbered among them. Leibniz himself wrote to Kircher on May 5th, 1670: "To you who, in the measure to which it can be acquired by men, are worthy of immortality, as the promise of your name announces [Athanasius in Greek means 'immortal'], I wish immortality in the prime of your youth."

What secret paths led the son of Doctor Johann Kircher, councillor to the Lord Abbot of Fulda and bailiff of Haselstein, to such studies, and what in particular attracted him towards Egypt?

Athanasius, as we have said, means "immortal". But it was also the name of the Patriarch of Alexandria, the saint who did so much for the defence of Catholicism against the Arians. The ever-increasing missionary zeal of the Jesuits was directed towards Egypt. The young student never lost sight of the example set by his patron saint, and thus Christian Egypt, by relinquishing the first key, ensured the basic knowledge for the future science of Egyptology.

Kircher's first decisive encounter with Egypt took place at Speyer. It was in the year 1628. Athanasius had just been ordained and had been sent by his superiors to Speyer for a "year of probation", of spiritual retreat. One day he was sent to find a certain book. The young scholar rummaged among the treasures of the library without discovering the book in question. As a reward, however, he unearthed a magnificent codex with beautiful engravings of the Egyptian obelisks, erected in Rome at great expense by Pope Sixtus V. Kircher was particularly intrigued by the curious designs on the surfaces of these mighty columns. At first he mistook them for arbitrary signs used by the ancient mason as ornament. But the text of the work, in which he was soon absorbed, immediately dispelled his error. Here in black and white he read that the mysterious hieroglyphic signs concealed all the wisdom of the Ancient Egyptians, cut in stone for the instruction and edification of the people. The key to this mysterious script had long since been lost, and no mortal had contrived to open this Book of the Seven Seals!

The future investigator yearned to decipher the hieroglyphs, to read and translate the epigraphs. Without the requirements today considered indispensable and without that caution which is a strict canon of modern scientific research, he plunged into the texts, and soon published his translations.

We give below an example from his *Sphinx mystagogica*:

FIG. 15.—dd-jn Wšjr "Osiris says".

Kircher interpreted these hieroglyphs as follows: "The life of things, after the victory over Typhon, the humidity of nature, through the vigilance of Anubis" (after J. Friedrich). Any layman can to some extent picture by what method he arrived at this transcription: for Kircher the wavy line signified "water", i.e. the humidity of nature, the eye symbolised "the vigilance of Anubis". On the other hand, he translated the Graeco-Roman imperial title Autocrator (= "master of oneself") written in hieroglyphics by a whole phrase (Fig. 16), giving an interpretation which, with the best will in the world, we cannot follow today. "The creator of fertility and of all vegetation is Osiris whose creative power was drawn from his kingdom in the sky by Saint Mophta."[11]

Kircher's translations have not without reason but with undue severity been classed as "absurdities" and "monstrous effronteries". It was obviously forgotten that Kircher, sharing the ideals of the scholars of his age, had to base his work on the "wild lucubrations" of Horapollo, whose fantasies corresponded not only to the mystic tendencies of decadent antiquity but also to the morbid predilection of the 16th and 17th centuries for allegories and symbols.[12] Clement of Alexandria already says expressly that the hieroglyphs, as well as verbal

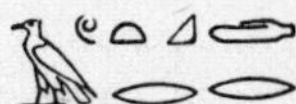

Fig. 16.—The imperial title "Autocrator" in hieroglyphic.

signs, consist of simple letters. But Kircher's age was less inclined than any other to admit such a statement. The hieroglyphs could not be anything else than symbols, and when a Greek translation of an inscription on an obelisk had no profound content (this case arose on one occasion) it was considered false, and Father Athanasius in turn promptly declared it to be false!

Nevertheless Athanasius Kircher did work of lasting value in this field (his other scientific achievements have received recognition). In a work published at Rome in 1643, he was the first man formally to define Coptic, the dying language of the Egyptian Christians, as the popular language of Ancient Egypt, an idea which at the period offered no evidence and was to be rejected with scorn by subsequent scholars of repute.

Kircher owed the foundations and materials for his Coptic studies to his close relations with the Roman Collegium de Propaganda Fide, the highest pontificial missionary authority, to which the missions distributed throughout the world were subordinate. Kircher published a dictionary and even a Coptic grammar, thus to a large extent helping to stimulate an interest in this old popular tongue. For more than two centuries his works were the point of departure for all Coptic linguistic studies.

In this lies the Jesuit Father's incontestable merit, for Champollion, the future decipherer of hieroglyphic, the classic incarnation of the decipherer, started in his youth from this acquired knowledge and pushed his studies of Coptic so far that it became for him a second tongue and at the same time the first and most important key to his decipherment work.

Athanasius Kircher, however, had a precursor, the Italian traveller, Pietro della Valle, whose Coptic grammar and lexicon he had received from an old friend. We shall discuss this very talented Italian in the next chapter.

Kircher was not merely an "Egyptian Oedipus" (although he once compared himself to the legendary Greek hero) wresting from the Sphinx, who had been silent for centuries, the key to her riddles; he was only occupied with the problems of writing in addition to his other studies (the best known of these is the "magic lantern"). He conceived a writing for deaf-mutes, and even outlined the bases of a universal script, allowing anyone to express his thoughts, so that all the races of the world could read them irrespective of their languages. Are we to see in him a precursor of Karel Janson and Professor Eckhardt? Why not? But those two scholars were themselves only late successors of a line of scholars intent upon freeing humanity from the curse of the general confusion of languages, and of conquering this Babel by a universal tongue. We need merely mention Raymond Lully and Trithemius, Leibniz himself and later the decipherer of Old Persian cuneiform writing, Georg Friedrich Grotefend.

The works of Kircher, therefore, brought nothing immediate to the decipherment and reading of hieroglyphs. He, too, was under the spell of Horapollo.

Once more the darkness threatened to descend. But the general upsurge of Orientalism in the 18th century allowed a few gleams of light to penetrate this obscurity and the young healthy shoots thrived among the tangled weeds of untenable hypotheses. Thus the English theologian, William Warburton, Bishop of Gloucester, the bellicose opponent of Voltaire, in the teeth of current opinion, maintained in 1740 that the hieroglyphs were not exclusively ideograms; that the texts were not solely religious in content but that the signs also possessed a phonetic element and that the texts could equally well apply to everyday matters. This theory of the phonetic value of hieroglyphs had already been put forward by the famous investigator and author of *The Journey of the Young Anarcharsis to Greece*, Abbé

Barthélemy, also by the sinologist, Joseph de Guignes (senior), who declared before the French Academy of Inscriptions and Belles-lettres on November 14th, 1756, that the Chinese were Egyptian colonists!

This same Guignes, in any case, was able to give an accurate reading of the hieroglyphic royal name "Menes". A colleague immediately attacked him and proposed the inaccurate reading "Manouph". This attack aroused the irony of the great wit, Voltaire, and inspired his biting diatribe against the whole corporation of etymologists (linguists and comparative philologists), for whom vowels did not matter and who cared not a jot for consonants. Tychsen and Zoëga also suspected the phonetic character of hieroglyphics.

These healthy ideas thrived amid the numerous and much-publicised hypotheses, devoid of all foundation, which were rife at the end of the 18th and the beginning of the 19th century.

Guignes held that the Chinese were Egyptian colonists. The English entering the fray reversed this theory and maintained that the Egyptians came from China. At this the Russians cocked an ear. Councillor Koch of St. Petersburg attributed no less than five alphabets to Egyptian antiquity. These fantasies and others of the same order resisted even the first concrete advances made on the path of decipherment. The demon of hieroglyphs was by no means dead, and he was visible simultaneously or successively in the reading of the texts: as epicurean mysticism; secret cabbalistic, astrological or Gnostic doctrines; practical hints for applied economy; entire paragraphs of the Bible, and even antediluvian literature!

The Chinese continued to haunt the brains of the scholars. A certain Count Palin invented this particular receipt: "Take one of the Psalms of David, translate it into modern Chinese, then transpose it into old Chinese characters and you will have before you a reproduction of the Egyptian papyrus." No wonder that Palin obtained "phenomenal results". He merely cast a cursory glance at the inscription on the Rosetta Stone, to which we shall refer later in detail, to know its character immediately, and then based his work on Horapollo, the Pythagorean doctrines and the Cabbala; the detailed translation which he published in 1824 at Dresden cost him, it is true, one whole sleepless night. But any longer reflection, according to him, would have been a grave error, for his rapid method enabled him "to avoid the systematic errors which invariably arise from prolonged reflection".

"Absurd!" wrote Abbé Tandeau de Saint-Nicolas, "it is as clear as day that the hieroglyphics are purely ornamental." Nor did anonymous decipherers conceal their opinions. An unknown Parisian managed to identify the 100th Psalm with an inscription from the temple of Denderah. Paris, therefore, considered that the biblical character of the hieroglyphics had been "proved". At Geneva they went even further by publishing a translation of the so-called Pamphylian obelisk in Rome which to an astonished world turned out to be "the story of the triumph of good over evil four thousand years before Christ"!

The voices of the serious scholars were stifled in this chaos of false erudition. As we have already said, the phonetic character of hieroglyphic writing had already been suspected. But even in specialist works a far more fertile indication was apt to be overlooked: in 1761–2 the brilliant Arabian expert, Carsten Niebuhr, who laid down the bases for the study of cuneiform writing, found himself obliged to kick his heels in Cairo. He resigned himself as best he could to this enforced idleness and, to pass the time, began to copy all the hieroglyphic inscriptions which were accessible. At the outset, on his own admission, this task brought him "nothing but boredom and disgust". "But soon", he went on, "I grew so familiar with hieroglyphs that I could reproduce them like an alphabet and found great pleasure in doing so."

Niebuhr began to look upon the monuments with a new eye. He noticed a difference between the "larger" and the "smaller" signs. "Only the large type", he maintained, "are true symbols; the small ones seem merely to serve as explanatory or to interpret the others; they often bear a marked resemblance to alphabetic letters." If this were true, then the decipherment could be attacked with the aid of Coptic.

Carsten Niebuhr made a second weighty observation which at first passed unheeded. He noticed that the number of hieroglyphs was rather meagre. There could not, therefore, be a sign for each individual word. By virtue of these two intelligent remarks, Niebuhr will always be ranked among the first decipherers of hieroglyphs, although his name is generally associated with the decipherment of cuneiform.

On the one hand futilities and pretentious assumptions, and on the other penetrating suppositions which still remained to be proved—this was the situation of the budding science of Egyptology when the key to the riddle suddenly appeared in the most unexpected manner. The saying that in times of war the Muses are silent does not apply in the history of decipherment.

FIG. 17.—Gottfried Wilhelm Leibniz.

Nevertheless the Rosetta Stone did not fall from the skies, so to speak. The background to its discovery is part of the history of European civilisation. At the source we do not find Napoleon, as popular belief has it, but Leibniz!

Leibniz was not only a great philosopher but a remarkable statesman, and his perspicacity in political matters decided him while in Paris in 1672 to divert Louis XIV's designs on his own country, Germany, by drawing up for the benefit of the "Roi Soleil" his *Consilium Aegyptiacum*, a document in which he suggested that the conquest of Egypt would ensure for France the primacy in Europe. Leibniz could not suspect that this memorial, destined for Louis XIV, absolute monarch by the Grace of God, would one day fall into the hands of a bold general, soon to become an emperor in his own right.

According to the testimony of eminent French historians, Napoleon knew of this memorial when, in the great hall of the

Institut before a galaxy of scholars, he outlined the scientific profit he hoped to gain from his Egyptian expedition. But although he had not lost sight of the main ideas of Leibniz, he had brought with him another book, the two-volume French translation of Niebuhr's *Travels in Arabia*.

If Napoleon's campaign on the military plane was a failure, through which the Corsican's dreams of power suffered a setback, the scientific results of the expedition surpassed all hopes.

The most valuable treasure of all was found on the 2nd Fructidor of Year VII of the French Revolution (August 2nd, 1799).

Napoleon's "Flight from Egypt" was imminent. The pressure of British naval forces had proved too strong. After their initial brilliant successes the French troops had been flung back on the defensive. But they still held the Egyptian coast and defended themselves stoutly against the English, who were operating at sea, and the Turks, who were attacking from the south.

Brigadier-General Bouchard had ordered his men to dig in by the old Fort Rashid, later called Fort Julien, about five miles from Rosetta in the Nile delta. Suddenly a soldier's pick hit against a hard body and glanced off with a metallic clang. The ruins of a wall brought to light a strange object: a basalt stele entirely covered with writing.

The unknown Arab soldier was probably greatly surprised by his discovery, and his comrades probably gathered round, a prey to superstitious fear. But thanks to Napoleon's foresight the army was not lacking in men who could at least read the portion of the epigraph written in Greek. The inscription turned out to be a memorial dated the 4th Xandikos = the 18th Meshir of the year 9 = March 27th 196 B.C. issued by the priests of Memphis in gratitude to Ptolemy V Epiphanes for gifts "which had increased the honours due to the king and his forefathers in the Egyptian shrines".

It was immediately recognised that the upper inscription was in hieroglyphs and the lowest in Greek. The intermediate script remained unidentified for a time, and it was erroneously believed to be Syrian. But the exceptional importance of this document was realised at once, because the colophon contained orders for the publication of the decree, whereby it was learned that it was a trilingual document.

The story of this wonderful find was published in the *Courrier de l'Egypte* No. 37 of the 29th Fructidor of the Year VII; its effect had the widest repercussions.

As was customary in the Ptolemaic era, this memorial was to be inscribed on a commemorative tablet in the three languages of the country: the literary language long since obsolescent but preserved traditionally on monuments, ancient Egyptian written in the "sacred signs", the hieroglyphs; then in the modern spoken language or demotic, a cursive script derived from hieroglyphs, and finally in the Greek tongue and script.

The matter was not so simple at first sight. Were we to be faced with a similar case today it would appear quite natural and familiar. The German Egyptologist, Georg Ebers, makes a very significant comparison on this subject:

> "Let us presume that instead of Egypt of that period we were dealing with an Italian province of the Austro-Hungarian monarchy, where the clergy had composed a resolution in honour of the imperial dynasty: it would undoubtedly have been published in Latin, in Italian and in the German language of the ruling house and its officials. This is precisely how the Rosetta Stone was composed. . . If we then imagine the Latin text in capitals, the Italian text in roman script and the German characters in Gothic type the analogy is perfect."

The stone was unearthed, the nature of the three writings confirmed. Now at last its bilingual—one might say trilingual—nature was discovered. Was the way now, broadly speaking, open for decipherment? Not a bit of it. Things were not nearly so simple!

As a start the stone was transported to Cairo so that the scholars of the Institut d'Egypte, founded by Napoleon, could study it. Copies were made of the text and sent to France, as though there had been a presentiment that the famous stele might get lost. Later it was transferred to Alexandria and installed in the house of the French General, Jacques François de Menou.

In 1801 the English landed an army and Menou was forced to capitulate. The French had to deliver to England all the Egyptian antiquities acquired in the Nile Valley in the course of the past three years. They tried their best to retain the precious Rosetta Stone, the importance of which was realised by the two warring nations, by declaring it the personal property of General Menou and thus not liable to the terms of the surrender. But the English General, Lord Hutchinson, with scientific zeal, insisted on the stone being handed over to him. Under a barrage of sarcasm, the French officers present at the operation, allowed Hutchinson's envoy, Turner, to carry away the document. The stone was landed at Portsmouth in 1802. It was then sent to the British Museum, "where we hope it will remain for many years . . . as a glorious trophy of British arms . . . not captured from a defenceless population, but conquered honourably and according to the rules of warfare", so concludes Turner's report.

A glorious trophy of British arms. . . . But the intellectual conquest was denied to British arms. Despite all the promising efforts of the English pioneer, Thomas Young, fate—equitable, doubtless, in the eyes of the French—reserved this triumph for the Frenchman, Jean-François Champollion.

But before Young and Champollion appeared on the scene the minister, Chaptal, had procured a copy of the inscription. He handed it to the famous French Orientalist, Sylvestre de Sacy, a scholar of international repute who, thanks to his erudition, was the father of modern Orientalism. Sacy was also renowned as a decipherer, having "broken" and successfully explained Pehlevi, the Middle Persian language and script. He was bluffed by the Rosetta Stone inscriptions. He was able to detect in the demotic text groups of signs corresponding to names quoted several times in the Greek—Ptolemy, Alexander, Alexandria, Arsinoë and Epiphanes—but his Demotic-Greek transliterations were wrong.

Sylvestre de Sacy was not only a great scholar but a man worthy of this title; he immediately confessed to Chaptal that he was incapable of deciphering the Rosetta Stone texts, and sent the copy to the Swedish archaeologist, David Åkerblad, a brilliant scholar who had served in the East as a diplomat and was now continuing his studies in Paris. Åkerblad was particularly interested in Coptic; he attacked the copy with great fervour and in addition he had at his disposal a sulphur cast of the inscriptions. Following Sacy, he mistakenly thought that demotic was an alphabetic writing and in consequence the best one for deciphering the hieroglyphs, the text which had suffered the worst mutilations. Åkerblad was a classical philosopher, a competent Orientalist, and he was lucky. He managed to recognise and to make a comparative reading in the demotic of all the names in the Greek text.

Then by transliterating the Greek names written in demotic characters he obtained an alphabet of sixteen letters, for thirteen of which he found the correct plurals. Moreover, he noticed that the same signs appeared outside the names and found, to his delight, that he could spell out whole words with which he was familiar in Coptic. He read: *erphêui*, "the temple", *ueinin*, "the Greeks", and at the end of several words he found in demotic the sign for the grammatical ending of the third person, the *-f*, which in Coptic means "he" or "his". Coptic writing, a Greek derivative, had borrowed a few demotic characters, as we know today.

The Swedish scholar happened to be poring over the hieroglyphic text when certain passages caught his eye: where the Greek text spoke of the "first", "second" and "third" temples, in the hieroglyphic passage stood a single, double or treble stroke above another sign. He had thus discovered the hieroglyphic ordinal numbers 1–3.

This promising start had been very rapid. With his alphabet Åkerblad now had at all events access to demotic writing and laid the bases for its decipherment. Two scholars impeded his further progress along this path. Their names were de Sacy and . . . Åkerblad.

Yes, he was a great hindrance to himself, and abandoned his line of discovery because he still believed in the alphabetic nature of demotic. Like Sacy, he paid no heed to the suppression of vowels—except eight (as we have already mentioned, Egyptian, like Hebrew, has no written vowels)—and was unable to recognise the numerous mute indicative signs known as determinatives. His alphabet was, therefore, only valid for reading the names which it had provided for him.

Åkerblad might well have continued on his own lines had not de Sacy poured cold water on his scientific hopes. He had communicated his results to the great French Orientalist who had entrusted this job to him, and received a courteous reply expressing his doubts. This thoroughly discouraged the sensitive Swede. Had de Sacy, embittered by the recent setback which he had been a great enough man to admit, made a snap and too hasty condemnation of his Scandinavian colleague's too hastily obtained results? It is quite conceivable. Even the great de Sacy was not innocent of scientific jealousy. Whatever the truth, David Åkerblad suffered from the scepticism of his colleagues just as he had suffered from a conflict with his own government, to which he had rendered valuable diplomatic services and from which his passion for Rome and his political principles alienated him more and more. His country had forgotten him so completely that fifty years later the German biographer of Champollion, H. Hartleben, was unable to procure a portrait of him, although she had all possible official support.

Thus de Sacy—unintentionally, of course—cut the thread hesitantly offered by Åkerblad and, apart from a few discordant echoes from a handful of amateurs, silence fell on the trilingual stone which endured until 1814.

That year the English naturalist, Thomas Young, went, as he did each year, to take his holiday in the country and to pursue his hobbies. Young, the natural scientist and doctor, was a scholar of the first order. By discovering the main phenomena of vision and the law of the interference of light he laid the foundations of modern optics. But his interests as a man and a scientist were catholic in the extreme.

While still a student at Göttingen in 1796, but already a doctor and physicist, he propounded the theory that only an alphabet of forty-seven letters could completely exhaust the possibilities of the human voice. In connection with these studies he later turned his attention to the alphabets of foreign languages, acquired a great reputation as a Hellenist and among other things continued his exercises in calligraphy. His various hobby-horses were known to a circle of friends and relations, and he was often given old damaged manuscripts to restore. All these occupations, outside his own particular field, were for him a pastime and a form of relaxation for his leisure hours.

Thomas Young never did things by half. Whatever he took into his head he carried it out. Thus during one holiday he had the bright idea of learning to dance on a tight-rope. He practised with great zeal and was soon able to give a performance on the rope, much to the horror of his Quaker community.

In the spring of 1814, then, Thomas Young went to the country on his holidays. A friend, Sir Rouse Broughton, gave him an old manuscript to take with him "to play with". But this time it was not a Greek text but a demotic papyrus.

As he examined it closely, Young remembered an article by a certain Severin Vater that had recently appeared in the third volume of Adelung's *Mithridates*, which, as an ex-Göttingen student, he always read regularly.

Johann Severin Vater (1771–1826) was successively Professor of Theology and Oriental Languages at Jena, Halle, Königsberg and once more at Halle. His academic activities had introduced him to Egyptian writing. As opposed to most of his contemporaries, however, he had started with the hieratic writing on mummy bandages. He concluded (a theory not yet proved) that the hieroglyphs should be read phonetically and consisted of an alphabet of rather more than thirty signs.

Young must have thought of this when in 1814, his appetite whetted by the papyrus, he studied a copy of the demotic inscription of the Rosetta Stone.

The Englishman was also acquainted with Åkerblad's work, because the Swedish scholar had once sent him from Rome an analysis of the five first lines of this text with a transcription into Coptic. But when Young tried to use Åkerblad's alphabet he soon discovered that it was false.

He saw, as Åkerblad had already seen, that certain words were repeated in the Greek text. Like his predecessor, he tried to isolate these same words in the demotic text. But Young went farther than Åkerblad. He divided not only the whole demotic text but also the hieroglyphic text to make the isolated words correspond to the Greek, and published the two texts anonymously in the review *Archaeologia*, so as not to endanger his reputation.

It was a bold step, but it had an unexpected success. The same year Young followed this up with *An Attempt at Translating the Demotic Text of the Rosetta Stone*, which he sent to de Sacy in Paris in October 1814. He believed that he would finish just as rapidly with the hieroglyphic text, which was still as "intact as the Ark of the Covenant".

A rash presumption, for what qualifications had this talented scientist to carry out a work in a field entirely unknown to him?

He possessed neither the necessary philological training nor the indispensable knowledge of oriental languages. He could, therefore, only make a purely material comparison; what guided him in the main was his mathematical instinct and, thanks to comparisons and analogies, he obtained really astonishing results, considering the inadequacy of the methods employed.

First: the groups of signs revealed by the division of the demotic text bore a striking resemblance to the group of hieroglyphs.

Secondly: Young could already indicate the meaning of a certain number of the group of hieroglyphs, but not as yet their phonetic value.

Thirdly: among the Greek names in the demotic text one at least appeared in the intact fragment of the hieroglyphic text, enclosed in the oval ring which cropped up several times in the inscription. (Guignes and Zoëga had already sensed that such rings or cartouches enclosed the names of kings.)

Fourthly: armed with this knowledge acquired, Young risked attacking other hieroglyphic texts and made some lucky guesses at the meaning of certain words. These results encouraged him in the summer of 1818 to produce a hieroglyphic lexicon of 204 words, a quarter of which were accurately translated and which in addition contained a list of fourteen phonetic hieroglyphic signs; among the latter five are perfectly correct and three others partially so. A modest result, it might be argued. But it does not detract from the undeniable progress attained and the great merit of Young in having been the first to recognise, against the general consensus of opinion, the existence of hieroglyphic phonetic signs among the purely ideographic!

Young now considered himself advanced enough to attack once more the trilingual inscription. He concentrated first on the cartouches which should have contained the name of Ptolemy.

Fig. 18.—Cartouche of Ptolemy.

He dismembered the hieroglyphs which composed it as follows: 𓊪 = p; 𓏏 = t; 𓍯 means nothing (!); 𓃭 = ole; 𓐝 = ma; 𓇌 = i and 𓋴 = os!

This analysis shows, on the one hand, how close Young got to the correct reading "Ptolmis" and, on the other, how greatly he was hampered by his ignorance of linguistics; moreover, he was looking for vowels in the hieroglyphs which, as we know, are suppressed in Egyptian.

By the same procedure he read in another inscription the name of Queen Berenice (actually *Brnikat*, *-at* being the feminine ending) thus gaining a few more letters.

FIG. 19.—Cartouche of Berenice.

Young had now really started to decipher the hieroglyphs!

But then something very strange occurred. Apart from his few lucky guesses, the man who had discovered the phonetic character of hieroglyphic was content with the results achieved and never crossed the threshold of the door he had opened. He halted on the fringe of so-called philology—not entirely of his own free will. When, for example, he met the name of the God of the Dead, Anubis, clearly written in phonetic hieroglyphs he did not recognise him and bestowed on him the name of the dog, Cerberus, the guardian of the Greek underworld! It is even more surprising that the name of another deity, Ptah, escaped him, although it appears several times on the Rosetta Stone in the Greek script, and that he himself had discovered from the Ptolemy cartouche the phonetic values of the two initial letters -p and -t.

Why did Young stop there? These studies, according to his own words, were the joy of his leisure hours, a joy which began to fade rapidly as he acquired a better knowledge of the Egyptians. He had hoped to discover the treasures of Egyptian natural science, which according to him had inspired Pythagoras. But the more familiar he became with the texts, the more evident it became that it was always a question of the gods, of Pharaohs and of the dead—the dead, above all—and never of astronomy or chronology. Moreover, his work never aroused, either in his own country or abroad, the applause he considered it deserved. In his prime and at the height of his intellectual powers he saw the star of his young rival, the Frenchman Champollion, in the ascendant, overshadowing his own light in the sky of European science.

Eight years before Napoleon outlined to the assembled scholars in the Institut de Paris his ambitious plans for the Egyptian expedition, the young wife of the librarian, Jacques Champollion, was fighting for her life at Figeac, the capital of the Lot department. She was pregnant and seriously ill. Her husband in his despair thought of their strange neighbour, the sorcerer Jacquou, who lived in the deserted Convent of Lundieu. Jacquou was reputed to know many secret remedies and had accomplished some remarkable cures. He laid his patient on a bed of burning herbs, of which he alone knew the curative properties; from various plants he then prepared a hot infusion and unguents, promising a rapid and complete cure on the birth of a son. He would not have been a sorcerer had he not added this prophecy: "From your travail will be born a boy who will be a light of the centuries to come."[13]

When the boy was finally born and the promised cure had been fulfilled, who could blame the family for not believing the sorcerer's third promise that little Jean-François would become immortal? The person who had the greatest faith in the future of this mite while still swaddled in its cradle was his twelve-year-old brother, Jacques-Joseph, one of the new-born baby's godparents.

A strange child indeed had been born to the librarian and his wife. When Doctor Janin examined the baby for the first time shortly after its birth he was surprised: the little face with its olive tint, two huge black eyes and heavy black curls was curiously oriental. To his amazement the doctor even noticed the yellow cornea, characteristic of the Levantines.

Jean-François Champollion was never to know the happiness of a peaceful youth in the bosom of his family. The Revolution broke out in France, and in April 1793 its eddies also reached the little town of Figeac, whose bitter struggle for liberty and indomitable pride had long since earned it an evil reputation. This reputation was upheld at the outbreak of the Revolution. From the Terror onwards, Jean-François's father entered the service of the new era; in the year III of the Republic he became a superintendent of the municipal police. His post allowed him to render valuable services; while the revolutionary notes of the Carmagnole, the frenzied jubilation of the apostles of liberty, welled like a flood about his house, his hearth became an asylum for several men whose lives were in danger, including the Benedictine Dom Calmet, the future teacher of his youngest son. Shouts of joy at newly won freedom, tears and complaints of refugees hidden in the house—these were among the first unforgettable impressions of the precocious Jean-François. The noisy fanfares of the Revolution, however, made the deepest and most lasting imprint on his sensitive mind. In the midst of this turbulent period, when the boy was two and a half, there was a very violent storm. In their anxiety the whole household began to search for him; the house was searched from the cellars to the attic, people rushed out into the blinding rain, to at last discover the child high in the attic huddled against the dormer window like a house-martin between the two beams, head outstretched and arms widespread. In this position, like some young Prometheus he seemed to be trying to catch a "little of this heavenly fire", as he explained to his terrified mother.

Jean-François, of course, had no idea that he would become a great decipherer. But, as the son of a librarian, he grew up surrounded by books, which fired his imagination long before anyone thought of starting to give him lessons. He constantly asked questions of his mother and, to quieten and amuse him, she read him long passages from her missal. The child remembered all he heard. Then he found a second missal and had the extracts in question pointed out to him. He compared the words he had heard with the printed text. He gave the letters imaginary names in order to distinguish them. At the age of five he invited his parents to a first reading of the missal and showed them his first attempts at writing—a curious script because he had copied the printed text.

Two years later the boy was given suitable teaching by his brother, Jacques-Joseph, who devoted his rare leisure hours to this task. But Jacques-Joseph was to be more than the first teacher, more than the loving and understanding elder brother, watching his pupil's progress. Probably unaware of the importance of his role, he was to become the first mediator between Jean-François Champollion and his Promised Land, Egypt.

In 1797, thanks to the good offices of a cousin, the talented elder brother was given an opportunity of going to Egypt with Napoleon's army. Jacques-Joseph was enthusiastic about this plan and gave his young brother, who listened open-mouthed, a vivid picture of this ancient and mysterious land. For the first time the seven-year-old boy had a vision of the miraculous land of Egypt. But it was still in the nature of an illusion, a mirage. The plan came to grief, and instead of going to Egypt, Jacques-Joseph found himself at Grenoble, employed in his cousin's business. Jean-François, greatly disappointed, remained at home with the good Dom Calmet, who guided him prudently and taught him to love nature. He collected stones, plants and insects. But he had soon outgrown this family instruction. At college he was a bad pupil, particularly weak in mathematics (this was to persist throughout his life). On the other hand, he delighted in Latin and Greek; he would recite by heart whole pages of Virgil and Homer merely for the pleasure of hearing the sonorous verses. And one fine day a second sign, a new call of destiny from far-off Egypt, was his reward; addressed to Jacques-Joseph, No. 37 of the *Courrier de l'Egypte*, in which the discovery of the Rosetta Stone was reported, arrived at the house.

Jacques-Joseph had been at Grenoble since 1798. Never in future would the two brothers forget this beautiful town and their favourite view of the snow-clad Alps. Grenoble, with its own university and excellent schools, was also the intellectual capital of the Dauphiné. In 1801 Jean-François, aged eleven, saw his ardent secret wish fulfilled: he joined his brother at Grenoble, where he went to a private school of good repute run by Abbé Dussert. To his great delight he embarked upon the study of Hebrew. A year later, at the age of barely twelve, he was to astound the school inspectors by his penetrating interpretation of a passage from the Bible in the original text.

The same year a third "ray of light" from Egypt illuminated the existence of the young Jean-François, when the new prefect of the Isère department settled at Grenoble. This man was neither an official nor some nondescript politician. He was the famous physicist and mathematician, Jean-Baptiste Fourier, the guiding light of the French scientific commission working in Egypt under the orders of Napoleon, and the author of the great historical introduction to the lavish memorial of this commission, the *Description de l'Egypte*. With the arrival of Fourier, Egypt was suddenly transported to Grenoble, and this was to prove a turning point in the life of Jean-François.

Several circumstances favoured the meeting of this talented

child with the great scholar. As Secretary of the Grenoble Academy, Jacques-Joseph was in close touch with Fourier. The new prefect insisted on making a personal inspection of the schools. He was struck by the personality of the young Jean-François and offered to show this pupil, who stood out above his schoolfellows, his Egyptian antiquities.

In the autumn of 1802 we find the boy at the Grenoble Prefecture spellbound, with flushed cheeks looking at Fourier's vast but choice collection. His enthusiasm, his intelligent questions, the obvious ardour of the born investigator in this shy boy induced Fourier to invite him to his scientific soirées.

For Jean-François this first visit to Fourier was a milestone. At this moment, as he often related in later life, a burning desire was awakened in him to decipher hieroglyphs—and at the same time the firm conviction that he would succeed.

"Enthusiasm alone is the real life," he was to say later. His own life justified this motto. And it was enthusiasm with all its power which for the first time seized this twelve-year-old boy in front of these Egyptian antiquities, still shrouded with mystery. The intoxication would never leave him.

How did it happen that such an enthusiasm manifested itself so early and in a childish manner? That his vocation was discovered at this moment and his store of energy and spiritual strength immediately sought an outlet?

He covered every surface within reach with strange signs which he called hieroglyphs: his restless spirit made him ply his brother with questions, and since he could not yet embark upon Egyptology he slaked his thirst elsewhere. The Lives of Plutarch inspired a whole gallery of heroes of antiquity, medallions cut out of board; he wrote a history of famous dogs beginning with Argus of the Odyssey. Next he assembled the material for a chronicle "From Adam to Champollion the Younger" because "he had to finish once and for all with the ineptitudes and uncertainties of the existing historical tables". One day his brother found him on the floor with whole pages torn out of Herodotus, Strabo, Diodorus Siculus, Pliny the Elder and Plutarch, dealing with Ancient Egypt. Jacques-Joseph, overcoming his grief at this barbarous desecration of his beloved books, praised the boy for his systematic scholarly studies.

Praise also poured in from his school. "I am very satisfied with the young Champollion," wrote Abbé Dussert. Jacques-

Joseph gave his younger brother the best possible reward—permission to learn three more languages—namely, Arabic, Syriac and Chaldaean! The child was led on a number of false trails, and the "Chinese ghosts" which Guignes had invoked gave him great food for thought, until the firm hand of the elder brother banished these phantoms.

Jean-François then attended as a boarder the semi-military lycée which in the meantime had been founded by Napoleon at Grenoble. A hard school! Despite the encouragement and the privileges he was given, the military discipline and the uniformity of the school regime weighed upon him, and he rebelled against certain of the teachers. At Fourier's house he met Dom Raphael, a former Coptic monk, who, as a reward for his services to Napoleon and the French army in Egypt, had been appointed Professor of Arabic at the School of Oriental Languages in Paris. This meeting was of serious importance to Champollion, who as a result of his private studies (at great detriment to his eyesight and his health: he spent his nights reading in secret) had just clarified one essential point. The writings of Guignes and Barthélemy had taught him the identity of Coptic with the language of Ancient Egypt, and a treatise written by Father Bonjour on the Vatican Coptic manuscripts confirmed his conviction that only a study of the practically extinct Coptic language could lead to the discovery and decipherment of the Ancient Egyptian language.

"I beg you to send me the first volume of the *Magasin Encyclopédique* or the *Mémoires de l'Académie des inscriptions et belles-lettres* [in which ten years before had appeared the theses of Guignes and Barthélemy] because one cannot always read serious matters such as Condillac . . ." (a well-known contemporary philosopher and psychologist).

Fourier finally rescued this "spirited colt who asks for triple rations" from the narrow stable of the lycée. Thanks to him, Champollion was able to read the *Consilium Aegyptiacum* of Leibniz, and the precocious youth earnestly hoped that the Emperor Napoleon would one day achieve what Louis XIV had failed to do: "to make Egypt the centre of the civilised world." "Everywhere I seem to be in Egypt," was the constant refrain of the young Jean-François as he began to prepare his first scientific work: *Egypt under the Pharaohs*.

He forwarded to the Grenoble Academy a general outline of

his work and a map; and on September 1st, 1807, read his introduction before this learned assembly. Mistrust, rebuttal and envy could be read on the faces of his audience as he stepped on to the platform to read his thesis. But when he had ended the President Renauldon embraced him, and in an enthusiastic speech welcomed him into this august circle. "In appointing you a member despite your youth, the Academy has taken into account the work you have already done, but looks forward to what you will achieve in the future. We like to think that you will justify our hopes, that one day your works will make a name for you and that you will recall that you received your first encouragement from this Academy."

At sixteen Champollion went to Paris to realise, of course, his plans concerning Egypt. But not for this reason alone. He also wished to find a job and the means to marry his sister-in-law, Pauline, his elder by six years, with whom he was passionately in love.

"Each to his tastes and leanings,
But I think in this life
The wisest man of all
Is the man who takes a wife."

he wrote sentimentally at this period.

Paris offered him the best teachers in the west for his Oriental studies. Jacques-Joseph introduced him to Sylvestre de Sacy, then at the height of his career. It was with unusual shyness that the young man approached this short, forty-nine-year-old scholar with the ascetic, awe-inspiring features. Sacy himself was deeply impressed by this encounter, but he judged the work of this sixteen-year-old boy as precocious.

In Paris Champollion took courses in Hebrew, "Chaldean" and Syriac; he studied Persian, Sanskrit, Arabic and Greek, and from 1808 occasionally deputised for one of his teachers. But the most beautiful language which Paris—which the whole world—could offer him was Coptic. He listened to the priest, Jeacha Scheftidschy, a member of the Coptic Union, saying Mass in that language at the church of Saint-Roche.[14]

"I want to know Egyptian as well as I know French . . . I am in fact a Copt who for his amusement translates into that language everything that comes into his head; I speak Coptic to myself so that no one will understand me."

On the other hand, he found partners for the other Eastern languages, and his frequent relationships with cultivated members of the countries where they were spoken was Paris's second gift to the young student. "He is perfectly at home with all these Orientals," his brother said of him and he himself wrote:

> "Arabic has completely changed my voice: it has grown soft and throaty. I speak almost without moving the lips and this must heighten my oriental appearance for Ibn Saoua . . . yesterday mistook me for an Arab, salaamed when I replied in his tongue and showered compliments upon me." And then Dom Raphael intervened.

Champollion's unwonted zeal and his relations with Orientals soon brought surprising results, which amazed the engineer and naturalist, Sonnini de Manoncourt, who had travelled extensively in the East. After meeting him he declared: "I was amazed to find that he knows the countries about which we spoke as well as I do." The spontaneous exclamation of Doctor Gall, the well-known phrenologist: "What a genius for languages!" would not have been necessary to inform the world that this young man possessed all the enthusiasm and obsessive passion of the born investigator.

The same year, 1808, still in Paris, a notable encounter took place between Champollion and the Rosetta Stone with which his name will always be associated. Not with the actual stone, of course, which was now in English hands, but with a copy.

Champollion did not yet try to decipher the hieroglyphs. He was content to compare assiduously the signs of the part written in demotic with a papyrus also purporting to be in demotic, but which was actually written in hieratic (*vide* below). He found that a certain number of the letters corresponded to those discovered by Åkerblad.

"I send you my first essays," he wrote to his brother. But this led him little farther than the Swedish scholar. The climate in which he wrote was far from favourable: on the one side his brother (who was now called Figeac to distinguish him from Jean-François) continuously encouraging him to greater things, and on the other Sacy, the circumspect teacher, advising him not to waste his time on decipherments which could not possibly succeed—except by some pure stroke of luck. It is not surprising that Champollion was occasionally discouraged. "I have spent seven whole days on the Egyptian inscription and I am convinced that it will never be translated in its entirety."

From 1809 Champollion's studies in Paris were interrupted. At the age of eighteen he was called to occupy the Chair of History at the newly created Faculty at Grenoble. He carried out his duties with the utmost zeal, but his audience were his former schoolmates, and several of the masters were envious of the "detestable pupil's" academic successes. Nevertheless, he found time to pursue his private studies and on August 7th presented the Grenoble Academy with a theory on Egyptian writing which broke radically with all the opinions previously uttered on this subject.

Champollion established that there existed not two but three Egyptian writings. Between demotic and hieroglyphs there was what he called "hieratic", a development which occurred when the hieroglyphs, instead of being employed solely for monumental writing, were written on papyri—an essentially new material which demanded a cursive script quite different from the original signs.

Champollion, by taking demotic for the oldest and hieratic for the youngest script, was still wrong in his chronological order. But he soon rectified this mistake and admitted it. He affirmed that the three Egyptian scripts were of the same nature. The two cursives were derived from the hieroglyphs and the decipherment of the latter must start from the demotic. Thus he embarked on his brilliant path of success four years before Thomas Young on the other side of the Channel had begun to busy himself with hieroglyphics.

In 1813 Champollion made his first discovery in hieroglyphics, a testimony to his perspicacity. Like so many great new ideas, the theory he propounded appears to us today to be simple. The Coptic language in which he constantly lived and worked has six endings for the six personal pronouns. According to Champollion these should also be found in Ancient Egyptian. In actual fact where the Greek text read "he" or "his" the hieroglyphic version of the Rosetta Stone used the horned serpent sign 𓆑 and the demotic text a sign he had long since known from his comparative philological studies. It was derived from this serpent sign and identical with the Coptic ϥ the "f" of the third person. Champollion had incontestably determined the first hieroglyph according to its phonetic value.

But he went no farther. On the contrary, he retrogressed, and fell once more into the error of mistaking the hieroglyphs for symbolical signs with no specific phonetic character. Had the demon of the hieroglyphs which had already baffled so many brains, feeling the approaching end of its rule, played its last trick?

Young had in the meantime published the hieroglyphic form of the name of Ptolemy, and to this Champollion constantly reverted. He concluded that the majestic lion enthroned in the centre of the cartouche could signify nothing else than "war", which in Greek is "p(t)ólemos", the eponym of the King's name.

If this "war" was only an hallucination, the real war soon knocked at the door of the decipherer. A tireless worker, Champollion had not become the erudite scholar, a stranger to the outside world. He had always been an ardent patriot. Napoleon's return from Elba had moved him greatly. The Hundred Days sufficed to make him politically suspect to the Grenoble police authorities; when he joined Didier's revolt at Grenoble and took up arms against the Bourbon Government (taking care to guard his Egyptian treasures with his life) he overstepped the constable. Forced to flee, he wandered for some time homeless and hunted in the Dauphiné Alps. His Chair and that of his brother were annulled and both men were ordered to reside under supervision in Figeac and subsequently in Grenoble, where Jean-François managed to get out of his difficulties fairly well, but without losing his ardour as a reformist school-teacher.

Now, unknown to Champollion, the scene of the historic decipherment was enlarged. During this interval there suddenly appeared on the scene an English diplomat, an English collector and traveller, a circus strong man and an obelisk. The latter played the leading role, but all the other actors are deserving of mention. It will not unduly surprise the reader to see appear on this stage an Italian giant, a variety star. Had not Thomas Young once performed on the tight-rope?

The diplomat was the British Consul-General in Egypt, Henry Salt, who, on his own initiative, undertook a number of investigations and amassed a valuable collection. In 1817 he wrote to Dacier, the Secretary of the Academy of Inscriptions, asking to be put in touch with French scholars—a letter which throws some light on Champollion's years in Grenoble as a school-teacher. It was written from the Valley of the Kings at Thebes, where Salt had just discovered five royal tombs. This forced labour had been carried out by the Hercules we have already mentioned.

His name was Gianbattista Belzoni, and he was born at Padua in 1778; he was a barber's son. To the surprise of all his neighbours, the boy grew to a Gargantuan size and soon overtopped all his neighbours. At the age of sixteen he was a positive Goliath. Since the family home became too restricted for him, he went to Rome on foot. Having learned only his father's trade, he continued to practise it until a flashing-eyed Roman lady crossed his path. She coldly rejected the clumsy advances of this Paduan giant. What was an Italian of seventeen to do in such a situation? He retired from the world and entered a monastery, where he studied hydraulics. At least he helped to dig an Artesian well.

Napoleon Bonaparte had led him by tortuous paths into the service of Egyptology.

As a general Napoleon had invaded Italy in 1796 and liberated Milan. Other French troops marched on Rome and treated the Pope Pius VI with short shrift. The armed patriots who opposed the invaders were shot, and squads of recruiting sergeants scoured the streets in search of strapping young men for impressment in the French army. For them Belzoni was a fine prize; he would make a splendid platoon leader. A troop commanded by a sergeant arrested him, but the soldiers had underestimated the strength of this giant in a monk's habit. With a single blow, the sergeant was felled to the ground, and Belzoni was able to save his skin. He did not stop until he reached Padua. But there the Doge was no longer in power: the new master of the country was the Austrian Emperor.

In Venice Belzoni learned to build bucket wheels and to dredge canals. He became an efficient hydraulic engineer. Then he conceived a taste for travel and wandered through Europe. At Hanover he was forced for a time to submit to the discipline of the occupying Prussian troops. It appears that he left their service with the permission of his superiors. A new and brief stay in his native Venice taught him that Central Europe was too hot to hold a man of his stature. He wandered to England. There an unexpected career awaited him: he became hydraulic engineer in a theatre; and in London a variety star—a circus strong man capable of lifting eleven men at a time.

After a trip to Portugal and Spain, avoiding the undertow of the European wars he landed in Malta, where he offered his services as a hydraulic expert to Mohammed Ali Pasha, the rising star and lord of Egypt.

It would be interesting to follow the details of this extraordinary man's career, but we must limit it to Belzoni's unwitting contribution to the decipherment of Egyptian hieroglyphics.

He had earned a splendid reputation as a transport specialist ready to use any methods—his hands, if necessary. He was therefore commissioned to transport to the Nile, by the methods used in that country, a twenty-six-feet-long overturned obelisk. This task was undertaken on the orders of the English collector to whom we have already referred—William John Bankes, a friend of Byron—to the indignation of the French Consul-General Drovetti, into whose clutches he nearly fell. A new monument came into the hands of an Englishman and a further obstacle arose to thwart the glory of French research.

On visiting Philae, the island on the Nile, Bankes had discovered what others had overlooked: an obelisk covered with hieroglyphs which had been erected on a plinth bearing a Greek inscription. The plinth and obelisk tallied. Now the Greek inscription on the plinth bore the name of Cleopatra.

In 1815 Bankes copied the hieroglyphs from the obelisk. The stone itself was available to Young for some years in England, but he had no idea what to do with it.

Champollion, however, worked like a slave. Despite being politically suspect, despite his failing health, he caused the dead to speak, or, to be more precise, the Books of the Dead written in hieroglyphic and hieratic which were discovered in the tombs and published in the luxurious volumes of the *Description de l'Egypte*. He continued to compare and contrast the signs of these two scripts. It was a painstaking and exhausting task. But in May 1821 he had reached his goal. He was now able to do what no one before him had done: to transliterate a demotic text sign by sign into hieratic and to transpose it subsequently into hieroglyphic. Figure 20 shows us quite clearly the enormous gulf that separated demotic from the other two scripts.

Thanks to this double transliteration, Champollion acquired a final proof which at one blow swept away all previous errors and felled the demon of hieroglyphic with a *coup de grâce*. Once again we cannot fail in restrospect to be amazed. Was the solution not simple, crystal clear and self-evident?

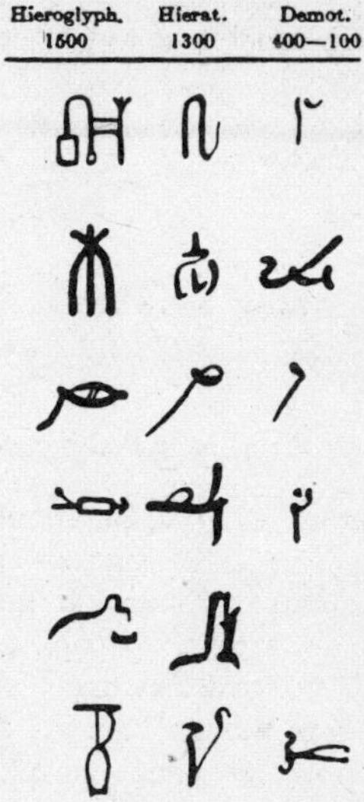

Hieroglyph. 1600	Hierat. 1300	Demot. 400—100

Fig. 20.—The evolution of Egyptian writing.

On his birthday, December 23rd, 1821, Champollion conceived the bright idea of enumerating all the signs of the text on the Rosetta Stone and of the corresponding Greek text. He discovered that the hieroglyphs far outnumbered the words of the Greek text; 1,419 against 486 words. A striking and irrefutable proof that the hieroglyphs could not be ideograms or symbols, because their number was too large for that.

This discovery was a great step forward towards decipherment, the lifetime goal which he had never lost sight of despite the turbulent times, sickness, persecution and poverty. He was ready to pluck it like a ripe fruit.

Reversing the process, he now transliterated all the demotic signs, the Greek names of which had provided him with the phonetic value, firstly into hieratic and then into hieroglyphic. His touchstone was still the name of Ptolemy. He discovered that the latter was also written phonetically in the hieroglyphic text and, avoiding Young's error, no longer read *Ptolemaios* but, according to the laws of the Egyptian language, *p-t-o-l-m-j-s*. Ptolmis. This substantial harvest, already reaped to a great extent in Grenoble and taken to Paris in 1821 by the ailing scholar, only required the proof of one example, the incontestable demonstration which was to silence the sceptics.

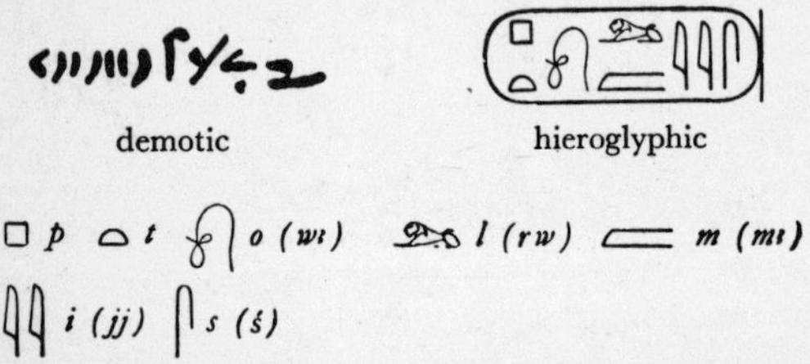

demotic hieroglyphic

p *t* *o (wı)* *l (rw)* *m (mı)*

i (jj) *s (ś)*

FIG. 21.—Analysis of the name of Ptolemy after Champollion.

Thanks to the demotic papyrus, Champollion knew the name of Cleopatra.

He had often practised translating it into hieratic and into hieroglyphic. He knew with no possibility of error how the name would read in the royal cartouche of a hieroglyphic inscription. But alas there was no such inscription available.

In January 1822, however, appeared a lithographed copy of the hieroglyphic inscription of the Philae obelisk, which Belzoni had managed to carry with all his sangfroid and prudence across the Nile cataract. Bankes had sent it to the Institut de Paris, where Champollion had aroused a host of petty jealousies. It was not he who received the copy, but Letronne, a Hellenist of some repute.

The latter, however, was a close friend of Champollion. He sent on to him the copy he had received from Bankes. This is what Champollion's biographer, H. Hartleben, writes on this subject:

> "On seeing it, the decipherer was electrified. There in the second royal cartouche stood the name of Cleopatra, sign for sign, as he had copied it himself a thousand times, reconstructing its form from the demotic and burning with impatience to see the confirmation of his discovery. Who else but he would have been able to do it?"

The two royal cartouches, Ptolemy and Cleopatra, furnished Champollion with twelve different hieroglyphic letters and gave him a good and solid basis for his future decipherment.

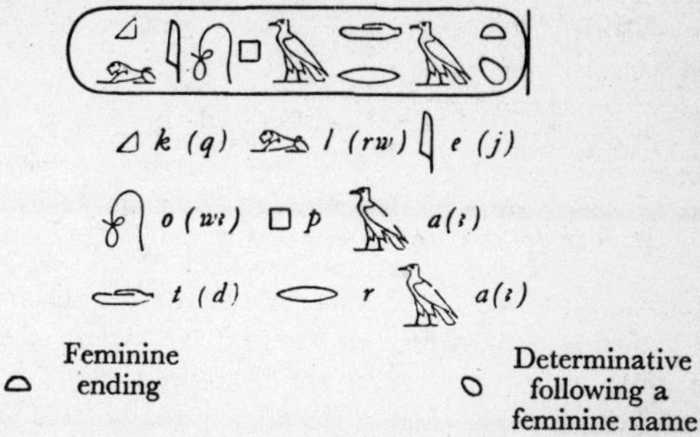

k (q) l (rw) e (j)

o (wꜣ) p a(ꜣ)

t (d) r a(ꜣ)

Feminine ending

Determinative following a feminine name

FIG. 22.—The cartouche of Cleopatra and its analysis.

The scholar's delight was not unqualified. Bankes had noted in pencil on the copy the name of Cleopatra—an easy supposition, since he had long ago read it in the Greek inscription. But when Champollion had proved letter by letter what the others (Bankes, Young and Letronne) had only presumed, they attacked him and disputed among themselves for the credit of decipherment.

But nothing could now deter Champollion. He collected all the royal hieroglyphic cartouches he could find and attacked them with the whole arsenal of his Egyptological weapons, lovingly forged at the expense of unremitting toil. Now the late Egyptian period came to life again, and the stones virtually began to speak: Alexander, Autocrator (Imperial title), Tiberius, Domitian, Germanicus and Trajan addressing him genially from their oval seals.

Familiar and yet at the same time alien, for among them was no true Egyptian name, and the scholar concluded—quite wrongly—that only foreign names of the Late Egyptian period were written with phonetic signs.

In August 1822 Champollion took another important step. He noticed that behind certain names (of stars) written in hieroglyphic stood a tiny star. A little star behind the name of the star! He suddenly had a flash of inspiration: he recognised the existence of what are called determinatives—mute signs added to the end of words to give a more accurate definition to words of the same orthography but different phonetically. These signs constituted a basic element of Egyptian script in its entirety.

a) b) c)

d) e) f)

FIG. 23.—The names of Alexander (*a*), Autocrator (*b*), Tiberius (*c*), Domitian (*d*), Germanicus (*e*) and Trajan (*f*) in hieroglyphic.

Champollion remained discreet about his discoveries; as a scholar and as a man he had learned the virtue of silence. But on August 22 he presented the Academy with a treatise on demotic, the fruits of several decades of study. He at last won a brilliant victory, and even received an unexpected acclamation —Sacy, the great Sacy, his former teacher who had soon turned

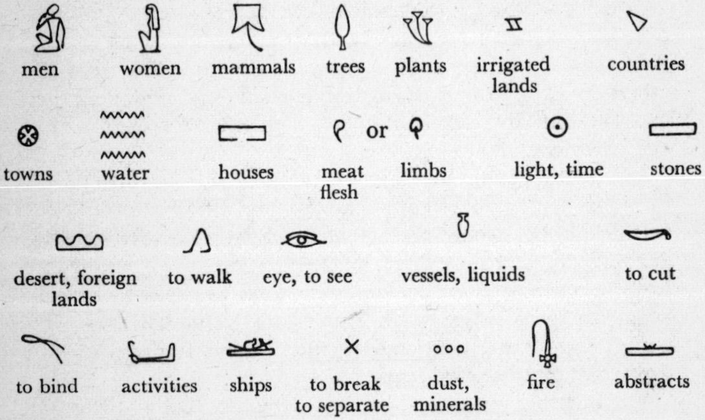

men | women | mammals | trees | plants | irrigated lands | countries

towns | water | houses | meat flesh or limbs | light, time | stones

desert, foreign lands | to walk | eye, to see | vessels, liquids | to cut

to bind | activities | ships | to break to separate | dust, minerals | fire | abstracts

FIG. 24.—Egyptian determinatives.

away from his gifted but over-confident pupil, jumped to his feet and without a word stretched out his two hands to the young savant. Then he proposed that Champollion's work should be published at the expense of the State.

Champollion never tired of collecting royal cartouches, a work which proved extremely fruitful. The inscriptions on the temples brought him dozens of the required names—but they were always Greek kings and Roman emperors of the late Egyptian period. Was it one of these names he was about to decipher on the morning of September 14th, 1822 as he feverishly bent over a consignment he had received from the French architect, Huyot, who at that time was travelling in Egypt and Nubia—very accurate reproductions of bas-reliefs and inscriptions from Egyptian temples?

FIG. 25.—The name of Rameses in hieroglyphic.

The decipherer picked up the first page and gave a start. Obviously the name of a king, but not one of the Lagidae or of a Roman emperor. He stared in fascination at the group of signs.

His brain began to work fast, his emotion increased and the hand which held the paper trembled. The name started with a sun (the circle top left). Now, the sun in Coptic ("I speak Coptic to myself") is *Re.* Next came an unfamiliar sign, then twice the folded cloth 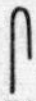, s. That meant—no, it was impossible!—R(e)-x?-s-s. Was this really R-m-s-s, Rameses, the most illustrious of the Pharaohs? Champollion turned over all the pages rapidly; a thousand thoughts ran through his head. His fingers trembled as he seized the next page. Soon his eyes fell on another name written in the following manner:

FIG. 26.—The name of Thutmosis in hieroglyphic.

This name once more finished with -s and its initial sign was the ibis, the bird sacred to the God Thoth. In the centre was once more this , which if R-m-s-s was correct could only be an m . . . Thot-m-s. . . . It was incontestably Thotmes or Thutmosis, another brilliant name among the Pharaohs.

There was no longer any doubt. Champollion had at last grasped the truth. What he had previously considered as a late degeneration, the use of hieroglyphs for a phonetic writing, had in actual fact been a fundamental characteristic of the ancient script. Not only did this discovery solve the last riddle, but it also opened to the scholar something he had never accepted in his wildest dreams—the key to ancient Egyptian history, which had been lost for 1,500 years. He now knew that the inscriptions did not belong to the late period at all but went back far earlier in antiquity.

The exhausted man could hardly control his feelings. He forced himself to remain calm and to concentrate. Everything had to be pondered upon, compared and checked. He could have shouted his victory from the housetops and given vent to his exuberance and joy. But science is a stern task-mistress, and Champollion had matured in her service. Furthermore, the numerous attacks and the petty jealousies he had suffered in specialist and lay circles had made him cautious and timid. With an almost superhuman effort he forced himself to make a cold and objective scrutiny. He remained the whole morning bowed over Huyot's drawings.

By midday he was certain. He rose to his feet, gathered up his papers and rushed to the Institut, where Jacques-Joseph was working. Flinging open the door of the library, he threw the bundle of papers on his brother's desk and in a voice hoarse with emotion proclaimed his triumph: "*Je tiens l'affaire.*" But his suppressed excitement was too much for his frail body. He collapsed in a dead faint.

For five days he remained in bed, listless, with no strength and deathly weary. Then he recovered. Within a few days he had composed his famous opusculus: *Lettre à M. Dacier, relative à l'alphabet des hiéroglyphes phonétiques*, which the addressee, his faithful friend, forwarded to the Academy on September 27th.

This work, in which we can read in simple and persuasive terms his readings of Greek and Roman names, shows that the *old* inscriptions contain in addition to the ideograms, alphabetic signs which constitute the ancient and essential part of the written script.

Champollion's discovery had the effect of a bombshell. For the French the decipherment of hieroglyphics had long become a matter of national pride and the subject of the day. The whole of France participated in the joy of its savant as soon as the news of this remarkable feat became known. Certain envious spirits slily maintained that people were beginning to write their love-letters in the hieroglyphs, using Champollion's alphabet.

The following year, 1823, Champollion published his *Précis du Système hiéroglyphique*, in which he gave the names of the Pharaohs, on the evidence of the inscriptions, back to the second millennium B.C.; the reading of numerous other names and translations of some fragments of the texts. The work is not free from errors, but none of them is of any importance in the practical field; they simply gave his adversaries an opportunity to attack him on certain points.

The best minds of the period (for example, Wilhelm von Humboldt in Germany and Baron von Hammer-Purgstall in Austria) assessed the unique discovery of the French Egyptologist at its true value. In England, Henry Salt encouraged him in person and in his correspondence. Thomas Young, on the other hand, did not evince the same generosity.

"But soon around his name there arose a chorus of howls" (Erman). In England the patriots wanted to award the laurels to Young. In France certain "decipherers" of the older school considered that they had been slighted. The sceptics of all countries found plenty to say, particularly the know-alls.

Of the German sinologist, Julius Klaproth—very competent in his own field, but possessing a hideous petty nature—Champollion said one day resignedly: "He is my evil genius." Klaproth supported the theory of so-called acrology, according to which the Ancient Egyptians were said to have written with one and the same sign all the words beginning with the same letter, just as if in English we were to write with the same symbol "sin", "seat", "season", etc.

At this juncture the Leipzig theologian, Seyffarth, intervened. Champollion had won a resounding victory over him in Rome at a tourney of "decipherers" before a galaxy of scholars, and Seyffarth had never forgiven him. Starting from justifiable objections, he arrived at the most fantastic conclusions on the subject of hieroglyphics; his divagations have become a byword in the history of German erudition. One of his works, for example, was entitled: *In which it is incontestably proved that on September 7th of the year 3446 B.C. the Deluge ended and the alphabet of the races of the world were invented.*

Marked by political and scientific persecutions, Champollion's career, which also brought him great honours, ended with the realisation of his lifelong ambition. In the vast collection of Egyptian antiquities owned by the King of Sardinia at Turin the decipherer acquired great mastery of his art.

Later he travelled to Egypt to pursue his studies. He entered the country as though returning to the land of his ancestors and explored it as his heritage. Here he spent the happiest hours of his life. It was there, too, in the tombs, that he caught the germ which was to cause his death.

He was made Chevalier of the Legion of Honour and was almost given a cardinal's hat in Rome! He transmitted his scientific heritage to his most talented pupil, the Pisan, Ippolito Rosellini.

Official France—at any rate, the Government and the Court—treated him with complete indifference. His adversaries did a fine job. Only after great difficulties was he appointed Professor of Egyptology at the Collège de France.

The strenuous work, his political adventures and his researches in Egypt had undermined his health. To his general debility were added tuberculosis and diabetes. Champollion knew that he was doomed to die, "My God," he cried one day, "give me another two years, just two more years. . . ." And on another occasion: "Too soon," and mopping his brow added: "There is so much inside my head."

On March 4th, 1822, he died of a stroke. When his remains were taken to the cemetery of Père Lachaise, the "big guns" of the scientific world, including Champollion's former teacher, Sacy, and Alexander von Humboldt, acted as pall-bearers.

"Archaeology is a beautiful girl without a dowry," Champollion once said. He could not foresee the wealth she would bestow upon him. "Enthusiasm alone is the real life," and Jean-François Champollion never for one day lost his enthusiasm; it had burned in his heart and illuminated him despite all the obstacles encountered in his brief existence.

At first it was believed that the young science of Egyptology which he had created would disappear with him into the tomb. The distrust aroused by his decipherment work, admittedly not free from error, gained ground. The merit for having ensured the survival and extension of his work is due to the scholar and diplomat, Karl Josias von Bunsen, and the philologist, Richard Lepsius.

Bunsen had met Champollion in 1826 at Rome and had been greatly impressed. He in turn encouraged Lepsius, a budding scholar, to devote himself entirely to Egyptology.

Initially possessing no luggage in the field of Egyptology,

Lepsius, with his Teutonic stolidity, had all the qualities necessary to increase his knowledge, to enlarge the breach opened by the brilliant Frenchman and to free Champollion's work from all its faults and weaknesses.

Born in 1810 at Naumburg on the Saale, he studied classical philology, archaeology and Sanskrit at Göttingen and Berlin under the best teachers of the period. Several of his contemporaries had done the same, but Lepsius had the advantage of them; he had won his spurs as a "decipherer", thanks to his private work and interpretation of the mysterious Iguvine Tablets, to which we shall return later in this book.

After this brilliant start the young man came in 1833 to Paris, the citadel of Orientalism, to complete his studies. With inflexible zeal and remarkable perspicacity he examined Champollion's works, and while confirming its value, discovered certain minor discrepancies, filled in the lacunae, proved the points in doubt and rectified the errors. He realised that Champollion would have done this himself had he been spared.

Discrepancies, lacunae, doubts and errors. . . . Certainly. As the foregoing illustrations show, Champollion thought that all phonetic writings consisted of isolated letters. In actual fact the majority contain a word sign of more than one consonant to which is often added a suffix of one or several consonants already contained in the sign. The sign 𓌻, for example, "the axe", represents "mr". To write the word "to love", which is also spelt "mr", the Ancient Egyptians added to the axe "mr" 𓌻 a second -r, 𓂋, which instead of "mr" gives "mr-r". The same applies to the signs 𓄟, the "whisk", "ms" and the "game of draughts", 𓏠 "mn". To Champollion these three signs 𓌻, 𓄟 and 𓏠, merely served to express a simple "m", but each had to be used in one of the families of the corresponding words! When he met it, which often happened, cases where 𓌻, 𓄟 and 𓏠 *alone* stood for "ms", "mr" and "mn" (without an added letter) he considered them merely as abbreviations of the usual forms. In this way, thanks to his great intuition, he avoided practically all errors; where the Egyptians had written "mr-r" to signify merely "mr" (as above in "to love"

𓂋 𓂋), Champollion from the outset only saw "mr"; on the other hand, when he read a solitary 𓌻, considering this as an abbreviation, he added on his own account the missing "r". We can safely say, therefore, that he was the first man to have read and understood hieroglyphic.

Lepsius recognised the weaknesses which had escaped the "Egyptian" of the Dauphiné. What a difference in character and method existed between the two men; between Champollion and the circumspect German with the "medallion head", as one of his colleagues said, referring to his well-chiselled features. He is reported to have said: "What is more impressive than the power of the mind, which expresses itself with reserved calm in a chastened language, as opposed to the unbridled passions of the same human mind?"

This "reserved calm", the goal of Lepsius's work, finds its classical scientific expression in his *Lettre à M. le professeur H. Rosellini sur l'alphabet hiéroglyphique*, published in Rome in 1837 addressed to Champollion's pupil. As the basis and synthesis of the new science this work dispelled once and for all the doubts attached to Champollion's work; it allowed an accurate and precise decipherment of hieroglyphic, and ensured a place for Egyptology among the other oriental disciplines.

Had it really been necessary to wait for further confirmation, to reinforce the results already achieved? At the beginning of 1866 Lepsius left on his second journey to Egypt and in company with his Viennese colleague Dr. Reinisch discovered at San, the "Zoan" of the Bible or Tanis of the Greeks, a second trilingual inscription, subsequently called the Canopus Decree.

This was a stele of hard limestone found among the ruins. It bore a hieroglyphic inscription of 237 lines and a Greek translation in sixty-six closely written lines. The same text was repeated for the third time in demotic on the margin of the tablet. Lepsius at first overlooked this.

Thus came to light what for many years the friends and partisans of Champollion had been waiting for: a new and brilliant justification of his work. The translation of the part engraved in Egyptian, carried out on Champollion's methods, and other methods evolved after his death, coincided perfectly with the Greek text. Lepsius at his first attempt could read both texts without any difficulty.

The decipherment of Egyptian writing was drawing to a close. Egyptian philology, on the other hand, the science of the language, was in its infancy. Scholars from various European countries, discoverers, translators, collectors, connotators and commentators, did great service to this study. The Englishman, Birch, Hincks of Ireland and H. Brugsch from Germany also made their more modest but conclusive contributions to the decipherment of this script; the former as regards the hieroglyphs, particularly the determinatives, and the latter, despite his youth, as regards demotic.

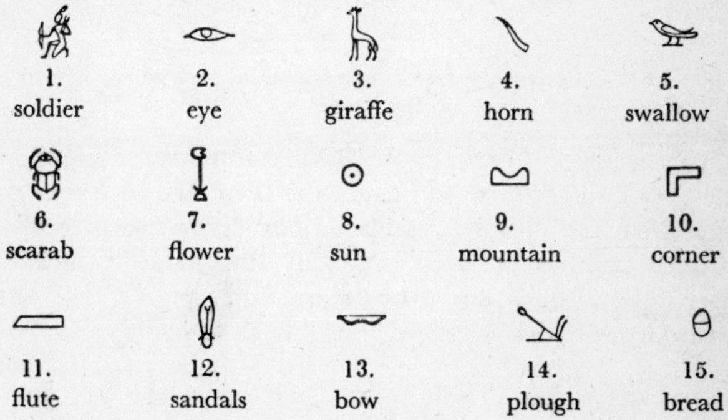

1. soldier	2. eye	3. giraffe	4. horn	5. swallow
6. scarab	7. flower	8. sun	9. mountain	10. corner
11. flute	12. sandals	13. bow	14. plough	15. bread

FIG. 27.—Egyptian hieroglyphs for concrete objects.

In conclusion let us examine the general situation of the subject more than a century after Champollion's pioneer work.

It has been proved that the three Egyptian scripts—hieroglyphic, hieratic and demotic—are in actual fact one and the same. To sum up their structure and nature we can resort to the hieroglyphs which have been the most transfigured and transformed down the ages.

Egyptian writing consists, as we have seen, of three types of signs: ideograms, phonetic signs ("isolated letters") and mute determinatives.

The ideograms or logograms represent some visible object (without taking into account the pronunciation). Egyptian possesses a great number of these.

It is striking how aptly these true-to-nature signs manage to conform to a simple and stylised outline; they have "an artistic perfection which is to be found among no other race" (H. Schneider).

The same remark holds good for the ideograms representing actions perceptible to the senses. These are portrayed by fixing their characteristic motion in an image. Thus the man with the raised stick (above left) signifies "to beat", the bird with its wings outstretched "to fly", etc.

FIG. 28.—Egyptian ideograms representing actions perceptible to the senses.

Abstract ideas were far more difficult to portray. Here once more they had recourse to images the sense of which was connected with the idea represented. The curved sceptre of the Pharaohs signifies "to rule", the lily, the heraldic flower of Upper Egypt, "the south", the dotard with his stick, "old age", the vase from which water trickles, "fresh or cool".

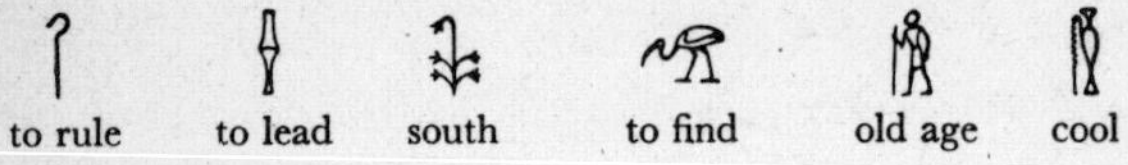

to rule to lead south to find old age cool

FIG. 29.—Egyptian hieroglyphs representing abstract ideas.

All these signs are still in the domain of pictorial writing: they are symbols, not phonemes. Fig. 30 shows that even in the dawn of history Egyptian writing was very well adapted to this procedure.

FIG. 30.—Egyptian hieroglyphic writing.

a high official (*b*) built (*a*) the vast dwelling (*c*). (That of King Menes, ca. 3500 B.C.) [15]

Nevertheless, the exact phonetic value of the written sign was often of vital importance. At a very early stage they had recourse to the phonetic rebus which we mentioned in Chapter I.

This was easy in Egyptian, since, the vowels not being written, the language possessed a number of homonyms, i.e. words consisting of the same consonants. Since the words were merely consonantal skeletons (the vowel sounds of all the languages of ancient Egypt are lost to us and can only be reconstructed approximately by analogy), they could, for example, with the sign for "lute" (n-f-r), also write the word "good", possessing the same consonantal skeleton n-f-r; or use the picture of a swallow (w-r) for "great" also (w-r). (Thus in English c-r would correspond to the words car, core, cur or care.) Moreover, since j and w as final sounds seem to have become mute at a very early date, they could even write with the hieroglyph signifying "house" p-r, the verb p-r-j, meaning "to come out".

As they departed progressively from the picture, the "swallow" (w-r) was no longer read only as w-r, meaning "great", but the single sign, without heed for its original meaning, considered phonetically (phonetisation) and used to write any other word with the group of consonants w-r such as w-r-d, "to be tired". W-r has become a simple syllabic sign or, if one prefers, since Egyptian possesses no vowels and no syllables according to our conception, a simple biconsonantal phonetic sign.

Here is a selection of these signs:

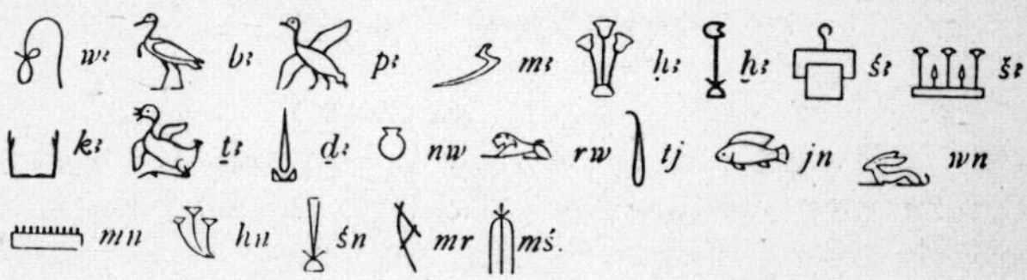

wꜣ bꜣ pꜣ mꜣ ḥꜣ ḫꜣ śꜣ šꜣ
kꜣ ṯꜣ ḏꜣ nw rw tj jn wn
mn hn śn mr mś.

FIG. 31.—Biconsonantal phonetic signs.

In the same way were born the uniconsonantal phonetic signs with which was achieved the last stage of evolution—that of alphabetic writing. These; too, stemmed from ideographic signs with a single consonant (and a vowel unknown to us). Thus the word "bolt" consisted of only the consonant s (plus a vowel which we do not know today; in Coptic it is šêi). The original sign was soon used for a certain syllable of the type s + vowel, and since the vowel did not count, as a simple alphabetic sign for the sibilant "s". It was in this way that the Egyptians built their alphabet of twenty-four letters (consonants only) which we give below.

Nothing prevented the use of a purely alphabet writing, but the conservative Egyptians clung rigidly to their familiar traditional signs and to their good and bad graphic customs.

Adopting the good, rejecting the bad and knowingly taking the final step towards an alphabetic writing—this final operation was left to the Ethiopian kingdom in the south of Egypt. Strongly influenced culturally by the North, this empire, where the spoken language differed completely from Egyptian, continued to use the Egyptian tongue and script for official purposes. But in 200 B.C., when Meroe became the new capital,

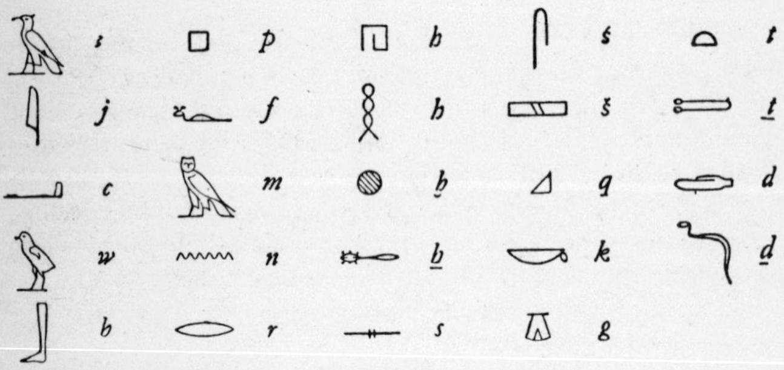

FIG. 32.—The Egyptian "alphabet".

and the empire seceded more and more from Egyptian influence in favour of an autonomous political life, the need for a writing more in tune with the local tongue became increasingly urgent. Then we see the birth, doubtless inspired by the Greek and Egyptian models, of Meroitic alphabetic writing, a happy combination of the two systems.

In common with Egyptian it has both a hieroglyphic and a demotic script. In common with Greek it consists of about twenty signs and a certain number of vowels. The Meroitic signs themselves have been borrowed from the Egyptians, but their meaning and value merely correspond to the Egyptian meaning of the same signs.

Although known as early as 1820, thanks to the reproductions of the French engraver, Caillaud, this language was long considered indecipherable.

Hierogl.	Demot.	Phonetic value	Hierogl.	Demot.	Phonetic value
		aleph. od. *a*			*l*
		e			*ḫ* [*γ*?]
		ê			*ẖ*
		i			*s*
		y			*š*
		w			*k*
		v [*b*?]			*q*
		p			*t*
		m			*te*
		n			*tê*
		ñ			*z*
		r			

: *wêši* : *ašêreyi* : *tktiẓ-mn* : *iqê* : *ẓêkrêr* : *erkelê* : *amnitêrey* : *eẓḇli*

"Isis (and) Osiris, protect Taktiz-Amon, (of) Zekarer conceived (of) Amon-tares born."

FIG. 33.—Meroitic alphabets (hieroglyphic and demotic) and a Meroitic inscription.

The distorted historical representations from the ancient and legendary kingdom of Meroe added to the difficulties of decipherment. Richard Lepsius was the first to dispel these illusions. Today we can consider that the writing can be read. The merit is due to the English archaeologist Griffith, who, in a matter of some twenty years (1911–29), taking the text on the Benaga plinth found by Lepsius, managed to read the inscriptions and partially to interpret them. The inscription in

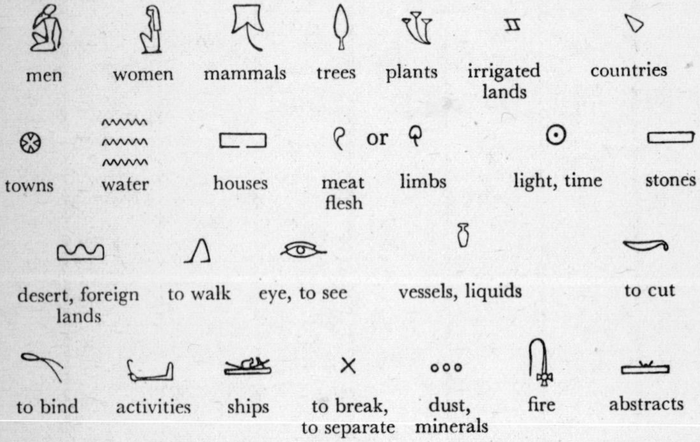

men | women | mammals | trees | plants | irrigated lands | countries

towns | water | houses | meat flesh or limbs | light, time | stones

desert, foreign lands | to walk | eye, to see | vessels, liquids | to cut

to bind | activities | ships | to break, to separate | dust, minerals | fire | abstracts

FIG. 34.—The most current determinatives.

question is written in the Egyptian tongue and script, but it also contains the names of the King and Queen in Meroitic hieroglyphs. This language being apparently unique of its kind, and its translation still being incomplete and a matter of controversy, we shall confine ourselves here to giving the Meroitic alphabet as an example of writing.

In Egypt, however, as we have explained, they were still far removed from an alphabetic writing. Each one wrote as he pleased. Thus a certain scribe could conceive the idea of writing the word "good", n-f-r, with the sign 𓄤 (which is the lute and on its own reads n-f-r), whereas a colleague deemed it necessary to string together n-f-r (lute) + f (horned serpent) + r (mouth); he would therefore write 𓄤𓆑𓂋, which was obviously more picturesque.

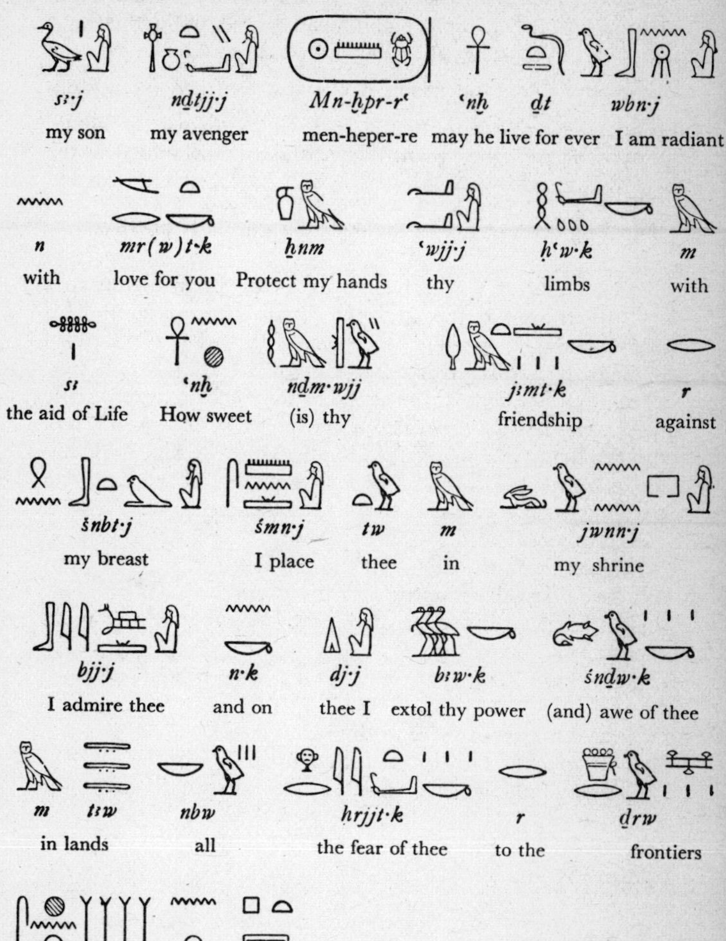

śḫnwt nt pt

of the pillows of the sky.

FIG. 35.—Text in Egyptian hieroglyphic: The God Amon-Ra speaks to Pharaoh Thutmosis III (1504–1450 B.C.).

How did they finally struggle against the homonyms? The group m-n-h, for example, could mean "wax", of the "papyrus plant" and in Late Egyptian "a youth". Even if they wrote the consonants 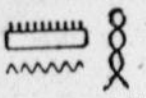 the problem was just as tricky. Only determinatives could remedy this evil. If m-n-h was to signify "papyrus plant", the "plant" determinative was added to the phonetic script: 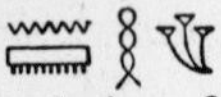.

Fig. 34 gives a choice of the most current determinatives.

To conclude we have given a text in Egyptian hieroglyphs with the transliteration and the English translation. This meagre example will give some idea of the oriental wealth of the language and its structure. (Fig. 35.)

The decipherment of the script of the ancient races of Nile dwellers has not only revealed a new phase of history, but has, as in the hymn of Amenophis IV, the "apostate king" Akhnaton, to his new God the Sun, given a picture of the Egyptian as a man:

Thy light rises in the mountains to the East,
And thou fillest the country with thy beauty.
Thou art beautiful and great, lucent and sublime over every land.
Thy rays burn them to the end of what thou hast created.

Thou hast subjected them to thy beloved son.
Thou art remote, but thy rays shine upon the earth
Thou dost illuminate mankind but none sees thy path.

Lord, how great and numerous are thy works,
Hidden from the face of men.[16]

CHAPTER III

AHURA MAZDA CAME TO MY AID

THE DECIPHERMENT OF OLD PERSIAN CUNEIFORM

"*King Darius proclaims: Ahura Mazda came to my aid!*"
—Rock inscription from Behistun.

IT was thanks to Darius I that in the 19th century we were able to decipher the cuneiform script which had fallen into even deeper oblivion than Egyptian hieroglyphs.

The writers of antiquity knew of the existence of this script. Herodotus and Strabo speak of "Assyrian characters", Diodorus of "Syrian", Athenaeus and Eusebius of "Chaldean". On verifying their sources we know today that they were describing cuneiform writing. But they all spoke of "characters" and of "writing"; among the writers of antiquity we find not the slightest indication that the Greek, Roman and Jewish scholars (the Talmud also mentions "Assyrian writing") were speaking from actual visual experience or had even recognised the nail or wedge as the basic element of this script. Later writers, too—Syrian Christians who should have been better informed—merely mention "Assyrian characters". The natives of Mesopotamia, the cradle of cuneiform writing, showed far more perspicacity and perceived what had escaped the erudition of the Greeks and Romans, the Jews and the medieval Arab geographers: they called these mysterious signs *mismari*—"nail writing". To show that these nails were more accurately described as wedges we had to await the arrival of a man from Westphalia.

But we are forging ahead of our subject. At the root of the history of this decipherment, as we have mentioned, stands Darius I, the Great (522–468 B.C., the Persian Daryavush), of the Achaemenid dynasty (founded by Achaemenes). Seizing the throne after a long struggle by suppressing sundry revolts, he ruled with a firm hand the kingdom of the Achaemenides, the vastest empire of the ancient world before that of Alexander, restoring its original frontiers and enlarging it to such an extent that it eventually comprised, in addition to the ancient kingdoms of the Medes and Persians, the Chaldees and Egyptians, a large part of eastern Iran as far as the Indus and even a large strip of the south-east European coast—for the period a gigantic, flourishing empire, well organised and brilliantly administrated, an empire which did not crumble to dust without bequeathing a number of valuable gifts to European culture.

This legacy, among other items, included the legendary ruins, which despite their decay served as a basis for the decipherment of cuneiform. Persian gifts to posterity included the pleasure-garden, horticulture, the domestic hen, the peach and the pigeon, coinage bearing the image of the sovereign and finally the post. This invention was not Roman, as has often been stated, but Persian; it was in this huge empire that the need for a postal service became essential. The system of the mail carried by messengers on foot and later on horseback, with fixed relays, came down to us after passing via Egypt and Rome.

Writing, however, was not a Persian legacy.

Such grandeur could not vanish without leaving some trace, and we can still see today, ravaged by the centuries and cruelly mutilated by the hands of men, the ruins which experts describe as the most grandiose of the ancient world: the Persian citadel, the Persepolis of the Greeks, the palace of which Alexander burnt, either in a fit of drunkenness or at the instigation of the courtesan, Thais, to avenge the destruction of Athens by the Persians.

There on a gigantic terrace about forty miles north-east of Shiraz on the slopes of Kuh-i-Rahmat, not far from the confluence of the Kur and the Polvar, rises the ruined palace of fine-grained grey marble, several buildings of which, as we can see today, were not completed. Popular tradition has never been at a loss to explain these ruins: it called them Takht-i-Jemshid, the throne of Jemshid, the legendary king of Ancient Persia. But the native guides also enumerate to strangers as possible builders Cyrus the Great, Darius and even King Solomon. Not far away tower the Chihil-Minar, the forty minarets or group of columns which we know today formed a suburb added by Darius I and Xerxes to their favourite residence.

Three miles away to the east of these palaces, reduced to ashes by Alexander, stood the wealthy city of Persepolis, which he fired and pillaged. But the city survived, and in the second century B.C. its inhabitants in a bloody battle repulsed the army of the Syrian King, Antiochus IV Epiphanes, as we can read in the Bible (Maccabees ix. 1–2). In the first centuries of our era the city of Istakhr, the residence of the Sassanians, stood on its site until 632, when it was destroyed by the Caliph Omar. The prosperity of nearby Shiraz prevented Istakhr from rising again. In the Middle Ages the environs of the city were famed for their rich meadows and market-gardens—at this period the Roman Capitol served as a "hill of goats" and cattle grazed in the Forum.

Opposite the ruins of the palace of Darius and Xerxes, a few miles along the north bank of the Polvar, rises the sheer cliff of Naksh-i-Rustam. The name means the "Portrait of Rustam", the Persian national hero; this was the native interpretation, on account of the portraits of the Sassanian kings carved in the rock-face. At the summit carved in the rock are the four tombs of the Achaemenian kings Darius I, Xerxes, Artaxerxes I and Darius II.

Some distance away—about thirty-five miles north-east of Persepolis—is the third imperishable monument of Ancient Persia at its apogee—the tomb of Cyrus the Great (Kurash II, 559–529 B.C.); situated in the old days in a park, it soon lay in the centre of the ancient city of Pasargadae, built by the King himself, the present-day Murghab. This "Tomb of Solomon's mother"—as local tradition has it—rests on six huge white marble steps; walls, cornices and roof are built of carefully aligned polished blocks, which have remained in position although the clamps which originally held them together have long since disappeared. The whole edifice resembles a cave with access through a narrow door.

This region alone, therefore, within a very limited space affords a silent yet expressive testimony to the grandeur and glory of the Old Persian Kingdom.

These, too, were the remains which first attracted the attention of European travellers. But at the outset the latter remained almost as embarrassed before these vestiges of ancient magnificence as their predecessors, the Arab geographers; the attempts at interpretation and theories on this period are reminiscent of the errors of the Christian pilgrims when faced with the Egyptian monuments.

Giosofat Barbaro, sent to Persia in 1472 by the Venetian

Republic, visited in succession Takht-i-Jemshid, Murghab and Naksh-i-Rustam and tried to explain what he had seen. Viewing the imposing rock sculptures of Naksh-i-Rustam, he mistook the central figure, which represents the Sassanid King Shapur I (A.D. 241–72) receiving homage from his prisoner, the seventy-year-old Roman Emperor, Valerian (260 B.C.), for the biblical Samson! Since Barbaro's account of his journey did not appear until 1543, the scholastic world learned at a rather late date of the existence of these rock carvings—too late to be able to correct this historical error.

More than fifty years after Barbaro's book appeared the Portuguese, Antonio de Gouvea, the first ambassador sent by Philip III of Spain and Portugal to the Court of Shah Abbas, tried in turn to give an account of the antiquities of Persepolis. He mistook Takht-i-Jemshid for the ancient Shiraz; it was not a serious mistake and his description of his journey, published at Lisbon in 1911, gives the first valuable observations on cuneiform writing. We can read in this "tale which deals with wars" that the writing was different from that of the Persians (contemporary), Arabs, Armenians and Jews.

The Venetian and Portuguese ambassadors were followed by an Englishman, John Cartwright, former Oxford student, who visited the Court of Shah Abbas the Great on a trade mission (1588–1629). Under the reign of this sovereign Persia had reached the height of its power and prosperity, and the English merchants hoped to profit from this wealth by obtaining a trade licence. But as far as Persian antiquities are concerned, Cartwright in his *Journeys of a Preacher* merely states that Shiraz lay on the site of the former Persepolis.

Don Garcia de Silva Figueroa, another son of the Iberian Peninsula, went further. He had read Diodorus and gives us a remarkable description of Takht-i-Jemshid. He recognised in it the remains of the palace of Persepolis, the architecture of which gave him a lot of trouble because he did not know how to incorporate it into the known Greek patterns. He conscientiously notes: "All the graphic signs are triangular, but extended like a pyramid or a small obelisk so that they are indistinguishable from each other except by their direction and arrangement." Don Garcia took with him a draughtsman who copied a whole line of cuneiform writing. These drawings were never published.

The man to whom we owe the first publication of this nature donned the garb of a pilgrim at Naples in 1614 and embarked at Venice the same year. He was accustomed to long sea journeys, for he had distinguished himself three years before with the Spanish fleet in the naval war against the Barbary States. Pietro della Valle's pilgrimage to the East led him through Turkey and Egypt to Jerusalem, then farther, via Syria and Persia, to India. On his entry into Rome in 1626 his gay and impressive oriental retinue delighted the curiosity of the Roman crowds; he soon became chamberlain of honour to Pope Urban VIII.

In the course of his years of travel he wrote numerous letters to his friends describing his impressions and adventures. The freshness of his tale resulted in these letters being later collected in a single volume; his *Reiss-Beschreitung* is still eminently readable, especially in the new translation published at Geneva. Pietro found time to explore in detail many ruined sites, in particular those of Ancient Babylon, and brought back to Europe baked and unbaked bricks collected from the ruins. At Persepolis he mistook the palace for the remains of temples, but he was nevertheless fascinated by the inscriptions, particularly the one not far from a stone lion in the colonnade covering almost the entire area of a wall. He describes it in his fifteenth letter.

The language and writing were completely alien to him. He remarks on the grandeur of the signs and thought that each one had its individual value, like Hebrew characters, and was not joined into words. He copied a recurrent series of five signs. This is the first specimen of cuneiform writing with which Europe was soon to make acquaintance.

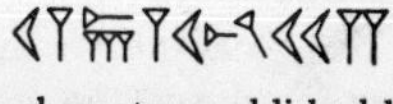

FIG. 36.—Cuneiform characters published by Pietro della Valle.

Pietro della Valle believed that the writing read from left to right. Since he was a man of imagination, he tried to draw all manner of conclusions from the frequency of certain characters.

But of what importance were five signs which no one knew, and which their discoverer himself could not even read? Of what use were the three lines of cuneiform mentioned in the account of Sir Thomas Herbert's voyage which was published in London in 1634? This author did, however, mention expressly the destructive activities of the natives, who had never ceased to use the monuments as quarries. Of little help, too, was the contribution brought by the *Beschreibung der moskowitischen und persischen Reise* (Schleswig, 1647), an account of the memorable and costly expedition sent to Perisa, via Moscow and Astrakhan, by Duke Friedrich III of Holstein-Gottorp; although the participation of Paul Fleming, a disciple of Opitz and of the Court librarian Adam Olearius, makes it a subject of interest in the history of German literature.

The first real progress was made by the journeys of the Frenchman, Jean Chardin, between 1666 and 1681. He was neither diplomat, archaeologist nor missionary, but the son of a jeweller who had sent him at the age of twenty-two to the East Indies to buy diamonds. Young Chardin's father had not over-estimated his son's talents when he sent him to the ends of the earth; he saw a great deal of the world, and was such a good sailor that after six years he brought his barque safely to Ispahan, where he was appointed, as we should say today, Purveyor to the Shah's Court. From 1671 to 1681 he travelled through Persia as far as India and then settled in London, where Charles II made him a baronet. He finally went to Holland as British chargé d'affaires and agent of the East India Company, whose activities and representatives played a far from negligible role in the decipherment of cuneiform. From 1693 to 1694 their agent, S. Flower, published in London the copy of a two-lined cuneiform text.

Chardin's *Travels* appeared in 1711 and contained the first accurate drawings by the illustrator, Grelot, of the construction, dispositions and extent of the ruined Achaemenian palace. Furthermore, they gave an accurate description of the Naksh-i-Rustam inscriptions and expressed the author's conviction that the wedges were not decorative motifs, but graphic characters.

A year later the *Amoenitates Exoticae* were published at Lemgo in Westphalia. The book was written by the "inventor" of cuneiform or, to be more accurate, the man who first coined the phrase (*litterae cuneatae*)—Engelbert Kämpfer.[17]

The life of this astonishing individual was original and colourful. He was a worthy citizen of Lemgo, an old Hanseatic town which exported cloth to Sweden, Livonia and Russia.

The breath of the outside world which had once animated the Hanseatic towns had practically been extinguished by the time Engelbert, the son of Pastor Johann Kemper (he later adopted the High German form of this name), was born. His studious youth was not always a very happy one. In this land, where the inhabitants had the reputation of seeing ghosts and of possessing second sight, the pastor continued to be a willing tool in the witch-hunts organised by the municipal council; it is all the more surprising, therefore, that the boy from his earliest years, with great self-assurance, escaped from this narrow *milieu* and discovered the road which was to take him round the world. Secondary studies, voyages and High-School studies led him successively to Holland, Lüneberg and Lübeck, then to Danzig, Thorn, Cracow and Warsaw. He ended at Koenigsberg by taking a four-year course in physics, natural science and medicine.

What motive urged him to go to Sweden, where, thanks to his good relations with the Puffendorfs, he soon obtained a post as secretary in Stockholm? It was apparently due to his keen desire to see the world and above all his great thirst for knowledge. In Sweden, the efforts of Charles XI to increase the might and prosperity of his country were translated into a vast political extension of foreign trade. The young King equipped a mission which was to travel via Russia to Persia with the object of entering into trade relations with the East. The Swedish mission set out on March 20th, 1683 (the same year that, farther south, eastern forces were invading Europe and the Turkish armies were destroyed before Vienna, the bastion of the West); Engelbert Kämpfer, doctor and secretary accompanied it.

Crossing Finland, the Swedes entered Russia. They were received at the Court of the Czars. We have no space to relate the encounter of Engelbert Kämpfer with the younger of the two Russian princes, Peter the Great, but we must recall another experience which awaited the Westphalian traveller before he came face to face with cuneiform; he was the first European to give us a description of the Baku oilfields where the burning liquid spurted from the earth.

"Following our paths, after half an hour we reached a strip of molten land, covered with white gravel and ashes. From a host of fissures spouted wondrous bright-coloured flames. Some of them burned with a great rumble and their powerful jets of flame terrified the onlookers. Others released more tranquil flames so that we could approach quite near them. Others again sent up clouds of smoke or vapour which, although barely visible, gave off a strong odour of naphtha.

"This strange phenomenon extended over an area of 90 paces in length and 26 paces wide. The vents of these gushers were extraordinarily narrow and did not measure more than the breadth of a hand. Some were quite short and oval while others meandered irregularly and were of great size. . . . Two Hindu fire-worshippers, Parsees, sat motionless within their semi-circular rampart, deep in contemplation of this fire in which they adored the eternal deity."[18]

By the end of March the expedition reached Ispahan. Months elapsed before the Court astrologer decided that the day was propitious for the Shah to receive the visitors.

This long wait was not unproductive for Kämpfer. He made friends with an old Capuchin friar, Raphael du Mans, head of the Christian Armenians in Ispahan; the friar was highly esteemed as their interpreter and taught the foreign visitor the language of the country.

Thus equipped, Kämpfer left the Swedish expedition to enter the service of the Dutch East India Company. On its orders he went to Ispahan and Shiraz. His route led him past Persepolis. "Next morning at daybreak we arrived within half an hour at the second curiosity—the ruins of the palace of Darius which is called Istakhr or Chihil-Minar, the Forty minarets."[19] Kämpfer explored, took measurements and made drawings. What attracted him most were the bricks engraved in cuneiform which Niebuhr was to copy accurately years later. Kämpfer copied only one inscription. It was placed very high, the sun was burning hot and blinding, time pressed and there were other things to see.

"To copy the sculptures and inscriptions of all these buildings with the measurements, decorations and all that is worthy of being noted would take more than two months. I shall communicate faithfully all I have been able to acquire during the brief delay of three days during which I did not even bother to eat."[20]

Kämpfer kept his promise in his *Amoenitates Exotiçae.* His account surpasses in adventures many of our modern globe-trotters' tales. Arabia and the Indies, Siam and Japan were the next stages of his nomad existence. After travelling for many years he arrived in Amsterdam weary and ill, old before his time.

He copied a whole inscription without knowing that it was Babylonian. That he thought the signs to be exclusively ideograms is a pardonable error. He was the first to publish an inscription of this length, and he invented the name under which these strange signs would soon be known to European scholarship.

In 1714 the Dutchman, Cornelius van Bruyn, who had visited the ruins in 1704, published his *Reizen* in Amsterdam. He took the time and trouble to copy not one but several inscriptions, and proved conclusively from a text engraved round a window that the inscriptions were to be read horizontally and not vertically, as had previously been supposed.

Men like Kämpfer and Bruyn, therefore, laid the foundations for the subsequent decipherment. To be more precise, the foundations of the foundation. Their works, following close on each other's heels, attracted the attention of their contemporaries, aroused and extended the interest of the public; in every country copies of their books invited scholars to study the subject more closely.

Despite the constant chaos caused by wars, art and science were encouraged in many lands, particularly in Denmark during the long and peaceful reign of Frederick V, known in Germany as the patron of Klopstock. This enlightened monarch also favoured trade and industry; a new commercial company was founded and ships despatched to the Mediterranean, West Africa and even to India and the West Indies.

Trade interests undoubtedly lay behind the government-sponsored expedition sent in 1761 to explore Arabia, Persia and the neighbouring countries. Among its members was the son of a Holstein pastor who was soon to win fame: Carsten Niebuhr (1733–1815), father of the great German historian Barthold Georg Niebuhr.

This promising young man, born at Lüdingworth, studied mathematics at Göttingen and, thanks to this education, became in 1760 an engineer officer in the Danish army. At

Göttingen he had discovered the works of Bruyn and Kämpfer; the world described in these two volumes excited him so much that he began to learn Arabic. He had thus received a double and excellent education when he set out in 1761 with the Danish expedition.

This ambitious mission, however, seemed to lie under an unlucky star. As a start it was held up in Cairo for several months. We have related in our chapter on Egyptian writing how Niebuhr profited by this period of enforced idleness to study hieroglyphics and what brilliant observations he contributed to the decipherment of its characters.

At last the expedition was able to continue on its way. It crossed Syria, Palestine and Arabia into the heart of the forbidden xenophobic South, as far as Sana. It was a death march. Fatigue, the incredible hardships and the hostility of the natives decimated the party. Carsten escaped death by a hairsbreadth, by going native: he disguised himself as an oriental, dressed and ate like the inhabitants of the country. Only the doctor to the expedition and Niebuhr himself emerged alive from this inferno, and when the two men at last reached Bombay the doctor succumbed to the privations suffered on this journey. Niebuhr landed alone at Bombay, the sole survivor of this expedition, which had set out with such high hopes.

Niebuhr refused to be discouraged. Less than a year later he set out once more across Mesopotamia and Persia. During the first days of March 1765, standing before the "Throne of Jemshid", he saw with his own eyes the ruins of Persepolis.

For three weeks, fascinated by these ruins, he drew indefatigably: he made sketches and copied inscriptions, achieving far better results than any of his predecessors had done in these regions.

His work was often criticised later on account of trifling errors and inaccuracies. Nevertheless he clarified a number of points left in doubt by Kämpfer and Bruyn. His well and clearly drawn copies are most attractive. With his *Description of a Voyage to Arabia and the Neighbouring Lands* which appeared between 1774 and 1778 (this is the book Napoleon held in his hand when announcing the creation of a Commission for Egypt, and which he took with him on his journey), Niebuhr was the first to present the scientific world with exact complete copies of several major inscriptions of Darius and Xerxes, copies, which as well as the pertinent and penetrating statements made in his text, contributed to the success of the first decipherments.

Niebuhr was the first to recognise that the surviving inscriptions were not written in a uniform manner but that there were three different scripts (he had not yet discovered that they were trilingual texts), and that the relatively few and simple signs placed next to two others in one of the writing systems were alphabetical signs (this observation was subsequently to be the key to the decipherment). He showed from certain judiciously observed indications that the writing was to be read from left to right and even established an alphabet of forty-two characters.

Of the forty-two letters recognised by Niebuhr thirty-two turned out to be correct, nine being definitely wrong and the tenth being the "word separator". An excellent result, if one considers that this expedition was under an unlucky star and that its real goal had nothing to do with the inscription.

Niebuhr's courage and tenacity found an echo in the young Persian Abraham Hyacinthe Anquetil du Perron (1731–1805). Originally a theologian, he was soon to lay the foundations in Europe for the study of the Zend religion. His theological studies in Paris, Auxerre and Amersfoort led him, like so many other investigators, to oriental languages. The centre of this study, of course, was Paris. He settled in the French capital to devote himself entirely to the study of these languages. One subject, however, he wished to study above all—influenced no doubt by the romantic ideas of his age—the scared writings of the Parsees, the last disciples in India of Zarathustra (Zoroaster), two worshippers of whom Engelbert Kämpfer had seen at the oilfields of Baku, sunk in prayer and meditation before the sacred fire.

For this enterprising Frenchman, India was not the end of the world; his country had long since been making great colonising efforts there. But it was almost impossible to envisage taking a pleasure trip. Anquetil du Perron, therefore, signed up on a French ship bound for India; his zeal and determination made the French Government decide to give him a grant. At Pondicherry, the French counting house on the Coromandel coast, he started to learn modern Persian. From there he made his way north (a dangerous journey, since the

Anglo-French naval war had spread to India) to Bengal, then across the whole country to the west coast to the town of Surate, at that time French. But he had not come here to shed tears over the French colonial tradition. A colony of quite a different type had attracted him to these parts: scattered throughout the north-west of India were the last adepts of the Old Persian religion, the Parsee fire-worshippers.

Thanks to his patience and sociability the young Frenchman managed to make friends with their priests, the *dasturs*. His enthusiasm won the hearts of these followers of Zarathustra, who themselves were incapable of reading the ancient texts except in modern Persian. The goal of this erudite scholar was the Zend Avesta, the sacred book of the Parsees. It is an anthology of all that survived of the sacred texts of the ancient Iranians, rescued from the foreign Greek, Parthian and Islamic dominations when they emigrated to India. When Pondicherry fell into the hands of the English in 1761 and Anquetil du Perron returned to Europe after a seven years stay in India, he brought back not only the Avesta in the original text (which neither he nor his Parsee friends understood), but also a translation in modern Persian which the *dastur* Darab had dictated to him letter by letter.

This was naturally not in cuneiform characters. The original itself is no longer transcribed in this writing. But the work of the pioneer, Anquetil du Perron, the translation of the Avesta, presented the decipherers of cuneiform with some exceptionally useful material: the forms in Old Persian of the historical names, which until then had been unknown to the world of scholarship except in their Greek guise (often seriously mutilated).

The first stones were laid both in the field of the language and the script. Count Caylus in 1762 (the year Anquetil du Perron had returned to Paris with his rich booty of 180 manuscripts) had provided a key to the mysterious cuneiform writing. He had in fact published an inscription from an alabaster vase of King Xerxes; this was actually engraved in four languages: Old Persian, Elamite, Babylonian (we shall deal with these two languages in the next chapter) and Egyptian! This key, however, remained unusable, since no one at the time could as yet read Egyptian. Another sixty years were to pass before Champollion's decisive letter to Dacier.

Among the new European travellers attracted by the monuments of the Achaemenians we must mention Sir William Ouseley, the English Orientalist whose secretary, James Justin Mourier, was the first to identify the "Tomb of Solomon's Mother" as the Tomb of Cyrus the Great; Sir Robert Ker Porter, the author of two quarto volumes with good drawings of the ruins; and the infant prodigy of Orientalism, the Englishman Claudius James Rich, the young resident Consul-General at Baghdad, who died in 1821 at an early age as Champollion was to do twenty years later; he succumbed to an outbreak of cholera at Shiraz. Rich must not be forgotten in the archaeological history of the ancient Orient. He showed complete confidence in the German decipherer Grotefend and regularly sent him copies of the inscriptions he had found. His influence extended even beyond the tomb; the two volumes of his journeys to Kurdistan, which did not appear in London until 1836, made such a profound impression on Orientalists that the French Government, swayed by this work and the private diaries of the dead man which were published in 1839, set up a vice-consulate at Mosul and appointed Paul-Emile Botta, the man who discovered Nineveh, to the post. It was also under the influence of Rich that a young Englishman decided to apply to the Porte through his embassy for permission to continue his researches. This was Austen Henry Layard, who rediscovered Nimrud. We shall mention both these men later.

At this juncture, the archaeological exploits of these investigators can only be mentioned *en passant*. At the moment of their triumph another deed had already been accomplished, to which at the outset no one paid the slightest attention and in fact expressly ignored it. It has its own fascinating story.

The copies of Carsten Niebuhr, the North German travelling under the Danish flag, whose work was also published in Denmark, were revised and assessed both in Denmark and Germany.

One of his contemporaries was Olaus Gerhard Tychsen (1734–1815), born at Tondern (Schleswig). This former student from Halle and teacher in the local orphanage later taught Oriental languages at Bützow, finally becoming librarian at Rostock. A great Hebraist, he was also the founder of Arabic palaeography and was interested above all in the burning question of Orientalism, so popular in his age. We have already mentioned that he attacked hieroglyphics without much success in a work published at Göttingen in 1790. In 1798, inspired by the theories of Niebuhr, he distinguished himself by publishing a treatise on the Persepolitan cuneiform script. His linguistic knowledge and a budding taste for comparative philology—at that time virgin soil sprouting with audacious theories—marked a turning point in his career. As opposed to Niebuhr, he attributed arbitrary phonetic values to cuneiform characters and then tried to discover a meaning in the groups of isolated signs, by comparing the phonetic composition of the "words" obtained with words of other Semitic and Indo-European languages.

This method led to numerous mistakes and even to one grave historical blunder: Tychsen mistook the inscriptions for an account of the exploits of Arsaces, founder of the Arsacid dynasty and the Parthian kingdom (247 B.C.); he thus post-dated the inscriptions by nearly 300 years.

But among the chaff in Tychsen's Latin treatise were several grains of rich corn.

He managed to see what had escaped Niebuhr: that the three different scripts must correspond to three different languages.

Again, more perspicacious than Niebuhr, he noticed the isolated oblique "wedge" which constantly recurs in the first script (it can already be seen in Pietro della Valle's five signs, Fig. 35); the sign was put there to mark the beginning and end of words and to separate words aligned without intercalary space. Tychsen had discovered what we call today "the word separator".

Independent of Tychsen, another scholar, the Dane Friedrich Christian Karl Heinrich Münter (1761–1830), arrived at the same conclusion. Born at Gotha and studying at Copenhagen and Göttingen, he became Bishop of Seeland. In 1800 he published his *Researches into the Persepolitan Inscriptions.* Basing his findings on historical arguments, he began by rectifying Tychsen's error and maintained that in all probability the inscriptions did not date from the Parthian Arsacids but from the Achaemenians, the great kings of Ancient Persia, who ruled 300 years later.

One may wonder what importance these 300 years could have had with regard to the 2,500 years age of the inscriptions in question. In actual fact they were of immense importance.

The new correct date established by Münter opened in effect two new vistas without which the future decipherment could never have been envisaged.

On the one hand, it was generally admitted that the inscriptions were written in Old Persian, a language related to that of the Avesta, upon which the efforts of Anquetil du Perron and Sylvestre de Sacy had already shed some light.

Secondly, it provided a new and absolutely invaluable landmark: it was now known what names to look for in the inscriptions. Let us recall the cartouche of Ptolemy, the nub of the decipherment of hieroglyphics. Let us imagine that Young and Champollion, taking an incorrect date, had looked in the cartouche for the names of other sovereigns—as, for example, Psammetichus or Necho. How many false steps would then have retarded the decipherment? The specialists were now on the correct path: they would no longer look for the name Arsaces in the inscriptions, as Tychsen was prepared to do, but names such as. . . . But do not let us anticipate.

Like Tychsen, Münter recognised the "word separator"; he, too, admitted the trilingual nature of the inscriptions. But where Tychsen had looked for Parthian, Median and Bactrian, Münter suspected Zend (Old Persian), Pehlevi (Middle Persian) and Parsi (an early form of New Persian). On the first score he was correct. Also on another theory which he shared with Tychsen: that the first version, on account of the number of signs, was alphabetic (Niebuhr had already spotted this); that the second must be a syllabic and the third an ideographic script. He was right once more when he concluded that the three texts must have the same context because multilingual texts were not a rare occurrence in antiquity, and because each time a word recurred in the inscriptions of the first version it was repeated in the two remaining scripts.

Although starting from a sound principle, Münter reached an *impasse*. He began to count the frequency of certain signs in Niebuhr's inscriptions and decided that those most often repeated must be vowels—in other words, representing a, ā, i, o and u. As it happened, only one of these vowels, the a, turned out to be correct, as was the case with the consonant, b.

Another trail in the meantime led the Danish theologian to his goal. Like Tychsen, he was struck by a group of seven signs, often repeated in the inscriptions. Both men thought that this must be a name. But Münter, familiar with Middle Persian titles, thought that they must signify "king" and "King of kings" —a random guess. The word preceding the title then, according to him, would be the name of the king. The group of seven letters which he suspected to be the king's name were:

𐎧𐏁𐎠𐎹𐎰𐎡𐎹 𐏐

Fig. 37.—The word "king" in Old Persian cuneiform script.

The word separator is on the extreme right. The word reads in the accepted transcription xsayaϑiya (pronounce chsājaϑija, ϑ = the English "th") and effectively means "king". Münter was close to his goal, but he did not solve the signs which followed the word "king" (in these he quite rightly looked for a flexional ending); the phonetic values which he attributed to the different signs are all incorrect. He strayed from the right path as soon as he had embarked upon it and had to abandon the struggle. . . .

"And then came Grotefend. Not even a specialist! Small fry, a school-teacher. Not the slightest idea of Orientalism. To win a bet made at a drinking bout he calmly set to and deciphered cuneiform."

This is the version one often hears. But it is not true—or only to a certain extent.

"A self-made man." This is the epithet one might apply to Grotefend after examining his life and scientific career. Obviously little Georg Grotefend, born at Münden, on the Weser, on June 9th, 1775, the son of a cobbler, could never have dreamed that his name would one day be of international renown. But he seems to have recognised very early in life that only indomitable zeal could help him in his rise. He already displayed this zeal at school in his native town and then at Ilfeld college. From 1795 he studied theology and philosophy at the university of Göttingen. Among the theologians at this university was a number of archaeologists and philologists. The ardour and conscientiousness with which Grotefend pursued his aims gained him influential patrons and friends who encouraged him, among them the head university librarian, a privy councillor and the secretary of the Academy of Science—the privy councillor Christian Gottlob Heyne, who included antiquity in his curriculum, with a will to enter into the spirit of it and, above all, to clear up the obscure points in archaeology. His attitude had a great influence on Grotefend and was admirably suited to his disposition. Two more of his patrons were Tychsen himself, who was the first to plead his name in the scientific field, and the famous historian, Arnold Hermann Ludwig Heeren, who in his *Ideas on Politics, Relations and Trade of the Leading Nations of the World* later gave Grotefend a platform for his somewhat neglected works.

Thanks to Heyne, while still a student the young man had found a post as assistant teacher and later from 1797 a permanent niche at Göttingen gymnasium and at the same time was given the opportunity to complete his studies. He made a profound study of classical philology and his application was soon to reap its reward. From his earliest youth he had shown unexpected talent in the most disparate interests. The pastime of the young Professor's leisure hours would, today, be called intellectual exercise: the solution of puzzles. Word puzzles, rebuses, acrostics—all were fair game to him. This passion led him slowly but relentlessly in a certain direction.

In 1799 he published at Göttingen a work which today is practically forgotten: *De pasigraphia sive scriptura universale*, on account of its trends and scientific direction one of his most significant writings, which a number of modern biographers and chroniclers suppress or ignore wrongly because it gives the key to the whole personality of the future decipherer. The title of course refers to a "common script" or "universal writing", and places Grotefend in the ranks of those men (quoted in the chapter on Egyptology) who have devoted their efforts to creating a "common language". It was not by chance, as some people maintain today, that Grotefend came to the decipherment of cuneiform writing.

It is not known at what precise moment he began to study Niebuhr's texts, nor when he obtained Sylvestre de Sacy's *Mémoires sur diverses Antiquités* (Paris, 1793). The Parisian scholar had published in this work a few short Pehlevi inscriptions discovered at Naksh-i-Rustam. Several of them agreed with the forms of the kings, as the epigraphs in the Niebuhr copies had agreed with the form of Darius and, according to Sacy, they contained the names of the kings and their ancestors and also the title "King of kings".

It is true that the goad which spurred Grotefend to start deciphering cuneiform was a bet made after a drinking session. But to maintain that he had never felt any scientific urge and that he had listened merely to the dictates of youth and pleasure would be to misunderstand him, to ignore his extremely serious preliminary studies, his personal dispositions and above all the influence of his teachers—in short, everything that subscribed to the intellectual development which made him what he was.

According to Sacy's treatise, Grotefend concluded—quite rightly—that this type of inscription was in the Persian tradition. But tradition is conservative. Why should not the inscriptions of Persepolis be based on the same models and also contain the names of the kings and the title "King of kings"? This supposition agreed with the hypothesis of Münter, whose works Grotefend knew. Why should it not apply to the group of seven signs which Münter took for the word "king"? (Fig. 37.)

Seven signs. "King." These characters had to be studied together, if possible in short texts. The young Professor turned once more to Niebuhr. He noticed in particular two short inscriptions which appeared to have several points in common (Fig. 38). Grotefend established for a start that Münter's group of seven signs, numbered 2, 4 and 6 in the upper inscription and 2, 4 and 7 in the lower, recurred on both in No. 5, prolonged in this case by several signs. This extension must be the long-sought-after genitive plural of the word "king", "of the kings".

Careful scrutiny enabled him to find the word No. 1 of the upper inscription in No. 6 of the lower, this time augmented by the sign [cuneiform sign] (the sixth place in the word). This word was in the initial position in the upper inscription and must therefore represent the royal name; in the second inscription it follows the title "King of kings", showing an ending augmented by a sign. Grotefend concluded that this prolonged form (on the model of the Sassanian Pehlevi inscriptions) must be the genitive form following the word "son", and immediately interpreted the second and shorter inscription as follows (the words of the translation are accompanied by numbers which the groups of signs in question bear in the cuneiform text):

"[1] Y, [2] the king, [3] the great (?), [4] the King [5] of kings, [6] of X, [7] of the king's, [8] son (?), [9] the Achaemenian (?)."

It was a great deal and yet very little; the words followed by a question mark in the transcription being the fruit of a simple hypothesis, nothing remained except the as yet unproved title "King of kings". Only the names X and Y could give the solution of the riddle.

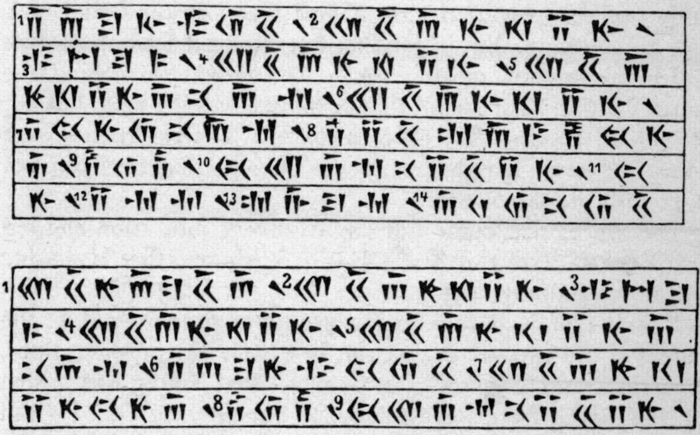

FIG. 38.—Old Persian inscription of Darius I and of Xerxes (below).

Grotefend was not worried. Had he not trained to be a humanist? He consulted Herodotus. And the Greek historian gave him the key. In the VIIth book of his history he relates how the uncle of Xerxes, Artabanus, wished to divert his nephew from his plan to attack the Greeks. Xerxes, inflamed with anger answered as follows:

'Artabanus, you are my father's brother; this will protect you from receiving the just recompense of your foolish words. However I inflict this disgrace upon you, base and cowardly as you are, not to accompany me in my expedition against Greece, but to remain here with the women; and I, without your assistance will accomplish all that I have said. For I should not be sprung from Darius, son of Hystaspes, son of Arsames, son of Ariaramnes, son of Teispes, son of Cyrus, son of Cambyses, son of Achaemenes, if I did not avenge myself on the Athenians."[21]

What a blessing this collection of the royal names of Ancient Persia proved to be! What a stroke of good fortune!

Grotefend tried to choose from among these names those which appeared to him best to correspond to the cuneiform words X and Y; he was guided in his search by an important observation which resulted naturally from the study of the two inscriptions:

Y is called in the second inscription "son of X the king". The author of the first inscription X was therefore the father of Y and himself king. But in the first inscription the group of signs which presumably meant "son" (No. 9) was *not* behind the word "king". That meant that X himself was the king, but not the son of the king (like his own son Y). The two names were about the same length, but it was obvious that they did not start with the same letter.

The wheel had come full circle. Every indication showed that Y was Xerxes and X was Darius I, whose father Hystaspes was never actually king.

Now it remained to read the groups of signs X and Y, the names of the two sovereigns, not in the Greek transliterations, "Dareios" and "Xerxes" (let us recall that Young was misled by the Greek form "Ptolemaois"), but in their Old Persian form. Grotefend compared the first seven signs of the first inscription with the name Darheush (as pronounced according to the Old Testament and to the Avesta), and proceeded in the same manner with the names Xerxes and Hystaspes, the father of Darius, who must correspond to the group of signs No. 8 of the first inscription. He thus obtained the phonetic values of thirteen cuneiform characters, four of which would later be slightly modified, Grotefend having used the Old Persian instead of Middle Persian forms. Fig. 39 shows once more the two inscriptions after they had become the decisive element in the decipherment, this time together with the transcription and the translation as it is accepted today.

Grotefend had, therefore, discovered the key to Old Persian cuneiform writing in record time, and one might be tempted to think that his discovery would immediately be recognised and acclaimed by the scholars all over the world (as was the case with Champollion's decipherment of hieroglyphics), and his work supplemented and advanced by other scholars.

Unfortunately, what occurred is a slur on the glorious history

(Spelt) (1) *D(a)-a-r(a)-y(a)-v(a)-u-š(a)* (2) *x(a)-š(a)-a-y(a)-ϑ(a)-i-y(a)* (3) *v(a)-z(a)-r(a)-k(a)* (4) *x(a)-š(a)-a-y(a)-ϑ(a)-i-y(a)* (5) *x(a)-š(a)-a-y(a)-ϑ(a)-i-y(a)-a-n(a)-a-m(a)* (6) *x(a)-š(a)-a-y(a)-ϑ(a)-i-y(a)* (7) *d(a)-h(a)-y(a)-u-n(a)-a-m(a)* (8) *Vi-i-š(a)-t(a)-a-s(a)-p(a)-h(a)-y(a)-a* (9) *p(a)-u-ç(a)* (10) *H(a)-x(a)-a-m(a)-n(a)-i-š(a)-i-y(a)* (11) *h(a)-y(a)* (12) *i-m(a)-m(a)* (13) *t(a)-č(a)-r(a)-m(a)* (14) *a-ku-u-n(a)-u-š(a)*

(Pronounced) *Dārayavauš xšāyaϑiya vazrka xšāyaϑiya xšāyaϑiyānām xšāyaϑiya dahyunām Vištāspahya puça Haxāmanišiya hya imam tačaram akunauš*

x = ch in loch *s* = ch in which *y* = y in yard ϑ = English th
c = tch *ç* = s in seep

"Darius the great king, the king of kings, the ruler of the earth, son of Hystaspes, the Achaemenian, (it is) who built this palace."

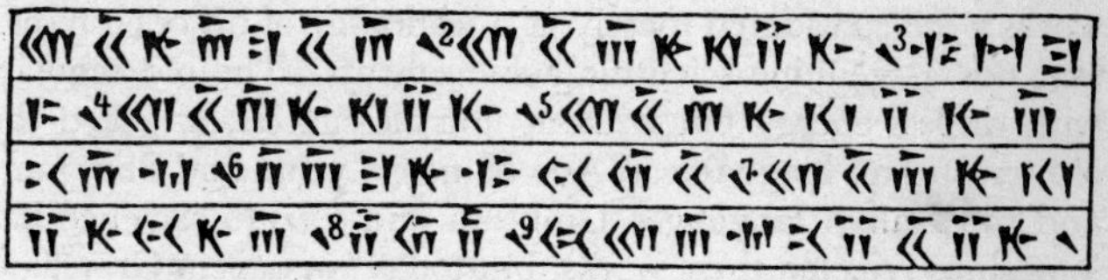

(Spelt) (1) *X(a)-š(a)-y(a)-a-r(a)-š(a)-a* (2) *x(a)-š(a)-a-y(a)-ϑ(a)-i-y(a)* (3) *v(a)-z(a)-r(a)-k(a)* (4) *x(a)-š(a)-a-y(a)-ϑ(a)-i-y(a)* (5) *x(a)-š(a)-a-y(a)-ϑ(a)-i-y(a)-a-n(a)-a-m(a)* (6) *D(a)-a-r(a)-y(a)-v(a)-h(a)-u-š(a)* (7) *x(a)-š(a)-a-y(a)-ϑ(a)-i-y(a)-h(a)-y(a)-a* (8) *p(a)-u-ç(a)* (9) *H(a)-x(a)-a-m(a)-n(a)-i-š(a)-i-y(a)*

(Pronounced) *Xšayāršā xšāyaϑiya vazrka xšāyaϑiyānām Dārayavahauš xšāyaϑiyahya puça Haxāmanišiya*

"Xerxes, the great king, the King of kings, son of Darius the king, the Achaemenian."

Fig. 39.—The inscriptions of Darius I and of Xerxes as they are read and translated today.

of Göttingen University. Grotefend's trail-blazing article: "Praevia de cuneatis quas vocant inscriptionibus Persepolitanis legendis et explicandis relatio" was published in part in the *Göttinger Gelehrten Anzeigen* of 1803–4, thanks to the influence of Tychsen, who had brought it to the notice of the university. But the authorities refused to publish the whole text written by this obscure Professor of twenty-seven because he did not actually belong to so-called university circles and was not a professional Orientalist! This fundamental work therefore remained unknown and despised until Heeren in his *Ideas*, already quoted above, allowed the decipherer[22] to publish his results at last in 1805. The original text had an even stranger fate; it was rediscovered in Göttingen ninety years later by Professor Wilhelm Meyer and finally published with due reverence in the University's *Gelehrten Nachrichten.*

Grotefend brought his official life to an honourable conclusion, but his subsequent scientific career was darkened by a tragic shadow; although he contributed in the following years at various intervals to the decipherment of cuneiform (also Babylonian) he never obtained, apart from a few articles of value, a decisive success, and until the end of his life persisted in various errors committed in his own researches. Some of these works were considered merely as a testimony of his open mind, and not as genuine scientific achievements. The old scholar, with tireless energy but without notable success, attacked the old scripts and languages of Asia Minor (Lycian and Phrygian) and the Italian languages Umbrian and Oscan. Science has long since rejected these works, but today we esteem Grotefend for his zeal and gallant attempts to throw some light into a very obscure field.

Let us recognise that he always admitted, without a trace of envy, the later successes of the specialists.

But the work and merits of Grotefend found no echo in the German-speaking countries. When an interest in Old Persian was revived a few decades later, the impulse came this time from the Scandinavian countries.

The Danish Professor, Rasmus Christian Rask (1787–1832)—with Franz Bopp and Jakob Grimm one of the founders of the new branch of science, comparative philology—paid a national debt of honour when in 1827 he established in the title "King of kings" the ending "a-n-a-m" of the genitive plural, which

Münter had merely suspected twenty years before and to which Grotefend had given the incorrect reading: "-a-tch-a-o."

Rask had embarked upon the study that interested him most—the study of the Germanic languages. From his voyages in Sweden, Norway and Iceland he produced his first great works: *Researches into the Origin of the Old Nordic or Icelandic Language* (Copenhagen, 1818), in which he demonstrated the close relationship between Ancient Nordic and the South Germanic languages (today West German), and its more remote relations encouraged him in 1816 to undertake a journey to India for which he received royal and private aid. He made his way, via Sweden and Finland, to St. Petersburg, and from there in 1819, via Moscow, Astrakhan, Tiflis and Persia, to India, which he explored between 1820 and 1822.

We find the young Dane on the trail of another European, Anquetil du Perron. Like his French predecessor, Rask made a profound study of the language and customs of the fire-worshippers, especially in Bombay and its environs. He was interested in the languages and customs of the Ceylon Buddhists and—a task most fruitful for the decipherment of cuneiform—he studied the sacred books of the Parsees.

In Europe, particularly in England, doubts had always been cast on the authenticity of the material collected at the cost of so much devotion by Anquetil du Perron. Rask was able to dispel this distrust once and for all. In a brilliant treatise on the Zend language he proved incontestably the authenticity of the documents published by Anquetil du Perron and the close relationship between this language and that of the ancient Indians. After studying Grotefend's alphabet and transcriptions he came to the conclusion that the language bore a slight resemblance to Zend, and proved that the latter was also as ancient, if not more so, than the Achaemenian inscriptions; his results far more than his explanation of the genitive opened the way for other scholars who were to complete the decipherment of Old Persian cuneiform—the Frenchman, Eugène Burnouf and the Germano-Norwegian, Christian Lassen.

But why did Rask himself not continue with the decipherment? The reason has already been indicated. Rask was a philologist. He was interested above all in studying the laws and construction of Old Persian and, for this reason, considered the study of the rich collection of manuscripts he took with him on his voyage to India as his most pressing task. He, too, died an early death.

Since Anquetil du Perron had brought back the fruits of his work to Europe, the study of Zend had become a matter of national prestige for the French. Eugène Burnouf, in studying the Avesta, was therefore only following the tradition. He and Lassen succeeded independently, but bound by a friendly exchange of views, in determining from a list of race-names nearly all the values of the cuneiform characters of Old Persian and its structure, thus pursuing and terminating the work of which Grotefend had laid the foundation stones.

They no longer worked exclusively from Niebuhr's copies. Documents in the meantime had multiplied. Among others there were copies from the estate of the German university Professor F. E. Schulz of Giessen, who was sent to Armenia by the French Government in 1829 and murdered by the Kurds. Then the existing material had increased to a surprising extent by the flair and circumspection of an erudite man upon whom his compatriots eventually bestowed the title "the father of Assyriology".

The British East India Company has often been decried by historians and even more by chauvinists on the Continent. But if one studies without prejudice the history of this commercial and political power in the service of a kingdom in full expansion, one must recognise—as in many similar organisations of the colonial powers—that despite present-day slogans the cultural factor was of prime importance. An idea of this nature would hardly have entered the head of young Henry Creswicke Rawlinson (1819–95) while he was wearing out the seat of his hose on the benches of Ealing School. A remarkable feature, though: the boy at this time flung himself heart and soul into the study of the Greek and Latin histories. There was, however, nothing of the model pupil or hypocrite about him. Strong and sturdily built, he made a name for himself at sport, which even in those days was a good point in the eyes of schoolmates and masters alike; the Battle of Waterloo, which according to British public opinion had been won on the playing-fields of Eton, was still alive in his memory. It is not surprising to hear that at the age of sixteen young Henry was called upon to serve in the East India Company. A year later he arrived in India.

On the boat the young man met the Governor of Bombay, Sir John Malcolm, himself a keen Orientalist, who kindled in him an enthusiasm which was to colour his whole life: the history of Persia and the language and literature of the Persians. In spite of his youth, Rawlinson knew what he wanted. Hardly had he arrived than he plunged into the study of languages. He learnt Persian, Arabic and Hindustani with such brilliant success that a year later we find him as interpreter and paymaster to the 1st Grenadier Regiment stationed in Bombay. But this was not his real goal. He wished to devote his life to Persian (Rask had already studied it at Bombay with the Parsees) and soon became an expert in this field. He learnt by heart long extracts from the Persian poets which proved a great asset to him later at the Court of the Shah. (Some decades later, in 1875, on the occasion of the Shah of Persia's visit to England, he was appointed political adviser to the Government, so that he could discuss political problems with the Iranian monarch in his own language.)

But for the moment Rawlinson served with the Grenadiers at Bombay as interpreter and paymaster. An excellent horseman, he soon won the friendship of all classes of the native population (still subjected to a very strict social hierarchy). These qualities earned him an honourable promotion. In 1833 he was sent on special missions by the Intelligence Service, and carried them out with such skill that two years later he was sent to Persia as military adviser to the Shah's brother, who resided at Kirmanshah, as governor of a province. In 1839 the extension of British domination on the right bank of the Indus provoked the First Afghan War and Kandahar and Kabul were taken; the following year the Emir Dost Mohammed was taken prisoner and replaced by a more amenable successor. The same year Rawlinson was diplomatic envoy of the British Government at Kandahar. Revolt was brewing in the country. The Afghans hated foreign domination and both the British and Henry Rawlinson were fully aware of this. He himself formed a troop of Persian cavalry and in May 1842 took part in the Battle of Kandahar, where he won a brilliant victory and followed this up with the same brilliance in the conquest of Ghazni. He returned to India at the end of the campaign.

Here the most favourable offers awaited the brave soldier.

A brilliant military career lay open to him. But he refused it. On the other hand, he did not reject a political future. When the British diplomatic envoy in Arabia, then under Turkish rule, Colonel Taylor, retired in 1843, Rawlinson succeeded him as Consul of Baghdad.

The two decisions—to abandon a military career and to accept Baghdad—were dictated by the same reason. Rawlinson had never forgotten an experience that had happened to him eight years before in Persia: his first encounter with cuneiform writing.

Appointed, as we have mentioned, military adviser to the Shah's brother, he went to Kirmanshah to learn that there were cuneiform inscriptions on the rocky slopes of Alvend (the "Aurant" of the Avesta and the "Orontes" of the classical writers). This mountain chain which rises to 12,000 feet due south of Hamadan (the former capital of the Medes, Ecbatana) has from time immemorial played a part in local tradition, the natives attributing magic powers to the herbs and stones to be found there. The inscriptions, incidentally, were called "Ganj-i Nameh", the "book of treasure"—for anyone who could read it would discover a fabulous treasure.

This proved true in a figurative sense. These monuments were for Rawlinson above price, a treasure trove.

He proceeded to copy two trilingual inscriptions (a methodical worker, for he returned a year later to check and correct his copies on the spot). But his arrival at Kirmanshah brought him a new surprise which made his heart beat faster—a treasure which eclipsed that of the "book of treasure". He learned that inscriptions and colossal sculptures adorned the rocks of Behistun some distance from that town.

The distance is, to be accurate, twenty-two miles—a good day's march. But what were twenty miles to a horseman like Rawlinson? Had he not once covered the 750 miles to Teheran in a single ride to inform His Majesty's ambassador of the arrival of the Russian envoy in Herat? During that summer and autumn he rode out a host of times to copy the inscriptions on the Behistun rock.

It was no easy matter to copy these inscriptions, particularly as he had to be lowered on a cradle down the rock-face to copy the epigraphy at his ease. Let us quote the explorer's own words, but before we do so let us examine the site and see what met his eyes and what had happened to it in the past.

Bagastana means "land of the Gods"—the sacred land. It is a tall mountain with twin peaks which today bears the ancient Iranian name Behistun or Bisitun. Its southern face, extraordinarily smooth, falls sheer to the famous Khurasan road, "the ancient road which led from Baghdad via Khanikin and Qasr-i-Shirin in the Zagros Mountains to Kirmanshah and Hamadan . . . the old trade route of the Asiatic peoples which caravans had followed for five millennia. For centuries in the spring the nomadic Kurds drove their flocks here to graze in the hills, and brought them down in the autumn to the plains of Germsir—the 'hot lands'. Each year the pilgrims from the East climbed these sacred heights, and descended to Najaf, Kasimein, Kerbela and Mecca, climbing again to Shah Abdul-Asim near Teheran, Kum and Meshed."[23] This route has always been the object of bitter battles. During the First World War the German troops occupied it. It had already witnessed the decisive battles of Darius the Great against the rebel princes and his victory over the insurgents. In this "land of the Gods" victory monuments commemorated the feats of arms of the sovereigns from time immemorial, and Darius I caused the record of his victory to be hewn on the sheer rock-face, to enshrine his memory for future generations.

Let us recount briefly the historical antecedents.

Since about 700 the Persians were governed by the Achaemenian dynasty, so called from their ancestor Hakhāmanish (Achaemenes). The son of Hakhāmanish, Chishpish (Teispes), divided the kingdom: Arijāramna (Ariamnes) received the eastern part, while the west was the portion of Kurash I (Cyrus), who later, like his son Kambushiya (Cambyses), would recognise the supreme authority of the Medes. We must wait for the son of Kambushiya, Kurash II (Cyrus II) the Great, to overthrow the King of the Medes, and conquer Media, Lydia and Babylonia.

The son and successor of Cyrus the Great, Cambyses II, banished his younger brother, Bardiya-Smerdis, and conquered Egypt. His long absence in the Land of the Nile was exploited by the magus Gaumata (a member of the priestly caste), a tax collector by profession, who proclaimed himself to be Bardiya (reported to be still alive) and usurped the title of King of Iran and Babylonia. Cambyses, returning post haste to punish him, died on the return journey in Syria in 522 B.C.

Thereupon seven Persian princes rose against the usurper, Gaumata. The rising was led by the grandson of Ariamnes, son of Vishtāspa (Hystaspes) and Dāryavush I (Darius) the Great (521–485 B.C.) who slew Gaumata with his own hand in his palace and became Great King. Civil war was inevitable. Rebellion broke out all over the country, inflamed and led by the exiled pretenders to the throne. Darius soon suppressed them. His victory over the rebels, "the false kings", and the world sovereignty bestowed upon him by Ahura Mazda are the subject of this other "queen of inscriptions", the sculptures and cuneiform epigraphy on the Behistun rock, recorded in the three languages of the Empire: Old Persian, Elamite and Babylonian.

On the bas-relief to the left can be distinguished two dignitaries of the Court; in front of them Darius himself, his right hand raised devoutly to Ahura Mazda (the winged solar disc). His left hand is reposting on a bow, his left foot on the neck of Gaumata lying at his feet and raising his hand in supplication; facing Darius are the "false kings" standing chained to each other by a cord passing round their necks and their hands tied behind their backs. Framing this bas-relief are the trilingual inscriptions.

How had this fabulous monument sunk into oblivion until it was rediscovered by Rawlinson in 1836? We know that the Aramaic alphabetic script had replaced cuneiform in the Persian kingdom. But the monument was too important and too close to the caravan route to be passed unnoticed. Evidence, therefore, should not have been lacking on the Behistun rock.

From some fanciful remarks by Diodorus Siculus (II, 13) we can extract this authentic piece of news: the mountain is sacred to Zeus (= Ahura Mazda) and bears a "Syrian" inscription. (We should obviously look in vain for the sculptured portraits of Semiramis and her hundred guardians mentioned by Diodorus.) Indications just as unproductive, given by the Arab geographers Yaqut and Qazwini, follow the ingenuous interpretation of Diodorus: the sculptures represent a school; the tallest figure is that of the teacher holding an "instrument" to chastise the pupils when they misbehaved! Certain Christian travellers risked giving their own interpretations. Thus Paul Ange Louis de Gardane, secretary to his brother the French ambassador at Teheran in 1807, pretended to see—the memorial is more than 300 feet above the ground—in the figure of Ahura Mazda a crucifix and in the remaining twelve figures the twelve apostles. The Englishman, Sir Ker Porter, was no better inspired by mistaking Darius for Shalmaneser III (859–824) and the figures before him for the ten tribes of Israel, the pointed bonnet worn by the rear figure being the mitre of the Levite priests. Nevertheless these interpretations belong in the history of culture; they are typical of the imagination of the archaeologists of this period, and it is only against this background that we can discover in their true light the achievements of the decipherers and translators.

All that had been said and written, then, so far rested on simple hearsay or on a very superficial examination of the actual sites. Before Rawlinson, no one conceived the idea of taking copies. This is what the English explorer has to say on the subject:

> "On reaching the recess which contains the Persian text of the record, ladders are indispensable in order to examine the upper portion of the tablet; and even with ladders there is a considerable risk, for the fort-ledge is so narrow, about eighteen inches or at most two feet in breadth, that with a ladder long enough to reach the sculptures sufficient slope cannot be given to enable a person to ascend, and, if the ladder be shortened in order to increase the slope, the upper inscriptions can only be copied by standing on the topmost step of the ladder, with no other support than steadying the body against the rock with the left arm, while the left hand holds the notebook, and the right hand is employed with the pencil. In this position I copied all the upper inscriptions, and the interest of the occupation entirely did away with any sense of danger.
>
> "To reach the recess which contains the Scythic (= Elamite!) translation of the record of Darius is a matter of far greater difficulty. On the left-hand side of the recess alone is there any foot-ledge whatever; on the right hand, where the recess, which is thrown a few feet further back, joins the Persian tablet, the face of the rock presents a sheer precipice,

and it is necessary therefore to bridge this intervening space between the left-hand of the Persian tablet and the foot-ledge on the left-hand of the recess with ladders of sufficient length; a bridge of this sort can be constructed without difficulty; but my first attempt to cross the chasm was unfortunate, and might have been fatal, for, having previously shortened my only ladder in order to obtain a slope for copying the Persian upper legends, I found, when I came to lay it across to the recess in order to get at the Scythic (Elamite) translation, that it was not sufficiently long to lie flat on the foot-ledge, and, as it would of course have tilted over if a person had attempted to cross in that position. I changed it from a horizontal to a vertical direction, the upper side resting firmly on the rock at its two ends, and the lower hanging over the precipice, and I prepared to cross, walking on the lower side, and holding to the upper side with my hands. If the ladder had been a compact article, this mode of crossing, although far from comfortable, would have been at any rate practicable; but the Persians merely fit in the bars of their ladders without pretending to clench them outside, and I had hardly accordingly begun to cross when the vertical pressure forced the bars out of their sockets, and the lower and unsupported side of the ladder thus parted company from the other and went crashing down over the precipice. Hanging on to the upper side, which still remained firm in its place, and assisted by my friends, who were anxiously watching the trial, I regained the Persian recess, and did not again attempt to cross until I had made a bridge of comparative stability."[24]

Here the account jumps a few years and records how Rawlinson in 1847 also managed to copy the Babylonian transcript:

"The Babylonian transcript at Behistun is still more difficult to reach than either the Scythic or the Persian tablets. The writing can be copied by the aid of a good telescope from below, but I long despaired of obtaining a cast of the inscription; for I found it quite beyond my powers of climbing to reach the spot where it was engraved, and the craigsmen of the place, who were accustomed to track the mountain goats over the entire face of the mountain, declared the particular block inscribed with the Babylonian legend to be unapproachable. At length, however, a wild Kurdish boy, who had come from a great distance, volunteered to make the attempt, and I promised him a considerable reward if he succeeded. The mass of rock in question is scarped, and it projects some feet over the Scythic recess, so that it cannot be approached by any of the ordinary means of climbing. The boy's first move was to squeeze himself up a cleft in the rock a short distance to the left of the projecting mass. When he had ascended some distance above it, he drove a wooden peg firmly into the cleft, fastened a rope to this, and then endeavoured to swing himself across to another cleft some distance on the other side; but in this he failed, owing to the projection of the rock. It then only remained for him to cross over to the cleft by hanging on with his toes and fingers to the slight inequalities on the bare face of the precipice, and in this he succeeded, passing over a distance of twenty feet of almost smooth perpendicular rock in a manner which to a looker-on appeared quite miraculous. When he had reached the second cleft the real difficulties were over. He had brought a rope with him attached to the first peg, and now driving in a second, he was enabled to swing himself right over the projecting mass of rock. Here with a short ladder he formed a swinging seat, like a painter's cradle, and fixed upon this seat, he took under my direction the paper cast of the Babylonian translation of the records of Darius."[25]

Now let us return to the inscriptions of Alvend. In 1836 Eugène Burnouf (1801–52) published his *Mémoire sur deux inscriptions cunéiformes*, one of which came from Alvend and the other from the estate of F. E. Schulz. He established a cuneiform alphabet of thirty-three signs, only a few of which were correct. His contribution to the decipherment is no less important on this account because, thanks to his profound knowledge of Zend and Sanskrit, he was able to define accurately the meaning of several words contained in the inscriptions (which he could only partially read). He showed, on the other hand, that the word "adam", which Grotefend took for a title, actually meant "I am". Among the newly acquired signs only the "k" and the "z" are due to Burnouf. But we must remember that he was primarily an Indologist and Sanskrit scholar and that his contribution to cuneiform formed only a small part of his lifework.

The same remark applies to his friend, Christian Lassen (1800–76). He, too, was a specialist in Indian dialects and Sanskrit who had been introduced to this study by A. W. von Schlegel, and Old Persian did not take first place in his activities. In the same year as Burnouf he published a treatise which has its place in the history of decipherment: *The Old Persian Cuneiform Inscriptions of Persepolis, Bonn 1836.*

In his search for new names—the point of departure of all decipherments—Lassen, in common with Grotefend, Rawlinson and many subsequent scholars, remembered that very useful guide—"Herodotus, my constant companion, a precious and respected friend," as the great German scholar and African explorer, Heinrich Bart, was to write as a dedication in his book. Herodotus also put Lassen on the right path. In Book IV, 87, we can read:

> "Darius also having viewed the Bosphorus erected two columns of white marble on the shore, engraving on one in Assyrian characters, and on the other in Grecian, *the names of* all the nations he had in his army, and he had some from all whom he rules . . ."[26]

Why should not this text, thought Lassen, be found among the inscriptions of Persepolis? He examined once more the copies of Niebuhr and discovered one which to all appearances contained no fewer than twenty-four proper names. Next he established an alphabet which, going beyond Grotefend and Burnouf, already contained twenty-three letters with correct phonetic values, eight of which were his discovery (two more letters were very nearly correct). Of the twenty-four proper names on the inscription he identified nineteen—a great triumph, as the assyriologist, Wallis Budge, was to insist a hundred years later.

But the palm must be given to Lassen for having, thanks to his Indian studies, removed the obstacle which had caused the first decipherers so much difficulty; he recognised that in Old Persian the vowel "a" had no particular meaning but, as in the Indian alphabets, was "inherent", integrated or an adherent to consonants so that the sign denoting "m" could mean either the consonant "m" or "ma". This immediately explained readings such as xšayϑiy vzrk for xšayaϑiya vazrka (see transcriptions in Fig. 39), where the written "a" represents ā, i.e. a double "a", the one which precedes the consonant being inherent, whereas the second is a true vowel.

When E. E. F. Beer and E. V. St. Jacquet independently determined several missing signs the decipherment of Old Persian cuneiform had practically been completed.

It was then that everything began again from the beginning. Henry Creswicke Rawlinson was not only an outstanding soldier, an energetic horseman and an adroit diplomat, he was also a scholar of the highest order.

When, at Kirmanshah in 1835, he copied the two trilingual inscriptions on Mt. Alvend, he barely knew that Grotefend had deciphered the names of Hystaspes, Darius and Xerxes. But we can imagine that thanks to his classical education he spotted the two names of the Achaemenides, Darius and Xerxes, as soon as he recognised that both inscriptions on Mt. Alvend were identical to within three groups of signs. It was he who, emulating Grotefend, deciphered the three names Hystaspes, Darius and Xerxes and in this way obtained thirteen letters. He, too, remembered the passage in Herodotus (VII, 11) where Xerxes relates his own genealogy.

But Rawlinson was in a far more favourable position than the Göttingen professor had been. He had at his disposal the fabulous Behistun epigraphy. The genealogy in Herodotus provided him with many more useful names: from the first lines of the Behistun inscription he extracted five groups of signs—the names Persia (Parsa), Arsames (Arshāma), Ariamnes (Arijāramna), Teispes (Chishpish), Achaemenes (Hakhāmanish)!

As though he had foreseen the difficulties of the decipherment, the Great King offered the archaeologist at the opening of his immortal inscription, the desired names:

King Dāryavush proclaims:
I (am) Dāryavush,
the great King,
King of kings,
King in Persia

King of countries
son of Vishtāspa,
grandson of Arshāma,
An Achaemenian.

King Dāryavush proclaims:
My father—Vishtāspa,
Vishtāspa's father—Arshāma,
Arshāma's father—Arijāramna,
Arijāramna's father—Chishpish,
Chishpish's father—Hakhāmanish.

King Dāryavush proclaims:
This is why we are called Hakhāmanishija
On our father's side we are of noble birth
Our fathers were a race of kings.[27]

When Rawlinson returned to Baghdad at the end of 1836 to receive from Colonel Taylor the cuneiform alphabets of Grotefend and Saint-Martin he had already established more phonetic values than the two scholars, whose results actually conflicted. Rawlinson worked throughout the following year on the Behistun inscriptions. In 1838 he sent the transcription and translation of the two first sections with notes to the Royal Asiatic Society in London. This work fell into the hands of the only connoisseur in the British capital—Edwin Norris—who sent a copy to Paris. Rawlinson was in close contact with the research work of his day, was in correspondence with Lassen and became acquainted with the work of Burnouf on the Jasna, the third part of the Avesta. He eagerly studied Zend and Sanskrit. At the beginning of 1839 he had translated nearly all the 200 lines copied from Behistun.

During this time European research had not remained inactive. When Rawlinson returned to Baghdad in 1844, he discovered a host of new works giving important results: an alphabet had been established, phonetic values corrected and translations improved. From London, Norris kept him informed of the progress of the Irishman, Edward Hincks (we shall meet both Norris and Hincks later), and when Rawlinson produced his magnum opus, *Memoir, on the Persian Version of the Behistun Inscriptions* (1844–5) he had to admit that European scholarship in this field had made great progress. This did not detract from his merit in having published (1846–9) the Persian version of his inscriptions. It represents a milestone in the history of the decipherment of cuneiform.

All these works gradually brought accuracy to the Old

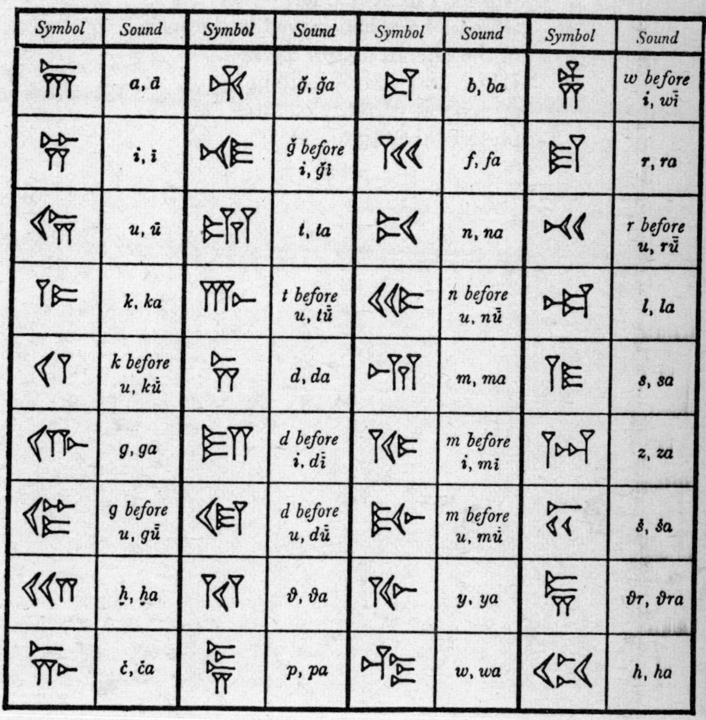

Symbol	*Sound*	*Symbol*	*Sound*	*Symbol*	*Sound*	*Symbol*	*Sound*
	a, ā		*ǧ, ǧa*		*b, ba*		*w before i, wī*
	i, ī		*ǧ before i, ǧī*		*f, fa*		*r, ra*
	u, ū		*t, ta*		*n, na*		*r before u, rū*
	k, ka		*t before u, tū*		*n before u, nū*		*l, la*
	k before u, kū		*d, da*		*m, ma*		*s, sa*
	g, ga		*d before i, dī*		*m before i, mī*		*z, za*
	g before u, gū		*d before u, dū*		*m before u, mū*		*š, ša*
	ḫ, ḫa		*ϑ, ϑa*		*y, ya*		*ϑr, ϑra*
	č, ča		*p, pa*		*w, wa*		*h, ha*

FIG. 40.—The Old Persian cuneiform alphabet.

Persian cuneiform, a consonantal alphabetic script which had retained certain elements of syllabic writing, and had undergone a transformation enabling it to suppress vowels. The "a" was inherent in the consonants and the "i" and the "u" characterised by the fact that the consonant preceding them adopted a different form in each case. Fig. 40 shows the Old Persian characters in the light of modern research.

Thus, after two and a half millennia, was accomplished what Darius the Great had written for future generations in his royal language:

> King Dāryavush proclaims:
> Ye who in future pass,
> will see this inscription,
> which I have had carved in the rock,
> of the human figures there—
> Efface and destroy nothing!
> As long as posterity endures
> preserve them intact! [28]

CHAPTER IV

IN CUNEIFORM ON SIX BRICKS

THE DECIPHERMENT OF MESOPOTAMIAN CUNEIFORM

"I must admit that . . . I was tempted more than once to abandon the study of Assyrian inscriptions because I despaired of ever obtaining a satisfactory result." [29]

—Henry Creswicke Rawlinson, 1850.

"I am the first man to read this text after two thousand years of oblivion."—George Smith after 1861.

THE decipherment of Old Persian cuneiform was practically complete, but in actual fact it constituted merely a beginning, the first step on the way to deciphering cuneiform in general; for Old Persian was only a kind of "late degeneration", a systematic yet practical shorthand and, apart from the wedge, had little in common with true cuneiform, although it did not entirely renounce its origin. Its clumsy way of transcribing vowels shows that it stemmed from a syllabic script.

Let us recall how the first copyists had already distinguished three scripts which they supposed to be three different languages; how at first they took the most simple of these scripts for alphabetical, and the second and third, based on their number of signs, for syllabic and ideographic respectively.

The decipherment of the Old Persian inscriptions thus gave the key to the reading of the other two.

Why had the great Persian kings addressed the world in three languages, and what were these three languages? The historical situation which had given rise to these inscriptions bears only a very remote resemblance to that found on the Rosetta stone.

As science knows today, the country of origin in the case of cuneiform was Mesopotamia, the country between the Tigris and the Euphrates, corresponding today to Iraq. The rise of its successive civilisations—Sumerian, followed by Assyro-Babylonian (Akkadian)—spread to the East and to the Western world of antiquity. We shall discuss later the Western sphere which came under their influence. To the East, the land of

Elam in the south-west of Iran, with its future capital, Susa (for a long time Elamite was called Susian), was in touch with Sumerian and then Babylonian civilisation, from which at an early date it borrowed cuneiform and at the same time the Akkadian language, i.e. Assyro-Babylonian. Later this country, with the aid of Assyro-Babylonian, began to write its own Elamite tongue (an idiom, neither Indo-European nor Semitic, still comparatively little known today). When the Persians invaded Iran through Armenia in the first millennium B.C., Elam was the first civilisation to the spell of which they were subjected. At the outset the Persian conquerors, together with the Elamite administration, which they considered very enlightened, preserved the language and writing of the country. The creation of a language of their own did not materialise until the reign of Darius the Great. It is in this Elamite or more accurately Neo-Elamite language and its script, the most ancient in the Persian kingdom, that the second text of Behistun is written.

And what of the third, Babylonian? The kingdom of Chaldaea had formed part of the Persian Empire since its conquest in 539 B.C. by Cyrus the Great; its language became the third language of the country. Proclamations concerning the whole realm were therefore written in these three languages.

The decipherment of the Elamite version certainly presented difficulties, but it seemed to promise better results than the Babylonian, which at first glance was very formidable. One hundred and eleven Elamite symbols were recognised, proving that this script was neither alphabetic nor ideographic; it looked to all intents and purposes to be a syllabic writing.

A first attempt by Grotefend had the merit of throwing some light on this large number of symbols which did not even possess word separators. His discovery once more bears witness, in this late work, to his extraordinary perspicacity; he recognised the determination of the masculine proper names, a mute sign placed before the name (not after it, as in Egyptian) in the shape of a vertical wedge.

The Dane, Niels Ludwig Westergaard, sent to Persia in 1843 to make copies, relied on a document acquired by his own investigations; a list of the names of countries from the tomb of Darius at Naksh-i-Rustam. He was the first to transcribe a part of the Elamite inscription. But in his eyes the writing was still in part alphabetic, partly syllabic, and he inadvertently entered on his list of eighty-five signs several determinatives of which he did not know the value. He believed that he was dealing with a Median language.

Here once more the decipherment started quite naturally from the proper names; the bases for the investigation were confirmed when Professor Edwin Norris, whom we have already mentioned, published the Elamite version of the Behistun inscription in 1853. Until then about forty proper names had been discovered, and now the number suddenly rose to ninety. This task could not have fallen into better hands than those of Norris. To show the almost intuitive reliability of this work we need only quote that in the old Persian text from which he worked he had managed to spot mistakes in Rawlinson's copies (he had never seen the originals), to recognise defective passages and make the necessary corrections. Rawlinson had inadvertently missed a line; back in London, Norris's eagle eye had immediately spotted this lacuna; he pointed it out in a letter to the scholar who, on comparing Norris's corrections with the original, found that they were correct.

Born at Taunton in 1795, Norris at the age of twenty had already learned Armenian and the various associated languages as well as several European languages. He was summoned, as Rawlinson and so many of his contemporaries had been, by the great organisation which knew how to exploit and develop the courage, initiative and intelligence of its employees—the East India Company. Norris entered its service at the age of twenty-three, and studied Indian, African and Polynesian languages. In 1838, thanks to his outstanding knowledge, he became joint secretary to the Royal Asiatic Society in London. It was in this capacity that he received the first treatise addressed by Rawlinson to the Society. Norris, thoroughly fascinated, plunged into the study of Old Persian and the related languages. His model translation of the Behistun Elamite version marked the second milestone in his scientific career. The first had been passed when in 1845 in India he had deciphered on his own initiative the rock inscription of the Emperor Açoka at Kapur di Giri. Let us mention *en passant*, to round off the portrait of this extraordinary man, that he faithfully encouraged Rawlinson's researches, sending him for years all the works concerning cuneiform writing with his own hand-written comments; in addition to cuneiform he knew to perfection several African languages and, being a Cornishman, also published several Ogham texts and wrote a book on Ogham drama (Ogham is a Cornish celtic dialect which became extinct at the turn of the eighteenth century).

But let us return to Elamite. Norris had based his work on the precious patrimony of proper names, which enabled him to determine most of the Elamite syllabic signs. Scholars now had at their disposal the Old Persian version to help them study the meaning of words and the grammatical forms.

We give below a specimen of the second script on the Behistun rock. It is one of the marginal notes on the figures on the bas-relief, and refers to the recumbent Gaumata.

Unfortunately even today Elamite has remained a sort of poor relation of Assyriology, a language which has not been entirely reconstituted. It would appear that an unlucky fate opposed its preservation, for we possess no Elamite monumental inscription from the post-Achaemenian period, although it is probable that the language remained alive until the end of the first Christian millennium.

There only remained to be solved, then, the most burning problem set by the Achaemenian inscriptions: the Babylonian text, an impregnable fortress which at first seemed to defy all attempts to decipher it. Then as the attackers pressed home their assault it lost this character and transformed itself into a treacherous labyrinth.

Naturally the similarity of this third script to the Babylonian monuments which reached Europe in even greater profusion had long since been noticed. Abbé Beauchamps, vicar-general of Babylon, who travelled the country between 1781 and 1785, was the first European to recognise a language in the symbols engraved on the clay cylinders, bricks and black stones he had picked up here and there. He sent a few specimens to his friend, Barthélemy, in Paris. But Babylonian research received a new impulse from another quarter and by a detour we have already mentioned. Several years after the premature death of her husband, the widow of Claude Rich had published in 1839 the private diaries of the explorer. The celebrated Franco-German Orientalist, Julius Mohl, discovered these a year later. With increasing interest he studied the scientific testament of the young Englishman.

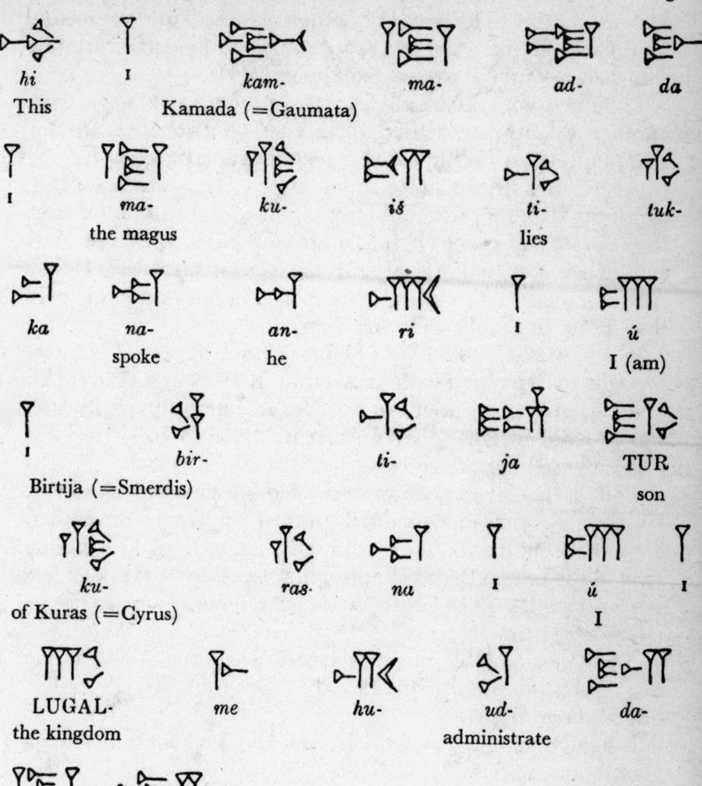

I is the determinative for persons. TUR and LUGAL are Sumero-Babylonian ideograms.

FIG. 41.—Neo-Elamite cuneiform inscription from the Darius monument at Behistun, with transcription and translation.

Fascinated by this reading, he felt a growing conviction, which soon become a certainty: Rich had discovered Niniveh—and anyone who started excavations there could anticipate an archaeological booty surpassing the wildest dreams.

Julius von Mohl enjoyed a certain influence in official quarters. At his instigation the French Government sent a vice-consul to Mosul with express orders to collect manuscripts and antiquities. The man in question was the Torinese doctor, Paul Emile Botta, who, in 1843, brought to light the magnificent palace of the Assyrian King, Sargon II.

Equipped with Rich's description of the great Nimrud hill, another Englishman visited these sites on two occasions, in 1840 and 1842. With no name and without means he approached the British ambassador at the Ottoman Porte, Sir Stratford Canning, who not only obtained permission for him to excavate but also gave him a little financial assistance. His confidence was well rewarded; the young man was Henry Austen Layard, who was soon to play a more important part than Botta in the discovery of Nimrud.

When, in the '40s, Botta at Khurasan and Layard at Nimrud brought to light the fabulous Assyrian palaces and sent copies of the lengthy descriptions to Europe, an extraordinary interest was aroused in what they mistakenly believed to be the last undeciphered cuneiform language.

This particular cuneiform had jealously guarded its secret. In 1850 Rawlinson, who had worked untiringly on copies, obtained from his young Kurdish climber, admitted, as can be read in the incipit to this chapter, that *he had more than once been on the point of giving up because he had lost all hope of ever obtaining a satisfactory result.*

An understandable discouragement when one considers the long Behistun inscription and the huge number of its five hundred odd signs.

Instead of reaping a goodly harvest could he not anticipate a very modest success?

This is probably what the Swede, Löwenstern, thought when, in 1846, he attacked the ancient inscription of Xerxes which had already been so propitious to Grotefend (see Figs. 38 and 39). He concentrated his attention on the Babylonian text and compared it with the Old Persian version. Its context was now fully known; it consisted of only proper names and titles (the latter having already been established by Grotefend); it was short—in brief, it constituted a promising point of departure.

It was in fact a simple and brilliant idea. No one had thought of it before Löwenstern. The Swede was, therefore, the first to see what today appears to us as obvious: the words for "king" (Old Persian, above Nos. 2, 4, 5 and 7) and "son" (idem, No. 8) correspond in the Babylonian text *to a single sign* ("king" below

Nos. 2, 4, 5, 8, "son" No. 6). One sign for a word—was Babylonian cuneiform ideographic?

Basing his investigations on the analogy with the Old Persian text, Löwenstern established correctly the two signs "king" and "son" and demonstrated convincingly that Babylonian cunei-

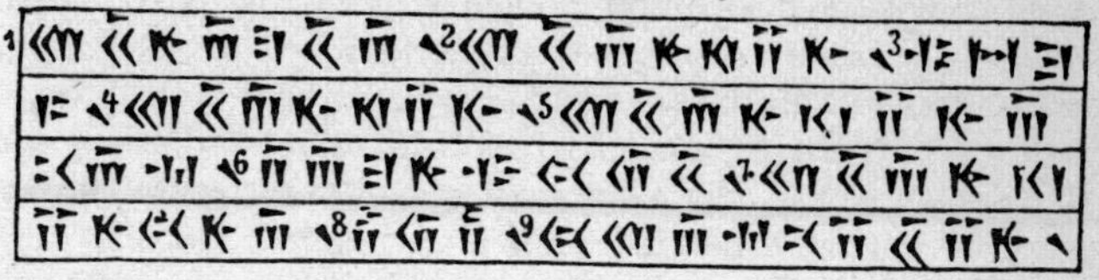

(Spelt) (1) *X(a)-š(a)-y(a)-a-r(a)-š(a)-a* (2) *x(a)-š(a)-a-y(a)-ϑ(a)-i-y(a)* (3) *v(a)-z(a)-r(a)-k(a)* (4) *x(a)-š(a)-a-y(a)-ϑ(a)-i-y(a)* (5) *x(a)-š(a)-a-y(a)-ϑ(a)-i-y(a)-a-n(a)-a-m(a)* (6) *D(a)-a-r(a)-y(a)-v(a)-h(a)-u-š(a)* (7) *x(a)-š(a)-a-y(a)-ϑ(a)-i-y(a)-h(a)-y(a)-a* (8) *p(a)-u-ç(a)* (9) *H(a)-x(a)-a-m(a)-n(a)-i-š(a)-i-y(a)*

(Pronounced) *Xšāyāršā xšāyaϑiya vazrka xšayāϑiya xšayāϑiyānām Dārayavabauš xšāyaϑıyaha puça Haxāmanišiya*

"Xerxes, the great king, the Kings of kings, of Darius, the son, of the king, the Achaemenian."

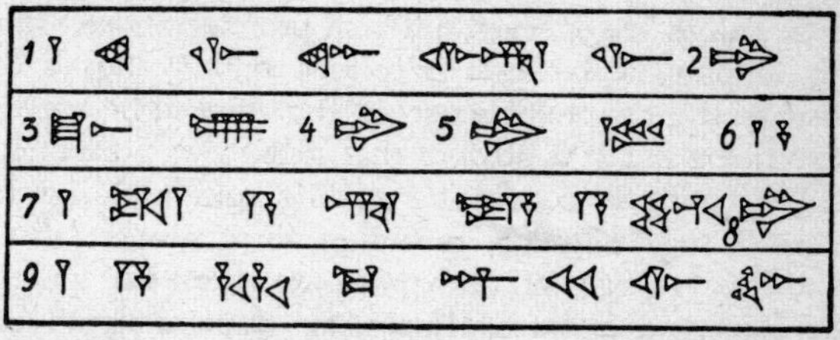

(1) ^{I}*Hi-ši-'ar-ši* (2) *šarru* (3) *rabû*^{u} (4) *šar* (5) *šarrāni*^{MEŠ} (6) *mār* (7) ^{I}*Da-a-ri-ia-a-mus* (8) *šarri* (9) *A-ha-ma-an-niš-ši-'*

"Xerxes, the king, the King of kings, the son of Darius, of the king, the Achaemenian."

FIG. 42.—Inscription of Xerxes in Old Persian (above) and in Babylonian (below) with transcription and translation.

form with letters in certain circumstances representing a whole word could only be an ideographic script. But this is precisely where the first difficulties arose. The name Xerxes, consisting of seven signs in Old Persian (two a's and five consonants), was in the Babylonian version composed of five signs (after deducting the initial determinative on the left). How was it possible not to deduce an alphabetic writing when five signs corresponded to the five consonants of the name in Old Persian? (It was known that the Hebrews and the Semites in general only wrote their consonants.) Other reasons led to the belief that they were dealing here with a Semitic language. In the same conviction Rawlinson studied Hebrew and Syrian from 1847. In February 1850 he presented the Royal Asiatic Society in London with his first results: he believed that he had found eighty proper names, about 150 phonetic values and nearly 500 Babylonian words. But eventually he had to recognise Hincks' work: it was the brilliant Irishman who cut the Gordian knot and opened the way to success in this jungle of conflicting readings.

The impossibility of using this method, which had been so propitious to earlier decipherments, had in fact been recognised, i.e. the application of phonetic values to new words, obtained from proper names. Was this not a discouraging proof that they had embarked on the wrong route? Each consonant could be expressed by a whole series of different signs, often up to six or seven. An attempt was made to explain this by homophony—the consonants effectively possessing all these phonetic values, six or seven different pronunciations. In view of this limping explanation it seemed that Voltaire's biting criticism of the Egyptologists could equally well be applied to the Assyriologists. It is obvious that such views prevented any unified, scientifically convincing reading, since each sign could have six or seven different meanings, for a simple "r" could respond to seven signs at a time, as Löwenstern had found.

The Reverend Edward Hincks, an eminent figure in the history of Assyriology, was a theologian. His portraits reveal him more as a scholarly theoretician than as a field archaeologist of an enterprising nature. In fact he had never gone excavating. But the battle was waged at his study desk between 1846 and 1850, and it was a decisive battle for the breaking of Babylonian cuneiform. The weakly little bespectacled priest came out a brilliant victor.

In 1850, the year Rawlinson had become discouraged, Hincks discovered the essential keys which could serve as a point of departure for this new science. He declared that Babylonian contained no simple consonantal symbols (no isolated letters, therefore), but was composed of syllabic signs of the type vowel + consonant—*ab*, *ir*, etc., or consonant + vowel—*da*, *ki*, etc. (Löwenstern's seven r's were merely syllabic signs *ar*, *ir*, *er*, *ur*, *ra*, *ri*, *ru*), and besides these syllabic signs there

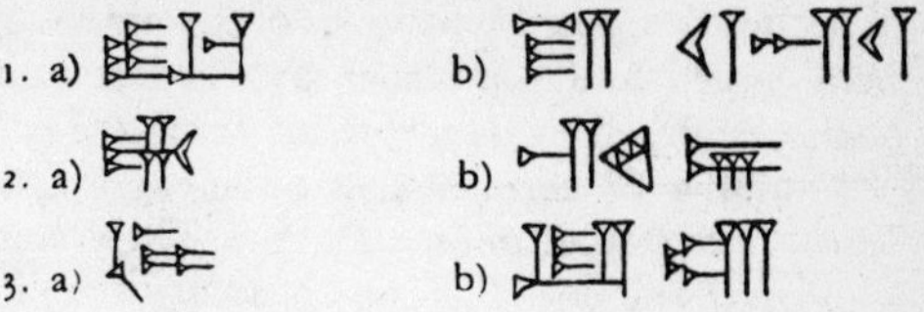

1. a) *šar* b) *ša-ar*
2. a) *gir* b) *gi-ir*
3. a) *lum* b) *lu-um*

FIG. 43.—Alternation of complex and simple syllabic writing.

were complex signs, of the type consonant + vowel + consonant such as *kan*, *mur*, etc. The latter in their turn could be rendered—an entirely new discovery—either by a complex script (*kan*, *mur*) or by a script split into two parts (*ka-an*, *mu-ur*).

Hincks further discovered with an almost unrivalled perspicacity (he had been trained in a good school) another peculiarity of Babylonian cuneiform which at first was far from reassuring to the hopes of lay and professional decipherers alike: a single sign could be used either as an ideogram, a syllabic sign or a determinative; the characters in this writing were in actual fact "polyvalent"!

Again Hincks had already recognised and established correctly a large number of the determinatives.

Dedicated to the study of hieroglyphs he would probably never have come to cuneiform had not the exciting discovery at Niniveh taken him along this path.

Two investigators raised two new columns in the temple of decipherment: a lucky find produced the third.

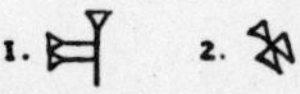

1. (*a*) ideogram *iṣu* "wood".
   (*b*) determinative before trees and wooden objects.
   (*c*) syllabic sign *iz* (*is*, etc.).
2. (*a*) ideogram *mātu*, "country" and *šadû*, "mountain".
   (*b*) determinative before the names of countries and mountains.
   (*c*) syllabic sign *kur*, *māt*, *šat*, *nat*, *gin*, etc.

FIG. 44.—Two signs which can be used either as ideograms, determinatives or syllabic signs.

The first of these was the excavator, Botta, of whom it was later said, rather unkindly, that he was no archaeologist. A man of talent, doctor, professional diplomat and naturalist from choice, he can also be considered as an eminent decipherer. Staking all his hopes on the inscriptions of the palace of Sargon, he had them copied and was struck by the fact that a great number of them offered evidence of the same context, one of the texts containing at certain spots an ideogram, while the other presented a group of phonetic signs. These comparisons led him to discover the pronunciation of some of the ideograms and allowed him to deduce the following formula: one and the same word is rendered alternately by an ideogram and a group of syllabic signs.

The conclusion was complete when Rawlinson, on the termination of his work in 1851 with the publication of the Babylonian version of the Behistun inscriptions, made this assertion: an identical syllabic sign can have several phonetic values; it may be polyphonous. Authentic, incontestable polyphony which had nothing to do with the first unfortunate attempts to admit the "homophony" of the isolated signs, nor with the polyvalence of the signs illustrated in Fig. 44. Thanks to a series of comparisons, Rawlinson recognised the polyphony of a great number of the Assyro-Babylonian cuneiform characters, supporting his theory by a list of more than 200 signs which, as a whole, still hold good today.

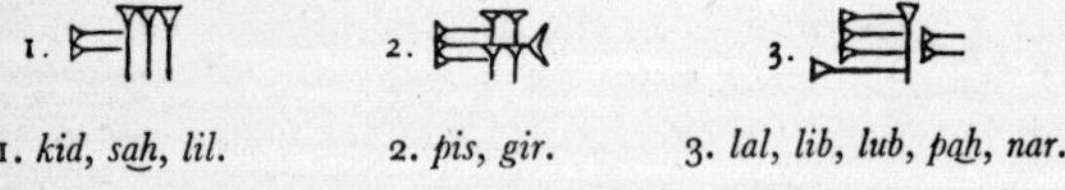

1. *kid, saḫ, lil.* 2. *pis, gir.* 3. *lal, lib, lub, paḫ, nar.*

FIG. 45.—Polyphonous syllabic signs.

Ambiguity, polyvalence, polyphony . . . no one need be surprised that distrust and even contempt greeted each new discovery on the part of the decipherers. Even more so when, prudently applying the newly acquired syllables to a group of signs which Grotefend had declared made up the name of the biblical Nebuchadrezzar, instead of the expected "nabu-kudurri-usur" (= God Nabu, protect my frontier stones), they obtained "Anakshadushish". And in the same way for Shalmaneser (Shulmānu-asharid), "Dimanubar"!

Had not Rawlinson recently declared: "because . . . I was in despair"?

In this *impasse* ancient Niniveh itself entered the stage, to provide what no investigator had ever dared to hope for: genuine already prepared syllabaries for budding scribes, in the form of clay tablets, were discovered in the archives of Kuyunjik (Niniveh) where the excavations started by Botta had continued.

On these tablets were found the Sumerian phonetic values of the ideograms, which no longer existed except in the language of the cult and of jurisprudence, figuring beside the corresponding names in the Semitic Assyro-Babylonian tongue. And on them were also found *an-ak* = Na-bi-um (God), *sha-du* = kudurru (boundary), *shish* = naṣaru (to protect), the imperative form of which was pronounced usur! Thus *an-ak-sha-du-shish* = *nabu-kudurri-uṣur!*

There are few occasions in the history of decipherment where efforts of a strict discipline have been so magnificently rewarded and confirmed.

Nevertheless philologists still nursed their doubts and suspicion of ideography and above all of its insidious polyphony. To end such a situation it needed a genuine intellectual revolution which the interested scholars themselves resolved.

To this school belonged two very different men: the first was English, William Henry Fox Talbot (1800–77), an Orientalist better known as a great mathematician and as the inventor of "Talbotype" photography. He was not the first English scholar to take up Orientalism as a side line; and if his compatriot, Young, the naturalist and doctor, gave the first impetus to Egyptology, the inspiration of Fox Talbot definitely led to the decipherment of Akkadian cuneiform.

Talbot was closely associated with S. Birch, the Egyptologist whom we mentioned in our chapter on Egypt. He worked at the British Museum with Edwin Norris, the eminent decipherer of Elamite. Fox Talbot revealed his plan to Norris, who did not hide his enthusiasm; the Royal Asiatic Society, of which he was secretary, would try an experiment by giving the same cuneiform text to several Assyriologists at the same time to translate without betraying that it was the same text. The result of their labours would decide the value of all the decipherment work done so far and the future of the new science, Assyriology.

A brilliant experiment—but who were to be chosen to take part? Rawlinson, Hincks and Fox Talbot, the originator of the plan, seemed particular suited for this task. But Assyriology, although strongly encouraged by the English, was no longer a purely British affair. There was one great man who could not be left out: the Franco-German scholar, Oppert.

Julius (later Jules) Oppert (1825–1905), born at Hamburg of a Jewish family, received a very unusual intellectual training. Like many linguists and philologists, he had abandoned mathematics in favour of Law at Heidelberg. After Heidelberg he went to Bonn, where Christian Lassen was lecturer. The young Hamburger was soon introduced to a new world in which he felt completely at home.

He studied Sanskrit and Arabic, spent two years in Berlin and submitted his doctor's thesis at Kiel, but Bonn still kept him on the staff. In 1847 at Berlin appeared his study *Das Lautsystem des Altpersischen*, in which he arrived at the same conclusions on the use of consonants as Rawlinson had published in 1846—Rawlinson later became his life-long friend.

The undisputed prestige that France enjoyed as the European centre of Oriental studies certainly influenced Oppert to be drawn towards that country in 1847. He did not go to Paris. Unknown to the public, he had first to show his mettle. In 1848 he was Professor of German at Laval and in 1850 at the Rheims Lycée.

A lycée professor as Grotefend had been, but a foreigner, Oppert soon embarked upon a brilliant scientific career.

In his new country he did not remain inactive. As early as 1852 a work on the Achaemenian inscriptions published at Paris aroused the attention of French scholars. Their influence resulted in his becoming that year a member of the French archaeological mission, sent to Mesopotamia under the direction of Fulgence Fresnel. A two-volume work on this expedition won him in 1860 the Prix de l'Institut, although Comte de Gobineau had seriously attacked the scholar and his system which, while admitting the broad lines of Rawlinson's decipherment, corrected and completed it in certain details. When Oppert renounced his Chair of Sanskrit to become Professor of Assyriology at the Collège de France, this promotion represented more than an outward progress: he had long since abandoned Ancient India in favour of the languages of the "land between the two rivers"—Mesopotamia.

One of Oppert's best qualities was a complete absence of any feeling of envy, of scientific or literary jealousy; already a well-respected specialist, and even considered a "big gun" in his own particular field, he was on friendly terms with younger scholars who in their own theses corrected certain doubtful points in his earlier works. "No one can reproach me that I stick to an earlier hypothesis when it has once been disproved," he said to one of his pupils on his last visit to Heidelberg towards the end of his life. This disciple, Carl Bezold, was to write his obituary notice:

> "Those among us who have been lucky enough to be on personal terms with this illustrious scholar, will never forget his impressive personality. No one could fail to admire his flashing eyes and handsome face, the extraordinary subtlety of his mind in a youthful body. A learned discussion between master and pupil, between the taciturn British General Rawlinson, a trustee of the British Museum, and the Parisian professor, a member of the Institut, renowned for his quick wit and brilliant repartee was, for an audience of Assyriologists, an unforgettable experience. . . ."[30]

Oppert never failed to voice his opinions, and his frankness was not always very popular among certain of his colleagues and friends, but "his genuinely noble and creative, scientific spirit" was impregnated by that high morality which characterised the man and the investigator: "it is not only the right but the duty of each of us to write and to teach solely the results obtained after conscientious examination."[31]

Oppert had to be won over for this plan. Now, chance decreed that in 1857 Rawlinson, Hincks, Fox Talbot and Oppert were all in London. The Royal Asiatic Society and its valiant secretary, Norris, set to work.

The copy of a cuneiform inscription was sent in a sealed envelope to four Assyriologists who could not have known of its existence because it had only recently been discovered. It stemmed from the three clay cylinders of the Assyrian King Tiglath-pileser I (1113–1074 B.C.). The four scholars were asked to translate it and to send their results to the Society.

Talbot, Hincks and Rawlinson worked from the same lithographed text. Oppert, independent as usual, made his own copy. The transcriptions were returned, also sealed, and the Society appointed a jury and called a solemn meeting.

Now the whole world was to be given the irrefutable proof that the young science Assyriology had been founded on solid bases.

The four texts agreed in all the essential points, although, naturally, there were slight divergences. The two transcriptions closest to each other were those of Rawlinson and Hincks. Fox Talbot had made a few blunders and Oppert translated his own copy into English; his version contained a few doubtful passages. But according to the findings of the jury the decipherment was adjudicated a *fait accompli*.

The decipherers could now have been left to their own devices, and merely study their results, had there not appeared at this initial stage a man who does not really rank among the decipherers of cuneiform (but among those of another writing), but whose name is indissolubly bound up with its history.

About the period when Rawlinson arrived at Kandahar as diplomatic envoy, George Smith (1840–76), a son of poor parents, was born in Chelsea. This precocious boy with an extraordinary talent for drawing was lucky enough to be apprenticed to Bradbury Evans in Bouverie Street, to learn how to engrave banknotes.

Apart from his profession, in which he soon distinguished himself, he had a single love—this is by no means exceptional in England—his favourite book was the Bible, with particular reference to the Books of the Old Testament. He read every work on Oriental literature he could find. He studied in admiration the antiquities which were arriving in great quantities at the British Museum. "The Bible is right." This refrain, which eventually spread to the general public, was largely due to the efforts and studies of Smith.

Copperplate engraving also had its advantages: it opened to the young man the road to European fame, although unfortunately he met with a premature and tragic death. His professional competence allowed him to collaborate in the illustration of Rawlinson's great work on cuneiform script. The symmetrical beauty of the "nails" and wedges, so mysterious at first sight, this immortal testimony of a remote past, acted on him like a charm.

A reader, tireless student and enthusiastic traveller, George Smith caught the eye of a scholar whom we have already quoted several times—Samuel Birch. He had recently been appointed Keeper of the British Museum, and now became his protector. Thus at the age of twenty-one Smith acted as restorer at the Museum; his task was to reconstitute the clay tablets which had often arrived broken from the excavations at Niniveh. Smith threw himself whole-heartedly into this new occupation, and his apprenticeship as a copperplate engraver stood him in good stead. At the end of a short time he was able to read the difficult Akkadian cuneiform script better than most of the specialists, deciphering the tablets without difficulty, as though he were somehow aware of their contents. In 1866 he became Assistant Keeper of Oriental Antiquities on the orders of Birch. Devoting himself entirely to his task, he had only one grumble: the London fog, which interfered with his reading. The faint gleam of the oil lamps hampered his studies and he was to a certain extent in bondage to the light.

The years 1872–3 marked the peak of George Smith's activities. By way of prologue he had succeeded in 1871 in partially deciphering the Cypriote syllabary. We shall be dealing with this in a later chapter. In 1872, as he was bending over his cuneiform tablets (sent to the Museum from Niniveh by Layard's successor, Hormuzd Rassam), Smith had a revelation which left him speechless: this was no inventory or monumental inscription but a tale shrouded in all the magic of the East, a grandiose epic from the mists of time celebrating the deeds of a certain Gilgamesh who had departed to immortality. A strange and disconcerting tale which grew very familiar as the able decipherer read further.

He read how the hero, Gilgamesh, two parts divine and one third human, built the walls and temples of the ancient capital, Uruk. The inhabitants groaned beneath the task and invoked the aid of the gods. The goddess, Aruru, in her compassion, created a hairy brute named Enkidu, who was to vie with Gilgamesh and dissuade him from his impious task. Tamed by the charms of a courtesan and defeated in honourable battle by Gilgamesh after a grim struggle, Enkidu became the hero's friend. Together they enjoyed a series of adventures. After overpowering the evil Humbaba, Lord of the Cedar Forests, they cut off his head; together they administered the *coup de grâce* to the celestial bull, a monster sent to torment them by Ishtar, whom Gilgamesh had scorned. When Enkidu succumbed to a serious malady Gilgamesh set out in search of eternal life.

He knew whom to ask for advice: his ancestor, Ut-napishtim, the sole survivor of the Deluge, the only man who had escaped the waters of the Flood.

George Smith could not believe his eyes: the Deluge—here on Assyrian clay tablets? There was no shadow of doubt. He continued to read feverishly. Ut-napishtim would certainly converse with Gilgamesh on this subject.

Alas! the secret was not to be found on the tablets and fragments that the impatient antiquarian examined. The documents suddenly came to an end. But where had these tablets come from? From the library of the palace of Ashur-nasirpal at Niniveh.

This "Chaldean Genesis" (for this is precisely what it was), thought Smith, who, like most of his compatriots, had been brought up on the Bible, must have a continuation and contain the tale to which the whole world would listen passionately—the story of the Great Flood!

The first audience to whom Smith revealed his discovery on December 3rd, 1872, were the members of the Society of Biblical Archaeology. His revelations aroused great emotion: the news of the Babylonian Deluge spread like wildfire. When Smith insisted that the missing passage must be sought at the place of origin, i.e. on the hill of Niniveh where Hormuzd Rassam's workmen were excavating, the applause was deafening. The *Daily Telegraph* offered a prize of £1,000 to the person who should find the missing fragments.

George Smith himself was the only man who could safely be entrusted with this task, for he not only had to find the fragments in question beneath a mountain of tablets but also be able to recognise them on the spot. It was even possible that the documents had already been dug up and rejected because their state of preservation had made them illegible.

Yes, George Smith was the only man capable of finding what England, what the whole world of scholars and most of the public waited for with impatience. Convinced of this, the

British Museum sent its most competent collaborator on the search.

In May 1873 George Smith held in his hand the object of his search: a fragment of seventeen lines of cuneiform, the missing lines of the opening passage of the Babylonian Deluge.

"Then the gods led by the evil Enlil took counsel. They would destroy the whole human race to punish it for its countless misdeeds. But Ea, still well disposed towards man, sent a dream to his protégé Ut-napishtim, revealing the threat which hung over the world. He was ordered to build a boat for himself and his family, the pilot and 'the seeds of life of all species'. Pious Ut-napishtim obeyed. Then the sluices of the sky opened and everything human was transformed into mud. But Ut-napishtim's boat drifted for six days and seven nights on the swollen waters until they started to subside, leaving the ark on the top of Mt. Nisir." Like Noah, Ut-napishtim despatched his messengers; after seven days a dove and seven days later a swallow. Both returned finding no place to settle. Then after seven more days he sent a raven. This did not return. Then Ut-napishtim left the ark. A rich sacrifice appeased Enlil who led Ut-napishtim, his wife and pilot "to the mouth of the two rivers where in future they lived like gods. . . ."

Smith, unlike Rawlinson, Botta and Layard, did not know how to make contact with the people of those far-off lands, with the natives, as they were called at that period, how to gain their confidence, to penetrate their mentality and gain their friendship. He understood the writing, the language and the thoughts of the ancient Mesopotamians, but the minds and way of life of their descendants remained a closed book to him, and he ignored the hands stretched out to him for "bakhshish".

His third and last expedition, for which he was given the necessary "firman" * in 1876, was under an unlucky star from the start. An outbreak of cholera was raging in Aleppo; a tribal war had broken out, and at Baghdad his companion and friend, the Finn, Enneberg, died.

But George Smith, mature, serious and entirely devoted to his task, was not the type of man to allow himself to be hampered by any obstacle.

* From the Persian *ferman* = order.

His closest collaborators knew this. While examining the Kuyunjik collections Smith was working on a large fragment of a clay cylinder with a long text. One of its sides, however, was covered with a whitish limestone crust, impossible to remove. Only Ready, the restorer, could have saved the situation, but to Smith's chagrin he was absent on a journey. He had to wait several days before Ready returned to scrape the cylinder scientifically and handed him the object of his quest. Smith was working with Rawlinson in a small room above the office of the Royal Asiatic Society's secretary at the British Museum, when the tablet was brought in to him. Impatiently he seized the cleaned fragment, studied it and found the text he had been looking for. Then this man, who was usually so reserved, burst out: "I am the first man to read this text after two thousand years of oblivion." Everyone looked up. Rawlinson and his colleagues wanted to congratulate him and to discover the reason for this unwonted emotion. But Smith, in a high state of excitement, had put down the tablet and was striding up and down the room. He even began, according to the English version, to take off his clothes, to the amazement of those present.

During his last expedition to Syria he worked himself without mercy, even braving the midday sun despite the warnings of the French consul; flouting all advice, he ate nothing but the native food, which he could not digest, and fell into a very weak state.

> "I'm not well. If we had a doctor here I'm sure I should be all right. But he hasn't come. I'm seriously ill. If I die, farewell. . . .
>
> "I have devoted all my efforts to my scientific studies. I hope that my friends will look after my family. . . . I've carried out my duty to the last. . . . I'm not afraid of death, but it grieves me to leave this world on account of my kin. . . . Perhaps I shall get well after all."

This was the last entry he wrote in his diary on August 12th 1876.

George Smith died six days later at Aleppo in the house of the British consul, where he had been brought in a state of complete exhaustion. His death brought the epic of the young Assyriologist to a close, but with it, too, ended the story of the decipherment of Assyro-Babylonian cuneiform.

All that remained was to interpret the languages which cuneiform has allowed us to discover—Hurrian, Urartaic and old Elamite. But this subject is beyond the scope of the present work; in all these fields research is still in full swing.

By way of conclusion let us examine the nature and characteristics of Akkadian cuneiform.

As regards its origin, recent excavations have proved the theory already put forward by antiquarians such as Hincks and Oppert; for the origins of cuneiform we must not look to the Akkadians, Babylonians or Assyrians but to a very much more ancient civilisation, the Sumerians, who transmitted it to the Akkadians! The Babylonian priests could hardly understand Sumerian, "the monastic Latin of the Ancient East" (J. Friedrich), and on this account recorded the vocabularies, grammars and Babylonian translations of the Sumerian texts, documents which enabled us to discover the secrets of this ancient language; thanks to the most ancient forms of Akkadian cuneiform we have been able to interpret even earlier Sumerian forms. At this stage science discovered a process of development, which would never have been suspected from the later cuneiform forms—the transition from the "picture to the letter". This could never have been understood without a knowledge of the materials employed.

FIG. 46.—Brick seal of King Naram-Sin found at Nippur (2270–2233 B.C.).

The land between the two rivers is alluvial. Here Nature offered in abundance the best writing material; they had only to select and smooth the local clay. On this they incised their signs with a wooden stylus or a pointed reed, and the clay tablets baked in the oven or by the sun would last for centuries.

In earliest times, when writing was in its infancy, the simple signs were chiselled for preference in stone: it is in this epigraphic linear that we find the oldest inscriptions, dating from the Sumerians and Akkadians. The brick seal reproduced in Fig. 46 is a good example of this.

It is obvious that in this type of writing it was easier to draw rectangles than curves. From this primitive form onwards the material (it is usually stone) exercised the first influence—an attempt to simplify and stylise which led to a departure from the curved in favour of the straight line. Nevertheless the original pictorial form of the signs is still unmistakable.

But the evolution did not end with the line. As writing grew more widespread and popular, the stone and chisel gave place to the clay tablet, the engraving reed and the stylus.

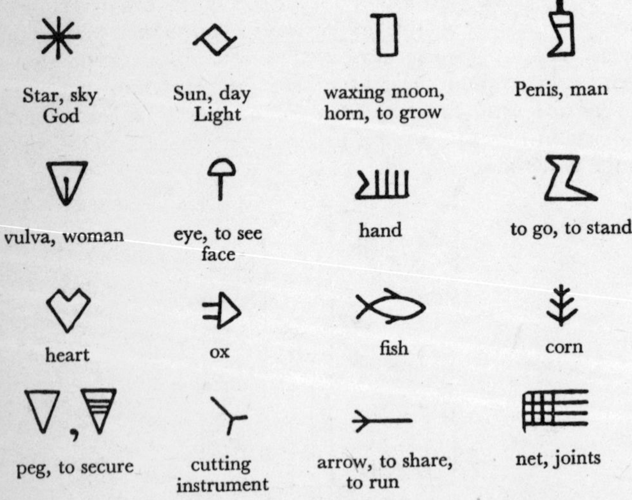

Fig. 47.—Early pictorial forms of cuneiform symbols.

The reed and the stylus were held obliquely to the written surface; in this way their points dug more deeply into the clay and produced the typical stroke, thickened at the extremity—the wedge; in the same way was born the other characteristic trait—the angular piece. Now we have come a long way from the original form of signs, and the uninitiated would be hard put to discover the original symbol in the end forms shown in Fig. 48. The successive stages already reveal that in order to facilitate the epigraphy the tablet which was originally inscribed vertically from top to bottom was now turned at right angles and placed on its left side.

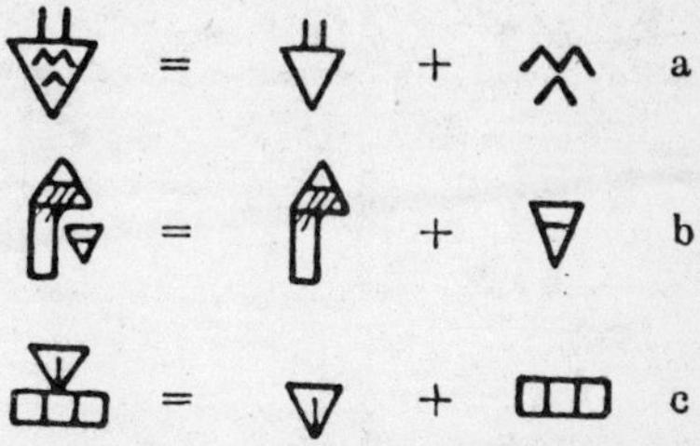

a

b

c

FIG. 48.—Combined pictograms.

The most striking example of this transitional stage from the picture to the wedge is afforded by the Old Akkadian inscription of King Sharkalisharri (Fig. 49). This is a monumental inscription of the sovereign from the temple of Enlil at Nippur, and contains the author's usual curse against profaners.

Differences occur in Akkadian cuneiform according to regions and periods: the earliest systems (Old and Middle Babylonian, Old and Middle Assyrian) are more complicated than Neo-Babylonian and Neo-Assyrian. But in conclusion, without dwelling on these refinements, barely visible to the layman, we shall endeavour to examine the structure of Akkadian cuneiform.

As a start let us point out what a superficial examination would never reveal: cuneiform script bears a striking resemblance (an inner resemblance as regards structure and nature) to Egyptian writing.

It, too, possesses three distinct groups of signs: ideograms, syllabic characters and determinatives. And this triple composition also has its history.

The Sumerians already used their ideograms as syllabic signs—a procedure which we have already seen in Egyptian writing. Just as in Egyptian *wr*, "swallow", was also used for *wr*, "great", so in Sumerian the sign *an*, "sky" (Fig. 50a), could also represent the simple phoneme of the syllable *an*, without regard for its meaning, and *mu*, "name", for the syllable *mu*. The Sumerians, whose writing was basically composed of ideograms, only used syllabic signs as an expedient. A relatively simple stage when we compare it with Egyptian writing.

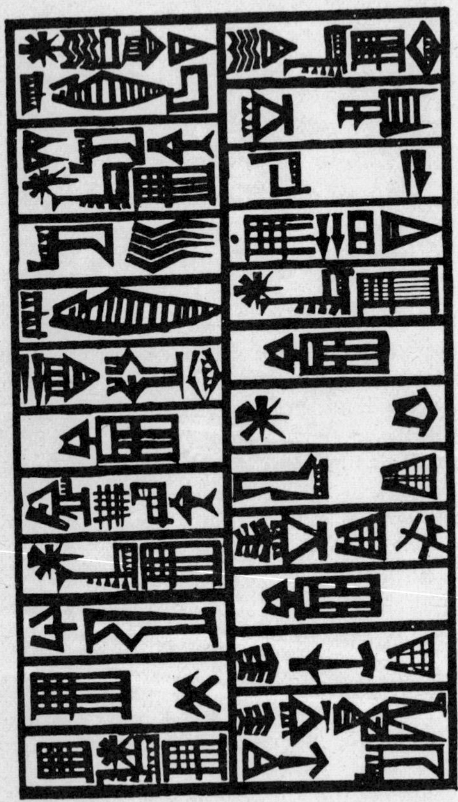

Fig. 49.—Monumental inscription in Old Akkadian.

But when the Semitic Akkadian borrowed cuneiform from the non-Semitic Sumerians and applied it to their own language (it resembled an ill fitting garment), they brought an irremediable confusion into this system which inspired the German Assyriologist, Carl Bezold (already mentioned in reference to his obituary notice of Oppert), to speak of: "that terrible cuneiform." We must not attribute to the Akkadians any premeditation, but must accept that they acted quite naturally.

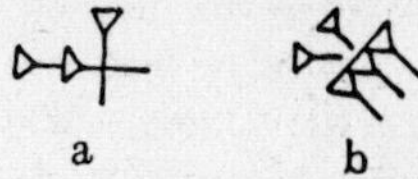

Fig. 50.—Sumerian characters used simultaneously as ideograms and syllabic signs.

They borrowed the Sumerian ideograms without changing their form, but—and this is quite comprehensible—applied to them their own Semitic phonetic values. Thus they no longer pronounced the Sumerian sign for "father" (Fig. 51a) as *ad*, in the Sumerian but in the Semitic manner, *abu*; *mu* = "name" (Fig. 50b) became *shumu*, etc. Chaos resulted when the Akkadians retained the Sumerian pronunciation of exclusively phoneme signs instead of rejecting them completely. The sign *mu*, for example (Fig. 50b), in Akkadian could be read *shumu*

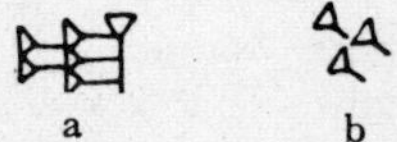

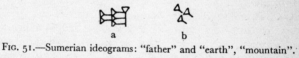

Fig. 51.—Sumerian ideograms: "father" and "earth", "mountain".

and mean "name" but at the same time retain its syllabic sign value and as such could only be pronounced *mu*. The fantastic results of this state of affairs can easily be imagined when one examines the sign represented in Fig. 51b.

In Sumerian it signifies: (1) "earth", "country" (*kur* or *kin*), (2) "mountain" (*kur*). We will ignore the other meanings of this sign. The Babylonians added to this their Semitic words of the same significance, so that for them this single sign could mean firstly *mātu*, "country", *irṣitu*, "earth" "country", and *shadū*, "mountain". Furthermore, it was retained as a syllabic sign for the two purely phonetic syllables *kur* and *kin* and even used as a syllabic sign for the syllables *mat* and *shad* of the Semitic words *mātu* and *shadū*.

This is one of the disturbing and varied aspects of these characters. Was not Carl Bezold right, then, in calling it "that terrible cuneiform"?

But he was also probably thinking of another common

phenomenon in Neo-Babylonian and Neo-Assyrian: one and the same sign can have several independent syllabic values. This is the terrifying polyphony of cuneiform, discovered by Rawlinson, the "chaos" mentioned above and illustrated in Fig. 45. The reader had to discover each time the nature of each syllable in question. He was successful when he was sufficiently familiar with the language and the text in question, but in a certain number of cases he could not be absolutely certain.

The most surprising feature is that this obscure, ambiguous, impracticable writing spread very rapidly, when in the second millennium B.C. the Assyro-Babylonian language was raised to the status of the international diplomatic speech. It served, among other usages, in the correspondence between the Egyptian Pharaohs and the petty Palestinian kings in the middle of that millennium as has been revealed by the world-famous finds at Tell-el-Amarna in Upper Egypt. Not to mention that races speaking another language adopted this difficult script, often, it is true, in simplified form, as we shall see in the case of the Persians.

But this ambiquity soon became a burden to the Ancient Babylonians and Assyrians themselves. They sought a means of re-establishing order in the chaos for which they had been responsible. And oddly enough they had recourse to the same remedy as the Ancient Egyptians chose: the "mixed script" and determinatives.

If for example they extended the sign *matu* = "country" (Fig. 51b) to be read in its true meaning to the exclusion of all others, it was written in a mixed fashion, i.e. to the ideogram itself was added the phonetic character with the following result:

mâtu + *ma* + *a* + *tu*

FIG. 52.—"country" in mixed script.

This example also serves to illustrate the main difference between the syllabic writing of the Egyptians and that of the Akkadians: the Assyro-Babylonian syllabic signs contain a clear and obvious vowel already betraying their non-Semitic origin; nor does there exist a sign representing a single consonant as in Egyptian.

As regards the determinatives which in Egyptian hieroglyphic script are placed at the end of the words, in cuneiform they usually occupy an initial position. Fig. 53 gives a few examples of this.

Thanks to these determinatives and ideograms, the Ancient Babylonians and Assyrians considerably facilitated not only for themselves but also for the 19th-century decipherers the reading of their writing. This script, as we have already mentioned, was widely distributed throughout the Near East and for a long time remained the principal instrument of communication between a great variety of races. The ideograms and determinatives, which remained the same in the different languages, immediately caught the eye of the reader even if written in a foreign tongue: the proper names, above all, stood out boldly, thanks to the determinatives, the first landmarks to guide the decipherers in their task.

Why, then, did the Babylonians and Assyrians fail to take the step which separated them from alphabetic writing? This would have been equally possible with cuneiform and with Egyptian hieroglyphs. But as with the Egyptians, this step which conservatism prevented was taken here, too, by a foreign power: on the one hand very late in Old Persia under Darius and on the other far earlier in Syrian Ugaritic, of which we shall speak in a later chapter. But whereas in Egypt the Greek alphabet accompanied the victorious march of Christanity, in the sphere of the great Persian Empire, to which later Babylonia and Assyria belonged, it was the Aramaic alphabetic writing which was ultimately to oust cuneiform for ever.

The results of investigation into cuneiform script changed our views on the history of the ancient world. One hundred years ago, history for us began with Homer; today with Babylonia, Assyria, Egypt. Vast empires, flourishing civilisations, known yesterday only by hearsay, have suddenly come to life. The bases of Western culture have been revealed to us with unhoped-for precision; the science of comparative religion, linguistics and the chronology of antiquity have been given new foundations, and world literature has been enriched by priceless treasures. Finally the cuneiform archives have allowed us,

^{d}*A-nu* ^{d}*En-lil* ^{d}*É-a*

Three names of gods with determinatives

1 ^{I}*Ha-am-mu-ra-bi*

2. ^{I}*Su-up-pi-lu-li-u-ma*

3. ^{F}*Pu-du-ḫé-pa*

Two names of men and one woman's name with determinatives

1. *māt Aš-šur* "Assyria". 2. *māt Mi-iṣ-ri* "Egypt".

3. ^{alu}*Ni-nu-a* "Niniveh". 4. ^{alu}*Kar-ga-miš* "Carchemish".

Two names of countries and two names of towns with determinatives

^{iṣu}*e-ri-nu* "Cedar" ^{iṣu}*e-lip-pu* "Ship"

A tree and a wooden object with determinatives

^{erû}*pár-zil-lu* "Iron" ^{erû}*pa-a-šu* "Axe"

A metal and a metal object with determinatives.

Fig. 53.—Words made more recognisable by determinatives.

as we shall see, to embark in turn upon the decipherment of a series of new writings, upon the discovery and transcription of other lost languages.

"What remains is man." We have already seen how apposite this remark was when applied to the inscribed monuments of Ancient Egypt.

To evoke man born in the ancient land between the two great rivers, we shall not quote the hymns to his gods, the son of the creation or the epic of Gilgamesh, not even the words of his sovereigns or the texts of the Law. No, we shall listen to his voice through two passages, one the song of Koheleth the Babylonian and the second from a didactic poem: one bitter and disillusioned, the other full of consolation and hope. These voices from the womb of time ring in our ears as an echo of the eternal duality of the human spirit. In contrast to one to whom life has dealt hard blows, and who groans: "All is vanity", rise the pious words counselling integrity and fear of God, reminiscent in their strict morality and limpid form of the spirit which breathes in the Old Testament images.

Let us listen first to the Babylonian martyr:

"Why do I weep, O Lord! Men never learn.
Take heed my friend and hearken to my words,
Preserve the substance of my counsel!
Prized is the word of the mighty man who has learned to kill,
While the weak who have not sinned are humbled.
Persecuted is the upright man who obeys God.
The evil man honoured and his crimes condoned
Riches are heaped upon the rich
the goods filched from a starving man
Power is the portion of the victor,
The weak are flogged and crushed.
I, too, who am weak, am persecuted by the rich."[32]

And then the exhortation of Ut-napishtim:

"Slander not, be fair in speech!
Speak no evil, say but good!
He who slanders, speaks but evil
And him the Sun God will punish by striking his head.

Open not thy mouth without watching thy lips!
Let not the words gush too swiftly from thy heart!
Once they are uttered perchance thou would'st recant.
Constrain thy spirit to keep silent.
Render homage to thy God each day
with a sacrifice, prayer and frankincense!
Bring to thy Lord, the love of the heart
For it is his due."

. . . .

"The fear of God engenders happiness,
Sacrifice prolongs life,
and prayer delivers us from sin.
He who fears God, will not be despised by his God."[33]

CHAPTER V

WEDGE AND SYMBOL OF THE LAND OF HATTI

THE INTERPRETATION OF HITTITE CUNEIFORM AND THE DECIPHERMENT OF HITTITE HIEROGLYPHS

"*Mysterious*
in a golden haze,
A prodigy
with sunny stride,
Asia unfolded
with all its scented peaks."
Hölderlin—*Patmos.*

No mystery seemed as inviolate as this. The decipherment of Hittite cuneiform and hieroglyphic inscriptions differed from the reading and interpretation of Egyptian hieroglyphs in one essential point.

Ancient Egyptians had remained alive down the ages. Greek history, literature and drama had raised imperishable monuments to the Persians. The Hittites had to wait to be rediscovered!

Their name, however, had not completely vanished into limbo. A book above price, the Book of Books, had preserved their memory: the Bible quotes the sons of Heth or Hittites in several passages, but usually in a purely non-committal manner. One of the passages, however, cannot be overlooked. It is the description of Sarah's death and burial (Genesis xxiii. 1 *et seq.*):

"And Sarah was an hundred and seven and twenty years old: these were the years of the life of Sarah. And Sarah died in Kirjathoarba; the same is Hebron in the land of Canaan; and Abraham came to mourn for Sarah and to weep for her.

"And Abraham stood up before his dead, and spake unto the sons of Heth, saying,

"'I am a stranger and a sojourner with you: give me a possession of a burying place with you, that I may bury my dead out of my sight. . . .'"

The sons of Heth agreed and from Ephron the son of Zohar Abraham received a field and a cave for the price of four hundred silver shekels . . and "the field and the cave that is therein was made sure unto Abraham for a possession of a burying place by the sons of Heth".

There is no doubt that the sons of Heth were the Hittites, the rightful rulers of the land of Canaan at the time of Abraham. It is by no means a negligible indication, and it is not the only one of its kind. The Bible speaks even more clearly in the Second Book of Kings vii. 6, describing the liberation of Samaria:

> "For the Lord had made the host of the Syrians to hear a noise of chariots, and a noise of horses, even the noise of a great host: and they said to one another, Lo, the king of Israel hath hired against us the kings of the Hittites, and the kings of the Egyptians to come upon us."

Here, therefore, the Hittites are associated with the Egyptian Pharaohs, the most powerful sovereigns of the ancient world; they are no longer mentioned in a list of insignificant tribes, but cited as a powerful armed force.

These indications could not have failed to arouse the interest of antiquarians had some monument, find or other testimony of antiquity proved the existence of this lost people; but in the eyes of 19th-century scholars the Bible was always considered to be an unreliable source.

When we consider the activities of the investigators, the brilliant achievements of the archaeologists and philologists of this period, this prejudice today seems strange and unjustified. The only valid explanation in retrospect seems to lie in the duality of the heritage of "the Age of Enlightenment": tireless search for knowledge and truth, allied to an uncritical contempt for everything which had for so long been considered the sole refuge of this truth.

Just as Christopher Columbus reached to America without being aware of it, 320 years later the "discoverer" of the Hittite empire died before he could suspect that he had made a find which would reveal an entirely new "Ancient World".

On his death this man was called Sheikh Ibrahim; he bore the title, well respected in the East, of Hadji,* and was buried

* Title reserved for those who have made the pilgrimage to Mecca and Medina.

in the Moslem cemetery of Cairo with all the honour due to a high-ranking Mohammedan. But when he was born at Lausanne on November 24th, 1784, his name was Johann Ludwig Burckhardt, and he came from an old patrician family of Basle scholars. At Leipzig, Göttingen and London he studied natural science and Arabic before taking up a post in Africa for the British African Society. In February 1809 he sailed for Malta, donned oriental dress and made his way to Aleppo, carrying despatches for the East India Company. He spent several years in Syria. For some time he lived at Aleppo, disguised as a merchant, and then at Damascus. He steeped himself in the history, geography and language of the Arabs, and travelled through the Lebanon, Hauran and East Jordania. From Cairo, where the amiable Mohammed Ali, whom we have already met in the chapter on Egypt, gave him several letters of recommendation, he went to Nubia; then, not entirely of his own free will, from Berber on the Nile, to Suakin and finally to Jeddah on the other side of the Red Sea. Here he was close to Mecca.

As an infidel he would never have obtained access to the sacred city. In the presence of two erudite Arabs he submitted to a thorough examination in the religion and laws of the Prophet, and showed such exceptional competence in this field that he was authorised not only to visit Mecca but to stay four months in the forbidden city and to make a pilgrimage to Mt. Ararat. In 1815 he visited Medina. The following year, while the plague was raging in Cairo, he explored the Sinai peninsula. Death overtook him on October 7th, 1817, in Cairo, where he was waiting for a caravan to continue his journey and studies. The Royal Geographical Society in London collected and published a certain number of his essays. They are of exceptional interest, distinguished by the simple writing, the truth and precision of the facts and an incredible wealth of penetrating observations.

But what of the Hittites? We said that it was unwittingly and quite *en passant* that he discovered them.

In the course of his travels he had visited the bazaar of the Syrian town of Hama, the biblical Hamath, and subsequent Epiphaneia on the Orontes. There he had noticed a stone covered with small figures and strange signs, a type of hieroglyphs fundamentally different from the Egyptian.

He referred to it on p. 146 of his *Travels in Syria and the Holy Land*, published five years after his death. It is easy to understand that among the profusion of geographical, historical, philological and archaeological documents left by Burckhardt, this discovery did not arouse very much interest. Burckhardt himself, far from assessing the importance of his discovery, devoted merely a few lines to it.

The rediscovery of the Hama Stones took place sixty years later. The Americans in turn had begun to discover the world of antiquity. Visiting the bazaar of Hama one day, the Consul-General Augustus Johnson and one of his missionary friends, Dr. Jessup, came across the object which had once aroused the attention of Sheikh Ibrahim—the stone set in the corner of a house. Greatly interested, they studied it as best they could from all angles and learned from the natives that this stone was by no means unique and that three others existed not far away. But when the two "infidels" tried to copy the inscription their native informants fell silent and a hostile crowd formed round them. Johnson and Jessup were forced to beat a hasty retreat. Drake and Palmer of the American Palestinian Exploration Society were no more fortunate in the following year, nor was Captain Richard Burton, the famous traveller, who did, however, manage to make some rough sketches. All these Europeans, by their manifest interest, had only aggravated matters, and the inhabitants of Hama, well known for their fanaticism, threatened to destroy the stones.

They might easily have done so had a higher authority not thwarted their black designs. Subhi Pasha, the new Governor of Syria, took up his post in 1872. He was a man of culture with an open mind. On learning of the existence of these stones he set out himself on a tour of inspection, inviting the British Consul at Damascus, Mr. Kirby Green, and the Irish resident missionary of the same city, William Wright, to accompany him. They found the stone in question and four others. They were all inset (one in a house in the painters' quarter, the second in a garden wall, the third in a small shop opposite the house of the French Vice-Consul), except the fourth, also in the painters' quarter, to which the inhabitants attributed miraculous powers. Sufferers from rheumatics used to lie on this stone and were cured—provided they had also invoked the aid of Mohammed and the Christian saints.

The Reverend William Wright and the Governor had both counted upon resistance from the natives. But Subhi Pasha was there in his title of governor. As a precaution against ill-will he had brought his soldiers, and armed sentries supervised the work. There were turbulent scenes when the stones, after being laboriously extracted, could finally be carried discreetly away. The stones left for Constantinople, capital of the empire (Hama was a capital of a *sanjak* in the Turkish *vilayet* of Syria), but William Wright was allowed to send casts to the British Museum.

The stones of Hama were now at the disposal of British antiquaries and accessible to all European scholars; Johnson announced the news to his American colleagues. The burning question which occupied the minds of two continents was: who had been the authors of these epigraphies? The answer was not long delayed.

The American, Hayes Ward, remarked that the engraved seals greatly resembled those found by Layard at Niniveh in 1849. The Reverend Wright, by profession a Biblical scholar, suggested a solution from the Bible: in his view it could only be the language and writing of the sons of Heth, a people known from the quotations we have already given at the beginning of this chapter, the former rulers of Syria and allies of the Egyptian Pharaohs.

Let us recall the date of the finds. Archaeology and research, after an extraordinary upsurge, had reached its highest development; the study of hieroglyphics and cuneiform scripts continually brought new results; Egyptian and Akkadian philology were born; Orientalism in fact, now a well-established subject, with all its various branches began to attract a wide public. Even the older generation which had witnessed the decipherment of hieroglyphs and cuneiform was still not extinct.

One name shines out in the years during which the decipherment of Hittite hieroglyphs was accomplished and the discovery of the two Hittite languages took place—Archibald Henry Sayce, a leading light in the young science of Assyriology.

Sayce was not English, as has often been maintained abroad, but from the old Welsh nobility. Welsh was his mother tongue. This perhaps accounts for his taste for metaphysical refinements and fairy tale (this played more than one trick on him in his writings) and for his warm, impulsive nature—so often to be found among his compatriots. Throughout the whole of his life he remained a very religious man with a passion for research.

No one had mentioned the Hittites when the frail and delicate boy first went to school at Bath. At the age of ten he read Virgil and Homer; at eighteen he had mastered Hebrew, Egyptian, Persian and Sanskrit. At twenty, after winning a scholarship, he went to Oxford; at thirty he was don at the same university where for fifteen years he held a Chair of Comparative Philology and for thirty years in Assyriology; he died a very old man on February 4th, 1933, after living sixty-four years in the same modest rooms in Queen's College.

But Sayce made many journeys abroad. With the aim of increasing his wide, practically inexhaustible knowledge he spared neither time nor money, and was never deterred by obstacles. At one time, up to the waist in water in the old Siloah tunnel near Jerusalem, he would be copying the famous Hebrew inscription of the building of the canal; next year he would be scaling the rocks of the burning South Arabian desert recording *graffiti*. The natives loved this foreign scholar. They called him "the crazy priest" or sometimes "the father with the flat turban", "Papa Spectacles" or "the gentlemen with the swallow's tail" because he never discarded the cloth during his travels and expeditions. Later Sayce fell seriously ill while travelling in the Pacific Islands; hardly had he recovered than he resumed his studies of the Polynesian civilisations. The cults of Java and the Dayaks of Borneo intrigued him as much as the primitive religions of Guinea; Japanese Buddhism, the introduction of Christianity into China by the Nestorians—everything interested this indefatigable scholar, who had the rare privilege of restoring to life in his numerous books the Near and Far East.

Sayce, despite his youth, was called in to arbitrate in the discussion on the Hittites. He maintained stoutly that it was certainly a question of this people. He was later reproached for being too orthodox rather than critical when it came to the Old Testament. It must be remembered that he was a staunch adherent of the Church of England and a doctor of theology. But Sayce produced new observations far exceeding all the simple theories which had so far been put forward regarding the inscriptions. Having acquired, even before leaving university, a sound knowledge of cuneiform and astonishing Hincks and Norris by an article on this subject, he deduced correctly that the known characters were far too numerous to entail an alphabet, and saw in the inscriptions a syllabic script with ideograms and determinatives corresponding to Akkadian cuneiform. At the height of his creative powers, and famed for his pioneer work in the discovery and decipherment of different languages and scripts of Asia Minor and Mesopotamia (including a vital article on Sumerian) Sayce further recognised a grammatical suffix in the frequently, repeated sign . It is the nominative ending -s.

But, as we have already said, existing documents were rare; they only started to flow in after 1876, thanks to the excavations undertaken by the British Museum, motivated by a remark of George Smith, who thus indirectly enters the story of the decipherment of a third language and a third script. In common with the British Consul at Aleppo—W. H. Skeene—Smith, during his last voyage in 1876, had recognised in the high mound which Egyptian and cuneiform sources designated as the centre of Hittite domination in northern Syria: Carchemish, on a bend of the Euphrates. Here texts were found bearing the same characters as those of Hama, and the archives of the British Museum soon brought to light a great number of other inscriptions and sculptures.

Now, these sculptures, far more than the inscriptions, opened Sayce's eyes. He suddenly recalled having seen similar ones: the same style characterised a whole series of neglected rock sculptures discovered in the old days by travellers in Asia Minor. They were in the village of Boghaz-Keui, about seventy-five miles east of Ankara and not far from Yazilikaya; at Marash in the north of Syria and at Karabel on the west Asia Minor coast. From this he concluded—with excessive haste, as we know today—that the Hittites, far from being, as had previously been believed, an insignificant tribe among many others in northern Syria, must have possessed a vast empire extending from Smyrna in the west as far as Hama on the Orontes to the south.

The rocky shrine of Yazilikaya, the "inscribed rock", near Boghaz-Keui was already known, as was the village itself, from the work of the French traveller, Charles Texier (*Description de l'Asie Mineure*, 1839–49). But these three lengthy volumes, full of remarkable illustrations for the period had never obtained the acclaim they deserved; they appeared at the wrong moment just as the general interest had been focused on Egyptian hieroglyphic and cuneiform scripts. Among the sculptures of Yazilikaya was a severe and imposing cortege of deities; several of these figures (as at Behistun) had short captions all beginning with the same sign. Sayce, trained in cuneiform, after comparing the captions with their subject, decided that this was a determinative (and at the same time an ideogram) for "god".

In November 1880 he had a brilliant idea which was to lead him to a new and wonderful discovery. He remembered having read in the German scientific reviews of a strange silver plaque.

FIG. 54.—The Tarkumuwa seal or Tarkondemos Boss, the point o. departure for the decipherment of Hittite hieroglyphs.

The man who had found the plaque was the Hamburg diplomat and Orientalist, Doctor A. D. Mordtmann, who was engaged on the decipherment and transcriptions of the cuneiform texts from Lake Van. Sayce, having done some successful spade-work on this subject, one day came across Mordtmann's description. This "silver seal", which Mordtmann considered to be the "most westerly offshoot of the Armenian system and of cuneiform in general", consisted of a thin plaque in the form of the segment of a wedge, 3·3 cm. in diameter and 0·7 cm. high, so that the diameter of the sphere of which it formed part must have measured about 4 cm. A numismatist of Smyrna, Alexander Jovanoff, had bought it, and today it is in the British Museum.

The inner surface is smooth; a few marks show the spot where it was soldered to a pommel. The raised surface is divided in two parts by a concentric circle; in the centre stands a warrior facing left, dressed in an embroidered cloak and wearing a close-fitting bonnet, turned-up shoes, his right hand to his breast; in his left hand he carries a lance and on his left can be seen the pommel of his dagger or sword—an obvious sign that it is a seal. The figure is surrounded by various symbols.[34]

Mordtmann's reading of this inscription had such fantastic repercussions that we must recount it here; it contains the germs of some basic ideas recognised by Sayce—and a fatal error which, adopted later by a German scholar and defended with great obstinacy, was to constitute the main obstacle to the decipherment of the Hittite hieroglyphic script for many years.

Here are the main points of Mordtmann's description.

"The outer circle contains a text in cuneiform composed of nine characters, starting at the spot to which the forefinger of the figure points; since it is a seal we must first take an imprint of the inscription which looks as follows:

1 2 3 4 5 6 7 8 9

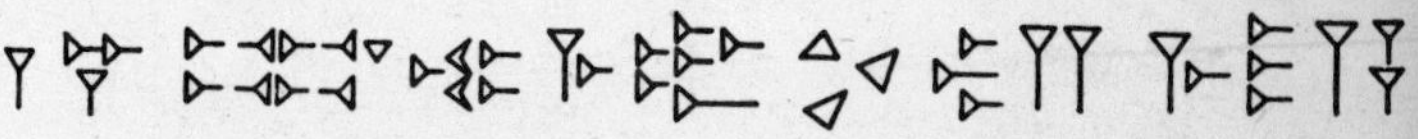

"The groups of signs 1, 6 and 7 are ideograms. Nos. 1 and 7 have the same meaning in the Babylonian, Assyrian and Armenian systems. No. 1 is the determinative for proper names. No. 6 in Babylonian is the ideogram for 'king' and No. 7 the determinative for names of countries. The meaning of the inscription is therefore: N N king of the country N N. It now remains to read the names themselves. The first name is:

2	3	4	5	
Tar-	ku-	dim-	mi	."[35]

Mordtmann concluded with a few reflections testifying to his clairvoyance, gift for combinations and erudition. We give here the most important of these reflections in a very abridged form, because learned journals generally attribute the merit exclusively to Sayce, while the latter, if I am not mistaken, only adopted them eight years later; also to show the origin of the disastrous error previously mentioned, the responsibility for which was unjustly laid upon the shoulders of the German investigator, Jensen.

Mordtmann, basing his judgment on his reading of the cuneiform text, obtained the name of the country Tarsun and read the entire inscription as: "Tarkudimmi king of Tarsun," giving his explanation which he considered "more than daring" on the following reasoning:

> "The monuments of Niniveh, Babylon and Persepolis bear little or no resemblance to our seal. If on the other hand we turn to the Near East the analogies multiply; we find them on the monuments of Ujuk, Boghaz-Keui and Eregli in Cappadocia and also on the Karabel monument at Smyrna; at Boghaz-Keui the same type of sword, at Karabel the lance as well as the beardless figure of the prince. The embroidered cloak and the helmet alone are attributes unknown on the monuments of the Near East.
>
> "These analogies alone force us to think of the Near East rather than of Mesopotamia or Persia, and to date the seal earlier than the Achaemenian period. Other direct proofs point to Cilicia."[36]

Mordtmann was in fact referring to Herodotus, Book VII, 91, where the Cilician mercenaries in the army of Xerxes are described:

> "The Cilicians wore on their heads helmets peculiar to their country, and had bucklers instead of shields, made of raw hides, and were clothed in woollen tunics; everyone had two javelins and a sword made very much like Egyptian scimitars."[37]

"This description fits in perfectly with the costume of Tarkudimmi," declared Mordtmann, pointing out the frequency of his name in Cilicia particularly in the form of "Tarkondemos" met with in Plutarch, which must have been conserved on this seal down to modern times.

But Mordtmann then made the error to which we have already referred. Forestalling possible objections to the weakness of his reading of the name "Tarsun", he tried to justify by proposing as an alternative "Zusun", "the undisputed form of the famous Syennesis, a ruler of this name who allied himself in 600 B.C. with Labynetus, king of Babylon . . . it is quite possible that the Tarkudimmi of our seal is actually this Syennesis. . . ."[38]

It was wrong, but it was believed for half a century until 1932!

But to return to the seal. Sayce suddenly recalling in 1880 the existence of the silver plaque immediately approached the British Museum; an official remembered that a similar seal had been offered to the Museum but was rejected because the Board thought it might be a fake (specimens of this kind had not been seen before). Although they had refused to buy it, they were prudent enough to take a galvanoplastic impression of it. This reproduction was given to Sayce for examination. It enabled him to make a brilliant discovery which would have sufficed to link his name for ever with the history of Hittitology.

His eye was caught by the hairstyle of the central figure and by his turned-up shoes; both these had in the meantime been recognised as Hittite. He gave a slightly different reading of the cuneiform text: "Tar-rik-tim-me sar mat Er-me-e, Tarik-timme, King of the land of Erme". This name is read today as Tarkumuwa, and the whole text as is to be seen in Fig. 55.

Tarku-muwa KING Me + ra—a COUNTRY
"Tarkumuwa, king of the land of Mera."

FIG. 55.—Phonetic reading of the Tarkumuwa seal.

We should like here to distinguish between the merits of Mordtmann and Sayce. The allusion to Asia Minor, the correct localisation of Cilicia, the accurate reading of the cuneiform text, at least as regards its structure and nature—all this can be placed to the credit of the German scholar. But the most important point had escaped him, and Sayce must be given the credit for having discovered it.

As familiar with the first Hittite finds and their strange signs as with cuneiform, Sayce recognised that the symbols of which Mordtmann spoke were graphic signs, Hittite hieroglyphs, and that the text itself should correspond to the cuneiform text; for the symbols  and  were to be met with also at Carchemish and at Hama. If the hieroglyphic text of the seal represented a transcription of the cuneiform text, they must correspond to the words "country" and "king". Moreover, the sign for "*tar*" was beyond doubt. Ideograms and syllabic signs had, therefore, been obtained—the first ray of light, the first essential revelation as to the character of the new script.

It was almost as though Mordtmann had never seen the hieroglyphs. He had certainly seen them but interpreted them in a manner completely convincing at the period, but no longer so except to the uninitiated.

> "The symbols on the seal bear all the marks of Cilician origin; the goats' heads denote the principal wealth of the mountainous region of Cilicia, while the adjacent symbol, the ears of corn, is an allusion to the extraordinary fertility of the Cilician plains; the obelisks reproduce exactly the buildings of the region west of Caesarea in Cappadocia which at that period . . . belonged to Cilicia . . . and the palm beach denotes these Syrian districts. The entire seal is therefore an interesting example of the earliest heraldry, an allegorical representation of the countries ruled by a monarch. . . ."[39]

An examination of this apparently convincing interpretation allows us to estimate the importance of the first step taken by Sayce and of his novel explanation.

Bilingual documents were extremely rare, and practically nothing was known of the phonetic values of the characters; the ideograms, as we know today, threw no light on this subject.

But in the meantime new documents had come to light: a seal from Niniveh, an engraved basalt cup; an inscription on an Aleppo mosque; and above all two remarkable specimens—an epigraphic inscription at Bor in Anatolia and a text in relief on the back and flanks of one of the two lions above the gate at Marash, a town in northern Syria.

Initially these discoveries did not help the decipherment, but as a whole they afforded the substance of Dr. William Wright's famous book *The Empire of the Hittites* (1884). Sayce, who contributed to its publication by writing a chapter on the language, rejected once and for all any idea of its being a Semitic tongue; the Hittites, he maintained, had come from Anatolia to Syria to conquer that country, which according to Egyptian and Mesopotamian sources, they dominated in the 14th and 13th centuries B.C. The sign , now definitely recognised as a nominative ending -s, the accusative ending -n, the determinative for the names of towns ▲, were *inter alia* Sayce's contribution to the decipherment. He also noted the word "Sandes", the name of a local god worshipped in the old days at Tarsus in Cilicia, which was to play its part in the subsequent decipherment as Santas.

The sensational finds of this period to which we have referred, and the increasingly evident kinship between Assyrian antiquities and the recently discovered monuments, unleashed a flood of voyages and expeditions to Asia Minor, which, in turn, resulted in new and inestimable finds. The Englishman, Sir William Ramsay, the Germans, Karl Humann and Otto Puchstein, the Austrians, Felix von Luschan and Count Lanckoronski, the Frenchman, Chantre, and the American, Wolfe, discovered and brought to light sculptures and new inscriptions. The period when only the stones of Hama were known, although a mere thirty years in the past, now seemed incredibly remote. When the German antiquarian, Leopold Messerschmidt, in 1900 published his *Corpus inscriptionum Hettiticarum*, he had already collected, examined and edited thirty-six major texts from Asia Minor and North Syria (a number later raised to forty-two) and about a hundred shorter and fragments of texts. This collection encouraged the whole world to push forward with the study of these documents, to decipher the writing and to translate the language.

Further progress is worth recording. The French investigator, J. Menant, had discovered in 1890 that the symbol of a human figure pointing to himself, placed at the beginning of many inscriptions, signified "I" or "I am" and corresponded to the Egyptian hieroglyph for "I".

Fig. 56.—Symbol for "I" in Egyptian and in Hittite hieroglyphs.

Sayce still believed that the figure in question was pointing to its mouth and that in consequence it meant "I say", "I speak" or in the third person "he says" or "he speaks".

The German Assyriologist, Peiser, on the other hand in 1892 added (in a book which proved a failure) a word separator |(and the sign | |, indicating the presence of an ideogram.

But the happiest attempt to penetrate the heart of the writing and finally to unveil its mysteries had been made in Germany even before the appearance of Messerschmidt's *Corpus*, by a man whose influence on the investigation was to be a two-edged sword. In his youth he had given it a decisive forward impulse, but his later works, on the contrary, acted as a brake and retarded the decipherment for many years; his personal attitude towards his colleagues and their work gave rise in the 20th century to a scientific polemic comparable in its violence with the quarrels of scholars prior to the 19th century.

Peter Jensen was the last representative of the first great generation of German Assyriologists. The son of a Frisian pastor, he followed the traditional path taken by the first specialists by taking a degree in theology at Strasbourg in 1880, subsequently being appointed professor at Marburg, where he taught for forty years. One of the last pupils of the old teacher, Eberhard Schrader, he became in turn the "magister" of the next generation, the influence of his personality and teaching lasting until 1940.

Jensen, an accomplished Assyriologist, rendered great service by his work on the Babylonian cosmology and his treatise on their epics and myths published in the *Cuneiform Library*. But the work he intended to be his *magnum opus* was the *Epic of Gilgamesh in World Literature*. In two heavy volumes he tried to prove that nearly all the Israelite accounts as recorded in the Bible are only local versions of the Gilgamesh myth and that to these Israelite myths of Gilgamesh can be traced more specifically the New Testament accounts of St. John the Baptist, Jesus, St. Paul, a great part of the Greek legends, the early Roman sagas, the tradition of Mohammed and of Buddha and even the Scandinavian sagas and the Indian epics! It is not surprising that Jensen aroused a great controversy; the scholar himself grew taciturn, surly and intransigent, wounded by the attitude of many of his colleagues.

The effort he devoted to Hittite seemed promising. He was a persevering and punctilious worker; his love of analogies and the tenacity with which he followed trails once discovered soon encouraged him to stray from his own field of Assyriology and attempt the decipherment of "unbroken" scripts. For years he studied Egyptian hieroglyphs. The Hittite finds then aroused and occupied his attention. A plaster cast of the lion of Marash stood on his desk. From 1894 (six years before the publication of Messerschmidt's *Corpus*) he wrote a series of articles on decipherment which he republished in 1898 in a revised and corrected version in his book: *Hittites and Armenians.* The title alone reveals his fundamental error; he thought that Hittite hieroglyphs were written in late Armenian. He did succeed, however, in basing his studies on the few solid results obtained by his predecessors, in particular Sayce, in giving the correct reading of the name of the city of Carchemish, which recurred

Kar - ka - me CITY

FIG. 57.—The name of the town of Carchemish in Hittite hieroglyphs.

frequently in the local inscriptions. He further recognised certain other titles mentioned in the texts and the demonstrative pronoun "this"; he finally established that "the aedicule" formed of a winged sun and the hieroglyphs for "Great King" surrounded the names of sovereigns on the pattern of the Pharaonic cartouche.

From the point of view of method, Jensen's attempt at decipherment blazed a new trail which could have proved decisive; later investigators who followed it with greater ardour and perseverance achieved the most success. Jensen himself only reaped the error. His principle was not to try at first to discover the phonetic values but to try to understand the inscription from outward criteria, and relying on historical evidence to presume—not to say guess—their content, before bothering about the pronunciation.

This method does not inspire whole-hearted confidence, and doubts are soon confirmed on examining Jensen's work in the light of his hypothesis. Influenced from the start by the fact that the small number of characters recognised with certainty were almost entirely ideograms, and having acquired in addition the erroneous conviction that the sign  (-s), already established by Sayce, could *only* be the nominative, Jensen thought that everywhere this sign was missing he was dealing with a genitive complement of the name. These two incorrect postulates led him into the error that all the inscriptions followed the same pattern, "X, Y, Z",[40] and could not therefore—even in the longest—constitute narrative or descriptive texts; they contained no verb, no single complete phrase, but were simple enumerations, monotonous lists of titles, an uninterrupted series of ideograms!

Jensen, alas, defended his theory until the end of his life with incredible tenacity and an inflexible will. Without dwelling upon his further mistakes we shall merely cite one of them, the bar which he put up against future decipherment; this was his reading of the signs [hieroglyphs] he misconstrued as Syennesis, the title of the Cilician Kings of the Greek era. Mordtmann perpetuated this error, as we have mentioned, thinking to recognise this word in the Tarkumuwa seal.

It was obvious that such a sterile hypothesis put forward by the best-respected specialist condemned German research to complete stagnation; the riddle of Hittite hieroglyphs remained unsolved. A new impulse given from another direction was like a revelation in the perfection of its unhoped-for clarity.

A precursory sign had manifested itself some thirty years earlier. The discovery of a considerable collection of clay tablets—texts engraved in cuneiform characters and written in Akkadian found in 1888 at Tell-el-Amarna in Upper Egypt—was a great event, equally rewarding for Egyptologists and Assyriologists. The tablets contained fragments of correspondence between the Pharaohs Amenophis III and Amenophis IV (the heretic King Akhnaton, whose hymn to the sun concluded our chapter on Egypt; Tell-el-Amarna was the site of the ephemeral palace built by this sovereign) and the kings of the Near East.

This priceless find, among many other letters engraved on clay tablets, contained two from the "Kings of Hatti", in one of which a certain Shuppiluliumash congratulated Akhnaton on his succession to the throne. Also numerous accounts of the warlike expeditions of the Hittites in northern Syria.

This discovery threw an entirely new light on the history of two races; but Hittitology for its part gained more than was at first recognised. Two of these letters, written, like so many others, in Akkadian cuneiform, and therefore legible, were almost entirely in an unknown and completely incomprehensible script. The mystery was soon cleared up in 1902. When the Scandinavian scholars, J. A. Knudtzon, S. Bugge and A. Torp, published these two documents, called after their country of origin *The Arzawa Letters*, they already expressed the opinion that it was a question of the most ancient Indo-European language so far discovered.

This was too much and yet too little to proclaim. Hardly a word could be read with any certainty, let alone a whole phrase. Moreover, the Indo-European experts were sceptical because "a few isolated and far-fetched etymologies could only arouse suspicion".[41] Knudtzon soon found himself forced to recant before the angry storm raised by the specialists.

Then suddenly, at the beginning of the 20th century, Hittitological research seemed to split into two divergent branches, as though the collaborative work between the British and German scholars, in particular, which had produced results in common, took two different courses. This disassociation was merely the consequence of the political situation.

A British expedition left Liverpool for Asia Minor under John Garstang. Its true promoter was Sayce.

For some years the latter had nursed a plan which in itself had nothing unusual about it: he proposed to excavate in the village of Boghaz-Keui, in the bend of the Halys,* well known since Texier as a magnificent ruined site where in 1883 Chantre had found inscribed tablets. As early as 1880 Sayce had submitted this promising plan to his German friend, Heinrich Schliemann, the discoverer of Troy, considered outside his own country as the prince of excavators. But Schliemann had not entertained the plan, and years passed before Sayce, after interminable negotiations, received permission from the Turkish Government to start excavations for Liverpool University. The expedition was already en route when it heard the surprising news that the Turkish Government had withdrawn its permission and allocated a new field of activity to the British—Carchemish—reserving Boghaz-Keui to a German expedition sent by the Berlin Oriental Society under the auspices of Kaiser Wilhelm II. The British paid a courtesy visit to the Germans at Boghaz-Keui on their way to Carchemish. Their efforts were not in vain. They brought to light new texts in Hittite hieroglyphic, more easy to decipher. The results of the German expedition were absolutely sensational.

Its leader was the Assyriologist, Hugo Winckler, a veteran expert in his field, but an erratic and difficult man to approach. An inveterate Pan-Babylonian (representing the new trend in

* The ancient name of the river Kizil-Irmak.

Assyriology to see in the Assyro-Babylonian civilisation the cradle of all civilisation worthy of the name), he had already made a reputation with several books and personal excavations before he came to Boghaz-Keui.

"Everything went off without undue difficulties and on the fifth day we reached Boghaz-Keui. Our arrival aroused no great emotion, for travellers are not rare here. Moreover, the Turkish peasant has too much intelligence to display undue curiosity at some unusual occurrence. . . . A presence as unexpected in Berlin would have aroused great excitement among the crowd and the need for police intervention. But the Oriental has an innate politeness. . . ."[42]

After a reception laid on with oriental hospitality and lavishness by a local landowner, Zia Bey, Hugo Winckler set to work. The expedition discovered in the great temple of Boghaz-Keui, the ancient capital Hattushah, 10,000 fragments of clay tablets; they were the official archives of the Hittite kingdom. A large number of the finds were in an excellent state of preservation. Since the sphere of influence of Akkadian as the diplomatic language had extended as far as this, and a great proportion of the tablets were written in this tongue, Winckler was able to decipher all his finds on the spot. From this moment a new and surprising light was thrown on the whole of the history of the Ancient Orient.

"A leafy shelter protected me from the sun and allowed me to examine the clay tablets. . . . A little below me a more spacious hut housed five creatures which had never known such a pleasant existence before—our horses! Their presence attracted swarms of flies and, as I deciphered the texts, I had to protect my head and neck and wear gloves unless I wanted to be held up at each sign to ward off the attacks of these little pests."

And Winckler adds ironically: "In our profession it is often difficult to ensure intellectual priority."[43]

But in the face of these sensational discoveries this embittered cynic changed his tune, and we will quote his own words to mark the significance of these finds.

From a study of the fragments in the Babylonian language, he was soon convinced that he had hit upon the site of the ancient capital of the Hittite kings, and that the tablets were the royal archives of these "Kings of Hatti" dating from their relations with the Egyptians.

"The first fragments did not yet contain the names of the kings in question. . . . But our hopes were soon realised. On August 20th, after twenty days work the break opened in the rocky hill had reached the first peripheral wall and here we found a perfectly preserved tablet which immediately aroused our highest hopes. A simple glance sufficed to see the collapse of all my past experience. This find surpassed my wildest dreams. The text was a letter addressed by Rameses to Hattushilish . . . on the subject of a bipartite treaty. In the past few days we had discovered a series of small fragments dealing with a treaty concluded between the two countries, but this tablet was the incontestable proof that the famous agreement mentioned in the hieroglyphic inscription in the temple of Karnak had also been ratified by the other party. Rameses, whose titles and genealogy corresponded exactly in the treaty, wrote to Hattushilish in person and the content of the document included all the paragraphs of the treaty. . . .

"The discovery of this exceptional document flabbergasted me. Eighteen years before in the Bulaq Museum I had seen the Arzawa letter found at Tell el Amarna. . . . I then believed that the original version of Rameses's treaty must have been written in cuneiform, and now I had in my possession one of the actual letters exchanged on this subject —in cuneiform and in pure Babylonian. Strange coincidence in one human life; the discovery already anticipated the first time I set foot on Eastern soil in Egypt, saw itself confirmed in the heart of Asia Minor. A coincidence as strange as the fabulous fate of a hero of the Thousand and One Nights. And yet, the balance sheet of the following year was even more fabulous, since all the documents were found in which all the characters who had occupied my mind during those eighteen years reappeared. . . . Yes, a remarkably strange chain of circumstances in one human life. . . ."[44]

Admittedly they were overwhelming historical documents. The results of the first expedition and second, led in 1911–12 by Winckler, now a dying man, surpassed all expectations. But a great part of the documents discovered—with the exception of the Akkadian ideograms (we have already mentioned the invaluable aid given by cuneiform to decipherers even in an unknown language, thanks to its ideograms and determinatives)—were illegible.

The investigators had taken into account that they might be dealing with the language of the mysterious Arzawa Letters, apparently identical with or closely related to that of hieroglyphs, as Sayce and Peiser had already suspected from the tablets discovered by Chantre.

The last years preceding the First World War were marked by a thorough exploration of the ruins, and by the time the shots rang out at Sarajevo the harvest of Boghaz-Keui had already been brought to safety in Berlin and Constantinople.

It was to the latter city that the German Oriental Society, after Winckler's death in 1914, just before the outbreak of war, had sent two young scholars to copy the texts of Boghaz-Keui: H. H. Figulla and Bedřich Hrozný. The latter—who died quite recently—had the opportunity of examining in the Constantinople Museum particularly long and well-preserved epigraphic documents from the site. And he won the jackpot: discovering and transcribing Hittite cuneiform, proving that it was an Indo-European language, although embellished by a number of foreign words, presumably of Near Eastern origin.

Bedřich (Friedrich) Hrozný, son of a Protestant pastor, was born in Lissa on the Elbe in Bohemia in 1879.[45] He attended the Kolin gymnasium, where one of his teachers, Dr. Justin V. Prášek, a professor of history and geography and a scholar of repute, followed with interest the progress of this very talented pupil. In obedience to his father's wishes, Hrozný began to study Protestant theology, and this subject aroused in him, as it had done in so many others, a love of the Ancient Orient. As a student he learned Hebrew and Arabic and after a semester decided to change Faculties, and from 1897, at Vienna University, devoted himself to the study of ancient oriental languages under the direction of the great Semitist, D. H. Müller, a cultured professor, very popular with his students. Some are still today brilliant representatives in particular fields. In 1901 Hrozný took his doctor's degree with a thesis on the "*Graffiti of Southern Arabia*".

We must mention here that from his earliest years Hrozný

MICHEL AUDRAIN—EDITIONS ARTHAUD

Cuneiform script

AUDRAIN AND SAMIVE

Karnak. Obelisk of Queen Hatshepsut

GEORGES BOURDELON

Darius I

GEORGES BOURDELON

Behistun. The Darius bas-relief

PHOTOS: YAN

(a) Royal Hittite family at a banquet

(b) Hittite hieroglyphic inscription from Hama

ULLSTEIN BILDERDIENST

(a) Jean François Champollion

DOBLH

(b) Ignace J. Gelb

(c) John Chadwick

DOBLHOFER

(d) Charles Virolleaud

DOBLH

G. FRANCESCHI—EDITIONS ARTHAUD

The back of an Etruscan mirror

MICHEL AUDRAIN—EDITIONS ARTH

The two sides of the Phaistos disc

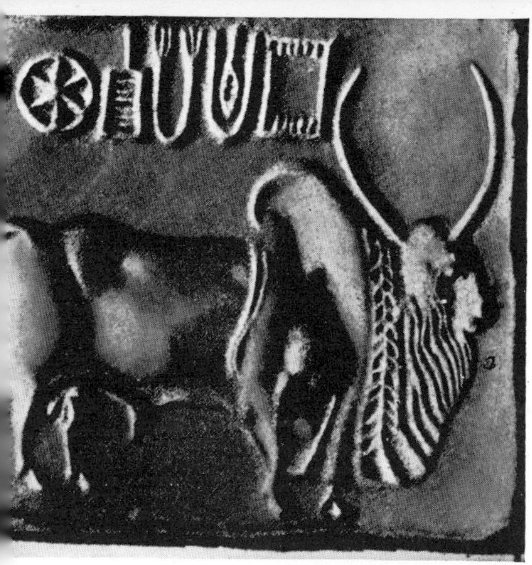

(a) and (b) Seals of the Indus Valley culture

PHOTOS: ULLSTEIN BILDERDIENST

BRITISH MUSEUM

Easter Island. Statue of Hoa-haka-nana-ea

ROSTAMY

(a) Ganj-i-Nameh

(b) Cretan seal: hunting scene, labyrinth

MICHEL AUDRAIN—EDITIONS ARTHAUD

MICHEL AUDRAIN—EDITIONS ARTHAU

Temple of Byblos

GEORGES BOURDELON

Naksh-i-Rustam

ULLSTEIN BILDERDIENST

Inscription of King Araras from Jerablus-Carchemish

AUDRAIN AND SAMIVEL

Akhnaton and Nefertiti

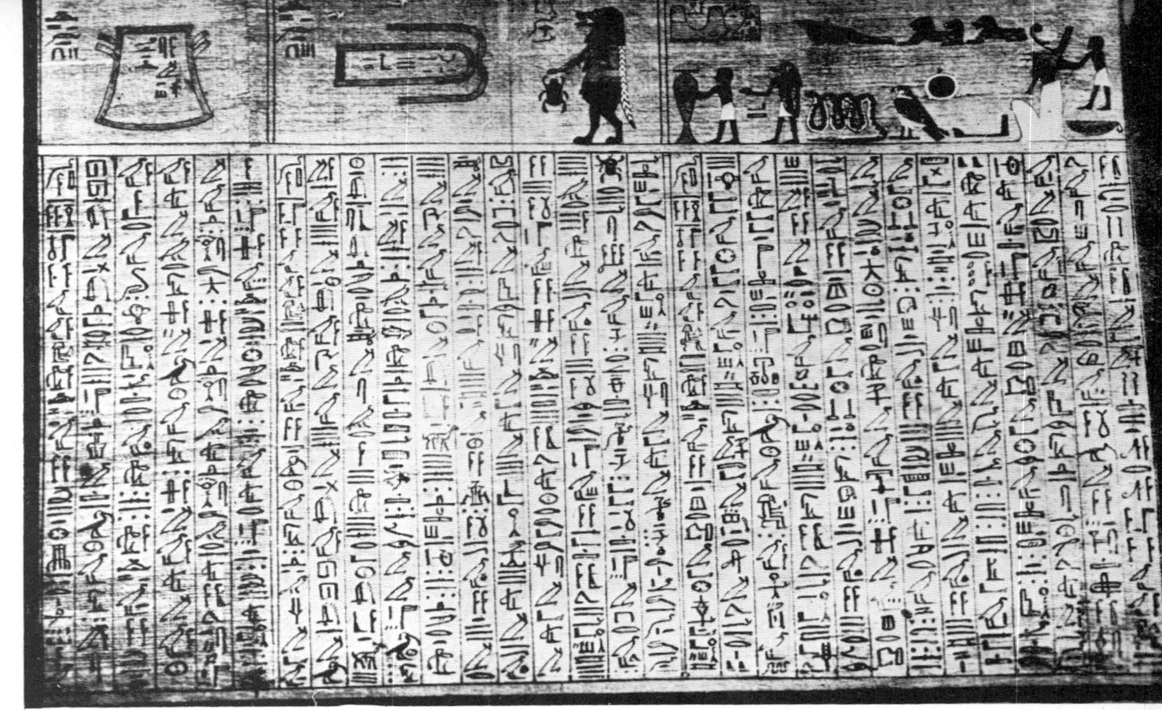

ULLSTEIN BILDERDIENST

Page from an Egyptian Book of the Dead

was not content to remain a mere Semitist philologist. Until the end of his life he only saw in the interpretation of texts a means of studying in detail the civilisations of Antiquity. But the expert Semitist also had to know at first hand one of the most important branches of his field: Akkadian (East Semitic) cuneiform script. This subject was not taught at Vienna at this period and Hrozný, equipped with an Austrian Government grant, went to Berlin to be initiated by F. Delitzsch, a teacher of several generations, in the art of cuneiform. The grant in question was money well spent, as Hrozný was to prove to the world ten years later. On his return he was appointed librarian to Vienna University, where he took his aggregation and became a professor at the age of twenty-four.

His works at this period are distinguished from the mass of contemporary Assyriologist literature by one outstanding feature. Whereas his colleagues were almost exclusively interested in the mythology and the religion of the ancient Babylonians and Assyrians, Hrozný was the first to focus his attention on the scientific aspect of his subject. In this domain he became a pioneer. In 1911 he wrote a profound study on the finances of the Babylonians and a work, which is often quoted, on cereals in Ancient Babylon. This important all-embracing work unfortunately remained uncompleted; he had conceived it as a preliminary study for a vast History of the Civilisations of Asia Minor. In the course of his long years of labour, interrupted only by a trip to the East with Professor Ernst Sellin, Hrozný increased his knowledge, used his prodigious memory and acquired that mastery of which he gave shining proof regarding the cuneiform tablets of Boghaz-Keui in the Constantinople Museum.

We know that he had to deal with particularly long and well-preserved texts. He also had at his disposal documents which afforded a remote analogy with bilingual texts: fragments of dictionaries, lists of vocabularies in the Sumero-Akkadian style, similar to those we shall meet with in the chapter on Mesopotamian cuneiform scripts, and which the Hittites had enriched with a third column in their own language—actually instruments of limited value, because they mainly included very rare words of little help to the scholar in his quest for everyday current words.

Hrozný then considered the texts as a whole, hoping thus to

recognise the structure of the language. His intuition and taste for combinations found plenty of scope in these precious tablets. Examining them with the utmost objectivity, he expected to find in them, in concordance with the state of research, at the period, a Caucasian language.

Certain ideograms were known to him, but they did not help him to understand the language because he could not determine the corresponding phonemes.

After a closer study of the modifications and inflexions of the words, and above all of certain variable endings, he came to the conclusion that Hittite contained grammatical forms proper to the Indo-European languages.

But Hrozný dared not publish the results, which he himself would have considered a piece of scientific bluff. Knudtzon, who had made a similar attempt in the language of the Arzawa Letters, had been forced to retract under the open fire of criticism.

Hrozný nevertheless carefully recorded all his observations and continued his studies until they gradually assumed the shape of an irrefutable proof.

The reading of a single phrase convinced him: the revelation was so abrupt that he himself was almost scared. A touchstone of decipherment, this discovery, like all other decisive turning points of the same order (one thinks of Champollion and the Ptolemy and Cleopatra cartouches and of the inscriptions of Darius and Xerxes solved by Grotefend), appear to us of surprising simplicity.

The phrase which caught and held his eye was:

"nu 𒃻 -an e-iz-za-at-te-ni wa-a-tar-ma e-ku-ut-te-ni."

𒃻, a Sumero-Babylonian ideogram, was pronounced as the phonetic script indicated *ninda*, and meant "bread". The phrase therefore ran (we shall now write the ideogram in English and give the cuneiform syllable script its true pronunciation):

"nu BREAD -an ezzāteni, wāsar-ma ekuteni . . ."

It referred therefore to bread (this example shows in a particularly striking manner the aid given by cuneiform to the decipherer of an unknown language), bread playing the part of object in the phrase, taking into account the ending -an. What verb could apply more aptly to the object "bread" than the verb "to eat"? Could there be anything more simple than a simple etymology based on the assonance? Was there a real relationship? Hrozný sought among the other Indo-European languages for a word where the consonance recalled that of the Hittite word. To eat in Greek was *ēdein*, in Latin *edere*, in High German *ezzan*!

Reconsidering the text once more as a whole, with his brain on the alert, Hrozný, as a consummate Orientalist, examined the construction of the phrase and was amazed to discover in it the parallel structure in two parts characteristic of Ancient Oriental language. Was not the "phrase" rather composed of two phrases of the same construction? And in this event would not *wādar* be the equivalent of the Old Saxon *watar* = water? On this principle would *ekuteni* mean "to drink"?

Hrozný had already thought that he had recognised elsewhere the verbal ending *-teni*, the adverb *nu* and the conjunction *-ma*. The pieces fell into place very rapidly and a picture formed in his mind. He seemed to hear in a three-thousand-year-old echo this legible and intelligible phrase: "Now you will eat bread and drink water."

Hrozný knew that this sensational discovery would arouse bitter controversy and would be a scientific event of the first magnitude. But it was even more indefensible to go back, now that the proofs of the Indo-European or, as we should say, today, Indo-Germanic character of the language to be deciphered accumulated with an almost crushing speed. The known interchange in Greek and Latin of the "r" and the "n" in the nominative and genitive (Greek: *hydōr*, gen. *hydatos* from *hydntos* = water; Latin: *femur*, *feminis* = thigh) "the best possible proof in favour of the Indo-European character of Hittite", added Hrozný[46]) and a certain number of really stupefying analogies between the pronouns and verbal flection.

On November 15th, 1915, Hrozný gave an account of his results before the German Middle East Society at Berlin. "That day", as the famous Assyriologist, Ernst Weidner, wrote in his stirring obituary notice to his colleague, "saw the birth of Hittitology."

In December of the same year, Bedřich Hrozný published this provisional report in *Mitteilungen der Deutschen Orientgesellschaft* under the title: "The Solution of the Hittite Problem." The definitive work, *The Language of the Hittites, its Structure and*

Appertainance to the Group of Indo-European Languages, appeared in 1917 at Leipzig. This classic work represents the peak of Hrozný's scientific achievements.

When the provisional report appeared in its final form, Hrozný was in the army.

In the K.u.K. army he was lucky enough to meet understanding superior officers, and during his service was able not only to correct the provisional report already referred to and his main work on the language of the Hittites, but also spend hours in the Constantinople Museum comparing and studying the cuneiform texts.

His work on Hittite cuneiform, however, contains one grave fault. He was an Assyriologist, or, to be more precise, a Semitist, who had been entrusted with the perusal of the Boghaz-Keui texts. He himself had from the outset felt only surprise and mistrust to see accumulate indications in favour of an Indo-European and not a Semitic language. Competent as he might be in reading the cuneiform texts, his qualification of strictly specialised Semitist did not make him quite the right person to study an Indo-European language. All the more credit to the results he obtained in the interpretation and decipherment of this unexpected language, although today people are inclined to judge Hrozný by the works of his old age, which were less successful. From his first works, however, he succumbed to the temptation of stating the existence of certain connections on the basis of simple assonances, taken incorrectly for true linguistic parentage; and his picture of Hittite cuneiform as an Indo-European language strongly mingled with non-Indo-European elements was fundamentally correct but questionable in detail.

It was in fact contested very violently, particularly by the specialists of comparative philology. But the latter sometimes overshot the mark, as Hrozný once reminded one of his adversaries, with smiling irony, in a lecture on the history and progress made in the decipherment of the Hittite texts, which he gave at the Sorbonne on March 14th, 1931. An authority on matters of philology had objected that *wādar* could not signify "water", since in Hittite the first vowel of the word is long, a phenomenon impossible in an Indo-European language. "This", he said, "makes an absurdity of Hrozný's theory."

It was not in the least absurd and represents an axiom which is no longer discussed today. But from a purely philological standpoint it needed to be revised and clarified by specialists. This task was undertaken by F. Sommer, E. Ehelolf, E. Forrer, J. Friedrich, A Goetze and E. H. Sturtevant on the basis of ideas recognised by Hrozný, and extended until Hittitology can today be considered a perfectly established science.

The excavation of the Boghaz-Keui archives was now complete. To the Akkadian tablets were added the Hittite, new eloquent documents admirably adding to both historical and philological knowledge of the Ancient East. We shall return to this subject later.

As an illustration of the strange mixture of Sumerian ideograms, Akkadian and Hittite phonetic words which characterises Hittite cuneiform, the following will serve to show clearly the obstacles against which Hrozný had to battle. It is taken from a popular book by the previously mentioned scholar, J. Friedrich[47]; the paragraph is taken from a legal code: "*ták-ku* LÚ. ULÙ^{LU}—*an* EL. LUM QA.AZ.ZU *na-aš-ma* GÌR-ŠU *ku-iš-ki tu-wa-ar-ni-iz-zi nu-uš-še* 20 GÍN KUBABBAR *pa-a-i.* ("If someone breaks the hand or the foot of a free man, he will give him (in compensation) 20 silver shekels.")

The root of the word for "man" is expressed by the Sumerian ideogram LÚ.ULÙ^{LU}, to which is added the Hittite phonetic accusative ending *-an*; EL.LUM, "free", is Akkadian, as is QA.AZ.ZU, "his hand", whereas in GÌR-ŠU. "his foot", the root is denoted by the Sumerian ideogram GÌR, and the ending by the Akkadian possessive suffix -ŠU, "his". The fine of 20 GÍN KUBABBAR, "20 silver shekels" is pure Sumerian, and the words *takku*, "if", *našma*, "or", *kuiški*, "someone", *tuwarnizzi*, "he breaks", *mu-šše*, "now to him", and *pāi*, "he gives", are Hittite phonetics.[48]

Research, therefore, did not remain the prerogative of the Central European countries; there was equal activity in the other camp. Here, they could not study the Hittite cuneiform inscriptions, for they were temporarily inaccessible (they were preserved in Turkey and Germany), but only the hieroglyphs which they had been able to collect in increasing numbers up to the outbreak of war.

Before the war the Englishman R. C. Thompson, encouraged by the British excavations at Carchemish of 1911, had announced his *New decipherment of Hittite hieroglyphs* and, by using the as yet undeciphered Hittite cuneiforms known only from the Arzawa Letters, tried to interpret the hieroglyphs. He failed in this interesting premature attempt because in these particular letters the Hittite words had to a great extent been read or classified erroneously. Thompson has to his credit, apart from the semi-correct reading of a few place-names (due to Assyrian sources), the discovery of the determinative for proper names (not categorically used).

Before a new attempt at deciphering the hieroglyphs was made, the Swiss philologist Emil Forrer, who was working at the time in Germany, attacked the flood of interpretations of Hittite cuneiform in an article published in the *Proceedings of the Berlin Academy of Science*, 1919, which bore the surprising title "The Eight Languages of the Boghaz-Keui Inscriptions".—A title even more astounding than the content of this important article. The eight languages in question obviously included Sumerian and Akkadian—but where were the six others? The texts contained a number of Indian technical words from the field of stud-farming and the training of horses. For the five other languages Forrer reserved a surprise which can be summed up as follows: Hittite is not a Hittite language!

This was the gist of Forrer's reasoning: by their language the Hittites were Indo-Europeans and could not therefore, in view of what we know of this linguistic strain, stem from Asia Minor, where they had arrived as simple emigrants. They would have found on their arrival an autochthonous population whose language indubitably figures in some of the Boghaz-Keui's tablets. Certain passages had mentioned *hattili*, "in Hattic", i.e. Hittite, a word doubtless derived from the name of the country Hatti. This race, then, which spoke a Proto-Hittite or Hattic tongue, comprised the true Hittites, and Forrer proposed to call the Indo-European Hittites language which dominated 90 per cent. of the cuneiform texts "Kanish", after the name of the town of Kanesh.

This designation was not adopted. The Indo-European conquering race—we still do not know today what they called themselves—were in future known to the world of science as the "Hittites"; the Biblical designation was too solidly rooted for it to be abandoned. And today we usually refer to the autochthonous population and its language as Proto-Hittite and Proto-Hattic respectively.

Forrer, who had arrived at these results after a general examination of the Boghaz-Keui texts, received in the following year the approval of Professor Hrozný.

The other newly discovered languages figuring on a few of the Boghaz-Keui tablets are Hurrian (formerly Hurrite) a non-Indo-European language which still remains "unbroken" today, Luvian or Nesite, closely related to Hittite cuneiform which has successfully been broken in recent years, and Palaic, also Indo-European, originally spoken in the town of Pala and its environs and which is now being studied.

Forrer's revelation of 1919 was confirmed by Hrozný in 1920 independently of the works of the Swiss scholar.

The same year saw a new attempt at decipherment of the hieroglyphs by the British Orientalist, A. F. Cowley. In his work he intentionally ignored the results obtained by Forrer and Hrozný as to the connection between Hittite cuneiform and the hieroglyphic language. He based his studies exclusively on the findings of Messerschmidt and the finds at Carchemish, also adopting the name of that city, but in addition to a number of errors could offer very few concrete results. He saw in the sign ⦶, often previously confused with the determinative for god, (ФD), the juxtaposed "and" (which is read today as *ha* and corresponds to the Latin *que*). He also suggested that the so-called "thorn", a slanting dash added to the signs, should be read as "r".

The German Assyriologist, Carl Frank, who embarked on the problems of Hittite hieroglyphs in 1923, took a different point of departure. Cryptanalysis used during the First World War had evolved a classification and systematic analysis of material, which allowed the decipherers to find the solution. With great circumspection and attention to detail Frank tried to establish lists of place-names, towns, gods and races. He succeeded in reading several geographical names correctly. But he was wrong in adopting as a certainty Forrer's simple suggestion and in regarding the language of the hieroglyphic inscriptions as Hurrian (the idea that this did not correspond to the Hittite cuneiform was gaining ground).

Carl Frank cannot be reproached for having directed his searches at the outset to the phonetic reading and neglecting the interpretation and comprehension of the inscriptions themselves; a certain number of errors can be imputed to him, but it is regrettable that Peter Jensen, a stranger now for many years in the field of decipherment although still interested in Hittite hieroglyphs, which he considered his own field, took it upon himself to utter the most violent and offensive criticisms. The old scholar, following his own false routes where contemporary experts could not and would not follow him, even forgot the cardinal rule of scientific objectivity and allowed himself to lapse into purely personal rudeness. "I blush as I lay down my pen," he wrote, commenting on Frank's decipherment. The latter defended himself in a more moderate tone. Jensen, with unqualified obstinacy, defended his theory of hieroglyphs considered as a series of ideograms or simple enumerations of honorific titles. Frank in turn lost patience and asked maliciously if the numbers of heads of asses or cattle recurring in the inscriptions were also part of these ideographic royal titles?

The only scholar, alas, who never failed to follow Jensen, even in his wildest surmises, was old Sayce, the pioneer of decipherment, the indefatigable initiator of several new generations of scholars. Now a very old man, he had continued to publish and to risk, even at this period, literal word-for-word translations. His articles of the years 1922–30 for the younger scientists, his successors, had the flavour of a voice from the tomb. But before he died in 1933, at the age of eighty-eight, the old scholar had the privilege of witnessing the real revolution which began about 1930. An almost simultaneous but autonomous effort by several antiquarians endowed Hittite hieroglyphs with a solid foundation and, as far as existing documents allowed, achieved remarkable individual results.

Five scholars of various nationalities were responsible for this revolution: an Italian, an American, a Swiss, a German and a Czech. Nearly all departing from different premises, they brought a new breeze into the history of decipherment which had remained almost stagnant since the lamentable Jensen–Frank polemic. One of them finally ventured on the snow cornice and brought down the avalanche. A native of Hamburg, although of Italian origin, his name was Piero Meriggi. Today professor at Pavia University and a linguist of international repute, he helped to decipher Hittite hieroglyphic writing and to interpret the Lycian and Lydian languages; he published Creto-Mycenaean texts and finally broke the mysterious Indus script and the even lesser-known Luvian tongue.

Piero's father, Cesare Meriggi, Professor of Italian at Pavia, was interested in the most disparate branches of science, including mechanics, approaching every subject he studied with so much skill and systematic intelligence that his son still speaks of him today as his "best teacher of the scientific method". He was preoccupied, like so many other research workers, with the idea of an international language, and works on general linguistics were his favourite reading matter. We are probably right in considering the rarefied atmosphere of the paternal house as the fertile soil in which the talents of young Piero developed at an early age.

The influence of this atmosphere turned out to be so powerful that after the First World War Piero Meriggi studied at Pavia University classical philology, in particular Greek, and took his Ph.D. in comparative philology. The Sanskrit expert who has recently died, L. Suali, by encouraging him to devote his thesis to the Lycian tongue—a controversial subject—pointed the way for him to the Ancient Orient. At the moment Suali drew Meriggi's attention to Asia Minor (Lycia is the southernmost province of western Asia Minor) his history professor, P. Fraccaro, was giving a course of lectures on the Hittites.

It was the burning topic of the day. Hrozný's recent decipherment was still being discussed with passion. Although Hittite cuneiform had been deciphered, the hieroglyphs had not yet been. Piero Meriggi therefore turned his attention to this new problem "from scratch", as he was to remark later, because he lacked the training in Assyriology indispensable to the study of Hittite cuneiform; but above all because he was fascinated by this still-virgin field.

Having completed his advanced studies, Meriggi became Gymnasium Professor for a year, then lecturer in Italian at Hamburg University, where, apart from his professional duties, he found time to carry on with his private research, receiving both encouragement and support from famous scholars. He produced what would have sufficed to ensure his reputation as a philologist: an important contribution to the decipherment of Hittite hieroglyphs. "What interested me above all were the hieroglyphs." Like several of his predecessors, Meriggi began with a close examination of the graphic system. In September 1927 he considered the results of his researches worthy of an official bulletin. At the beginning of March 1928 he visited

H. Ehelolf in Berlin, and the latter confirmed that his main discovery had its analogies in Hittite cuneiform. Encouraged by this, Meriggi submitted his work for public approval. "When the young Italian linguist, Piero Meriggi, announced at the Congress of Orientalists in 1928 at Bonn a new preliminary study to the decipherment of this script (Hittite hieroglyphic) . . . the author of these lines felt a strong mistrust of this bold enterprise," wrote J. Friedrich in retrospect in 1939.[49] But this mistrust was soon dispelled, and it was actually Friedrich who facilitated the young scholar's first contacts with the German *Zeitschrift für Assyriologie*, which published the lecture he had given at Bonn.

In his article Meriggi dealt with particular emphasis on questions of principle, gave statistics of the use of the basic signs, their position within the limits set by the word separators and their relation to the "thorn".* Then he endeavoured to determine the nature of the signs (phonetic or ideograms?) and examined the frequency of each character. His readings usually concurred with the views of his predecessors, and he remained so much beneath the spell of Jensen's theories that he did not even dare to reject the faulty reading of Syennesis. But in conclusion he was able to announce:

"I now have to impart a final essential piece of news: I think that I have recognised in a group of signs the word 'son'."[50]

When we recall the first efforts of Grotefend we realise the importance of the results acquired: not only a major insight into the syntactical articulation of the language, but also historical data of the greatest value. Now complete genealogies were legible. The dynastic lists from Carchemish, Hama and Marash allowed new comparisons with names found in the cuneiform texts and a definitive reading of certain royal names.

What procedure had Meriggi followed? He had carefully compared and analysed the initial lines of two inscriptions. At the start of both (they stemmed from Carchemish and were at the time the longest known bilingual texts) he encountered three names, followed by sundry attributes, one of which, common to the three names, was the title "prince" recognised by Meriggi [hieroglyphic signs]. Placed at the end of the honorary titles, it was followed in the case of the first name by no other word (cf. Fig.

* A small oblique stroke or perpendicular beside a syllabic sign to express the closed syllables ending with "r". Other decipherers call it "the tail".

58). In the second and third cases, on the other hand, "prince" was each time followed by another word invariably beginning with the same sign: it was therefore a question of two words with the same root. "In these circumstances it was reasonable to postulate in these two groups the terms for 'son' and 'grandson' and the obvious etymological connection gave support to this theory." [51] Professor Meriggi could already be sure of his facts when the second inscription confirmed his discovery.

"This systematic part of my article, which at least led to an initial comprehension of the syntactical construction of the

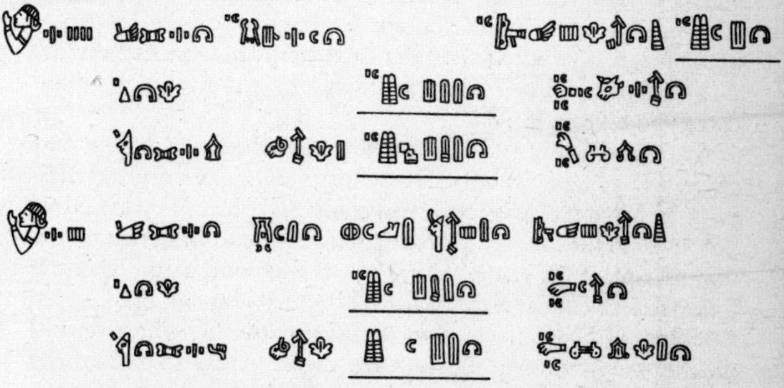

FIG. 58.—The opening texts of the two inscriptions from Carchemish in which Professor Meriggi discovered the word "son" (each three rows contain three names); the title "prince" is underlined; then come the words meaning "son" (2nd row) and "grandson" (3rd row). Note the variations in the signs and in the script.

texts, to the clear establishment of the words for 'son', 'grandson', etc., and the genealogies, I believe to be of value," said Meriggi with undue modesty in a recent lecture at Vienna. In actual fact this work already confirmed certain of the determinatives for names suggested by Thompson, the attribute "beloved of the gods", the title "Prince", and words "son", "grandson" and "great grandson", etc., and was in the words of the British investigator, R. D. Barnett "the final touch that starts an avalanche". The avalanche itself was the work carried out by the Gelb–Forrer–Bossert trio.

Ignace J. Gelb, professor at the Oriental Institute of Chicago University, was born on October 14th, 1907, at Tarnow in Poland. At an early age he conceived a passion for the most abstruse scientific subjects. He was fascinated by the unknown and something attracted him towards unexplored domains. While still a student he read a book by the Hungarian novelist, Maurice Jokai, a *roman à clef*, the hero of which, Paul Barko, scours the wilds of Asia in search of the original home of the Hungarian people. Gelb studied at Florence and then at Rome; his schoolboy dreams found their outlet in predetermined studies, and at Rome in 1929 he obtained his Ph.D. with a thesis on the early history of Asia Minor.

This history was closely allied to that of the Hittite civilisation, still little known at the period and still shrouded in mystery. The same year the young doctor began to study the Hittites—at Chicago, the advanced post of American Oriental studies, largely founded by German scholars. Emil Forrer was taught there some years later.

At Chicago other tasks soon occupied the mind of the new professor, who could only devote his evenings, nights and holidays to his secret passion, Hittite hieroglyphs. He succeeded, however, in mastering this particularly difficult subject, and the manuscript of his *Hittite Hieroglyphs I* was soon in the press; it appeared at Chicago in 1931. The same year, at the Leyden Congress of Orientalists, a memorable gathering where several pioneer decipherment works were presented, Gelb announced the results obtained after two years' hard work.

He followed to a certain extent the trails blazed by his predecessors. A number of his readings of names remained mere essays. But he also produced new and substantial results. He proved, for example, something that prior to him had been a mere hypothesis: that the "thorn" is an "r". Then he recognised in the group ∩↑∩ a verb, *a-i-a*, meaning "to make" (he actually read it *a-wa-a*), a particularly important result because it provided incontestable proof of the close kinship between Hittite and Luvian hieroglyphs and also with Hittite cuneiform which Gelb, following Thompson, compared with Hittite hieroglyphs. This was a promising start now that great strides forward had been made in the decipherment of Hittite cuneiform. Gelb also maintained that certain strips of lead covered with Hittite hieroglyphs recently found beneath a house at Assur, and which had been considered to be a kind of amulet, were in fact letters. This discovery was important because it was more or less known by comparison with other oriental languages what kind of introductory phrase might be expected on such documents.

The most vital contribution brought to decipherment by *Hittite Hieroglyphs I*, however, was the discovery that Hittite ideographic writing in addition to its numerous ideograms contained about sixty signs, each formed by a syllable of the type consonant + vowel or open syllable. In view of the fact that the number of signs considered to be phonetic amounted to about sixty, Gelb was convinced that the Hittite syllabary must be of a structure similar to, or even identical with, the Cypriote syllabary (cf. Chapter VII). Another conclusion imposed itself: ideographic Hittite writing, like Cypriote writing, made no distinction between voiced, mute and sibilant consonants (e.g. b, p and ph).

Since the characters of the Hittite hieroglyphic syllabary were revealed to him during an evening stroll, Professor Gelb believes unshakeably in this recipe for good inspirations and new ideas, without being convinced of its traditional medicinal value:

> "From that evening I have been convinced that the best ideas come to us while we are walking. I think of a man striding along, his chest thrust slightly forward, placing his heels firmly in the ground, his spinal column receiving electric charges favourable to swift and profitable reflection."[52]

Other problems could not be solved by the simple method of walking, as for example the reading and function of the relative pronoun in Hittite hieroglyphs. Even if he considers that it was largely responsible, Professor Gelb still maintains today that this problem caused him his greatest difficulties. It was primarily a question of assimilating a whole by no means consistent literature and of testing the results, a mental gymnastic in the course of which the Professor admits that he nearly lost his patience.

Gelb's undeniable progress was to be followed by two other attempts in the grand style.

We have already mentioned the Swiss linguist, Emil Forrer, professor at Berlin, later at Chicago and today at San Salvador, the discoverer of the eight languages of Boghaz-Keui. His study of the cuneiform texts had been very revealing. No less vital for the decipherment of the hieroglyphs was his work *The*

Hittite Ideographic Writing (Chicago, 1932), the major importance of which was recognised by J. F. Friedrich.

The method used by Forrer marks a decisive phase in the work of decipherment, and we give here the broad outlines. Prior attempts (with the exception of Jensen's, quoted above) had as their goal the phonetic reading of the characters, thus departing from the true path; in future, Forrer maintained, an objective comprehension of the content of the inscriptions was essential. He quoted in this respect the ideograms of Chinese writing read in Japan in Japanese, in Korea in Korean, in Annam in Annamite, and the Sumerian ideograms, which, as we know today, were pronounced in Assyria in Assyrian and in Hittite among the Hittites. He remarked later that we still use a certain number of such ideograms which are universally understood, although they represent no determinate phoneme, each reader attributing to them the phonetic value to which he is accustomed (signs for money £, $, Fl., etc.). Objective comprehension, therefore, must take precedence over the reading.

But how to acquire this objective comprehension without being able to read a single syllable? There is in practice, maintained Forrer, one method: the observation of parallel phenomena. Parallels can occur:

(1) between the symbolical representation and the text;
(2) between the written object and its designation;
(3) between the written symbol itself and its meaning.

A few brief examples will help to illustrate what Forrer means. The first case applies when their attitude, costume and attributes obviously predict them as deities, possibly several figures on a rock sculpture each accompanied by the same hieroglyphic sign; we deduce that the sign in question means "god". Better still: when in a sculpture representing the family of a prince, as at Carchemish, the ruler holds his son by the hand and above the prince's arm is written: "I hold him by the hand." Case 2 applies when one sees engraved on a sacrificial axe: "Axe of the High Priest"; we shall soon encounter one of these revealing instruments in another context. Case 3 is that of all ideograms which have remained comparatively close to their original form, as for example the Old Sumerian symbolical character ✳ = "a star".

These three parallelisms, continues Forrer, already lead

without phonetic reading to twenty points of the lexicon of the language to be deciphered, in this case Hittite hieroglyphics, and, by mutual comparison, to four essential points of grammar. But these are not the only possibilities afforded by observation of the parallel phenomena. There is another priceless key: the similarity throughout the Ancient East of certain portions of the inscriptions. Forrer quoted three particular features:

(1) the opening of royal inscriptions (the initial formulae had already allowed Meriggi to read the genealogies);
(2) the formulae of the curses;
(3) the introduction to the letters.

Royal inscriptions usually begin with the genealogy of the princes and their titles, often in conjunction with the names of gods and localities.

The curse formulae are composed of co-ordinated relative clauses the verb of which is either in the present or the future tense ("Whoever . . . destroys . . . breaks or . . . mutilates in any way . . . will himself be destroyed . . . broken . . . mutilated . . . , etc.") with a complementary clause usually in the imperative to express the divine curse ("May the gods destroy . . .").

The opening of the letters usually observes this stereotyped formula: "A to B; I am well. My family is well, I hope the same applies to you, to your family, etc."

A simple comparison of these texts will reveal the signs employed for case-endings, pronouns and personal suffixes, demonstrative pronouns, relative and interrogative pronouns; also the adverbs, prepositions, conjunctions, particles and verb forms—in short, the basic features of a grammar intelligible to the eye if not to the ears.[53]

Let us now choose from these theoretical points the one which most clearly shows the way in which Forrer put into practice his theory and which at the same time constitutes his most valuable contribution to the decipherment of Hittite hieroglyphs.

We have mentioned that a few formulae of curses were in current use in the Ancient Orient. Thanks to a profound study of their structure, Forrer discovered one which was to put him on the right track.

This formula serves as colophon to the famous stela of the

Babylonian King Hammurabi (1728–1686 B.C.), a legal codex of 300 paragraphs; written in Akkadian and engraved on a block of basalt six and a half metres high, these laws were designed for the newly-founded empire which included the whole of Babylonia and Assyria. The code dealt with important questions of penal, civil and commercial law and ended as follows:

> "... If this man does not hearken to the words I have here engraved, forgets my curse and no longer fears the gods, abolishes the code I have established and substitutes for my words other words and defaces my sculptures, erases my name from this inscription and writes his own upon it (or) on account of the maledictions which will ensue, charges another (with this task), this man:—the end of the text is now in spaced type and is also written in Babylonian:
>
> "*lû sharrum* — *lû bêlum*
> be he a king — be he a lord
> *lû iššakkum* — *û lû awîlûtum ša šumam nabi'at*
>
> a governor or some other person worthy of being named[54] ...—may Anu, the powerful father of the gods, take from him the title of king, break his sceptre and curse his fate."

We have chosen this phrase from the curse formula because, on account of the spacing of the characters, Forrer selected it. It contains the word "king" and two other titles. But the titles "king" and "prince" were already known as ideograms of Hittite hieroglyphs.

Faithful to his method of making parallels of Eastern curses, Forrer now searched the Hittite pictorial inscriptions for a clause of the same construction. And he came across this one:

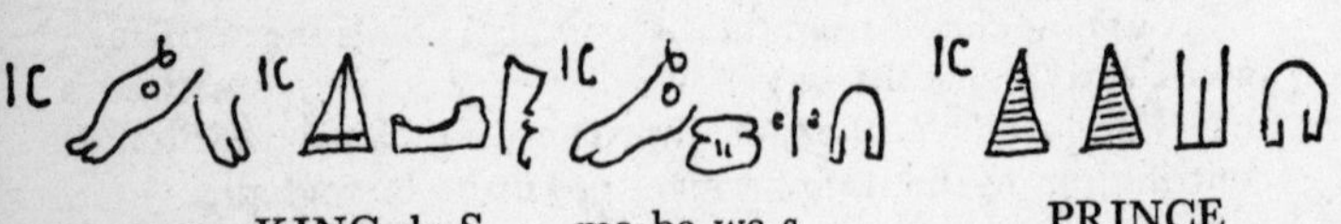

ma-n KING-da-S — ma-ba-wa-s — PRINCE
"be he a king — or a — prince ..."

thereupon followed the second part of the phrase: Hammurabi said: "Let Anu, father of the gods wrest from the criminal his title of king, break his sceptre and curse his fate—and 46 pious wishes of the same nature."

Why should the second phrase not also begin with the same words in Hittite: "May the gods . . ."? The subject of this phrase immediately caught the scholar's eye in the shape of the group ⓓ c↑, the first sign of which was already known as the determinative for the names of the gods; ↑ could only be the sign for the nominative plural! Moreover, the last word of this conjuration ended regularly with the well-known phonetic sign ⌐ or ⌐, *da* or *tu:* and the ending -tu must, therefore, denote the imperative of the verb corresponding to the Old Indian imperative *astu*, Latin *esto*, Greek *éstō*! The endings of the ablative and the past participle were discovered by this same method, which also allowed Sayce-Cowley's justaposed ⓓ, *ha*, to be read in the light of the Indo-European equivalent and in the Latin quis *que*, "each man".

In presenting these results before the assembled Orientalists in two lectures given at Leyden and Geneva (the text was later published in the work we have already quoted), Forrer at one blow revealed "the grammatical structure of the hieroglyphic language with all its particles".[55] He was also able to give the correct reading of the royal name: Muwatallish.

The originality, intelligence and lucidity of Forrer's work received the praise it deserved. But the work of the German scholar, Helmuth Theodor Bossert, which appeared almost simultaneously with that of Forrer and completely independent of the latter, was no less original and substantial. The name of Bossert, today of international renown, is most often quoted in respect of Hittite hieroglyphic writing.

In the course of his varied and chequered career, Bossert applied his scientific talents to a number of fields. The feature which characterised him from his very early youth was his passion for palaeography.

His first interest was his own family tree. Born on September 11th, 1889, at Landau in the Palatinate, while still a pupil at Karlsruhe gymnasium, Bossert spent his summer holidays, from 1902 onwards, searching parish records for traces of his ancestors. But these became more and more difficult to decipher as he went back in time. The boy was not discouraged. His imagination was fired by the old scripts which were to charm him throughout his life.

But Bossert, who never did things by half-measures, did not intend to remain an amateur in this field; he learned his profession from A to Z. Slowly and patiently he familiarised himself first with the manuscripts of the 17th and 18th centuries. He was fortunate enough to find well-disposed teachers who took a paternal interest in him, initiated him into the love of their own science and showed him the paths to follow.

There was the famous Celtic expert, Alfred Holder, Keeper of the Karlsruhe National Library, a great scholar and a man of good will who, at the time Bossert passed his baccalaureat, was working on a catalogue of the Reichenau convent library. He invited his pupil to help him in this work. Bossert had pushed his studies to a point where he could read Latin and German manuscripts back to the Carolingian period. Holder at times even went to the young student for help, for he had recognised his capabilities in reading texts and palimpsests in a bad state of preservation. The most difficult script which the scholar expected his pupil to decipher was without doubt the letters which the Celtic authority himself wrote to Bossert when he was at the front (he served with distinction in the First World War in France, Belgium, Russia and Serbia). These letters were in fact so illegible that the recipient, despite his training, had to ponder over them for hours on end before finally getting their meaning.

The well-known art historian, Max Wingenroth, a friend of the Bossert family, also had a decisive and benevolent influence on the boy, and among the luxurious volumes of his splendid library awakened in him a taste for art history and archaeology. It was Wingenroth, too, who drew Bossert's attention to the importance and necessity of learning languages. At school, apart from the obligatory languages, Latin, Greek and French, he had learned Hebrew and English, and had even copied Egyptian hieroglyphic texts which he could not afford to buy. At the universities of Heidelberg, Strasbourg, Munich and Freiburg-im-Breisgau, Bossert devoted himself with equal ardour to art history, archaeology, medieval history and Germanistics. In addition to these main subjects he studied all the details of his profession, i.e. ancillary historical sciences: diplomacy, palaeography, heraldry, genealogy and sphragistics. He even published (while still in the top form) short historical articles and the results of his research into German flamboyant Gothic.

At the time art history was his favourite subject, and his doctor's thesis, published at Innsbruck in 1914, was entitled: *The Old High Altar of Our Lady of Sterzing in the Tyrol.*

It is a long way from Sterzing in the Tyrol to Boghaz-Keui, the ancient Hattushah, the capital of the Hittites, from the altar-piece of Our Lady to the fire altar of the legendary Mopsus. How could Bossert have foreseen his future path? Freiburg University, where he worked as assistant under Wingenroth, now director of the museum of that town, had become his spiritual home, where he wished to take his degree in medieval art history.

A few months stood between the young Ph.D. and his military service. He called up on October 1st, 1913. Before his release, the First World War had broken out. Bossert fought for four years on all fronts, as we have mentioned. In the summer of 1918 he was ordered to Berlin, where he witnessed his country's defeat and saw a decisive turning point in the direction of his studies.

The post-war world witnessed a revival of interest in the Hittites, based on Winckler's finds and Hrozný's decipherment. This gave a new impetus to international research. The young art historian also turned his attention to the Hittites and the old Mediterranean civilisations. Once more he approached his new task with his vast knowledge and his usual competence. At the age of nearly thirty he embarked upon the study of cuneiform languages and mastered Egyptian. To finance his undertaking he became scientific adviser to the Berlin publishers, Wasmuth Verlag, and for a certain time to the *Sozietätsverlag* run by the *Frankfurter Zeitung*. For his private studies he had only his evenings and the long journeys to and from his house to the office. It needed a great effort of will, as those who have done the same will realise, considering that he had no access to the public libraries, which were open only during the day. To keep up to date, Bossert had to buy his own scientific journals and the indispensable new publications.

He was particularly attracted to scripts which had not yet been deciphered; first and foremost of these was not Hittite hieroglyphic, but Cretan. During 1929–31 he wrote articles on the decipherment of this "Minoan" writing and hazarded a guess at the reading of proper names in Ancient Cretan. He had come to the same conclusion as other scholars—that there was an affinity between this script and Hittite hieroglyphic. Since the inscriptions in the latter script were far more plentiful, he hoped that they would help him in this new decipherment. This was the task he undertook in his book *Šantaš und Kupapa. A New Contribution to the Decipherment of Cretan and Hittite Hieroglyphs* (Leipzig, 1932). Piero Meriggi, to whom, with J. Sundwall, he had dedicated this work, announced in a review that Bossert's work represented a great extension of the knowledge already acquired, especially regarding Hittite hieroglyphs, and that the problem of the writing had now reached a point which no one had expected to reach so swiftly.

His predecessors had started either with phonetic readings or on an objective comprehension of the inscriptions. Bossert, on the other hand, began from a magic formula in Egyptian, which he had learned at school. It was from a medical papyrus in the British Museum which contained this interesting passage: a spell designed to conjure the Asiatic pox, written in the tongue of the Keftiu, who were none other than the Ancient Cretans. The formula ran: "*sa-n-ti ka-pu-pu wa-i-ia-im-a-n ti-re-ka-ka-ra.*" Bossert, recognising it as an invocation of the god Šantaš (Sandon, Sandes) and the goddess Kupapa, tried to determine these names in the Hittite hieroglyphic texts. Here his vast knowledge of archaeology and his training in palaeography were of immense help. By studying the different styles he succeeded in dating the hieroglyphic monuments and made a decisive contribution to palaeography. R. D. Barnett called this work "an invaluable palaeographical study of symbols". As far as the readings were concerned, Bossert exercised his traditional prudence, giving no translations of lengthy texts. He accepted the readings of the names of towns which had already been made: Carchemish, Gurgum (= Marash) and Hama; but he was the first to give a correct reading of the town of Tyana in Asia Minor, according to the cuneiform text "Tu-wa-nu-wa", and above all he rejected Jensen's error which had so long troubled investigators and hindered all progress; the king of Tyana was no longer called Syennesis, as according to Jensen, but Wa-r-pa-la-wa-s.

This discovery was of equal value to history and to the decipherment. Bossert immediately recognised in Warpalawas the King of Tyana whom Assyrian cuneiform sources named Urballa—an adversary and vassal of Tiglath-pileser III.

We have no space here to study in detail the advance thus made for history and Ancient Eastern chronology; this rich harvest was no less precious for the acquisition of new phonetic values. Bossert published a whole series of readings of hieroglyphic signs, only a very small number of which had to be subsequently abandoned. His brilliant work brought him an offer

FIG. 59.—The name of Warpalawas in Hittite hieroglyphs.

from the Berlin Assyriologist, Bruno Meissner, at the request of the Prussian Academy of Science, of editing a "Corpus" of Hittite hieroglyphic inscriptions. In the summer of 1933 he went to Turkey to collect rock inscriptions. Here he was invited by Kurt Bittel, Director of Excavations, to take part in an expedition to Boghaz-Keui. He had already visited Istanbul and Izmir in 1922 and also knew the hieroglyphic inscriptions of the Berlin, Paris and London museums. But it was not until he himself worked on the Nishantash inscriptions at Boghaz-Keui and on the texts of the Yazilikaya bas-reliefs that he realised the difficulties that faced the scientist working on these petroglyphs.

The decisive influence for his subsequent career, more than this practical apprenticeship, was an encounter on his return journey at Ankara. Here he was introduced to Doctor Reshid Galip, the Turkish Minister for National Education, who had been ordered to organise the Kemal Atatürk's new university of Istanbul on European lines. The Minister offered the brilliant scholar a chair, and he accepted. From April 1934 Bossert was Professor of Languages and Asia Minor Civilisations at the Faculty of Letters at Istanbul University and at the same time director of the Archaeological Institute for New Eastern Studies.

Istanbul had followed all the decipherment works, including Bossert's *Šantaš and Kupapa*; it was now known that Bossert had definitely "dethroned" the old Syennesis in favour of Warpalawas. The way was free, and Meriggi, who had subscribed to the famous error in his early work, now began to establish in turn a new list of phonetic signs. In a series of minor works he corroborated the main results of Bossert, although, as opposed to the German investigator, who believed it to be Hurrian, he considered it to be Indo-European language. In the attempt to discover its syntactic structure, Meriggi in a series of more ambitious articles in French and German learned journals interpreted whole texts; despite a few conflicting details his results coincided by and large with those of Bossert. This kind of common platform, erected by two independent scholars, was reinforced by the readings of Hrozný, who, from 1932, had also turned his attention to Hittite hieroglyphs. Friedrich in retrospect described the state of research at this period as a kind of "common front" represented by Bossert–Meriggi–Hrozný. Hrozný's greatest contribution, perhaps, was to have drawn attention to certain analogies between Hittite cuneiform and hieroglyphic and thus to have pointed out the close relationship between the two languages.

While the younger generation of decipherers were forcing this victorious "breach", an old Englishman of eighty-eight was on his sickbed, which he was never to leave. He was Archibald Henry Sayce, the former "pope" of Hittitology. He continued to take an active part in the decipherment, but luck failed him. Nevertheless the old man's memory and alacrity of mind, which he retained to the end, were quite remarkable. Until his death he followed with the keenest attention the progress of research, and during the last weeks of his life, relying entirely on his memory, he annotated a Phoenician text from Râs Shamrah (we shall speak of this later) in Hebrew, Phoenician, Arabic, Akkadian, Egyptian and other related languages. He never had a harsh word for his often hostile critics and on the eve of his death his last intelligible question was: "When is Virolleaud going to publish the new Râs Shamra texts?"

New texts—this was the constant cry of the Hittitologists. After 1933 research did not remain inactive. As a start the existing documents were collated and made accessible to everyone. Editions appeared of the Hrozný, Meriggi and Gelb texts, the fruits of long years of study and extensive field work. Professor Gelb, for example, had travelled to Turkey several times between 1932 and 1935 bent upon discovering new Hittite hieroglyphic monuments: "the trips on horse or mule back across the ancient Hittite countryside were some of the happiest moments of my life."[56] He often set out on false trails. "Yes, over there near the village [this was sometimes several miles away] there are some of the inscriptions you are looking for," the natives would say to him. But when he arrived at the spot indicated he would find that the characters carved in the rock were merely natural erosion caused by the wind and the rain. Magnificent finds rewarded him richly for his pains; such as the discovery of the inscription on the old crusader's citadel of Yilankale at Sirkeli in Cilicia, and the hardly won text of Kotukale which two previous expeditions had been forced to abandon because it was engraved on a cliff face which fell sheer into the water. The intrepid American, wishing to take photos and copies, cut the Gordian knot by engaging a troop of sappers to blast a way up for him with dynamite to the inscription of his dreams. Like the other foreigners travelling in Anatolia, Gelb was full of praise for the good-will and hospitality he met with in all the Turkish villages. He was all the more surprised when, in the course of his second trip to Emirgazi, a village in Central Anatolia, his questions were greeted with impassive, hostile faces. Upon insisting, he learned that there were no inscriptions in the neighbourhood and that had there been they would certainly not have told him for fear of tempting Providence. Thirty years before some Hittite hieroglyphic inscriptions had been found in this place and sent to the Istanbul Museum. Hardly had they left than the village was visited by the plague.

The methodical Professor Meriggi in 1937 was able to publish a complete list of signs (at least for the period) which is still indispensable today. As early as 1934 the Germans, K. Bittel and H. Güterbock, had resumed excavations at Boghaz-Keui and found in the former royal palace a store of nearly 300 clay seals, a third of which were genuine bilingual documents (some of them were short and in a bad state of preservation). From these could be read, as on the famous Tarkumuwa seal, the names of the kings in cuneiform and hieroglyphic script. The main prize was not the new linguistic knowledge obtained but the fact that from now onwards the hieroglyphs of most of the Hittite kings' names were known. Composed for the most part of ideograms, these names threw no light on the pronunciation, but among them were a few names in syllabic writing (including that of Queen Puduhepa, read by Bossert in 1933). For historical research in general the discovery of the royal name Shuppiluliumash was of major importance.

In 1944 Bossert made this particular seal an object for special study. He now asked himself a new question: Do characters which are normally syllabic signs also have an ideographic value? Starting from this hypothesis he arrived at a satisfactory explanation for the name Shuppiluliumash, which has not as yet been universally accepted.

The later works of Gelb (1935–42) brought a new and extremely fortunate revision, or rather a new determination of certain signs which had so far remained in doubt. The American scholar presented a list of phonetic signs which in common with his theory of nasalised vowels is still controversial.

Even with the discovery of these seals, so precious at first sight (the German excavators previously mentioned had

(*a*) Tarkumuwa of Mira.

(*b*) Indilimma.

(*c*) Tabarna of Hatti

(*d*) Queen Puduhepa of Hatti.

FIG. 60.—Hittite hieroglyphic and cuneiform seals.

already found a second in 1939), decipherment had not made very much progress. The Second World War brought little interruption; several scholars continued their work, as can be judged from the dates of publication of the works quoted above. At the end of the war nothing had happened to revise the judgment of J. Friedrich on the results obtained in 1939: "The decipherers of hieroglyphs, both in their theoretical studies and their readings, are on the right track."[57]

Some light had been thrown on the fundamental traits of this writing. About fifty regular syllabic signs mostly of the type consonant + vowel were known; opposed to these almost universally recognised signs were a very much larger number of ideograms the pronunciation of which was unknown. It was also known that the syllabic signs were often used as "phonetic complements", serving to express phonetically the ending of words represented by ideograms or even other parts of words. It had been admitted, without actually being proved, that the Hittite hieroglyphic script was an Indo-European language.

> "The different readings should constantly be reviewed and eventually corrected. New finds are still bringing us surprises. But we cannot consider Hittite hieroglyphs today either as undeciphered or undecipherable."[58]

The new finds in question could only refer to the fine bilingual documents which Sayce already dreamed of deciphering and upon which the efforts of all linguists, archaeologists and historians were concentrated.

The man who revealed them to the world was Helmuth Theodor Bossert.

During a journey in south-eastern Turkey in 1945, undertaken at the request of Istanbul University with the aim of discovering traces of ancient civilisations, Bossert, from conversations with nomads, learned of the existence of a "lion stone" situated, according to them, in the neighbourhood of the little town of Kadirli.

Now the lion was one of the symbolic animals favoured by the Hittites and the most frequently encountered. Bossert's interest was aroused, and in February 1946 he set out in search of this stone. He would probably never have discovered it without the aid of the Turkish schoolmaster, Ekrem Kusçu, the only man on the spot who knew of the existence of this stone and had himself seen it on several occasions. Bossert, therefore, saw the "lion stone" (a lion which eventually turned out to be a bull) and discovered that it had apparently served originally as a plinth for a statue. The statue itself, very much damaged, lay not far away and bore a Semitic inscription. At the same spot—on the Karatepe or "Black Mountain", formerly called Aslantash on the River Ceyhan, the Pyramos of antiquity in the south-east of Turkey, i.e. Cilicia—Bossert discovered during his first rapid survey fragments carved with Hittite hieroglyphs.

Semitic writing and Hittite hieroglyphs: a new hope was

immediately born. Did the "Black Mountain" really conceal bilingual documents written in both scripts?

Bossert returned to Karatepe the following year. He excavated for a whole month with his assistant, Doctor Bahadir Alkim, an erudite young Turk who had been educated in Europe, and was now teaching at Istanbul University.

To him must be given the credit for disinterring what had been sought for more than seventy years, something which

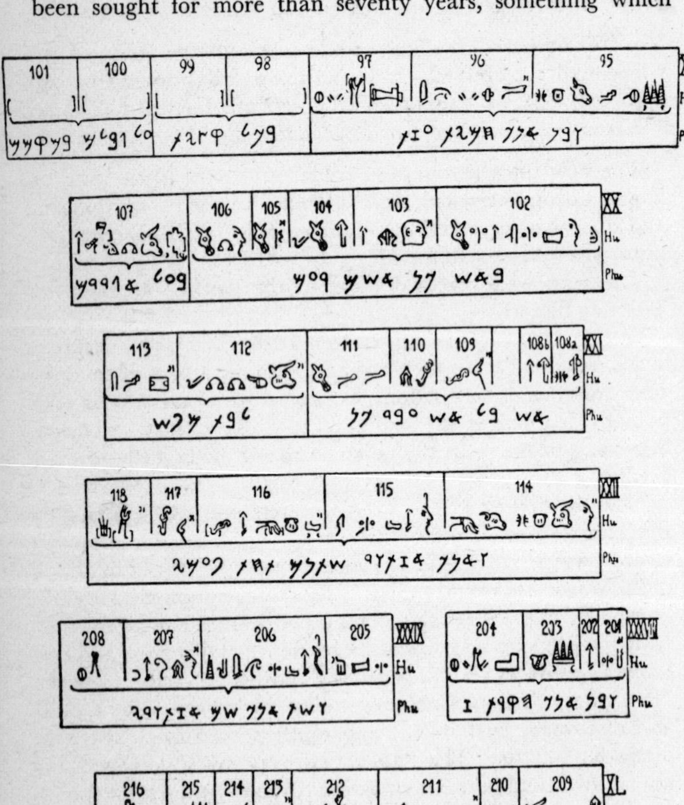

FIG. 61.—Phrases XIX–XXII and XXXVIII–XL of the Karatepe bilingual.

Bossert had secretly hoped for despite all his successes: intact stelae, well-engraved reliefs (orthostats) with sculpture and inscriptions in Phoenician and Hittite hieroglyphs—*the bilinguals.*

"He found the bilinguals." It sounds so simple! Actually this sensational find, to borrow J. Friedrich's comment, was the reward of arduous work, privations and countless deceptions, the culminating point of a series of dramatic incidents and a stroke of good fortune because Bossert's collaborator, Franz Steinherr found, one might say in his sleep, that the texts written in these two languages had the same content.

The Karatepe inscriptions have sometimes been compared with the Rosetta Stone.

In actual fact the Egyptian epigraphic document more deserving of this comparison would be the Canopus Decree. The bilingual Karatepe stele was the touchstone required to confirm the accuracy of decipherment, the seal to crown all that had hitherto been accomplished.

Here is a translation of this inscription, according to the Phoenician text:

> XIX. "And I built stout walls at all the boundaries, on the frontiers, in the places where lived evil men, chiefs of robber bands, none of whom had served the house of Mopsus, but I, Asītawadda, I placed them beneath my feet."
>
> XXXVIII. "And I built this town, and I placed (on it) the name Asītawadda. For Baal (in Hittite hieroglyphs, the God of the Storm) and Resheph of the Birds sent me to build it."[59]

Since the Hittite hieroglyphic version was expressed in two languages it furnished, for comparison, the values of fifteen phonetic signs and the meaning of sixteen ideograms. Furthermore, this bilingual document revealed many new ideograms; more than forty words were read for the first time, twenty of which had prior to this been hypothetical.

It also brought some surprises: for example, the affirmation that certain ideograms could also appear as vowels or as syllabic signs in the middle of a word; an inverse polyphony to that which occurs in cuneiform was even discovered: in Hittite hieroglyphs the same phonetic value could be expressed by different signs.

This discovery enabled us to penetrate farther into the syntax of the language and was a considerable aid to its comprehension. The language turned out to be closely akin to, although not identical with, Luvian and also to differ from Palaic and Hittite cuneiform; it originated in the south-west of Anatolia. Thanks to knowledge acquired from Bossert's bilingual, we can consider the decipherment as a *fait accompli*, although much remains to be done in this field.

The inscriptions, however, were not as fruitful as historians had hoped.

Their author was not Phoenician; he bore the Anatolian name of Asītawatas and styled himself king of the Dananiyim and vassal of Awarakus, a Cicilian sovereign who, according to cuneiform sources, was called Urikki or Uriaik and surrendered to the Assyrian Tiglath-pileser. According to the Karatepe inscriptions the kingdom of the Dananiyim was the plain of Adana. We have seen that Asītawatas speaks of the town founded by him and to which he gave his name (identified with the ruins of Karatepe). He also relates how he brought peace to the land in the east and west and built powerful fortresses.

As we have indicated, since the inscriptions date from the 8th century B.C., in the year 1000 B.C. Cilicia had become the scene of a mixed Hittite–Phoenician civilisation, thus only a reflection of past glory of the powerful Hittite empire ("Ancient Empire from *ca.* 1600–1470, the New Empire from *ca.* 1440–1200"). From the historical point of view the discoveries were on the whole disappointing.

The bilingual stela, however, gave some valuable indications to the classical philologist. In the translation of the Phoenician version Asītawatas styles himself as belonging to the "mpš" dynasty. This gave food for thought.

It was immediately recognised that the Dananiyim could be synonymous with the already known Danauna or "dnwn", who invaded Egypt in the 12th century B.C. A letter from El Amarna calls them the Danuna, a people from Canaan. They settled in Cilicia or in the immediate neighbourhood. And here we come to another point taken from Greek antiquity.

Homer called the Greeks of Troy "Danaoi", the Danaans and Greek tradition maintained that the word derived from a dynasty of Argos of Oriental origin. Danaos, the founder, must have been the son of Belos. Now Belos is synonymous with the Babylonian god, Bel, and whoever was called Belos (-os being merely the Greek ending) undoubtedly came from the East. Asītawatas also styled himself the descendant of the "mpš" dynasty. According to the judgment of several scholars this must be Mopsus, a name well known in Greek mythology. His parents were legendary deities, one of which had ties with Asia Minor. He is reputed to have built the town of Mallos in Cilicia, and to have died there. Cilicia actually possesses a town with an even more revealing name. Situated on the Ceyhan, on the ancient route from Tarsus to Issus, Turkish Missis was in the old days called Mopsuhestia, a Greek word signifying "hearth" or "fire altar of Mopsus".

We know from Assyrian sources that in the 11th century the King Ashur-nasirpal I conquered the land of Daununa and took five towns.

Since the inscriptions of Karatepe go back to the 8th century, the dynasty and realm of Mopsus should have been 300 years old when Asītawatas wrote his text. Mopsus therefore emerges from the mythical mist of Greek legend and, thanks to the testimony of the Karatepe inscriptions, becomes an historical figure.

Professor Bossert combined these results with another passage from the Karatepe texts where mention is made of Pahri, an important town of the Hittite empire of which the Karatepe fortress formed the outpost, and tried to prove that Mopsuhestia, the town of Mopsus, was in the olden days called Pahri.

To do this Mopsuhestia had to be discovered!

In 1956 excavations brought to light among other things an ancient mosaic pavement from the old episcopal church of Mopsuhestia. The search continues.

Let us now take a final look at Hittite hieroglyphic and its evolution from cuneiform and the Egyptian script. Here once more it is a question of hieroglyphs—but very different and unusual, to say the least of it, when compared with the Egyptian hieroglyphs with which we have grown familiar. From the artistic standpoint, the Hittite examples are very inferior, but if the Egyptian signs strike the observer by their beauty of form, harmony and their severe drawing, the Hittite characters for their part have a certain carefreeness, incompleteness and strangely chaotic charm.

"The comparison in fact is hardly justified. The Hittite inscriptions are written boustrophedon, i.e. the direction of the writing changes at the end of each line, a system which recalls the progress of an ox harnessed to the plough. It is read from left to right and then from right to left without the reader having to hop back to the beginning. This peculiarity gives the writing a cursive character. In the case of the Hittites it runs effectively in all directions: sprawling over the margins, turning corners, encroaching on the neighbouring block, on the bodies of the animals, at the whim of the scribe. This could never be said of Egyptian writing. The Egyptian scribe composed rather than wrote, and the aesthetic effect counted far more in his eyes than the actual content of the most conventional phrases. The Hittite was expansive by nature. When his heart was full his writing overflowed. He wrote for the love of what he wanted to say and the outward appearance mattered little to him. The ideograms were not always placed according to a set scheme.[60] At the Syro-Hittite epoch, even in the monumental inscriptions, the margin which separates the naturalistic original hieroglyphs from the partial or total cursive abbreviations is left to the whim of each individual. The characters wander over the stone rather than fall into regular lines. It needs a long experience of Hittitology to be able to read them in their correct order." [61]

As we have already indicated several times in this book, we find in Hittite hieroglyphs elements of the Egyptian script and Akkadian cuneiform: ideograms, phonetic signs and determinatives placed partly before and partly after the determined word. Hittite hieroglyphic is related to Akkadian cuneiform (but not to Egyptian) by the fact that its syllabic signs also contain a clearly determined vowel. A word separator exists, which is only sometimes used. In addition to the symbolic signs—miniature masterpieces in their careful drawing—more simple cursive signs are often met with.

The determinative for proper names can be clearly distinguished on the Carchemish inscriptions (see above, Fig. 58); it is a small oblique stroke placed before and above the name (there are six in all); it may have been copied from the Babylonian cuneiform, the vertical wedge preceding the names of male persons. Apart from images of outstanding naturalism (above all the heads of animals) other signs are stylised to the point where it is impossible to recognise their symbolic origin. Let us take a few typical examples of the words meaning "house" and "sun" as well as the mysterious determinative for the names of gods, simultaneously determinative and ideogram, as in the cuneiform script.

The Hittites of the "Ancient Empire" (*ca.* 1600–1470 B.C.)

FIG. 62.—Inscription from Carchemish, of a pictographic nature.

already used hieroglyphs as well as cuneiform not only for their monumental epigraphy, but also for private use; the scribes who wrote on wooden tablets certainly did not engrave wedges. Throughout the duration of the Ancient and New Hittite Empires (from about 1600 to 1200 B.C.) cuneiform, such as we find it in the records from Boghaz-Keui, and the hieroglyphs existed at one and the same time.

FIG. 63.—Hittite hieroglyphs for "house", "sun", "god".

The Hittite hieroglyphs, far from disappearing after the fall of the New Empire about 1200 B.C., survived and continued to develop in the small states, the Neo-Hittite diadochs in south-east Anatolia and Syria, perhaps in a conscious attempt to preserve the national tradition among these scattered communities. It is precisely to the survival of these small states that we owe the vital finds of the Hama stones, the Carchemish inscriptions, the lions of Marash and the bilingual stela of Karatepe.

Let us cast a final glance at the material used. We have seen that the decipherment of Hittite cuneiform was comparatively easy because as soon as the store of clay tablets found by Winckler were made available the legibility of the script was an advantage; we have also shown how the laborious decipherment of the hieroglyphs and their language took more than eighty years and how difficult and halting was the progress until the discovery of the great bilingual texts. Why, then, are the hieroglyphic texts, with the exception of the royal monuments, so rare?

Most of the inscriptions illustrated in this book show the characters drawn in painstaking relief. But there also existed an incised writing, vestiges of which were found at Carchemish dating from the 9th century B.C. which seems to have been widespread until it disappeared in the 7th century with the Assyrian conquest. All the older texts are engraved in relief on stone.

This technique is not suited to such material. Inscriptions on stone are usually chiselled. The fact that the Hittite characters have an elegant regularity when carved in relief on stone makes us conclude that they were originally produced by another technique and that the stonemasons had merely imitated an earlier process—engraving in relief on wood. Wood was in fact the chief material used in the earliest periods, but in a special form, as the tools and the writing materials depicted in the sculptures teach us.

"The Hittites wrote with a brush and ink on tablets of wood backed with whitewashed white linen. Thus the scribe who traced his cuneiform characters with the same gesture as the Babylonian used when he plunged his stylus in the moist clay was a wood engraver, as though cuneiform writing were merely an ancillary art subordinate to that of writing hieroglyphs. The Hittite children learned to write at an early age. The small prince, standing at his mother's knee, in addition to a bird on a string carried a 'copy book' and an inkpot.[62] It is in fact a wooden folding tablet with a lock. These tablets could also serve as letters. But letters were also written on strips of lead which could be rolled up neatly and repeatedly used because the characters were easy to erase.

"Official documents were engraved on silver, iron or lead

and there is no existing material that was not 'painted' or inscribed, but the main material was wood and that is why no hieroglyphic document of the third millennium has come down to us."[63]

The rare Hittite literary documents which have survived give us a very incomplete yet strangely evocative picture: that of a healthy, vigorous people, intellectually honest, loving life and its pleasures, endowed with an innate sense of humour but capable of deep emotions, as we find in the moving plague prayer of King Murshilish II:

"God of the Storm of Hatti, my Lord, and you (other) gods of Hatti, my Lords! The Great King, your servant, has sent me; Go speak with the Storm God of Hatti, my lord, and to the other gods my lords, tell them this:

"See what you have done. You have sent the plague to our land of Hatti and the land of Hatti has suffered death and poverty from the plague.

"People died of it under the reign of my father, under the reign of my brother, we continue to die since I became the priest of the gods twenty years ago.

"And the death that lies over the land of Hatti, and the plague have not left us.

"But I, I cannot master the torment of my heart. I am no longer master of the agony that invades my soul."[64]

"God of the Storm of Hatti, my Lord, and you, o Gods, my Lords, is it thus: we have sinned.

"My father too sinned; he transgressed the word of the Storm God of Hatti, my Lord, but I, I have not sinned.

"But it is thus: the sins of the father fall upon his children.

"The sins of my father have fallen upon me.

"This is my confession to the God of the Storm of Hatti, my Lord and to the gods, my Lords: that is what we have done.

"And since I have confessed the sins of my father, let the spirit of the Storm God of Hatti, my Lord, relent and may the gods, my Lords, be benevolent and banish the plague from the land of Hatti.

. . . .

"I entreat you, hearken unto me. For I have committed no evil.

"And of all those who of old have sinned and committed evil, there rest not one because they are all dead long since, and the errors of my father have fallen upon me.

"So that you may banish the plague, o gods, my Lords, I bring you gifts and sacrifices.

"Banish the torment from my heart, solace the agony of my soul."[65]

CHAPTER VI

"CAPE FENNEL" AT "WHITE HARBOUR" AND GUBLA THE "CITY OF PAPER"

THE DECIPHERMENT OF UGARITIC AND GUBLITIC

"*How many sleepless nights* . . ."—Edouard Dhorme.

RÂS SHAMRA, "Cape Fennel" in Syria, is situated about half a mile inland to the south-west of Minet-el-Beida, the "White Harbour".

Anyone consulting a modern map would have difficulty in finding either the cape or the harbour in question, but an imaginary line traced across the sea from the extreme north-easterly point of Cyprus in an easterly direction would come to the coast and to the "White Harbour", which today has lost all its lustre and importance. Eight miles to the south lies the town of Latakia, the Laodicea of antiquity.

Cape and harbour were discovered by archaeology barely thirty years ago. But in this short space of time they have become famous and have opened to science a series of surprising prospects. One of these surprises was the discovery of a new writing.

In March 1928 a peasant, while tilling his fields at "Cape Fennel", found by chance a vaulted subterranean cave. The news soon spread that in this tomb a number of valuable objects had been found, and the report came to the ears of the Governor of the Alaouites, in which Râs Shamra lies. The latter informed the French authorities at Beirut, and the director of the French Archaeological works in Syria and Lebanon, Professor Charles Virolleaud, left in haste with one of his assistants for the scene of the discovery; there the two scholars brought to light a certain number of ceramic fragments which they called in the well-known archaeologist, Maurice Dunand, to identify. The result left no doubts: they were Cypriote and Mycenaean vases of the 13th and 12th centuries B.C.

Were they important wares? It was easy to conjecture that they had arrived by the White Harbour. Minet-el-Beida must have been an important intermediate port carrying on an active trade with Cyprus and the Aegean. Convinced of this, Dunand persuaded the Academy of Inscriptions to send an expedition to Minet-el-Beida and Râs Shamra. The excavations began in 1929 under the direction of C. A. F. Schaeffer and G. Chenet and are still in progress today. They can be considered as one of the most rewarding archaeological undertakings of our age. They have provided a host of unexpected and lucid information on a new colony of antiquity Râs Shamra: the ancient Ugarit, whose name and existence the Tell-el-Amarna Letters had revealed. New indications on ancient Syria had certainly been anticipated, but not these sensational discoveries, for this region had been comparatively well explored. Disappointed so far, the excavators saw themselves richly rewarded in another quarter: their finds spoke a crystal-clear language. In this northern Syria town, once flourishing and prosperous, foreign influences had a lasting effect on the Syrian character; and the important and obvious Egyptian strain was still dominated by Aegean influences, and the excavations soon revealed the presence of an Aegean colony.

The earliest stratum went back to the third millennium B.C.; the second stratum (20th–16th century B.C.) revealed beneath the great temple of Râs Shamra an ancient necropolis; the absence of pottery among the artifacts found in the tombs suggested that at this epoch it had not known the cultural influence of the large neighbouring isle. The upper stratum (from the 14th–12th century B.C.) was even more eloquent. On the site of the ancient necropolis had been erected a large temple which was discovered in 1929. It had at first been mistaken for a royal palace: traces of burning showed that it had perished in the flames already in antiquity. In addition to Egyptian sculptures and a votive inscription were discovered images of two local deities, the embodiment of this "cradle of civilisations", Ugarit: the erect figure of a goddess in Egyptian dress, and a well-preserved stela representing the "god with the feathered crown", the style of which could not be determined with accuracy. The god held a lance in his left hand and a sceptre in his right, which the Egyptians usually bestowed on foreign rulers (their Pharaohs carry the crook); a curious crown of feathers adorned his head; an apron and belt were round his waist; a pommelled dagger and pointed shoes, copied no doubt from the Hittite mode, completed his costume.

This sacred image undeniably bore traces of Egyptian, Syrian and Asia Minor influences, but afforded no unity of style. It could not with certainty be attributed to any of these cultures and was obviously the expression of a mixed culture. Could it not perhaps be the symbol of a fusion of civilisations of which Râs Shamra had been the centre? This theory was confirmed by another find which fell into the hands of the excavators in 1932: the Baal of Râs Shamra, a well-preserved stela measuring at least three feet high and portraying Baal as the god of the storm. His right hand brandishes a club and in his left he holds a spear which he plunges into the ground; the shaft of the spear develops at the top into a leafy branch. The god wears a horned helmet, an apron round his waist and a long, curved scimitar, in his belt. In the small Syrian garbed figure standing in front of him one could probably recognise the dedicator, the king of some Ugaritic town.

In addition to the Egyptian, Hittite and Syrian, the Creto-Mycenaean influence is strongly visible in these sculptures. The nearby necropolis of Minet-el-Beida provided among other riches a particular jewel: the lid of an ivory pyx on which was carved a figure of the Creto-Mycenaean goddess of fertility, *pótnia thērôn.* She is depicted with bare breasts, holding ears of corn, simply dressed in a broad, wide skirt and flanked by two kids standing on their hind legs. Minet-el-Beida and Râs Shamra also possessed several large tombs of Mycenaean princes; the artifacts found in all these graves eventually provided a complete picture of the cultural influences to which Ugarit had been subjected: numerous cylinder seals, and other funereal appurtenances of Egyptian, Mesopotamian, Anatolian, Cypriote and Cretan origin along with objects of a characteristic local mixed type.

For archaeologists and general historians, but in particular for the epigraphists of the world, the soil of Râs Shamra offered at first excavation one more gift of greater significance than any previous find.

When the large temple of Râs Shamra, which was mistaken for the royal palace, was excavated in 1929 the expedition found a number of small, cell-like rooms which in a palace could have served as storerooms for provisions. This interpretation became dubious when on May 14th of the same year cuneiform tablets were discovered in a corner of one of the rooms under a pile of ashes and rubble; the excavations carried out between 1930 and 1932 having revealed the presence of a large number of cuneiform texts, this spot was recognised as the library and school of the scribes. The tablets discovered had been seriously damaged by the heat of the great fire, and had to be treated very carefully before being removed. Some of them looked familiar; they resembled the tablets from Tell-el-Amarna and bore Babylonian cuneiform signs; there were also lists of equivalent words which supported the scribes-school theory. But the majority of the tablets were to cause a far greater surprise than the discovery of the Boghaz-Keui archives twenty-two years before: they were texts written in an absolutely illegible and incomprehensible cuneiform, which had disappeared and been forgotten for more than 3,000 years.

The gods of ancient Ugarit, after showering their gifts on the 20th-century archaeologists, did even more: they offered almost at the same time a kind of key to decipher the secrets of the tablets. During this first expedition, in fact, several depots of bronze weapons were discovered, among which were five axes with inscriptions in the mysterious cuneiform.

The excavations at Râs Shamra mark a culminating point in the rich history of French archaeology. French scholars, however, did less in discovering the solution of this dark mystery, the decipherment of the Ugaritic cuneiform and language. At Beirut there were specialists who naturally took part in all the searches. But while Schaeffer and Chenet, during the second expedition, dug up and removed to safety treasure after treasure, while the cautious Virolleaud published the first cuneiform texts and prepared to publish more, at Halle on the Saale a German scholar at his work-table began to decipher the new writing and discovered independently the greater and most important part of this language.

Hans Bauer, the son of a Grasmannsdorf innkeeper near Bamberg, was born on January 16th, 1878. He attended the gymnasium at Bamberg, and after passing his exams went to the Gregorianum, the papal university at Rome, where he studied philosophy, theology, natural science and languages, without as yet bothering with oriental tongues. On his return home he was for two years administrator of Bamberg Hospital, and not until 1906 did he begin his oriental studies in Berlin, where among other teachers he knew Delitzsch, who had once taught Hrozný.

He continued with these studies at Leipzig under Zimmern, took his degree at Berlin in 1910 and his aggregation at Halle in 1912. Bauer, who in the course of his career became one of the leading specialists in Oriental languages, was a pure linguist—one of the few of his generation—guided for the most part by the historical ideological aspect of oriental investigation. His philological studies already showed him as the master of a method which was later to bring him fame as a decipherer.

He had a great talent for analogy and an almost uncanny flair for all the aspects of philology. The first of these qualities was combined with a profound taste for mathematics, and his catholic knowledge in all branches of learning, rare in a Semitist, rendered him untold service.

Well versed in astronomy and zoology, he had some knowledge of medicine and in addition an excellent grasp of medieval philosophy. He knew to perfection the principal Semitic languages (which few Semitists today can boast), read nearly all the European and numerous Far Eastern languages—Chinese, Malay, Korean, etc.—which allowed him to do comparative research in the field of semantics and to discover new analogies.

Such an extraordinary diversity of knowledge could not fail to open new paths for him. Hans Bauer's two grammars—Hebrew and Biblical-Aramaic—have not received world-wide recognition. Nevertheless, these works represented a bold step into the still-dark regions of the history of language and a new point of departure in the conception of two Semitic "times", and their development. What instinctively drove Bauer to such bold undertakings, apart from his love of analogies, was an instinct for the mysterious cogs and internal movements of a language that would not be denied. It was this urge combined with his mathematical and philological intuition which allowed him to give one of the most astonishing performances that has ever been witnessed in the history of decipherment: the "breaking" of Ugaritic cuneiform and the discovery of the language in which the inscriptions were couched. An even more remarkable scientific *tour de force* since Bauer, somewhat of a recluse, accomplished it entirely on his own.

Let us now follow his work and the successive phases of his decipherment, based on the lucid and comprehensive exposition given by himself.[66]

The expert who happened to be on the site, Charles

Virolleaud, had already noticed that the new writing contained a relatively small number of characters (at the time twenty-seven were known, but today scholars distinguish thirty and sometimes thirty-two). He deduced quite correctly that it must be an alphabetic writing: this restricted number could not apply to syllabic signs or ideograms. An alphabetic cuneiform, then, like old Persian, that final offspring of Mesopotamian cuneiform, but more than 1,000 years older and stemming from a region which passed for the motherland of all alphabets, the oldest known at the period in the Semitic sphere being Phoenician. Influenced apparently by other finds, Virolleaud classified the language of the new documents as Cypriote or possibly Mitannian, known from the El Amarna Letters. But a first glance at the tablets immediately gave Bauer the impression that it must be a Semitic language. He accepted this hypothesis as a principle (although it was no more likely than a dozen others), and fortune smiled upon him. On April 27th, 1930, after a few days' work, he had succeeded almost on his own, without bilingual texts, in deciphering the writing, although he had only that month seen the first texts published by Virolleaud.

Bauer's method clearly reveals the happy conjunction already mentioned of his mathematical talents and his wide linguistic knowledge.

Postulating *a priori* that the unknown script must conceal a Semitic language, he applied the Semitic structural laws to the texts before him.

The only landmark which could be of aid to him was a word separator represented by a vertical wedge. In the space between two of these separators Bauer often found a single cuneiform sign. He thought that this must apply to words of a particularly common letter in Semitic, since that language, as we know, employs no written vowels and only consonants. The purely outward aspect of the script gave him a second hint: the word-separators obviously indicated the beginning and end of words; but at the beginning and end of Semitic words were prefixes and suffixes. This, then, was Bauer's reasoning: in West Semitic the prefixes could only be the letters *alef* (explosive guttural before vowels) j, m, n and t and sometimes b, h, k, l and w; the suffixes the letters h, k, m, n and t and eventually w and j; the single-letter words l and m, sometimes also b, k and w! Thus certain well-determined cuneiform signs—those at the end or beginning of words or isolated between word separators—should correspond to the phonetic values which we have just enumerated. Bauer was now in a position to approach the actual reading. In his attempt he used an extremely simple and well-tried method—an examination of sign frequency.

He collected in columns the phonetic values which, according to his reasoning, corresponded to certain determined signs and obtained the following picture. In Semitic we find:

As prefixes	As suffixes	As single letter words
I	II	III
Aleph	h	l
j	k	m
m	m	(b)
n	n	(k)
t	t	(w)
(b)	(w)	
(h)	(j)	
(k)		
(l)		
(w)		

By means of this picture Bauer carefully studied the frequency of the various signs in the texts. He noticed that in the three categories quoted above two particular characters constantly occurred. He therefore looked in the table of signs usable in the three categories and found three: the "k", the "m" and the "w". He immediately crossed out the "k", which is rare in Semitic; there remained, therefore, the "m" and the "w".

Scrutiny of the texts showed that two more very frequent signs, simple and triple horizontal "nails", appeared to be prefixes and suffixes but not single-letter words; they must therefore figure in column I or II and not in column III; these conditions, as we can see, were fulfilled by the "n" and the "t". Let us remember that Bauer, arriving at this point of his demonstration, still did not know which was the "m" and which the "w", just as he could not distinguish between the "n" and the "t". His table offered him two pairs of signs—a double alternative. But four signs were not so limited that each of them now afforded only two possibilities. This greatly facilitated the work of the decipherer.

Charles Virolleaud had noticed that a group of six characters engraved on several bronze axes recurred at the start of a cuneiform tablet, but preceded by another letter. He concluded that the group of signs on the axe represented a proper name and the cuneiform tablet the opening of a letter addressed to this same person, the first isolated letter representing the preposition used as a form of address before the name of the recipient; the signs therefore corresponded to the Akkadian preposition *ana* (English: to).

Hans Bauer knew how to take advantage of this clue. In West Semitic, he said to himself, the preposition "l" corresponds to the Akkadian (East Semitic) preposition *ana*; the sign placed at the beginning of the above mentioned letter could, therefore, only be the letter "l".

Strong in the knowledge of the "l" and of his double alternative, Bauer, the mathematician, worked out what could be called a "table of probabilities" and an equation with one unknown quantity. The calculation of probabilities was born of a reflection which for a Semitist was obvious but may give the layman an idea of certain advantages of Semitic writing, which in other respects is very defective. Bauer looked for the word which would be most likely to figure in the texts, the word "king", in Semitic *mlk*, which we shall meet again in our chapter on the Cypriote syllabary. He started with the first of his two alternatives for "m". He then came across in the text a word the reading of which in his opinion gave "ml" + an unknown sign, which, following his favourite method, he called "x". Was "x" in fact "k" and the word in question the sought for *mlk* or "king"? The hypothesis became a certainty when, a little farther on in the text, he found the form *mlxx*, which must obviously correspond to the word *mlkk*, "thy king". Bauer was now convinced that he had discovered the "k" and now definitely established the "m".[67]

Bauer continued his search for words whose presence in the text seemed to be the most probable. His next objective was "son". After long and fruitless efforts he finally discovered on a tablet presumably containing a list of names two signs repeated fifteen times without word separators in front of other different groups of signs. Obviously names. The second of these two signs, a triple horizontal "nail" in his eyes, no longer represented an unknown quantity but must be, according to his table, "t" or "n"; the first seemed to be a single-letter word—a glance at column III confirmed that it was a "b". Bauer had discovered the word "son" and established the letters "b" and "n".

At this stage of the decipherment we see that the scholar "had scented the game"; now he laid a trap to catch the next letter. Bauer had been particularly lucky with his "b"; where there was a "b" and an "l", Baal could not be far away. The word comprises three consonants in Semitic because the epiglottic explosive *ayin*, often written "'" is also considered as a consonant. Therefore "b-x-l", this was the series of the letters forecast by Bauer. He found them on a small tablet not once but seven times. The *ayin* had been established.

With the aid of similar observations Bauer in his initial work was able to establish the correct value of seventeen signs. He believed that he had pinpointed twenty for certain and a probable five more; two signs he decided had to be left in abeyance on account of their rarity. As he himself stressed, the progress of his work was naturally not as quick as it sounded when related later in cold print. It is obvious that this intellectual *tour de force* realised in a few days could not be attributed to pure luck: it was in actual fact the fruit of twenty years' constant preoccupation with problems of writing. But it is interesting and very instructive to see Bauer at work, at the moment he had made a mistake.

In establishing the table illustrated on p. 209, which groups the characters in their category of prefixes, suffixes or single-letter words, Bauer had been mistaken on one point. The scribes of antiquity had unwittingly played a trick on him by juxtaposing a single letter word without a word-divider to the preceding word, so that Bauer, taking it for a suffix, classified it wrongly in column II of his table and gave it a wrong value. This naturally led to several more mistakes.

Secondly, the bronze axes, the key to the decipherment, the gift bestowed by the Ugaritic deities and used as such by Bauer, were also perfidious, and two of them proved fatal to the scholar. We reproduce them here not only to illustrate his error but because this picture will enable the reader, letter by letter, to decipher an original text in Ugaritic cuneiform.

The left-hand axe has in all six cuneiform characters; the example on the right has the same signs preceded (above) by four others. Anyone who takes the trouble to find the six characters of the left-hand axe on the right-hand one will have some idea of how difficult it is to read the simplest cuneiform. Hans Bauer suspected in this group of six signs, common to both axes, the name of their owner, and concluded, not without reason, that the group of four signs preceding the "name" on the right-hand axe represented the word "axe" itself. He drew this conclusion methodically from the parallelism between the inscription and the object "written" already used with success by

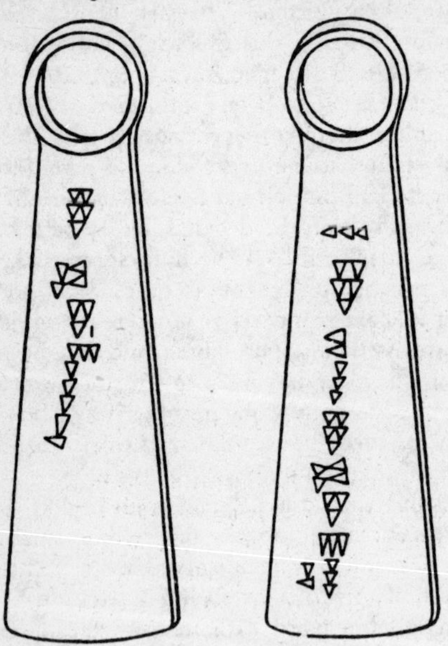

FIG. 64.—Engraved Axes from Ugarit.

Emil Forrer in the decipherment of Hittite Hieroglyphics. One of the four signs which according to Bauer's theory must signify "axe" was already known. If we turn the picture 90° to the left and lay it on its left side, the inscription being written from left to right, it is sign No. 4, the triple horizontal "nail" = n. Bauer had already discovered from other analogies that the sign No. 2 = r. We can understand therefore that he was convinced that he had before him the Hebrew word *garzen*, "axe", written in Semitic *grzn*, thus allowing him to identify the still-unknown signs Nos. 1 and 3 as "g" and "z". He applied these values to other groups of signs and plunged ever deeper into his error.

Later works on this alphabet have shown in fact that Ugaritic is an autonomous Semitic dialect not identical with but very closely related to Hebrew. The Ugaritic word for axe is not *grzn* but *ḫrṣn*; the complete inscription of the right-hand axe reads: *ḫrṣn rb khnm*, i.e. "the axe of the high priest", and that of the left hand the shorter *rb khnm*, "high priest". An attentive reading of the two texts reveals in the word *rb* an old friend, the "Rabbi".

Having obtained these results by the end of April 1930, Hans Bauer published in the June supplement of the *Vossische Zeitung* an introduction to his decipherment giving the translation of four letters, *alef*, "t", "r" and "n", readings of the names of the deities Ashera, Astarte and Baal, the divine titles El and Eloah and the adjectival numbers three and four. He had already noticed the presence of two signs for *alef*. In *Forschungen und Fortschritte* of August 20th, 1930, appeared an exposition of his decipherment method designed to reach a wide public, and at the beginning of October 1930 his first important work: *The Decipherment of the Cuneiform Tablet of Râs Shamra*. This work contains a complete transliteration of the known texts, interpreted according to his alphabet, which is partially incorrect, as we have seen, as well as an *Important Supplement*. Important because it represents the second stage of the decipherment, the decisive stage of the inevitable corrections made to Bauer's original system and an account of further knowledge acquired.

Before the appearance in the *Vossische Zeitung* of his introduction: "The Decipherment of a New Cuneiform Language," Professor Bauer had informed René Dussaud, Keeper of Oriental Antiquities at the Louvre and editor of the Oriental review *Syria*, in which the Ugaritic texts had appeared, that he had accomplished the theoretical decipherment of the texts, and later acquainted him with the essential results of his work. The latter were reported and approved by René Dussaud at a session of the Academy of Inscriptions shortly after the introduction appeared in the *Vossische Zeitung*. This article also fell into the hands of Edouard Dhorme, professor at the École Biblique et Archéologique Française in Jerusalem. To check the phonetic values established by Bauer, Dhorme had at his disposal not only his vast specialised knowledge but also the practical experience he had acquired as a decoder during the First World War.

He managed to raise to twenty the number of signs known, eliminating Bauer's unfortunate errors. The way in which he corrected his colleague's results shows his tact in scientific matters. Dhorme placed at the disposal of the Halle scholar the proofs of the article which was to appear in the *Revue Biblique*, and thus Bauer was able to add to his book, which was already in the press, the *Important Supplement* quoted above, in which he incorporated the new values and readings discovered by Dhorme. The Frenchman's work and the knowledge obtained in the interval by Bauer himself resulted in the latter's alphabet, known as the "5th October alphabet 1930", which already contained twenty-five accurately established signs. In a bare six months Hans Bauer and Edouard Dhorme had completed the essentials of the decipherment, merely from the meagre texts published to date (1929), lists of little linguistic interest.[68]

Theoretically, the decipherment was now a *fait accompli*. Certain values remained to be discovered and others to be clarified. This embellishment was to be the work of the scholar who had published the texts, Professor Jean Charles Virolleaud, whom we have already quoted in this book on several occasions.

Virolleaud was born on July 2nd, 1879, at Barbezieux, Charente. Future *docteur ès lettres* and *Directeur d'Études* at the *École pratique des hautes Études* of the Sorbonne, he had been interested in Oriental languages from his earliest youth; he had studied Arabic and Persian, the history, geography and archaeology of the Ancient Orient, carried out research work in the Constantinople Museum, travelled in Asia Minor and Persia, and on October 1st, 1920, was appointed Director of Archaeological Works in Syria and the Lebanon. Showing great activity in this capacity, he organised all the archaeological missions despatched during his term of office in that part of the Levant then under French mandate, and made a number of important contributions to the ancient history of the Near East. It was also to his initiative that we owe the creation of several museums, including that of Damascus and Aleppo, which have themselves become active centres of research.

In the course of the second excavations at Ugarit in the spring of 1930, C. F. A. Schaeffer and C. Chenet discovered a number of new clay tablets which surpassed in value the finds of the previous year. It was no longer a question of further incomplete lists, but of long narrative texts, which enabled the

decipherment to be completed. Virolleaud gave the Râs Shamra alphabet its definitive form. When he presented his preliminary reports within the framework of a full account of

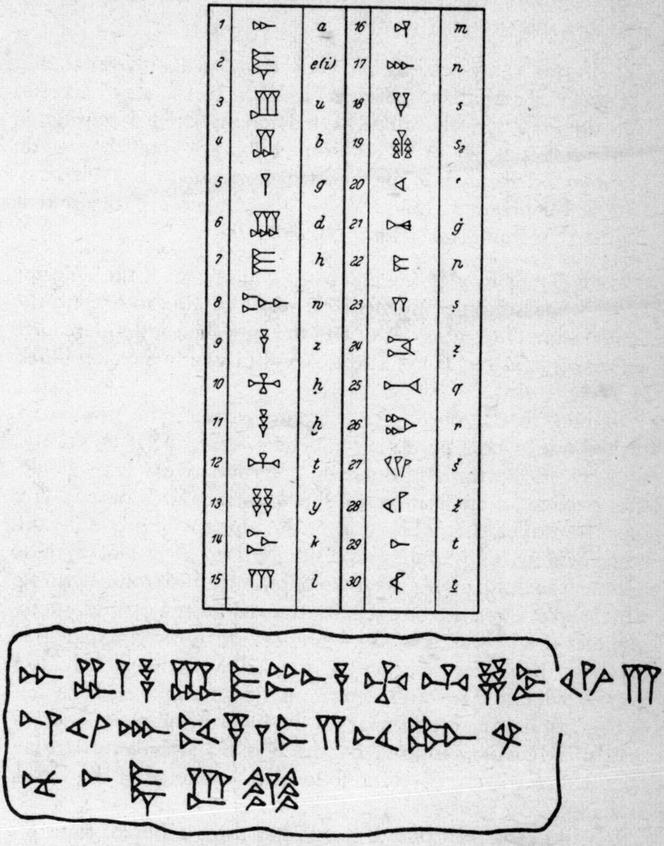

1	a	16	m
2	e(i)	17	n
3	u	18	s
4	b	19	s_2
5	g	20	ʿ
6	d	21	ġ
7	h	22	p
8	w	23	ṣ
9	z	24	ẓ
10	ḥ	25	q
11	ḫ	26	r
12	ṭ	27	ś
13	y	28	ƶ
14	k	29	t
15	l	30	ṯ

FIG. 65.—The alphabet of Râs Shamra.
Above: as modern research sees it.
Below: as it appears on a clay tablet from Ugarit.

his work,[69] he had added to the work of Bauer and Dhorme, the determination of the sign "z" and also a third sign for *alef*. From now on complete light had been thrown on the nature and structure of the writing.

The progress of Virolleaud's studies shows us clearly the type of man he was. It is here that we must look for the secret cells of his work, for the key to his personality. When questioned on his early beginnings and the driving force behind his work and activities, he wrote:

> "As far as my profession is concerned I will only say that at the age of seventeen I decided to learn Hebrew. I had read in the *Pensées* of Blaise Pascal this maxim which I considered and still consider to be sublime: 'I think it good that we do not go too deeply into the theory of Copernicus: but this . . .!' It is important to one's whole life to know if the soul is mortal or immortal.' *Pascal III*, 218."[70]

Hans Bauer lived to see his work triumph with the Dhorme and Virolleaud amendments. He was also able to help in the exploitation of his discoveries and to assess their full significance before his death at Halle at the age of fifty-nine after an illness of a few weeks.

Similar to the north-west Semitic writing, the new script turned out to be a purely alphabetic system; it has no syllabic signs, no ideograms and not even determinatives. Like the entire particular civilisation of the Ugaritic kingdom, it is a mixed product, a combination of the alphabetic principle and cuneiform writing similar to Old Persian; it is also akin to another no less interesting mixed product—Meroitic writing, which, like Ugaritic, uses as an outward form Egyptian hieroglyphics originally alien to its essence and to its language. In creating their new writing Ugarit and Meroe rejected ideograms, syllabic signs and determinatives, using the characters of the original pictorial script on the inner principle of another system—Ugaritic, inspired by the Semitic alphabetic writing denuded of vowels, Meroitic following the model of the Greek alphabet.

It will be noticed that Ugaritic has three different signs for the letter *alef*, according to whether it comes before "a", "e" and "i" or before "u", as the tables of Fig. 65 show. A strange phenomenon which gave rise to a series of hypotheses on the origin of this singular alphabet.

In 1935 Hans Jensen considered that the problem of the origin of Ugaritic cuneiform had not yet been solved. No great advance seems to have been reached today. Investigators have considered Ugaritic from several angles: as an imitation or development of the northern Semitic alphabet, of the so-called Sinaitic writing, or even as the simplification and reduction of the Babylonian syllabic signs. All these attempts can be considered as failures. Another more plausible theory is meeting with great approval today: that the Râs Shamra cuneiform script is not an inherited and adapted system but a free creation, the autonomous invention of a man who, while knowing the north Semitic alphabet (whence the principle of alphabetic writing without vowels, cf. Fig. 65), was used to writing with the aid of a sharpened reed on wet clay tablets. The use of this material, unsuitable for reproducing a linear script, forced him to adopt cuneiform characters. Since the script includes three different signs for the letter *alef*, and since, furthermore, tablets have been discovered at Râs Shamra written in Hurrian, a language hardly known at the period, even Hans Bauer concluded a non-Semitic origin.

The finds at Râs Shamra have provided a host of new information in the political, historical, artistic, economic, epigraphic and linguistic fields. Thanks to these documents we have today a precise picture of a royal city of northern Syria about 1500 B.C. A rich and flourishing community, relatively independent, although under Egyptian domination about 1200 B.C. it fell a victim to the "Peoples of the Sea", the invaders from the north-west. We know that its precious and often-refined works of art bore traces of Cypriote, Mycenaean, Hittite and Babylonian influence. The city was an important centre on the trade route from west to east, from the Aegean via Cyprus to the Euphrates and beyond. Here was discovered a new cuneiform alphabet, the origin of which still remains a mystery today. To this must be added a new language possessing its own features, although it was closely related to all the other known Semitic languages.

The discoveries at Râs Shamra constituted an inestimable addition to the history of religion. Texts were brought to light referring to the cult, the gods and sacrifices, purification rites and lists of sanctuaries. Another group of tablets contained lengthy epic texts relating to the battles of the gods, the birth of the gods' children, etc.; the results of these finds threw a completely new light on the Phoenico-Aramaic religion of northern Syria in the second millennium B.C. and on the land of Canaan, the cradle of the Israelite religion. The elements collected were of a magnitude and depth hitherto unknown. Divine epithets used in the Old Testament were found here as genuine names of gods; references to fertility gods dying and being resurrected, types familiar in Greek mythology; certain documents seemed to authorise new conclusions as to the origin of the Râs Shamra gods and the Homeric Pantheon—an unexpected confirmation of the old tradition which insists upon the profound influence exercised by the birth of the world and of the gods in the mythology of the ancient Phoenicians on that of the Greeks. These texts in fact corroborated the reality of a sentiment, very precious to religious historians: the nostalgia for a transcendental conception of the deity, of the "god in himself". Sayce had foreseen this revelation when he cried on his deathbed: "When is Virolleaud going to publish the new Râs Shamra texts?"

The extract from the myth of Mot and Alijan, the son of Baal, which we give here as an example of Ugaritic literature, naturally contains nothing of that eternal human nostalgia, but by the power of its words, the vigour of expression and its undeniable poetic charm it gives a glimpse into the religious epic of the north-west Semites of antiquity and at the same time into a fragment of their most ancient cultural heritage:

The days sped by,
The love of Anat overwhelmed her.
As the heart of an antelope for her fawn,
As the heart of an ewe for her lamb,
So was the heart of Anat for Baal.
She seized Mot. . . .
Raising her voice she cried:
'O Mot, render (me) my brother!'
And Mot son of the gods replied:
'What would you, O virgin Anat?'
The days sped by . . .
As the heart of an antelope for her fawn,
As the heart of an ewe for her lamb,
So was the heart of Anat for Baal.
Anat seized Mot, the son of the god
With her sword she cleft him
With a flail she threshed him

With a fire she grilled him
With a mill she ground him;
She scattered his body in a field
That the birds might devour it . . .

Here there are lacunae, and the text becomes difficult to read. The ensuing columns tell us that Alijan Baal reappears, but that Mot, his adversary, also returned to life in spite of the cruel death inflicted upon him by Anat.

Mot is powerful, Baal is powerful!
They charge like the wild bulls.
Mot is powerful, Baal is powerful!
They bite each other like serpents.
Mot is powerful, Baal is powerful!
They kick each other like horses.
Mot cries, Baal cries!
Sopas calls the halt which condemns Mot:
Now Shor-El thy father hears thee not!
Verily he will tear the door hinges from thy dwelling;
He will overthrow thy kingly throne
And break the sceptre of thy sovereignty.[71]

Now we come to another scientific performance which was accomplished alone and unaided, to the third investigator who contributed to the decipherment of Ugaritic—Edouard Dhorme.

A specialist in comparative philology, Dhorme from his schooldays was fascinated by words. He adored Latin and Greek, dead languages, which for him were vivid and capable of new life; but in addition to them—and this feature characterised the future scholar—the living language, English, and above all German exercised a great attraction for him.

The end of the century also marked a turning point in the young man's career. He was born on January 15th, 1881, at Armentières. After completing his wide linguistic studies he was appointed to the *École Biblique* at Jerusalem. He embarked upon an active career as teacher and investigator, devoting himself in particular to the Semitic languages—Hebrew, Aramaic, Arabic—and to the study of Babylonian, Assyrian and Sumerian cuneiform texts. Among his principal works which appeared at this period we must quote his *Choix de textes assyro-babyloniens*, 1907.

His personal tastes as well as his professorship at the École Biblique opened up a wide new field for Dhorme; biblical studies. The exegesis of the Old Testament above all encouraged him to study in detail the scripts as well as the Semitic languages. The result of his researches appeared in his well-known book *Langues et écritures sémitiques*, 1930.

The scope of these works reveals a mastery of all the fields relative and ancillary to comparative philology. Edouard Dhorme could call upon his wide experience as an archaeologist and excavator in Palestine, Cisjordania and Transjordania, Egypt, Sinai and the Lebanon as well as the Tigris and Euphrates basins.

To this must be added another type of training which, even if at first sight it does not seem to be connected with philology and archaeology, nevertheless represents for the decipherer of ancient unknown writings a kind of special training. After his return from the French expedition of the Dardanelles and Macedonia during the First World War, Dhorme was employed on a task admirably suited to his talents: the decoding of intercepted enemy messages in cipher. He himself insists today that this activity was of great help to him later in his decipherment of unknown languages.[72]

At the end of his professional term at Jerusalem, Dhorme taught at the *École pratique des hautes Études* at the Sorbonne (where we have already met another professor, Charles Virolleaud) and from 1945 at the Collège de France.

We have followed the rapid and brilliant successes of Dhorme, the Orientalist, and seen how, in addition, he revealed himself to be a great decipherer when the French excavations at Râs Shamra in 1929 brought to light unknown cuneiform writings. He was also present when the explorers on the site of ancient Byblos found a number of treasures of consummate interest—two stelae, two bronze tablets, several spatulae and fragments also covered with hitherto unknown signs. This time it was not cuneiform scripts but signs which bore a certain resemblance to Egyptian hieroglyphs, as a result of which it was given the ill-chosen name of "pseudo-hieroglyphic writing of Byblos".

Byblos was one of the main cultural centres in ancient Phoenicia. But the name Byblos, borrowed by the Greeks from the word which in their language meant "paper", is of more recent date than the town itself; the Greeks imported Egyptian paper from this important trading centre. As the city originally bore the Old Semitic name of Gubla (in Hebrew Gebal, today Jebeil), it is possible that the assonance bublos-Gubla contributed to this new name. From Gubla is also derived the term "gublitic writing" given to it by the Bonn Semitist, Anton Jirku, which is preferable to "pseudo-hieroglyphic" or "Proto-Byblic".

The finds from Byblos, a city to which we already owed the oldest inscriptions in Phoenician alphabetic writing dating from *circa* 1000 B.C., were collated and published by the archaeologist, Maurice Dunand, in his book *Byblia Grammata* (Beirut 1945). A year later Dhorme presented to the French Academy of Inscriptions (August and September 1946), and in the Review *Syria* (25, 1946–48) the completed decipherment.

Dhorme had started from a premise and an observation. The premise consisted in presuming the inscriptions to be in the Phoenician language—not without reason, since our knowledge of the history of Gubla-Byblos forbids us seeing any extra-Semitic linguistic influence. The observation was the result of the use of a basic rule of all decipherment which, as we have seen, has been applied on many occasions. Dhorme recognised slightly more than seventy signs (excluding variants) and concluded a syllabic writing—the number 70 being obviously too high for an alphabetic and too few for an ideographic script.

He did not try to identify the phonetic values of this presumed syllabary; if his suppositions that it stemmed from a Phoenician language were correct the reading would be a *fait accompli* as soon as he had established the simple consonantic skeleton of the text. Although he reckoned on syllabic signs (of the type consonant + vowel, ba, bi, bu, but also vowel + consonant, ab, ib, ub) he was quite content for the moment to study the consonants inherent in each of these signs, since all Semitic languages are read, as we know, solely by the aid of consonants. Strong in this reasoning, Dhorme next grouped the signs so that there was no longer question of bi, ba, bu or mi, ma, mu, etc., but only b, b^1, b^2. In this way was born the glossary in Fig. 67.

Let us now turn to the actual process of decipherment, a perfect illustration of the story of Columbus's egg. To follow

(a)

(b)

Fig. 66.—(a) Stone stela with Gublitic inscriptions.
(b) Bronze tablet with Gublitic writing: *above* recto; *below* verso.

Fig. 67.—Glossary of Gublitic characters.

[1] l and l_2 are perhaps the same sign.

Dhorme's reasoning, let us take the verso of the bronze tablet which served as his point of departure (Fig. 68). On the extreme left of the picture will be noticed the seven 1's which caught his trained eye. The scholar immediately translated this as seven times 1 = 7!

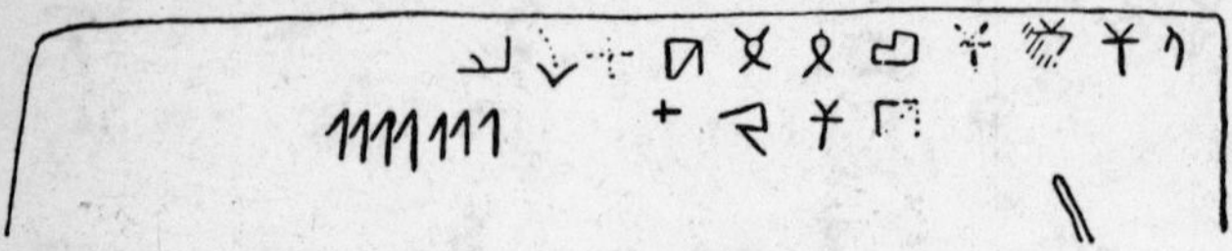

FIG. 68.—Verso of the Byblos bronze tablet.

He therefore considered these seven strokes aligned to be the number 7. But could this 7 possibly conceal a date?

Before the number 7 (i.e., on the right, since the inscription reads from right to left) stood the four signs 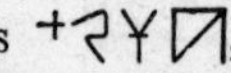, the first of which  on the extreme right is a form of "b", as we know from earlier chapters. Dhorme reflected: could this be an indication of a date? "In the year" would then be represented by the four consonants b-šnt; this made four signs of which the first could be a "b" preceded by the number. The group 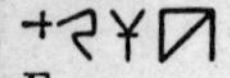 might correspond to tnš-b or its palindrome b-šnt. Four new consonants won!

Provisionally Dhorme accepted these four values as a point of departure and sought confirmation of his theory. In the same inscription he met a series of signs n-x-š. From his wide experience a further reflection struck him, which had struck Forrer during his decipherment of Hittite hieroglyphs: the parallelism between the content of the inscription and the written object. The text was engraved on a bronze tablet and there is a Semitic word nḥš for bronze or copper. Dhorme accepted this as a new value "ḥ", which soon helped him to read the word mzbḥ, "altar". The "m" discovered in this way was to prove very useful and to bring confirmation; thanks to it he discovered in line 14 (the first line of the verso, the second line, 15, of which contains as we have shown the date) the indication of the month b-tmz, "in the month of Tammuz". This gave him for z a second sign now classified as z_1.

The year and the month were known, so why should not the day be there in the form of a numeral?

Let us look once more at line 14; the four last signs on the extreme left, [glyphs], are composed, as we know today and can check by Fig. 67, of the consonants z_1, mt-b, or according to modern transliteration b-tmz[1], "in the month of Tammuz". There was every reason to suppose that the sign placed in front on the right concealed the numeral in question.

Before the two successive notations of the sign Y, already identified as "š" according to the last line, separated by a sign as yet not known, Dhorme, the expert Semitist, did not have to hesitate long; he translated it at once: šdš, six(th) and looked beyond this group—i.e. to his left—for the word jm-m, "day", whereby two signs slightly different from each other came to light as "m". The date on this verso then was: b-šdš jm-m b-tmz[1], b-šnt 7, in other words "the sixth day of Tammuz in the seventh year"!

We can guess how delighted he must have been.

> "My finest moments were when I had recognised a Phoenician alphabetic script in the Râs Shamra texts and a Phoenician syllabary in the 'pseudo-hieroglyphic' inscriptions from Byblos. But how many sleepless nights I spent during the period of decipherment before I had solved it." [73]

Dhorme still had to verify a host of details, and to make corrections before he could present his results to the Academie des Inscriptions on August 2nd, 1946. In his article "*Déchiffrement des inscriptions pseudo-hiéroglyphiques de Byblos*" [74] he produced convincing readings of all the documents published by Dunand the preceding year, and gave weight to his argument. One of the most persuasive of these is the simple content of the first deciphered inscription (Fig. 66). It treated neither of kings, warlike deeds nor of good works. Had this been the case would not the decipherer have been suspected of having invented such plausible contents, even if with the best will in the world he had deceived himself? Nothing of the kind in Dhorme's inscription: it was the report of the engraver on his own work and that of his colleagues decorating the temple—a theme *a priori* so unexpected that no decipherer could possibly be suspected of having invented it.

A second convincing proof: thanks to the reading of the first bronze tablet inscription, he was able to read the far longer one on the second bronze plaque, which provided a similar tale.

Thirdly, this last inscription contained a stupefying number of Egyptian names of deities—a fact which the decipherer could certainly not have anticipated when he began his work. To support his results he gave a series of philological, and in particular grammatical reasons, with which we shall not bother.

We can accept with all confidence the picture of this script as Dhorme discovered and outlined it. Gublitic writing is still not a perfect instrument, and this can easily be explained by its very character. Its inventor (the monuments date from 1900–1700 B.C.) undoubtedly had in mind, as Dhorme shows, Assyro-Babylonian cuneiform script—hence the syllabary; it is imperfect because the original syllabic signs, conforming to the Semitic character of the language, were soon difficult to distinguish strictly from each other and were often used at random, merely with regard to the consonants they contained—a state of affairs which the table of graphic signs reflects (Fig. 67) with their many consonantal variants.

We have presented in this book, borrowed from languages and literatures which have become available thanks to decipherment, certain examples which typify the language and the people. Others which, thanks to their universal human message, are capable of moving the modern reader; in some cases they play a dual role. Sovereigns' decrees and prayers, sacred myths and prophecies echo down the years. Let us listen in the name of ancient Gubla to the voice of the good workman who, happy to have completed his task, consigns to a bronze tablet the tale of his efforts, without suspecting that it would be rediscovered 4,000 years later and would become the key to the decipherment of this primitive writing which vanished at such an early date.

These are the words of Lilu: I have rolled the copper of Tophet.
With the point (= the tooth) of iron I have engraved
These objects (or these vases). The key to
the temple, Ikarrenu has engraved with signs
and he has written its name (of the temple) Aton-Yahaki.
The crown of orichalc of the altar I have engraved.
This work Lilu has done for the honour of his family . . .
I did this in the time of the governor Ipush,
The sixth day of Tammuz
In the seventh year.[75]

CHAPTER VII

OF GODS AND PRINCES OF COMMERCE

THE DECIPHERMENT OF THE CYPRIOTE SYLLABARY

"*One of the most brilliant discoveries of modern times.*"
—Moritz Schmidt on Johannes Brandis' decipherment work.

"THE bill for the torches was the business of Zovar . . ., Megalotheos and Philodamos; that of the collections the business of Zovoros and Aphrodisios."

This phrase can be read on a votive inscription from northern Cyprus dating from the 5th century B.C. It shows that at this period, or perhaps even earlier, the inhabitants of the island already knew how to calculate coldly; other finds have taught us that Cyprus, already populated in the third millennium B.C., kept up active trade relations with Egypt and Palestine. It was "the great metallurgical centre of the ancient world" (Diringer), an object of envy, the bastion of Asia Minor and Syria in the Mediterranean, a few days' sail from Egypt and Crete. At the turn of the second millennium B.C. the Greeks set foot on Cyprus (Kupros, as they called it), but not as armed conquerors. Their peaceful penetration naturally caused a progressive decline in the autochthonous art and civilisation. Its situation at the crossroads of three main cultural centres—Asia, Syria-Palestine and Egypt—resulted in the island having a very lively history; the feet of the foreign sovereigns never ceased to tread the soil of this ancient civilisation. To the south, where the mountain chain falls gently to the sea, leaving room in the plains for important urban settlements, the Phoenician colonists settled at the beginning of the first millennium. Then at the end of the 8th century came the Assyrian domination. Cyprus beheld the arrival and departure of the Persians, and Macedonians; the Romans and later the Byzantines governed her, and among her rulers was also Richard Coeur de Lion; an Englishman ruled the island centuries before his descendants in 1878 leased it to the Turks, to whom it had belonged for more than 300 years, to protect the Suez Canal and the route to India, and finally annexed it in 1913. But the Greeks knew how to preserve the

Hellenic character of Cyprus, as another monument testifies—a monument which played a decisive role in the history of the decipherment of the Cypriote syllabary: a bilingual votive inscription in Phoenician and Greek stemming, in the 4th century B.C., from a Phoenician noble in the reign of a local Phoenician king. The Greek version was written in Cypriote syllabic script, and we now possessed the coveted bilingual document, the key to the decipherment.

It seems incredible that in Cyprus, with its restless history, apart from a number of antique treasures, no inscriptions, coins or medals engraved with this curious script had been brought to light before 1850. The British were reproached for having done very little as regards the historical exploration of the island. This reproach, as will be seen, was hardly justified.

The first explorer of the island was in any case not an Englishman. Nor was he a Cypriote, Greek or Turk, but a Frenchman. Honoré Theodore Paul Joseph d'Albert, Duc de Luynes (1802–67), archaeologist and numismatist of repute, lived for many years in Naples and often visited Rome in 1825 when his friend, Champollion, was in Italy. He evinced great interest in Champollion's work. It is probable that from these meetings the Duke's enduring interest was aroused. He was furthermore a brilliant artist, and the penetrating eye of the artist has its advantages when it is a question of studying graphic forms. A number of decipherers have been excellent artists.

The Duc de Luynes was the first to draw the world's attention to the remains of Cypriote writing. In 1852 he published at Paris his work *Numismatique et inscriptions chypriotes*, in which he had conscientiously assembled all the existing documents. This collection contains a certain number of coins and inscriptions, one of which became a kind of scientific Waterloo for the scholar. It was an inscription of thirty-one lines engraved in bronze unearthed at ancient Edalion. Since in his work he had given an index of all the known graphic signs, the comparative length of the text encouraged him to ask the German investigator, Röth, to try his hand at deciphering it. The German was only too pleased to do so. But he did not hesitate to break all the laws: he set to work without even knowing the writing or the language of the documents which had been sent to him. The result of his work is one of those "scientific curiosities", as the German numismatist, Brandis, charitably remarked.

Röth, who naturally knew of the Phoenician period in Cypriote history, thought that he could determine the phonetic value of the fifty odd signs correlating them with the twenty-two letters of the Phoenician alphabet. By this purely external comparison he obtained words in which he purported to recognise Semitic forms. His translation—again we quote Brandis—"made a mockery of all human intelligence"[76] and has often served as a warning to posterity.

In the meantime the activity of the Italian collector, Palma de Cesnola, who lived in Cyprus from 1865 as United States Consul, had produced a rich harvest of new finds (35,000 items), which are today in the Fine Arts Museum at Boston; and another diplomat, R. H. Lang, at that time British Consul at Larnaka, discovered at Edalion the bilingual votive inscription in Phoenician and Cypriote, quoted above. Although incomplete it served as a good basis for the decipherment.

Lang's scientific podium was the *Proceedings of the Biblical Archaeological Society* of London. George Smith, one of the leading lights of the Society (as we know his name is closely associated with the investigations into cuneiform), took the greatest interest in the new discoveries. Smith never denied the scientific training he had received from Rawlinson; he attacked the bilingual Phoenico-Cypriote inscription in the same way as his teacher had approached the Persian text of the Behistun rock inscriptions.

He looked for groups of signs liable to contain proper names. Lang thought he had recognised in a certain group the name and title of King Milkjaton. The Phoenician version provided the name itself. Fig. 69 shows it, greatly damaged, but gives some idea of the content of the missing portion, thanks to analogous and contemporary inscriptions of the same King. Now the Phoenician version says that the noble Phoenician Baalram, son of Abdimilk, in the year 4 of King Milkjaton, King of Citium and Edalion, dedicated a statue in gratitude to his god Reshep of *mkl* (Apollo of *Amyklai*). It provided, therefore, the proper names of Milkjaton, Edalion and Citium. Smith next compared the phonetic values of the groups of Phoenician letters with the Cypriote groups in which he suspected proper names. The number of fifty-five signs eliminated the possibility of an alphabetic in favour of a syllabic script. Thanks to his wide experience of cuneiform, Smith was convinced of this. He soon found the syllable *li* (≤) of the word Milkjaton (*mi-li-ki-ja-to-no-se* according to the Cypriote writing, the genitive of the proper name) again in *e-ta-li-o-ne* of Edalion.

At this point Smith's adviser, Samuel Birch, whom we have often mentioned, intervened and remarked to the decipherer who in his youth had studied copperplate engraving, but not Greek, that the Phoenician word *mlk* = "king" should correspond to the Greek word *basileús*. Smith then examined the group of Cypriote signs and tried with Lang to determine the word for "king". This word which appeared twice had each

Fig. 69.—Phoenico-Cypriote bilingual document from Edalion.

time a different ending, and Smith correctly took one of the two forms for the genitive and the other incorrectly for the nominative.

If the premise was correct that it was a syllabary, the Cypriote word would modify its penultimate sound; but the Greek *basileús* does the same; its genitive is *basiléôs*. Smith decided rather hastily, but justifiably, as it was soon to be discovered, that the language of the Cypriote inscriptions was Greek.

Smith had found the key to the inscriptions. The proper names quoted and the word *basileús* had already given him a total of eighteen syllabic values. He applied these to short inscriptions on medals which he thought would offer him the best chance of finding Greek names. He did in fact discover a series of new masculine names. Some of his readings were false, but among the correct names was that of Evagoras, the greatest King of Cyprus (411–374 B.C.), whose memory still lives in Cypriote popular tradition.

After this Smith found himself at the end of his knowledge of Greek. His incomplete education and the weakness of his Hellenic knowledge forbade him any investigation beyond proper names. That year, on the other hand, marked the zenith of his career as an Assyriologist with the discovery of the Gilgamesh Epic and the episode of the Deluge; it is understandable, then, that he should have abandoned the Cypriote vein.

For the second time Samuel Birch entered the scene and provided absolute proof that the Cypriote language, despite all earlier theories, was neither Semitic nor Egyptian, but Greek. This Greek it is true had a very barbarous and unusual look, for a number of reasons.

First, it was easy to make slight errors in decipherment because the number of signs was far greater than in the case of an alphabetic writing. Secondly, the Cypriote dialect was very different from the other types of Greek so far known; and thirdly, the writing had its own orthography, the weakness of which clearly indicated that it was not a Greek creation but borrowed from a primitive non-Greek Cypriote population. For example, let us compare a few Cypriote words with the corresponding Greek forms (both in transcription): *pa-ta* is the Greek *pánta*, "all", *te-o-i-se* signifies *theôis*, "to the gods", *a-ra-ku-ro* = *argýrō* (for *argýrou*) = "of silver".

It is easy to grasp that this writing was an instrument of expression for which it had not originally been designed. In many cases the obscurity remains. Johannes Friedrich notes, for example,[77] that the Cypriote *a-to-ro-po-se* reads in Greek *ánthropos* = "man", *átropos* = "invariable", *átrophos* = "badly nourished" and *ádorpos* = "fasting". We have no space to deal with these complicated orthographic rules at greater length: we shall confine ourselves to one example: *A-po-ro-ti-ta-i* signifies "Aphrodite"!

When George Smith published the results of his work in the *Proceedings of the Biblical Archaeological Society* of London in 1872, he had established thirty-one syllabic signs and given convincing proof of the syllabic character of the writing. As we have said, he was unable to conclude his task because he lacked a knowledge of Greek.

By a strange stroke of fate the accomplishment denied to him had to wait for his successor, then in the cradle.

Johannes Brandis, son of a Rhenish University professor, was born at Bonn in 1830. His father was a philologist and philosopher, and the boy's university career seemed assured. But in 1837, thanks to the good offices of Schelling, his father was appointed councillor to the Greek Cabinet by the King of the Hellenes, Otto 1st, son of the King of Bavaria. Here, under the tutelage of his father and due to his talented teacher, the archaeologist and historian Ernst Curtius, later famous as promoter and director of the German excavations at Olympia, the young Johannes received an indelible impression of Athens and its monuments, the Greek people and their language. These formative years under the blue skies of Hellas, his searches for bright-coloured ceramic fragments, the summer holidays at Cephisia, the bathes between the old harbour towers of the Piraeus and cruises in the Aegean remained the dearest memories of his life.

As a student at Bonn, Brandis in a competition essay set by the philosophy Faculty had tried to compare the tradition of antiquity with the finds of Botta and Layard. This earned him a post in London in 1854, as private secretary to Bunsen, one of his father's friends. We have already met him as the friend and benefactor of Richard Lepsius. In London Brandis met Birch and Norris.

Brandis's Assyriological studies which had begun with this competition essay led him to the chronology of antiquity. His later appointment as private secretary to the Princess of Prussia did not interfere with his new investigations on the history of weights and measures and the closely allied subject, coinage. His crowning work, a basic study on the systems of weights, measures and coinage in the Near East of antiquity, was published in 1866.

For this work Brandis had made a deep study of Cypriote history. The news of R. H. Lang's recent discovery—a bilingual document—reached him in the midst of his studies. As a testimony to his superlative knowledge of the literature dealing with this subject he drew attention to a classical author, the lexicographer Hesychius of Alexandria, who, at the end of the 4th century A.D., compiled a kind of general encyclopaedia which for us today, although it has survived in a seriously altered form, is one of the most important sources of our knowledge and critical study of authors, and even of Greek dialects. In Hesychius there is an indication that among the ancient inhabitants of Cyprus the word "and" was not pronounced as *kai*, as in other countries of Ancient Greece, but as *kas*. Many specialists had cast doubts on the accuracy of this statement. Brandis adopted it, and it became the main key to the decipherment.

A little word like "and" naturally recurs constantly in the texts. Brandis recognised the word *ka.s* in the group of signs [sign] 𐠊 (read from right to left: 𐠊 = ka).[78] This was the modest pebble that released the avalanche.

At Edalion a bronze tablet had been discovered written in a single tongue, and with the advantage over other documents of being well preserved. This became an object of Brandis's later investigations and was to confirm for the first time the *ka* in question.

The tablet consisted of a rather long group of signs, recurring six times in the inscription. Starting with the title of king (already known since Smith), it was followed by the *ka.s* cited above and a series of other signs. Having recognised the *ka.s*, Brandis resolved this group of words as *basileús kàs agotólis* and, familiar with Greek and its dialects from infancy, recognised the Greek words *basileùs kas* (*h*) *a gotólis*. The last word, rather unHellenic in appearance, soon relinquished its secret, revealing a phonetic law of the Cypriote dialect, confirmed by similar phenomena in other Grecian dialects: *gotólis* was merely *ptólis*, "the city", and the six times repeated formula meant "the king and the city".

First step, first satisfactory solution; the inscription stemmed from the king of a city. But Brandis went farther. His key *ka* also applied to another group of signs corresponding to the Phoenician word "he built". Syllable by syllable he discovered the Greek *katéstase*, "he built", and a little later *kasígnetos*, "brother", two words of great importance to a complete understanding of the syllabary; a whole new series of syllabic values had been won.

Brandis, who had recently assembled his provisional results in *An Attempt to Decipher the Cypriote Script*, was unable to present his work before the Berlin Academy, as he had intended. Hardly had this tireless worker reaped his harvest than he received a visit from a grimmer harvester. He died on his return from Vienna on July 8th, 1873, at Linz, in the prime of life and at the peak of his scientific powers. His former teacher and friend, Ernst Curtius, had the privilege of presenting his work to the Academy.

But Brandis had been carried off in the midst of his work, and his results were neither complete nor accurate on all points.

Among the German scholars who had to assess the work of Brandis was the Jena Hellenist, Moritz Schmidt, who described the dead man's work as "one of the most brilliant discoveries of modern times".

This was praise indeed from Schmidt, a kind of child prodigy, who had beaten Champollion by doing his first decipherment at the age of three.

Little "Mor", as he was called at home, was born at Breslau on November 19th, 1823. His father was the High Court judge, Moritz Wilhelm Eduard Schmidt. The child was amazingly precocious. At the age of three he decided to learn to read, and his aunt, Juliette, to help him made a series of cardboard letters. But the child, one learns, soon rejected them impatiently and procured an alphabet with a Moor's head on the cover. This became his favourite toy.

His father was then appointed Assize Court Judge at Schweidnitz, and the boy was lucky to find a few remarkable teachers in the local school. The headmaster was Carl Schönborn, whose brother, Augustus, played an eminent part in the decipherment of Lycian writing (Schmidt himself later published his posthumous works); a second professor taught the talented child Hebrew so proficiently that after two years the boy could read the original text of the Old Testament in an edition which did not mark the vowels.

The next stage in his intellectual formation was also propitious. There was but one fly in the ointment: his youth. He had to wait two years before he could sit for his baccalaureate and three years before he could be admitted as gymnasium teacher. But to offset this he attended Berlin University at its most brilliant period. Chairs were filled by such scholars as

Böckh and Lachmann, with whom Schmidt was soon in personal contact. Furthermore, he frequented a Sunday Club in company with such men as Theodor Fontane and Count Moritz Strachwitz, both wealthy patrons.

Of Schmidt's scientific legacy as a whole we shall only mention here two of the highlights: works which although on the surface seem disparate are closely bound up with each other. His main work (he became professor at Jena in 1857, after teaching for eight years with devotion in the Gymnasia) was a revision of that inexhaustible mine of information, Hesychius. It was published in five volumes at Jena and later in an abridged two-volume edition.

We can be certain that when Moritz Schmidt drew attention to and commented on Brandis's work he was greatly interested to see the latter's reference to the lexicographer of antiquity, and his enthusiastic agreement (in spite of some reservations on a few points) marked the start of his next decipherment work. Schmidt took up the torch and pursued the task begun by George Smith and left uncompleted by Brandis.

Without going into detail let us mention *en passant* that Schmidt also started from *ptólis* or *gotólis* and *kasígnetos*, but due to certain comparisons obtained results very different from those of his predecessors. Endowed with perseverance and an astonishing capacity for work, he had deciphered by January 1874 almost the complete syllabary. The same year he published the previously quoted great bronze inscription from Edalion; his interpretation of this text cast a definite light on the nature of Cypriote writing. It is composed exclusively of syllabic signs (cf. the transcriptions of Brandis), both in the case of the open vowels (i.e. of the type consonant + vowel) and in the case of simple vowels!

The German scholars, Deecke and Siegismund, added a corner-stone to this work which had been accomplished in so short a time (as regards the essentials between 1872 and 1874) and, by discovering the syllabic signs with the initial sounds j and v, removed the last difficulties from the script.

The famous Edalion bronze tablet contains a contract between the king and the city on the one hand, and a family of doctors on the other, rents and properties being conveyed to the said doctors and their descendants instead of cash fees.

The result of all this work and these many comparisons in all its modesty is of a certain historical value.

But the Cypriote syllabary still conceals a mystery. In 1910 a few Cypriote inscriptions not in the Greek language were discovered, not in Cyprus but in two museums where they had lain until this date—at the Ashmolean in Oxford and in the Louvre in Paris. Professor Sittig of Tübingen, who died recently, even discovered at Amathus (on the south coast of

Vowels	a	e	i	o	u
j	ja	je	–	–	–
v	va	ve	vi	vo	–
r	ra	re	ri	ro	ru
l	la	le	li	lo	lu
m	ma	me	mi	mo	mu
n	na	ne	ni	no	nu
Labials	pa	pe	pi	po	pu
Dentals	ta	te	ti	to	tu
Gutturals	ka	ke	ki	ko	ku
s	sa	se	si	so	su
z	za	–	–	zo	–
x	xa	xe	–	–	–

Fig. 70.—The characters of the Cypriote syllabary.

Cyprus) a genuine, unfortunately very short, bilingual document of the 4th century B.C. in Cypriote syllabic writing and ordinary alphabetic Greek. Obviously the elements are far too scanty to allow a reading and an interpretation of the vanished language, although attempts have been made to do so. But there will come a day when it will be done, because it is now generally admitted that the Cypriote syllabary is derived from Cretan linear scripts, some of which have recently been deciphered. A transitional writing has also been found (still undeciphered) called Cypro-Minoan or Cypro-Mycenaean which represents the link between the Cypriote syllabary and the Cretan Linear scripts. The study of the latter may soon throw some light on Cypro-Minoan and on the documents written in Cypriote syllabic, and again the unknown language. Of the twenty-six letters and the five numerals of this script known today, ten to twelve are identical with the classic Cypriote syllabary and eight others could equally turn out to be. We cannot make any forecasts on this subject because we

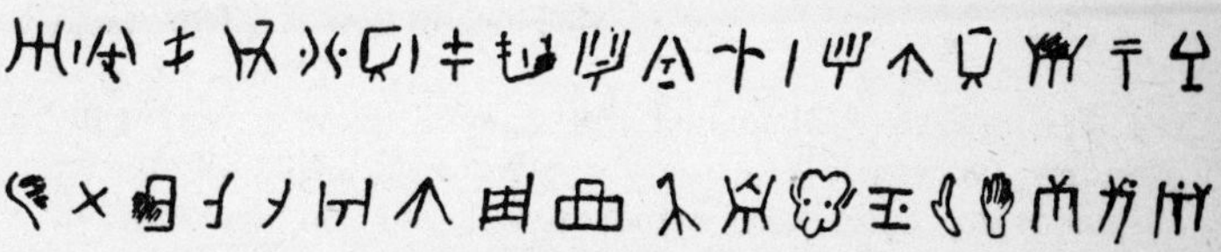

FIG. 71.—Cypro-Minoan characters.

know Cypro-Minoan only from a few texts on vases—short inscriptions which, once deciphered, would doubtless reveal no more than the content of the vases or the identity of the owners.

More than eighty years have elapsed since the discovery of the writing of Ancient Cyprus, the copper island of the eastern Mediterranean. A few days' crossing away (we speak of sailing-vessels) lay the land of origin of an even more ancient writing which recently gave a star performance in the history of decipherments—Crete, the land of Ariadne and the Minotaur, the sea-girt cradle of the most ancient European civilisations.

CHAPTER VIII

WAR CHARIOTS AND BEAKERS

THE DECIPHERMENT OF CRETO-MYCENAEAN LINEAR B

"*A stately cup, too, which the old man had brought from Pylos:*
Its golden curves shimmered, but the handles were four . . ."
—Homer, *Iliad* XI, 632–34.

It all began in 1889 when the English traveller and antiquarian, Greville Chester, made a bequest to the Ashmolean Museum at Oxford of a carnelian seal, the four oval sides of which bore stylised symbolical characters similar to hieroglyphs. They were reputed to have come from Sparta. The man who examined this gift was the Keeper of the Museum, Arthur Evans.

Evans immediately noticed a certain similarity with Hittite hieroglyphs, especially in the head of the dog or wolf with the protruding tongue (third oval). But at the period no parallel had been established with the testimonies of one of the oldest spheres of ancient civilisations, and Evans examined the possibilities of the most disparate origins, including "prehistoric" Greece.

Four years later, in the spring of 1893, Evans travelled to Greece, and in the course of his investigations at Athens found several examples similar to this prototype. He was able to collect seals with three or four faces, often pierced in length, and the results of his inquiries invariably attributed them to the same origin: Crete. On approaching the Berlin Museum, Evans received impressions of similar examples, including that of a cameo discovered by A. H. Sayce at Athens. He was thus able to announce in November of that year to the Greek Archaeological Society in London that he had discovered some sixty hieroglyphic symbols apparently belonging to a pictorial writing of Cretan origin. He visited the island the following year.

After exploring the interior and the eastern part of the island his hopes were crowned with success. He collected a considerable number of remains of an ancient civilisation which he believed to be the Crete of the Hundred Cities sung by Homer, the kingdom of Minos. A particularly lucky find stirred his collector's passion and reinforced his opinion: he discovered here in Crete a reproduction of the "Sparta" carnelian (Fig. 72) acquired by his own museum, in the hands of its original owner.

If twenty-five years earlier Wright's discovery of the Hama stones in Syria had encouraged the superstitious natives to destroy the stones and to do violence to the persons of the discoverers, it was quite another just as deeply rooted superstition which came to the aid of Evans. He was looking as usual for his seals and cameos when, to his surprise, he noticed that the peasant women and village girls wore these objects as amulets

FIG. 72.—Carnelian four-sided seals from Crete ("Sparta").

and necklaces on a chain: they prized them as *galópetrais*, "milkstones", or *galóusias*, "givers or dispensers of milk", and wore large ones when they were pregnant. On the strength of this Evans began to comb the villages in his path. He visited house after house, hut after hut, admiring these village jewels, and had an opportunity of examining fine specimens of pierced seals dating from Cretan antiquity. With skill and patience he managed to persuade some of the women, particularly the older ones, to part with their "milkstones" and to sell him the amulets. Many of them who were attached to their jewels were only too pleased to exchange them for more beautiful modern tinted cameos of the prized creamy tint.

When one of them categorically refused to part with her lucky charm, Evans had to be content with a copy. At the same time he came across many other "written" specimens which, as opposed to his first finds, bore linear or quasi-alphabetic characters. The British antiquarian recognised two systems of primitive native writing, one pictographic and the other linear; a discovery of such importance and of such consequence that

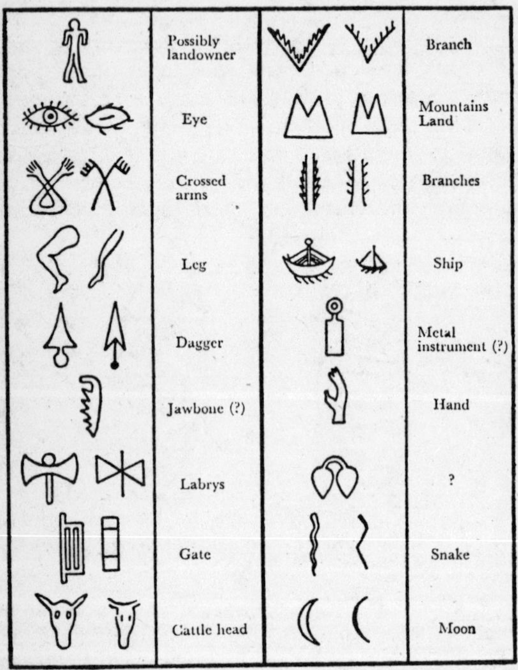

Fig. 73.—Selection of signs from the 140 Cretan hieroglyphs established by Evans with their probable meanings. The more ancient forms of a very marked pictorial nature are figured next to stylised signs.

he decided to supplement his investigations by starting excavations in Crete.

Excavations in Crete! Evans did not even know where to begin. He wanted to broach the work which Schliemann had outlined before his death as the crowning glory of his life without ever having time to accomplish it.

"Knossos, the city of Minos, the legendary site of the palace built by Daedalus, the cunning architect, filled with works of art, with the dancing hall of Ariadne and even the labyrinth, was naturally my first objective." [79]

The site of Knossos was known from indications given in the fifteenth century by Buondelmonte. It was the village of Makroticho or Makritichos ("long wall"), three miles south of Candia, the modern Heraclion, in an enclosed valley which plunges deep into the interior. But the island was still under Turkish rule and only the owner of the land had the right to excavate; Schliemann had had experience of this in 1877. The Spanish Consul, Minos Kalokairinos, a native of Candia, had discovered storerooms full of great jars (*píthoi*) and also a small incised tablet. The American, W. J. Stillman, had started excavations with the permission of the Ottoman Porte, but when the firman did not arrive and the right to excavate was withdrawn, work was stopped. Moreover, another interested party had appeared to buy from the various landowners the whole royal hill "the *kephála tselempê*". Before the greed of the landowners and the obstruction of the Turkish authorities he had to abandon his plan in 1889. The man in question was Heinrich Schliemann.

Evans met with similar obstacles. During his search for the milk stones he had been able to buy a plot of land on the *kephála*. When the Turks finally left Crete in 1899 he was able to acquire the whole property and obtain permission to start excavations.

The name of Sir Arthur Evans is today famous; his great exploit, the excavation of the Palace of Minos at Knossos, has been related a host of times in scientific and popular magazines, and has become the property of the whole cultured world.

Evans was called upon to decipher the ancient Cretan writings. At Knossos he discovered a large number of small clay tablets covered with linear script similar to the reproductions of the seals of the "milk-stone" type. In 1909 he published at Oxford in a luxurious magnificently illustrated volume, *Scripta Minoa I*, in which he dealt mainly with his hieroglyphic discoveries. In the foreword he announced his intention of publishing in Volumes II and III the linear documents, which he divides into two classes: A and B.

In addition to the hieroglyphic documents, *Scripta Minoa I* already contained all the Knossos material in Linear A and fourteen documents written in Linear B. But it was twenty-six years before Evans fulfilled a meagre part of his promise and, in 1935, published in the fourth volume of his *Palace of Minos* 120 of the 2,800 Linear B tablets he had discovered. It was, therefore, justifiable that Evans should have been reproached for having delayed this publication and for having entrusted no one with the task of pursuing his work (from 1909 to 1952, the year in which *Scripta Minoa II* appeared, revised and corrected by his former pupil, Sir John Myres). During this time investigation was not only paralysed and from lack of material embarked upon false routes, but arbitrarily stopped. Johannes Sundwall, a Finnish scholar of the first order, the modern Nestor of investigation into Cretan writing, had incurred the displeasure of Evans for having copied on his own initiative thirty-eight new tablets at Heraclion between 1932 and 1936.

The judgments of the two British decipherers, Ventris and Chadwick, are easy to understand: "Two generations of scholars were thus deprived of the possibility of doing any constructive work on the problem." (Linear B script.) [80]

A study of the attempted decipherment of this writing between 1900 and 1950 will allow the reader to judge to what extent this reproach was justified. It is obvious that the mysterious documents exercised a charm on specialists and laymen alike, "scholars of repute, talented amateurs, restless spirits of all types, from those domains where archaeology degenerates into madness". [81] Following Evans, the vestiges of all these languages were presumed to be the same language, the classical Cypriote syllabary was consulted and every continent was scoured for races who could have been the originators of this writing: the most diverse nations of the ancient world were suggested: Hittites and Egyptians, Basques and Albanians, Slavs and Finns, Hebrews and Sumerians. The most staggering error was the one that blinded Friedrich Hrozný during the last years of his life without detracting from his great merits. He died in 1952. The circumspection and critical faculty of which he had given so many proofs abandoned him in the years 1940–9. He fell a victim to the dangerous "professional malady" to which not even tried decipherers are immune; he launched a concentrated attack on all the undeciphered languages of the world! Hrozný's solution of Cretan Linear B script was only a hotch-potch of easily refuted hypotheses of Hittite and Babylonian words.

Arthur Evans had seen far more clearly and assembled with far greater objectivity and caution theories on the external characteristics; in his view the tablets were for the most part

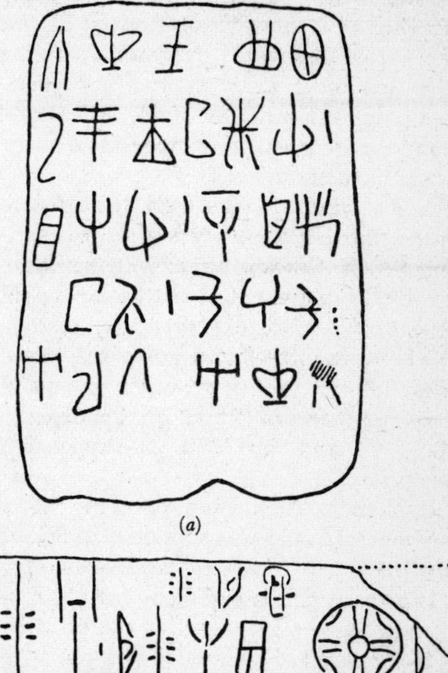

(*a*)

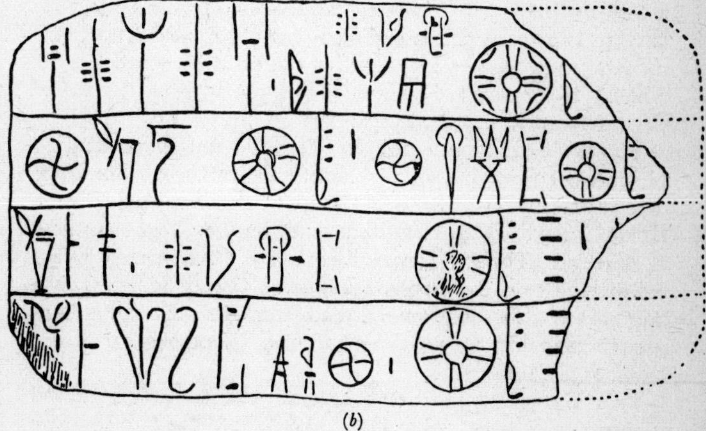

(*b*)

FIG. 74.—Tablets from Knossos: (*a*) Linear A script; (*b*) Linear B script.

inventories, catalogues and lists of persons, animals and objects; symbolical ideograms placed at the end of groups of signs or lines revealed the subject; the system of measures was decimal. The opening lines of the actual writing consisted of groups of two or more (up to seven) signs and manifestly represented words of the "Minoan" language. Fig. 75 (*a*) and (*b*) give us a clue as to how Evans arrived at these conclusions. 75 (*a*) is a tablet discovered by Evans in 1904 in the Knossos arsenal or armoury; here we can recognise twelve words (separated from each other by small vertical strokes) and in the upper right-hand corner the pictogram of a war chariot at the side of which is the number 3.

The team of scientists who worked on the Mycenaean language in the course of these years of stagnation is dominated by the name of A. E. Cowley, already known from having collaborated in the decipherment of Hittite hieroglyphs. In 1927 he gave the purely hypothetical meaning of six signs: three of them 𐀵𐀰 𐀵𐀭 were to be found before the totals of the Knossos inventories and in the three other groups 𐀒𐀷 and 𐀒𐀺 he thought to read the word "child" in the masculine and feminine forms "boy" 𐀒𐀺 and "girl" 𐀒𐀷 —a supposition which turned out to be correct.

The era of mistakes had not yet come full cycle. The languages to which Cretan was supposed to belong now included a "Proto-Greek", a "Pelasgic" and Aegeo-Asiatic dialect related to Hittite. A young eighteen-year-old English student hit the jackpot in 1949 by investigating the Etruscan content of the tablets! He persisted in his opinion until, in 1952, he deciphered Creto-Mycenean Linear B.

The prologue to this decipherment did not devolve in the philological field, but in the archaeological field. For some decades documents written in a script then called Minoan were already known. Thanks to finds made on the Greek mainland at Mycenae, Thebes, Tiryns, Eleusis and Orchomenos, Evans maintained that the Mycenaeans were Cretan invaders who had gained a foothold on the mainland; the philologists baptised them in turn, as we have mentioned, Pelasgians, Etruscans, Illyrians or Hittites.

Then in opposition to these conservative experts (so embittered that a man of outstanding merit like A. J. Wace had to retire in favour of Evans and in 1923 give up the direction of the

British School) the British Archaeological Institute at Athens, a new conception and a new school of thought, was born, according to which the Mycenaeans had spoken and even

FIG. 75.

(*a*) The "War Chariot" tablet from Knossos.
(*b*) Some Creto-Mycenaean ideograms: (*a*) man, (*b*) warrior, (*c*) cuirass, (*d*) woman, (*e*) garment, (*f*) tissues, (*g*) pig, (*h*) calf, (*i*) sheep, (*k*) lance, (*l*) arrow, (*m*) sword, (*n*) bronze?, (*o*) copper bar?, (*p*) honey: combination of the two syllabic signs *me-ri*, Greek *meli*, cf. Latin *mel*, French *miel*, (*q*) war chariot, (*r*) wheel.

written Greek. In support of these theories came the works and results of a Graeco-American archaeological expedition sent in 1939 to western Messenia. Here at Ano Englianos the American, Carl W. Blegen, discovered the remains of a great Mycenaean palace and identified it as the palace of King

Nestor, who figures in the Third Book of the *Odyssey*. Blegen took several soundings and was lucky enough to hit immediately upon the archives, consisting of 600 clay tablets. The finds were sent to Athens to be cleaned and the fragments assembled. In June 1940, after Italy's declaration of war on the Allies, when the last American ship left the Mediterranean for home, he took this treasure back to the States under the care of Mrs. Wace. The tablets were published a little later by the young American scholar, Emmett J. Bennett.

The writing on the Pylos tablets from the palace of Nestor were incontestably identical with Cretan Linear B.

Blegen's discovery was given a mixed reception. Certain people saw in the new finds imported wares from Crete and, as such, a confirmation of Evans's "Knossocentric" theory. Hardly a voice was raised to suggest that the Pylos tablets, like those of Knossos, could be written in Greek.

Here again, as often occurs in the initial stages, too much circumspection was to delay the tangible results.

On May 16th, 1950, Alice J. Kober died at Brooklyn. She had taken her doctor's degree at Columbia University with a thesis on mathematics, physics and natural science. A passionate linguist, she had included in her curriculum Sanskrit, Hittite, Old Persian and other Indo-European languages, including Semitic, Sumerian and Basque. She evinced the greatest interest in Creto-Minoan. It can be considered as an example of the irony of fate that Alice Kober, who insisted that this language was indecipherable, should be the one chosen to lay the first solid bases for the decipherment.

> "In any attempt to decipher documents written in an unknown language and script the first step is to examine the facts resulting from all existing documents. The second consists in discovering by careful analysis and logical reasoning the deductions to be made from these fundamental facts."[82]

A cautious and sober programme which stops short of the decisive step of introducing phonetic values.

Alice Kober drew up practical lists of established signs. Then she started to compare the written words, and thus made her first important discovery: the language inherent in this writing had grammatical inflections.

From a certain number of the tablets she took and assembled

a series of words each figuring in three different forms: on examining these words they were apparently distinguishable from each other only by the endings. In each case it was a word repeated in three versions, since the three forms figured together in a list or were found in the same position in one and the same type of tablet.

Alice Kober grouped the words for comparison in a systematic table. The different types of tablets (determined by their content and their aim such as they stemmed from the excavation site, pictograms and other secondary indications) gave the following results:

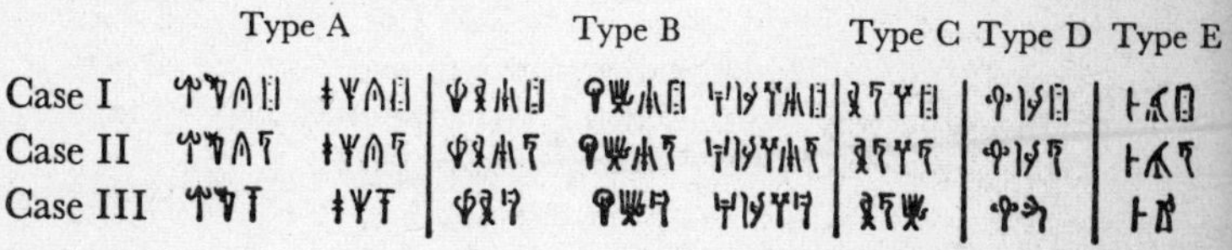

	Type A		Type B			Type C	Type D	Type E
Case I	[illegible]	[illegible]	[illegible]	[illegible]	[illegible]	[illegible]	[illegible]	[illegible]
Case II	[illegible]	[illegible]	[illegible]	[illegible]	[illegible]	[illegible]	[illegible]	[illegible]
Case III	[illegible]	[illegible]	[illegible]	[illegible]	[illegible]	[illegible]	[illegible]	[illegible]

Fig. 76.—Dr. Alice Kober's triplets.

We are now in the stage of looking round the workshop and of studying the evolution of a reasoning, the logic of which is dubious. The process of this discovery suddenly reveals itself, as is the case with so many discoveries, to be of extreme simplicity.

The table (Fig. 76) reproduces in all eight groups of three: two of the Type A, three of the Type B and one each of the Types C, D, and E. Each group represents one and the same word in three different cases recognisable by their variable ending. Case III offers in each group the shortest form. To Case I invariably belongs the terminal sign [illegible], to Case II the sign [illegible], and this process of annexation produces in Cases I and II the transformation of the sign which in Case III serves as the terminal sign: the [illegible] of Type A becomes [illegible] the [illegible] of Type B becomes [illegible] and a similar transformation occurs in Types C, D and E.

These variations are of the greatest interest, for they correspond exactly to the transformations which arise in a flectional language in the declension of nouns, for example. The American investigator established comparisons with the Latin words for "slave", "friend" and "good", all of the second declension, divided them into syllables because Mycenaean writing could certainly be considered as a syllabic writing and placed beneath her "triplets" for comparison the Latin groups of four words below:

ser-vu-s	*a-mi-cu-s*	*bo-nu-s*
ser-vu-m	*a-mi-cu-m*	*bo-nu-m*
ser-vi	*a-mi-ci*	*bo-ni*
ser-vo	*a-mi-co*	*bo-no*

A careful comparison of the Mycenaean table with the Latin declensions makes it easy to envisage Dr. Kober's next step.

If we now try to compare (naturally without trying to draw conclusions as to the true phonetic values of the Mycenaean syllabic signs) the Latin *ser-vu-s* with Case I of Type A, we shall see (by starting with the ending, the rational point of departure, thus from the right) that the [sign] corresponds to "s", the [sign] to "vu" and the rest of the Mycenaean word [signs] to the rest of the Latin word *ser*; just as *ser-vo* corresponds to [signs]. To make this comparison even clearer, let us place our equation on two superimposed lines:

ser	- *vu* -	*s*	*ser*	- *vo*
[signs]	[sign]	[sign]	[signs]	[sign]

FIG. 77.—Experimental equation.

The syllables "vu" and "vo" offer the first "fix": they have a common consonant. According to the Latin example it is the "v"; in reality an unknown consonant. Since we do not know a single sound of the Mycenaean syllables we overcome this by calling the "v" "consonant I" the "u" "vowel 1", the "o" "vowel 2". This gives the table the following fragment:

	Vowel 1	Vowel 2
Consonant I	[sign]	[sign]

We know, then, that the two syllabic signs represented have a common consonant but different vowels. A meagre result, but any solver of crossword puzzles knows that a contemplation of this fragment of the table gives a promising start. This embryonic table does in fact offer of its own accord a chance of pursuing further objectives in order to complete it.

Let us begin with the extreme right column "vowel 2". Vowel 2 was "o". The word [signs], which was compared with *ser-vo* (it could have been done equally well with *ser-vi*), is found in Case III of Type A. If then we examine the last line of the Latin table, corresponding to Case III, we find the terminal syllable (ser)*vo*, (ami)*co*, (bo)*no*—syllables which all contain vowel 2. The same can be accepted of the terminal syllables of all the Mycenaean words in Case III, i.e. the syllabic signs [sign], [sign], [sign], [sign] and [sign]; they all contain vowel 2, but each has a different consonant. We complete the able in the following manner:

	Vowel 1	Vowel 2
Cons. 1	[sign]	[sign]
Cons. 2		[sign]
Cons. 3		[sign]
Cons. 4		[sign]
Cons. 5		[sign]

To resume. In the still-empty column, vowel 1, will now appear the same signs containing vowel 1 or the "u", according to the hypothesis announced above. According to the Latin table they are syllables vu, cu, nu; the same which in Cases I and II of the Mycenaean table precede the terminal sign of the words. We find here the signs [sign] (Type A), [sign] (B), [sign] (C), [sign] (D) and [sign] (E). If we enter them in the table it will be complete for the first time:

	Vowel 1	Vowel 2
Cons. 1	[sign]	[sign]
Cons. 2	[sign]	[sign]
Cons. 3	[sign]	[sign]
Cons. 4	[sign]	[sign]
Cons. 5	[sign]	[sign]

This modest table was no more nor less than the kernel, the original cell for future decipherment, the primitive form of the "grid" of which the British and their American colleagues speak today. It is clear that this grid was capable of extension in all directions, according to the principles we have just shown.

Alice Kober, who died young, was not permitted to pursue her theory to the end or, if we may use a phrase, to close the meshes of the net for the capture not only of the vowels and undetermined consonants, but of real phonemes. In 1949, however, she was able to bring a new and important contribution to the decipherment by showing that the group of signs already suggested by Cowley 𐀵𐀰, 𐀵𐀭 and 𐀒𐀺, 𐀒𐀷 as the masculine and feminine forms were one and the same word; this was a valuable indication as to the character of this mysterious language, for languages which modify the vowel of their syllable ending to express the genders (instead of adding for example another syllable) are almost exclusively Indo-European.

It might be thought that Alice Kober's successors only had to follow up the solution she bequeathed to them in 1950. But we must point out that at this period we were unable to read with certainty a single syllable, no word of the unknown language, and that the most conflicting theories were still put forward as to the character of this language. The brilliant doctor's thesis in which the American, Emmett J. Bennett, Jnr. (Cincinnati, 1947), treated the Pylos documents as Alice Kober had treated the Knossos tablets; his publication of *The Pylos Tablets 1951* and of the Knossos tablets (*Minoan Linear B Index*, 1953), and his explanation and codification of the system of weights and measures in 1950 did nothing to change the position.

The decisive impetus to the decipherment was given by Sir Arthur Evans, although he did this neither scientifically nor intentionally. He could not suspect in 1936, on the occasion of the Jubilee of the British School of Athens in London, when he lectured on Minoan questions, that among his audience the future decipherer followed his explanations with passionate interest. The man who eight years ago discovered in a single blow the riddle of Creto-Mycenaean Linear B at the time he listened to Evans was a boy of fourteen wearing out the seat of his pants on a school bench.

Naturally it was not by chance that he was present to hear

the much-admired discoverer of the Palace of Knossos. From early childhood Michael Ventris (1922–56) displayed a marked predilection for strange idioms and mysterious scripts. With a great gift for languages, the young man later surprised his friends and colleagues and won the heart of many foreigners by speaking to them with perfect ease in their native tongues.

During his studies he was constantly interested in what was then called "Minoan". He had already left school and begun his architectural studies in 1940, when, at the age of eighteen, he published an *Introduction to Minoan Writing*, in which from an examination of the tablets he maintained in principle that they could be written in Etruscan—an opinion which he abandoned only twelve years later.

But events of another nature were to occupy Ventris during those formative years. His architectural studies were interrupted by the war. He served four years as a navigator in the R.A.F. and spent some time with the British Army of Occupation in Germany. In the course of his travels his copies and reproductions of the Minoan documents never left his possession. In 1946 he was demobilised and returned to his architecture. The ex-sergeant navigator soon settled down in his new *milieu*. He took part in all the active demonstrations staged by the students, and distinguished himself in the last two years of study by obtaining a grant for both years.

Architecture was the career he had chosen, and certain of his biographers are incorrect in maintaining that this was only a second choice, his preference being for Cretan writing. When Ventris was killed in September 1956—a more premature end than that of Champollion—architectural circles mourned the loss of one of the most talented of the younger generation.

With Bennett's above-mentioned article seven more Pylos tablets were published, thus increasing the number of known documents. They encouraged Ventris to jettison his previous theories and to embark upon a "series of attempts", a certain number of detailed studies of the script. His privately printed *Work Notes*, addressed between January 1951 and June 1952 to a few dozen colleagues and interested persons—notes designed to record his attempts and to stimulate collaboration and criticism—contained phrase by phrase the results of his efforts and his evenings of tireless investigation. Commissioned by the Architecture and Buildings Section of the Ministry of

Education, he worked all day on the plans for a school and in 1952 built a house for his wife and himself, "a piece of simple, logical, pleasant and unaffected architecture".

His *Work Notes* at the outset contained a few errors. He continued to envisage the possibility of Aegean and Etruscan words and readings—since the very idea of a Greek language was forbidden by orthodox history and archaeology. But notes 2, 8, 10, 11 and 12 contain the seeds of several essential points of the decipherment—observations and theories already uttered by Alice Kober, by the young Cambridge philologist, Chadwick, by the Greek, K. D. Kristopoulos and the American, Emmett J. Bennett. Notes 1, 13 and 14, dealing with proper names, point out at least six declensions recognisable by the vowel of the last syllable of the nominative. Ventris adopted the grid system invented by Alice Kober for his comparisons and classifications. Other tablets containing numerical indications allowed him to differentiate between the forms of the singular and the plural. In Note 9 he tries once more to explain his observations by the forms of Etruscan declensions—but this attempt met with increasing difficulties. Notes 1, 15 and 17 finally illustrate the successive stages to the birth of Ventris's grid, which, in 1952, appeared as we show it in Fig. 78.

The results obtained were, as we have seen, very imperfect and incomplete; not even the exact number of vowels was known; moreover, certain signs had been included in several categories—for the good reason that at this period Ventris still envisaged, in these particular cases, the existence of two distinct meanings.

This provisional picture, laboriously worked out, had, however, two advantages, and we stress this point in view of subsequent attacks. Defective and obscure in certain respects, the grid had been elaborated from certain characteristics visible in the documents themselves; that is to say, it rested on observations of facts resulting from a simple examination of the tablets according to their place and circumstances of discovery, from the simple enumeration and comparison of the written signs. No theory of any kind on any language apt to be recognised on the tablets had been of help to set the ball rolling, no case had been fulfilled by taking into account that the known elements could be integrated within the framework of any specific language.

We must stress this point: the striking argument for one of the most violent attacks lately launched against the Ventris system consists in the affirmation that the documents written in Linear B contained no Greek and that the little Greek he wished to see in it at all costs had been introduced by Ventris himself.

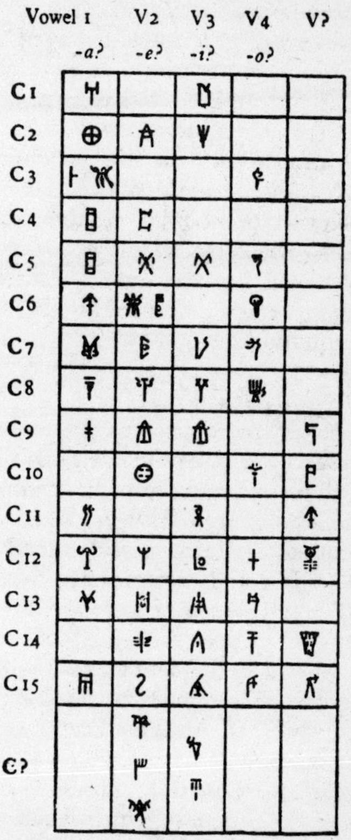
Vowel 1
V2
V3
V4
V?
-a?
-e?
-i?
-o?
C1
C2
C3
C4
C5
C6
C7
C8
C9
C10
C11
C12
C13
C14
C15
C?

FIG. 78.—The grid in February 1952, before the decipherment.

The same year Ventris abandoned his Etruscan theory. At the start, unwilling and incredulous because he was forced seriously to envisage the possibility of a Greek language. February 1952 brought the fulfilment of the promise made by Arthur Evans in 1909 and not kept by his former pupil, Sir John

Myres. The latter was unable to avoid in his edition of the Knossos tablets *Scripta Minoa II* (a thorny and unrewarding task when one considers in retrospect the material left by Evans, some dating from half a century before) certain faults and lacunae which Bennett and Chadwick corrected in 1952, 1954 and 1955. But the new publication was a confirmation of the provisional grid compiled by Ventris (Fig. 78). Moreover, a comparison of the words of the now-enlarged vocabulary gave Ventris an idea which was to play a decisive part.

According to his first grid, the lack of symmetry of which had never ceased to worry him (and others with him), certain words of the same type afforded in their endings variants which could be considered as flexional endings of declensions, whereas other words of the same type showed notable modifications (for example -so and -i) which could not be variations according to the context. Wherein lay the error? Certainly not in the tablets themselves. Ventris examined his grid once more.

This was the equation:

𐀀 = a, 𐀊 = ja, 𐀃 = o, 𐀍 = jo.

If correct, it would be of great consequence. The frequent termination of masculine names in the genitive, -𐀍 or 𐀍𐀍, then read -(o) jo and (-i) jojo and therefore resembled the ancient forms long since known from Homer, such as *Autolykoio* and *Ikaríoio*; the genitive feminine plural already envisaged -𐀊𐀃 was in this case -(i)ja-o and corresponded to the ancient forms *gaiáōn, theáōn*! If these values were introduced into Alice Kober's triplets, the first five (Types A and B) offered a skeleton of vowels and semi-vowels so eloquent that without much imagination the missing consonants could be filled in; thus five of the most important cities of Ancient Crete were subsequently found, including its capital: Lyctos, Phaistos, Tylissos, Knossos and Amnisos (Fig. 76, Case III, Types A and B, in the incomplete script of the originals, which recalled Cypriote writing, *ru-ki-to* (r appeared in the place of l, u in Ancient Greek is y), *pa-i-to, tu-ri-so, ko-no-so, a-mi-ni-so*).

If these new values were correct they would cause a chain of reactions in the grid, inevitable in such cases: the phonetic value of thirty-one signs at least could be determined. In spite of all these confirmations Ventris in his 20th Work Note still believed that it was an illusion, a mirage. His last pronouncement of June 1952 was still in the post when he started work again trying to introduce new phonetic values into a number of the tablets. He then had an inspiration and at the same time the irrefutable evidence of the Greek solution. A host of new words, emerging from the darkness, awoke from their milleniar sleep: he saw appear a -po-me, genitive po-me-no (Classical Greek *poimén*), "shepherd", a ka-ke-u (*chalkeús*), "forge", a ke-ra-re-mu (*kerameús*) "potter", a ka-na-pe-u (*gnapheús*), "fuller", and even an i-e-re-u (*hiereús*) and i-je-re-ja (*hiéreia*) "priest" and "priestess".

Obviously the divergence between the new script and the traditional forms of Classical Greek was enormous. The initial sound of the syllable and the vowel was written; the sound ending was discarded. Thus pa-te could mean *patér*, "father", but also *pántes*, "all". A word like *stathmós*, "stable"), appeared in the form ta-to-mo: the initial "s" falls; there was no sign for an isolated consonant. The same applied to the "th" before m; but here the reverse occurred, the "th" was joined to a silent vowel "jo"! No distinction between long and short vowels, nor between "b", "p" and "ph" and "g", "k" and "ch"; it could already be surmised from the city names Lyctos and Tylissos that the "r" and the "j" were rendered by the same sign.

Ventris, an architect and not a philologist by profession, decided that in such circumstances everything or nearly everything was now possible and that this "everything" could just as well be "nothing". He felt an ever greater need to call upon the aid of some specialist who had learned his profession from A to Z.

Sir John Myres came to his aid. He introduced him to a young man who had studied at Cambridge, collaborating later at Oxford in the publication of a Latin dictionary. He had met Myres, and in 1952 was appointed Reader in Classical Philology at Cambridge. This was the origin of the Michael-Ventris–John Chadwick team of decipherers whose two names are inseparably linked in the story of the decipherment of Linear B.

John Chadwick, born in May 1920, was the second son of an official. He was educated at St. Paul's School in London and then at Cambridge. Two years younger than Ventris, Chadwick's studies were interrupted by the war. He served five years in the Royal Navy.

From his school days Chadwick had taken the greatest interest in languages, and his excellent Greek teacher at St. Paul's, G. E. Bean, today professor at Istanbul, knew how to encourage this particularly promising pupil. From the outset he was fascinated not only by foreign languages but also by incomprehensible or little-known tongues. Whereas in 1940 Ventris, at the age of eighteen was trying to prove the Etruscan origin of Cretan, Chadwick at the same age, two years before, had started on Tibetan.

> "During the war I spent my spare time studying modern Greek and Sanskrit. The war also gave me the opportunity of learning Japanese and a knowledge of their writing (quoted in the first chapter of this book as a syllabary). Japanese helped me greatly in revising my former opinions and adapting them to a language written in a syllabic, ideographic script." [83]

Demobilised in 1945 at the age of twenty-six, Chadwick returned to Cambridge and passed his exams with honours in classical philology.

The same year he teamed up with two colleagues to study privately the Cretan texts. When this work at the outset gave no tangible results his two friends tired of the subject, but their defection did not discourage Chadwick. He pursued his studies without any hard-and-fast plan. He collected extracts and notes, made a few cautious conclusions in 1946 and waited for the appearance of new documents. At the very start of his work in 1946 he envisaged the possibility of a Greek language, but achieved no results worth publishing. When Ventris announced his discovery in 1952 and through Sir John Myres met Chadwick, the announcement of the decipherment reached the new reader in the midst of his university tasks; he was little prepared to receive it despite six years of study devoted to Creto-Mycenaean writing.

Sir John Myres, who showed him Ventris's latest work note, was not particularly impressed. Chadwick, too, at the outset displayed some scepticism, although, as one of those who wished to see in the Minoan texts a Greek language, he was more disposed to accept the results of Ventris. Sir John allowed his young colleague to copy Ventris's grid as it appeared at that time.

"Those four days were the most exciting of my life. I was so absorbed by this affair, that my wife reproached me for forgetting the anniversary of our marriage."[84]

Chadwick began to introduce into the texts the values established by Ventris and, to his intense surprise, recognised that they contained, in the orthography admitted by Ventris, far too many Greek words for it to be purely a matter of coincidence. He met with several meanings which he had already encountered in his own studies—a brilliant justification of the work of the young architect. A certain number of unclassical forms, which had doubtless aroused doubts in Ventris's mind, at first sight appeared clear and familiar to Chadwick with his great knowledge of Greek dialects. A lively correspondence ensued between the two scholars (later they wrote their letters in the script they had deciphered), which was ended only by the tragic death of Ventris. Chadwick in turn was able to produce the phonetic values of several as yet unidentified signs. Their observations complemented each other or gave the partner some new food for thought. Chadwick was the first to read the names of the gods on one of the Knossos tablets—one of the rare cases in which Ventris showed scepticism.

> "I have always endeavoured to make it clear that all the merits of the discovery are due to Ventris; my role was that of the first infantry division sent in to widen the breach and the advanced guard of tanks which gives the necessary support. The simple determination of the phonetic values was only a start, and in the extremely difficult task of transcribing into comprehensible Greek the words deciphered, we worked as equal partners. We never concealed our plans from each other and often came to the same conclusions simultaneously.
>
> "It was an unqualified delight to work with Ventris and, even when we did not agree, we were always able to see each other's points of view and either to find a compromise or to renounce our conflicting opinions."[85]

Before the end of 1952, Ventris and Chadwick had finished their first important publication, the article "*Evidence for Greek Dialect in the Mycenaean Archives*", which appeared the following year in the *Journal of Hellenic Studies* (LXXIII 1953, pp. 84–103), "a memorable publication as rich in content as it is modest in form. It stood up to the cross fire of criticism and in the first two years inspired other scientific works on the Mycenaean-Greek language, an additional confirmation of the importance of the discovery."[86]

This article contains the key to the writing; it is no longer a colourless table of vowels and consonants, designated merely by numbers, but a record of the concrete phonetic values of sixty-five of the ninety-eight previously established signs; we produce here this "experimental syllabic grid" in the still incomplete form it showed at that period.

a	e	i	o	u
a, a_2	e	i	o	u
ai				
ja	je		jo	
wa	we	wi	wo	
da	de	di	do	da_2
ka	ke	ki	ko	ku
ma	me	mi	mo	
na	ne	ni	no	nu, nu_2?
pa, pa_2?	pe	pi	po	pu
	qe	qi	qo, qo_2?	
ra, ra_2	re	ri	ro, ro_2	ru
sa	se	si	so	
ta, ta_2?	te, pte	ti	to	tu
	z?e		z?o, z?o_2	

FIG. 79.—The decisive table of the syllabic signs reproduced from *Evidence*.

Ventris and Chadwick had already made known their decipherment in a series of lectures before the appearance of the article *Evidence*. They won over to their theory scholars of repute from Sweden and Great Britain to whom the results of their work had been sent beforehand. Among their first partisans were R. D. Barnett and Ignace J. Gelb, whom we have already met in earlier chapters.

But the success from the article *Evidence* was slight; most of the specialists reserved their judgment and there was considerable criticism.

Among the archaeologists who, according to their principle,

considered with cautious reserve the concrete solution presented by Ventris and Chadwick was the American investigator, Carl W. Blegen. He had started work again in 1952 at Pylos and discovered more than 300 new tablets which naturally could not be studied on the site. In the spring of 1953 Blegen was in Athens studying them in detail and comparing them prior to publication.

We have not forgotten how Lepsius silenced those who cast doubts on Champollion's decipherment by the discovery of the Decree of Canopus, nor the striking confirmation brought at Karatepe by Bossert to his own work and to that of his predecessors in Hittite hieroglyphs.

The role which the Decree of Canopus played in Egyptian hieroglyphs and the bilingual epigraph of Karatepe in Hittite hieroglyphs was, in the case of Linear B, an insignificant tablet before which Blegen stopped in amazement, in May 1953, to study it with growing interest. This is the tablet in question:

FIG. 80.—Inventory from Pylos of tripods and vases—a brilliant confirmation of the decipherment.

On May 16th, 1953, Blegen wrote to the decipherers telling them that he had discovered a tablet where it was obviously a question of vases some of which had three feet, others four or only three ears and others with no ears at all.

> "The first word (an ideogram according to Blegen) according to your system should obviously read ti-ri-po-de; it recurs twice in the form ti-ri-po (singular?). The vessel with four ears is preceded by qe-to-ro-we, that with three ears by ti-ri-o-we-e or ti-ri-jo-we, and that with no ear by a-no-we. All this seems too good to be true. Can we consider this a mere coincidence?"[87]

It was no coincidence. This is obvious if, with the Viennese scholar W. Merlingen and according to the Ventris system, we systematically analyse the inscription on the tablet and if we present it in a phonetic transcription, in Classical Greek and

English.[88] We shall recognise word for word, in cases of doubt appealing to the syllabary in Fig. 79, and read with our own eyes the first specimen of Linear B script.

Line of the Tablet	Transcription	Ideogram
1	ti-ri-po-de ai-ke-u ke-re-si-jo we-ke *trípode Aigeùs krē̂sios (w) érge* *Tri*pod, Aegeus the Cretan made (?) it (?)	 Tripod: 2
1	ti-ri-po e-me po-de o-wo-we *trípous henì podì oi (w) ōwēs* *Tri*pod, with one foot and one ear	 Tripod: 1
2	di-pa me-zo-e qe-to-ro-we *dépas me (î) zon tetrō̂wes* Jug: rather large with *four* ears	 Vessels: 1 with *four* ears
2	di-pa-e me-zo-e ti-ri-o-we-e *dépae meízoe triō̂we* (Two) jugs: rather large with *three* ears	 Vessels: 2 with *three* ears
2	di-pa me-wi-jo qe-to-ro-we *dépas meîon tetrō̂wes* Jug: small with *four* ears	 Vessels: 1 with *four* ears
3	di-pa me-wi-jo ti-ri-jo-we *dépas meîon triō̂wes* Jug: small, with *three* ears	 Vessels: 1 with *three* ears
3	di-pa me-wi-jo a-no-we *dépas meîon ánōwes* Jug: small with *no* ears	 Vessels: 1 *without* ears

This irrefutable confirmation, this decisive proof, as can be imagined, aroused the most tremendous interest. Leading scholars in every country were loud in their praise: among those who agreed at least in principle with the new decipherment were Johannes Friedrich, Piero Meriggi and the old Finnish expert, Johannes Sundwall. The Tübingen professor, Ernst Sittig, who had attacked the tablets with statistical-cryptographic methods from the First World War without much success, abandoned his theory and added new confirmation. The reading *dépas anóuaton* for *di-pa a-no-wo-to* met with on another tablet beside the ideogram ◊ "earless jug", thus the

Basic values										Homophones	
a	𐀀	*e*	𐀁	*i*	𐀂	*o*	𐀃	*u*	𐀄	*a₂* (*ha*)	𐁀
da	𐀅	*de*	𐀆	*di*	𐀇	*do*	𐀈	*du*	𐀉	*ai*	𐁁
ja	𐀊	*je*	𐀋	—		*jo*	𐀍	*ju*		*ai₂?*	[illegible]
ka	𐀏	*ke*	𐀐	*ki*	𐀑	*ko*	𐀒	*ku*	𐀓	*ai₃?*	[illegible]
ma	𐀔	*me*	𐀕	*mi*	𐀖	*mo*	𐀗	*mu?*	𐀘	*87 (*kwe?*)	𐁌
na	𐀙	*ne*	𐀚	*ni*	𐀛	*no*	𐀜	*nu*	𐀝	*nwa*	𐁅
pa	𐀞	*pe*	𐀟	*pi*	𐀠	*po*	𐀡	*pu*	𐀢	*pa₂*	𐀣
—		*qe*	𐀤	*qi*	𐀥	*qo*	𐀦	—		*pa₃?*	𐁖
ra	𐀨	*re*	𐀩	*ri*	𐀪	*ro*	𐀫	*ru*	𐀬	*pte*	𐁇
sa	𐀭	*se*	𐀮	*si*	𐀯	*so*	𐀰	*su*	𐀱	*pu₂?*	𐁆
ta	𐀲	*te*	𐀳	*ti*	𐀴	*to*	𐀵	*tu*	𐀶	*ra₂* (*ri-ja*)	𐁈
wa	𐀷	*we*	𐀸	*wi*	𐀹	*wo*	𐀺	—		*ra₃* (*rai*)	𐁉
za	𐀼	*ze*	𐀽	*zi*		*zo*	𐀿	*zu?*	𐁙	*ro₂* (*ri-jo*)	𐁊
*22	𐁒	*47	𐁔	*49	𐁕	*63	𐁗	*64	𐁘	*85 (*si-ja?*)	𐁂
*65	𐀎	*71	𐁃	*82	[illegible]	*83	[illegible]	*86	[illegible]	*ta₂* (*ti-ja*)	𐁋

FIG. 81.—Mycenaean syllabary according to Ventris and Chadwick. *Documents in Mycenaean Greek.*

same word as we find on our first tablet, which means "without ears" or without spouts.

In 1954 Ventris and Chadwick planned a vast work in three volumes, the first of which was to deal with the script, the language and Mycenaean civilisation, the second—the bulk of the work—was to present 300 selected tablets from Knossos, Pylos and Mycenae with transcriptions and comments, and the third a Mycenaean vocabulary and various indexes.

The manuscript, with a preface by Professor Alan Wace, was finished at the end of 1955. It contained, augmented and revised the key to the script, leaving unexplained only a very few signs by reason of their rarity.

In 1956 Ventris was mainly busy with his architecture. But this year also marked at Easter the zenith of his career as a decipherer: the Mycenaean Colloquy, organised by the *Centre National de la Recherche scientifique* at Gif near Paris, where he and his collaborator, Chadwick, came in personal contact for the first time with some of their most illustrious colleagues. The image of the young scholar impressed itself indelibly in the memory of all those who met him.

On September 6th, 1956, Ventris was killed, at the age of thirty-four, at Hatfield, not far from London, in a car accident.

> "It was typical of him that he sought no honours and of those he received (and these were a great many) he spoke unwillingly. He was always modest and undemanding, and his winning personality, his wit and humour made him a most pleasant companion and colleague. He was always ready to work for others and to give them generously of his time and assistance. Perhaps only those who knew him could really appreciate the tragedy of his early death."
>
> (John Chadwick in *The Times* of September 17th, 1956.)

> "The picture of Ventris radiates with particular brilliance. The author of these lines had the pleasure of meeting him this year at Gif. Ventris had come from Zermatt and he was very sunburnt. He was a keen skier and a great friend of our country, with which he had ties from early youth. Simple and natural in his behaviour, he expressed himself with lucidity and precision showing no animosity to ideas which differed from his own. He gave a detailed account of his recent investigations and with good grace furnished the necessary explanations with a calm assurance, in which there was no trace of pride. It was surprising to find in an architect such a profound knowledge of Greek philology, and to notice with what speed and alertness of mind he approached new problems. With extraordinary ease and charm he spoke to Greeks in modern Greek and with us in Swiss German, giving an impression of youth and yet maturity.

Although his discovery had brought him premature fame, he had not lost the noble sense of moderation."

Ernst Rich in the *Neue Züricher Zeitung*, September 26th, 1956.

And finally his mentor and benefactor, Alan Wace, wrote in the Greek newspaper *Kathemerini* at Athens:

"Michael Ventris achieved immortality during his brief life, so brutally cut short by his tragic death, by deciphering Mycenaean Linear B and discovering the most ancient known form of the Greek language such as was spoken 700 years before Homer. . . ."

It is impossible today to assess the importance of this discovery. The documents discovered have certainly not produced the great literary inscriptions which a number of scholars and lovers of classical antiquity no doubt hoped; thus we shall refrain here from drawing from these inventories so far deciphered, vestiges of a huge accountancy, any lengthier examples than we have already shown. But we must stress one feature which appears to us almost as a tragedy. The tablets are generally "invoices", probably designed to be added to lists at regular intervals (perhaps at the end of each accounting year?) and subsequently destroyed. Their preservation is due to the sudden destruction of the palace, in all probability at the hands of an enemy, and it seems that at Pylos even the last mobilisation orders for the invasion were preserved. But there is no doubt that these new unsuspected testimonies of the earliest historical European era are closely and more directly tied up with the origin of what we call the West than all the famous monuments of Babylonia and Egypt.[89]

Let us mention that the discussion as to the accuracy of the decipherment principle of Linear B has recently been revived in a somewhat bitter form. To the earlier opponents, whose spokesman was A. J. Beattie, the Edinburgh philologist, were soon added the two German investigators, E. Grumach and W. Eilers, both of whom rejected the methods and the results obtained by Ventris and Chadwick. We cannot deal here even summarily with this erudite polemic; but the essence of the objection rests on the reproach addressed to the two decipherers for having introduced *a priori* in the texts the Greek language, deciphered in the tablets. The readings of Ventris and Chadwick certainly have a weakness; but this is merely a matter of detail. The system—as far as we can judge today—will only be found water-tight when an adversary can provide an absolute proof that this "intrusion" of a language in the signs is not in the origin of the signs. We should therefore, by means of an ancient language—Latin, for example—by deduction and point

Fig. 82.—Signs written in ink on the inside of a beaker from Knossos.

by point prove this intrusion, with the same stupefying results that faced Ventris and Chadwick and, moreover, experience the satisfaction of seeing appear a stream of new, longer and polysyllabic Latin words, as is the case today with the Greek. Until this convincing proof has been found we shall follow the opinion of most scholars on the unique performance accomplished by the decipherers.

We now come to the other Minoan scripts which we mentioned at the start of this chapter. Neither has yet been deciphered.

Investigation began with Linear B script, and there was a sound reason for this. The writing does in fact offer an infinitely greater and more interesting documentation than the others—Linear A and the Creto-Mycenaean hieroglyphs.

Linear A, the first documents of which were found by Evans at Knossos on tablets and other objects (for example in the form of signs written in ink inside beakers), was obviously more widely distributed than Linear B. Whereas at Knossos only a small part of the finds are in Linear A and the majority in Linear B,

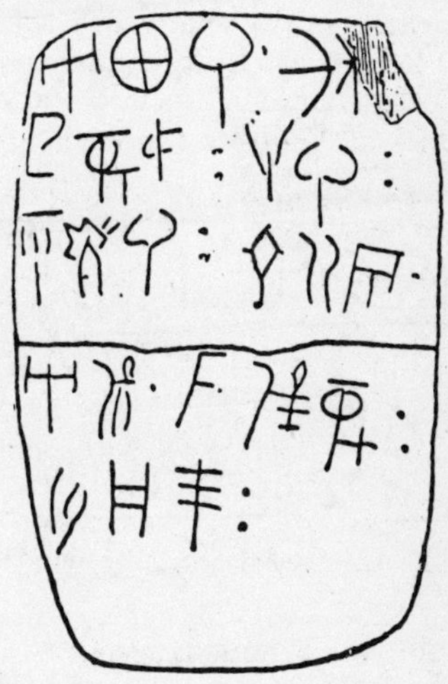

Fig. 83.—Small clay tablet in Linear A script from Hagia Triada.

the Italians discovered the former script on tablets and clay discs in the small palace of Hagia Triada (the site of more recent and plentiful finds) and at Phaistos in southern Crete; then at Mallia in 1923 the French found archives of clay tablets bearing side by side later hieroglyphs and initial Linear A. Several other sites in Crete have delivered further finds to excavators. The particular interest of this writing is that on the one hand it must be considered to be related to the even more ancient Cretan hieroglyphs, and on the other as the forerunner or sister of Linear B. A and B actually have in common forty-eight signs, twenty of which stem from the old ideographic writing. The documents in Linear A date back to a period *ca.* 1650 B.C.; it must have still been in use about 1350 B.C. This script is generally believed to convey the non-Greek language of the autochthonous Cretan population. This theory is confirmed by the fact that the elements of Linear B, originating from Linear A, adapt themselves as badly as a borrowed garment to Mycenaean Greek.

It is not surprising, therefore, that the latest attempt at decipherment by the American Orientalist, Cyprus H. Gordon, whose audacious equation: Linear A = Akkadian, on its appearance (two articles in the review *Antiquity,* September and December 1957) unleashed a lively controversy and was almost unanimously rejected. Gordon's method was simple; applying the syllabic values in Ventris's Linear B to similar signs in

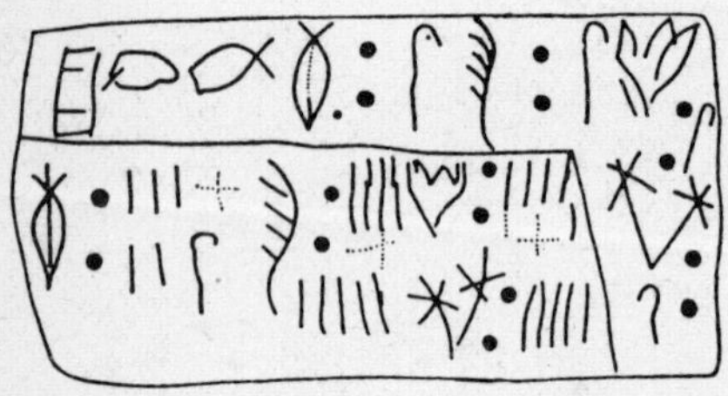

FIG. 84.—Hieroglyphic inventory from Phaistos.

Linear A, he deduced a Semitic language by experiments with various languages of the same family and thought to recognise Akkadian. Without going farther into the historical, archaeological and epigraphical reasons which invalidate this system, we shall merely state that the method of transferring the syllabic values of Linear B to the signs of Linear A, while the latter script shows every evidence of a strongly ideographic character, does not seem above criticism, and that moreover the equations of the Semitic words so far established (already by reason of their number) are far from convincing.

Cretan hieroglyphs were mentioned at the start of this chapter and they are the oldest source of Cretan writing. Figs. 72 and 73 give some examples. Fig. 84 illustrates a hieroglyphic inventory tablet. The top line is supposed to indicate twenty and a half units of each of the four wares represented by the ideograms , , and , probably corn, oil, olives and figs.

If we succeed in deciphering Cretan hieroglyphs and Linear A script, we shall discover the language of the mysterious and legendary folk that settled in Crete before the migration of the Mycenaean Greeks.

We have not so far explained a find which has been available

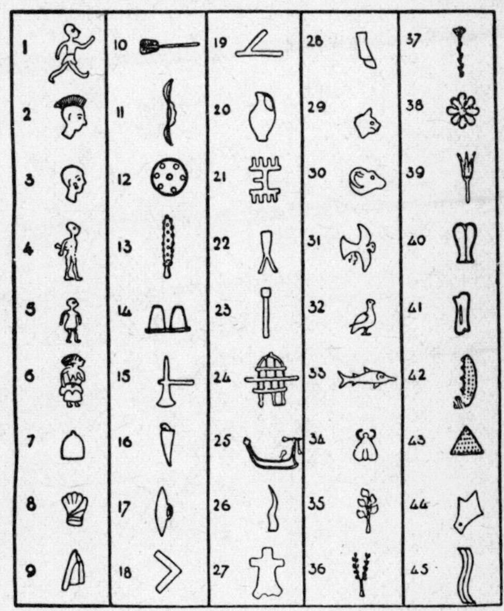

Fig. 85.—The signs of the Phaistos Disc.

to us for fifty years and yet remains as enigmatical as on the day of its discovery: the famous Phaistos Disc.

It was discovered by the Italian archaeological mission of 1902 led by Professor F. Halbherr which, as we have mentioned, also worked at Hagia Triada. On July 3rd Doctor L. Pernier, in an outbuilding of the Phaistos Palace, brought to light a square storeroom. Next to a broken tablet incised with Linear A was a mysterious disc made of fine clay. According to some experts it is not of Mycenaean origin. The disc is not completely round, but irregular in contour. The signs were in all probability pressings of individual seals. They number forty-five. Fig. 85 gives a table of these figures.

If we refer to specialist literature we shall find a host of theories and attempted interpretations for nearly all these forty-five signs. The curious hair style of the man (No. 2 in

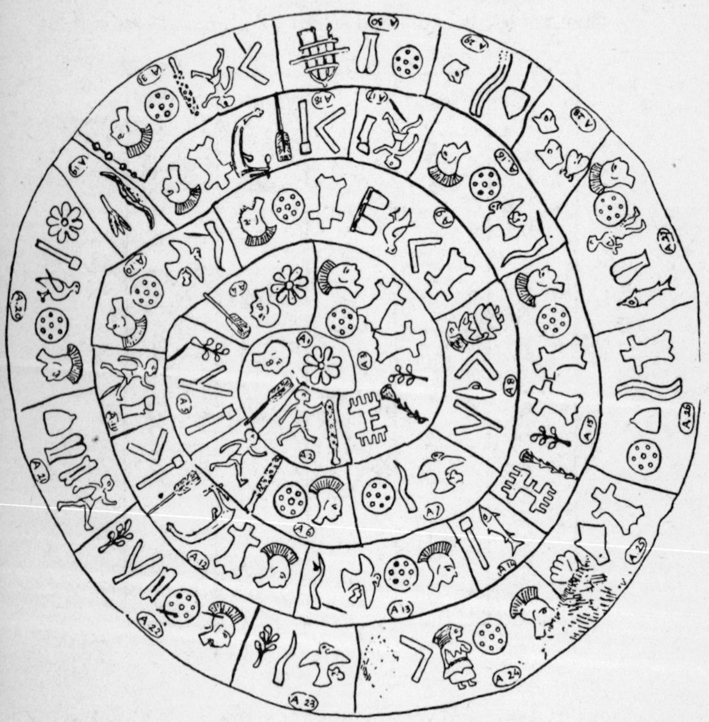

FIG. 86*a*.—The Phaistos Disc. Recto.

Fig. 85) plays a particular role. From the warrior element discernible, without too much imagination, in the different symbolical signs Sir Arthur Evans concluded a hymn of victory and suggested that the whole was the text of a sacred song.

We are no nearer to a solution of this ancient Cretan riddle (if it is Cretan, as has been questioned) since Evans's day. People have tried to recognise in it Philistine, Lycian, Carian,

Cypriote, Libyan, Anatolian and Semitic origins. The disc still awaits its decipherer. The two sides which never fail to attract the eye, and not only invite new attempts at decipherment but also afford the layman a visual pleasure exempt from

Fig. 86*b*.—The Phaistos Disc. Verso.

all speculation, remain mute but eloquent, as they must have appeared to the discoverer.

For those who would like to try their talent for combinations, clairvoyance and luck we reproduce here both sides of the Disc. Possibly a professional investigator will sooner or later win the laurels promised to the one who solves the riddle of this clay plaque which can be seen today in the Heraclion Museum. Or perhaps a brilliant amateur will solve the mystery of these spiral images and, like a modern Theseus, find the way out of this new labyrinth of the island of Minos.

Or has fate decreed that they shall remain silent and guard their secret—preserve a mystery in this world where mysteries become ever more rare?

CHAPTER IX

PRINCE KÜL-TIGIN, BILGE KAGAN AND THE SAGE TONJUKUK

THE DECIPHERMENT OF THE OLD TURKISH RUNIC SCRIPT

"I, the heaven born, wise Turkish Kagan have ascended the throne. Hear my words from the beginning to the end . . .—" Inscription from Orchon.

THE word *türk* or *türük* originally meant "strength" or "vigour".

The people who bore this name—rightly, as we shall show—appeared for the first time in history towards the middle of the 6th century A.D. Relatively modern, their written documents cannot be compared with the testimonies of the pre-Christian millennia of the ancient Orient with which we have dealt so far. But they are of great interest because they stem from a country situated beyond Western civilisation, from the heart of Asia and from a race of which for a long time we knew nothing and still largely ignore.

The reason that for Western Europeans the origin, destiny and very essence of this people remained so long a closed book like the Apocalypse is because the sources were too remote from our normal field of vision. They remain the same today. The historical awakening of the Seljuk Turks, and their first pre-Islamic splendour, found an echo in the old and rich Chinese literature which, while of cardinal importance to the ancient history of Central Asia, remains almost as unknown in Europe as the Byzantine historical sources, no less rich, diverse and instructive, which have recently been discovered and are gradually being made available.[90]

Since earliest times the race which we call by the generic name of "Turks" lived in the vast regions of Central Asia. Originally it consisted of a few nomad tribes whose horizon was confined to their tents and pasturages, bound together by a very weak link. Possibly one of these early tribes, or even one single chief, called himself "strength" or "vigour". The Turks enter history as subjects of a powerful race which the Chinese historiographers call Ju-Juan or Juan-Juan.

Around the year A.D. 646—this is the period when the Chinese Empire was split into north and south, when in the north under the Wei dynasty Buddhist sculpture blossomed for the first time in the cave temples, and under the Emperor Liang Wu-ti Buddhist literature and philosophy reached a remarkable peak; the period, too, when in Byzantium the emperor Justinian and his consort, Theodora, ruled as absolute monarchs over Church and State—about this date the Turks tried for the first time to shake off the yoke of their tyrants, the Juan-Juan. Powerful Turkish tribes of the north, whom the Chinese call Thie-le, attacked towards the south. Turks, in the pay of their foreign masters, led by Tou-men opposed their brothers and repulsed them. But the victory made them aware of their own strength, and a few years later, led once more by Tou-men (this is his Chinese name; on the Turkish inscriptions he is known as Boumin), they overthrew the Juan-Juan. Thus Tou-men became the founder and builder of the Ancient Turkish kingdom. Under his supreme authority his younger brother reigned as head of the western Turks and founded a dynasty. The Chinese called it Se-tie-mi, the Istemi of the Turkish inscriptions.

When Boumin died in A.D. 552 his three sons succeeded him in turn. Their reign sees the rise of Mukan, the most famous of all the Turkish kagans, a general and conqueror who enlarged and unified the kingdom, bringing it a hitherto unattained prosperity. After conquering the "White Huns" or Ephthalites, this powerful realm extended west across the ancient land of Sogdiana to the Iaxartes (Sir-Darja), the Yenčü-ügüz or "river of pearls" of the Turks, and to the Iron Gate, the pass already known in antiquity between Samarkand and Balkh; to the east as far as present-day Manchuria.

Maturing in permanent contact with the old civilised nations this people in the sixth century reached an astonishingly high level of culture, no longer enforcing a blind, belligerent policy but carrying out far-sighted and intelligent trade negotiations. Thus Istemi—his brother's vassal if we accept his name, but virtually absolute ruler of the West Turkish zone—on his own initiative entered into relations with the Byzantine kingdom with a view to acquiring the silk trade, previously in the hands of the White Huns. An incredibly vivid, bright-coloured and suggestive picture is afforded by the Byzantine trade and diplomatic mission sent to the Turks in August A.D. 568 by the Eastern Emperor, Justinian II, a fascinating mixture of barbarian uncouthness, superstition and Shamanism combined with the most refined luxury and sensuous delights of the Orient. The following passage from the report of the delegation is taken from one of the most remarkable works of Byzantine literature—*The Story of Menander, the Protector*:

"When Zemarchos (a Byzantine high official, head of the delegation) and his retinue after several days journey reached the land of the Sogdians, they dismounted from their horses and saw approach a party of Turks sent specially to offer them iron; in my opinion (this is the author, Menander, speaking) the Turks wished to show that their country possessed iron mines. Iron being considered to be one of the rarest metals they had recourse to this method to prove that they mined this mineral. Other members of this same race, the so-called 'exorcisers' also came to greet the delegation. They approached Zemarchos, laid down their packs, lit a few sticks of incense and muttering incomprehensible words in their barbaric tongue carried round in a cup leaves of frankincense which burnt and crackled. Whipping themselves into a frenzy and foaming at the mouth they feigned to chase away the evil spirits. In the obvious intent of averting some threat of misfortune they made Zemarchos himself pass through the flames. They also believed themselves to be purified by this ceremony. Then led by their own chiefs they repaired to the residence of the Kagan. This was situated on a mountain called Ektag, which means the Golden Mountain. In the valley at the foot of this mountain dwelt Sizabulos." [91]

The "Golden Mountain", actually the "White Mountain" (Ak-dagh), is in the Altai region. Sizabulos, whom Menander in another passage calls Silzibulos, is none other than Istemi; we learn from the Byzantine historian, Theophylactos, who knows him by the name of Stembis-Kagan. Let us hear how this ruler received the delegation:

"On their arrival the envoys were taken before the Kagan, who sat in a tent on a two-wheeled golden throne which could if necessary be drawn by a horse. They solemnly saluted the barbarian prince and, according to the custom, offered him gifts brought in by servants specially employed for this purpose. Then Zemarchos said: 'To you O sovereign of so many peoples, friend of the Romans (Eastern Romans or Byzantines) to whom you wish naught but good, the emperor offers through my lips his greetings and good wishes. May good fortune attend you always. May you always triumph over your enemies and reap the fruits of your victory. Far be it from us to feel any jealousy, the enemy of all friendships. The Turks and the peoples who obey them are for us as friends and relatives and do you not nurse the same sentiments for us?' Sizabulos replied to this greeting of Zemarchos in similar vein. Then they repaired to a banquet and in the same tent enjoyed the pleasures of the table. The tent was adorned with sumptuous, bright-coloured silks; drinks were served but not the juice of the grape for this land knew neither the vine nor the taste of wine. The guests then returned to their quarters, to drink a barbarian brew, a kind of cider. Next day they feasted in another tent adorned with similar embroideries. Sizabulos lay on a couch of pure gold and in the centre of the tent were ewers and vessels of gold and vases filled with spring water. They feasted once more with great revelry before taking leave of each other. The following day the encounter took place in a third tent, this time decorated with gilded wooden columns; the couch supported by four gold peacocks was also gilt. Outside this tent had been placed carts laden with rich silver utensils, plates and chargers, in addition to many statues of animals which, in refinement and taste, vied with our own. So great was the love of luxury of the Turkish Kagan."[92]

Seven years later the picture had changed. The peace treaty between the Eastern Roman Empire and the Avars, the former vassals of the Turks, had embittered the latter against Byzantium, and when in A.D. 575 a Byzantine delegation led by Valentinos visited the Turks it was received with hostility.

"At the end of a long and exhausting journey, they reached the camp of Turxanthos, one of the princes of the Turkish tribes. The Turkish sovereigns had in fact divided their realm into eight parts; the supreme prince was called Arsilas (Arslan = lion). Valentinos advanced towards Turxanthos who had come to meet the delegation and told him the joyful news that the Romans had a new emperor. . . . Turxanthos immediately cut him short. 'Are you not one of those Romans who know ten languages and think only in the language of lies and deceit? You approach me as a messenger full of ruse and perfidy, and he who sent you is no less of a hypocrite. But you shall die and that with all speed; among us Turks lies are not customary. Your sovereign will receive a well merited chastisement. . . . The whole earth obeys me from the extreme East to the extreme West. Think, O wretched mortal, of the fate of the Alans and the Uitgurs! Confident in their own strength they declared war on the invincible Turks; their hopes were dispelled and today they serve as slaves." [93]

The leader of the Byzantine delegation, an experienced diplomat and accustomed to dealing with Turks, was able to pacify the Prince's anger. Turxanthos (also known as Turxathos; the word is actually a title incorrectly used as a proper name: Türk-šad = Šad or leader of the Turks) changed his attitude and addressed to the Representative of the Eastern Romans a request which is of the greatest interest to ethnologists, the exact replica of which is found in documents written in Old Turkish. It ran:

"'Romans, you find me sorely afflicted. My father has just died—you must in consequence cut your faces with your dagger blades to conform to the laws and customs of our funereal rites.' Valentinos and his companions immediately cut their cheeks with their daggers. During these days of mourning Turxanthos also sent four Hun prisoners (in their language these traditional sacrifices to the dead are called *dochia*), led the poor devils in person to the centre of the square and sacrificed them to his dead father together with their horses: in his barbarous language he exhorted them to inform his father, the late Silzibulos, that . . . he . . . (here the text is incomplete).

"After his father's solemn funeral, Turxanthos had several discussions with Valentinos; then he despatched him to the interior of the Turkish kingdom to see his brother, Tardu. Tardu lived on Mt. Ektel, which means the Golden Mountain." [94]

Under Silzibulos-Istemi's successor (Ta-t'au in Chinese) the great Turkish kingdom was divided into two parts, West and East. The Chinese, harassed by the constant incursions of Turkish brigands, sowed discord between the two parts of the kingdom; as a result of this astute policy they exhausted themselves towards the middle of the 7th century and within a short period of time were reduced to the rank of provinces, subject to the power of China. But after twenty years of foreign domination a sibling of the old dynasty once more won by arms the title of Kagan of the Eastern Turks—this was Kutluk, the "fortunate", or, to give him his real name, Elteriš Kagan, "the Kagan of the unification or founder of the kingdom", who by a succession of victories and an energetic administration succeeded in uniting and consolidating the realm.

Elteriš Kagan died in the course of this constructive work, leaving two small sons of six and eight. His brother, Kapagan Kagan, now had a free hand. Dissatisfied with the results achieved, he pursued his dream of restoring the ancient Turkish kingdom to its erstwhile power and magnificence; he wanted to extend his domination as far as Persia, as his ancestors had done, and to subject the hostile and rebellious Western Turks, who had seceded from China at the same time as their Eastern brothers. An impulsive, irresponsible man, Kapagan Kagan as a statesman was not of the same calibre as his deceased brother. He showed himself to be so cruel and devoid of scruples that his own subjects deserted him and emigrated in swarms to China. His assassination by a rebel tribe in A.D. 716 was a red-letter day in the lives of his two young nephews, the legitimate sons and heirs of Elteriš Kagan. The eldest son of Kutluk ascended the throne under the name of Bilge Kagan, the "wise sovereign". His younger brother, Kül-tigin (Prince Kül), his active and resolute supporter, began by executing various members of his uncle's family and of his own, all dangerous pretenders to the throne. A single member of the old guard was spared: Tonjukuk, who had distinguished himself under Elteriš Kagan, the father-in-law of Bilge Kagan and his counsellor during the latter years of his life.

Bilge Kagan, the "wise sovereign of the Turks", "the divine", "the heaven-born", lived up to his name. He turned out to be a gentle, intelligent and cautious ruler. Most of the Turkish emigrants returned to their own country. He became on friendly terms with the Emperor of China. His brother, Kül-tigin, more energetic than the sovereign in peace and war, was a stout supporter of his throne, and his death in A.D. 731 was a grievous loss to his elder brother.

Bilge Kagan did not long survive his brother: he was poisoned in 734 by his own minister at the very moment the Emperor of China had promised him the hand of a Chinese princess. Eleven years later this early Turkish supremacy was annihilated except in the eyes of the Chinese, whose friendship Bilge Kagan had managed to preserve by his able policies. The mortal blow came from another Turkish race, the Uighurs, who were about to play a prominent role in Central Asia.

The wise, reflective rule of Bilge Kagan brought his subjects the last great flowering of their ancient realm. It is due to his enlightened political views that we owe a heritage particularly valuable for science. The result of the good relations existing between the Turkish Kingdom and the T'ang dynasty in China was that, on the death of Prince Kül-tigin not only his brother, Bilge, but also the Chinese Emperor honoured his memory by erecting to him an imposing monument. When Bilge himself followed his elder brother to the grave, his son and successor, once more together with the Chinese Emperor, erected a magnificent tomb to his memory. The inscriptions on these two monuments enabled us, in 1896, to decipher the Old Turkish script.

For nearly a thousand years they remained forgotten and neglected—in common with all similar documents of the other regions of the Russian Kingdom to which during this period these Old Turkish residences belonged. It was not until Peter the Great's occidental spirit and desire for progress that life returned to these silent testimonies of a remote past. From 1719 to 1727 the German naturalist, Daniel Gottlieb Messerschmidt of Danzig, explored Siberia at the request of Peter the Great. His travels led him from Nerchinsk to the frontier river of Manchuria, the Argun-kerulun and on the banks of the Upper Yenisei near some ancient tombs discovered two remarkable stones bearing inscriptions and bas reliefs of animals, human faces and decorative ornaments. The characters of the epigraphs were reminiscent of Nordic runes. Copies of these and other stone inscriptions, which at the time were attributed to the Scythians, reached Europe by the grace of Catherine the Great's envoy and were duly published.

At the beginning of the 19th century finds of this type continued to accumulate in Paris, the future citadel of Orientalism. The importance that they might have for the history of Central Asia became apparent, and the first attempts at decipherment were made. Abel Rémusat and J. Klaproth, both contemporaries and adversaries of Champollion, were among the first decipherers. Their efforts were fruitless. All manner of theories were advanced on the subject of the new writing: it was Scythian or Chudic or related to the Nordic runes; it was even assumed to be a Celtic or a Gothic script. None of these attempted interpretations came to anything and silence soon fell once more on these documents.

Among the scholars who had studied and published the inscriptions and tried to decipher them in the first half of the century, was the Finnish investigator, M. A. Castren. His work was resumed after some time by the Finnish Archaeological Society, which sent, around 1875, two expeditions to Minussinsk to search for and examine inscriptions. The result of these two expeditions was a luxurious volume published by the above-named Society, *The Inscriptions of the Yenisei* (Helsingfors, 1889), with seventeen folio pages of text and fourteen illustrations, thirty-two reproductions of inscriptions and eight photographs; three years later a supplement and a glossary completed this work—everything an archaeologist could desire with one exception: the decipherment of the script.

Apart from the remarkable illustrations the work included a spirited account of the discovery of the documents; in this way it achieved another important object for any publication of this type: it aroused a keen interest among specialists.

Shortly after this, at the eighth Russian Archaeological Congress, N. Jadrinzev, who had explored nearby Mongolia, drew attention to the wealth of this country in antiquities of all kinds, and especially to the inscriptions discovered in the region of the River Orchon. The journey undertaken in the spring of 1890 by the Finnish scholar, A. Heikel, accompanied by his wife and brother, led him to the old bed of the River Orchon and to Lake Kosho-Tsaidam (south of Lake Baikal). Here he found two weatherbeaten and partially mutilated monuments—imposing ruins which, to all appearances, had been forgotten for centuries and were completely unknown to European scholars.

They found a huge stela, obviously an overturned commemorative stone, a four-sided monolith, carefully hewn in a kind of limestone or indifferent quality marble 3·50 m. high, 1·32 m. broad at the base and 1·22 m. at the summit; the thinner sides measured between 0·44 and 0·46 m. Two of the sides were seriously defaced. The tapering stone was crowned by a rather clumsy ornamental motif representing two dragons: the broadsides bore a small pentagonal epigraph tapering to a point. The stone broadened out towards the base into a powerful cone which fitted admirably into a well-preserved plinth, carved in the shape of a tortoise. The form and execution were of contemporary Chinese monuments and the work was without doubt Chinese.

The four sides of the monument were entirely covered with inscriptions. The western face bore a lengthy Chinese inscription, and the remaining three were decorated with symbols in the runic alphabet already discovered in the regions of the Yenisei and the Orchon.

About forty yards away from the stone stood a tall sacrificial altar joined to the monolith by a slightly raised terrace twenty-five yards long, obviously the remains of an earlier edifice. Closer inspection showed that it was in fact the remains of a Chinese brick wall. Not far away Heikel noticed seven marble statues of obvious Chinese work, representing Turks, as could be seen from the costumes and attributes of the figures; the statues had been decapitated. On the reverse side of the monument two badly damaged carved animal figures must have originally denoted the entrance to this building, which was later identified as a necropolis. Extending over a distance of two and a half miles was an important line of stone statues at intervals of ten to thirteen yards, the faces turned to the east; these represented the enemies slain during the lifetime of the person buried here.

Half a mile from the spot Heikel and his companions found a similar, rather larger, commemorative stone, not only overturned but unfortunately smashed to pieces. For this reason the sides had suffered more severely than those of the first monument. Great portions of the inscriptions had been completely defaced and erased; the surface that remained was also engraved in Chinese characters and the same unknown runes; the surroundings had been appointed in the same manner.

A. Heikel and his collaborator had stumbled across the tombstones of Prince Kül-tigin and his brother, Bilge Kagan.

In 1892 they published at Helsingfors the inscriptions they had discovered. Two years earlier, before Heikel had set out, the Russo-German philologist, Wilhelm Radlov, of the Imperial Russian Academy of Science, had worked out a detailed plan for the exploration of the sites of these finds; the following year he himself led an expedition which included, among others, N. Jadrinzev and the Siberian specialist, D. A. Klemenz. From Kiachta they entered Mongolia to explore the ruins on the banks of the Orchon and its tributaries, in an attempt to prove that a close relationship existed between the Yenisei and the Mongolian inscriptions. At Kara-Balghassun, the remains of the flourishing Mongolian residence of Karakorum, the travellers discovered an impressive granite monument engraved with three inscriptions: one in Chinese, one in Uighur and the third in "Siberian" runic.

In 1892 the results of this latest expedition were published in the learned journals. On December 15th, 1893, the Danish scholar, Vilhelm Thomsen, submitted to the Danish Royal Society of Science in a foreword of a bare fifteen pages entitled "*Descriptions of the inscriptions of the Orchon and Yenisei*" the broad outline of the decipherment and the alphabet of the new script.

The Chinese inscriptions of Orchon, translated and interpreted by G. von Gabelentz, revealed the nature of these stones. They were tombstones, the first and best conserved being of a man named Kiu te (k)-ch'in, son of Kut-te-luk kho-han, and younger brother of a reigning prince named Pi(t)-kia kho-han. In these Chinese names it was not difficult to read the previously quoted sovereigns, Kutluk, "the fortunate", Bilge, "the wise" and Prince Kül-tigin. Chinese literature had already mentioned the building and lay-out of these memorials. Some distance away was eventually discovered on two columns of stone still standing the inscription of the tomb of the great statesman and general, Tonjujuk.

How did the archaeologists know before the inscriptions were deciphered that they referred to sepulchral buildings? It was only by studying the remote past that they could throw light on the cruel and barbaric ancient rites which form the historical and cultural basis of the Mongolian burial-grounds. The hard, weatherproof stone tombs, which had survived for centuries on the banks of the Orchon, are the late echoes of an antiquity which raised to its dead not only monuments of granite but also human flesh.

The ceremonial ritual is known to us from Herodotus. He describes in Book IV, Chapters 71–2, how the Scythians (a general term in his works) were accustomed to bury their dead; if we compare this text with Menander's description of the burial given to his father by Silzibulos-Istemi, son of Turxanthos, and if we recall the Orchon tombs, the stones of which speak eloquently of the same traditions, we shall see a ray of light—even if the centuries which separate Herodotus from the Orchon tombs had mitigated the ancestral customs and barbarous cruelties to which Turxanthos himself was obliged to subscribe.

Here is Herodotus' account:

> "The sepulchres of the kings are in the country of the Gerrhi, as far as which the Borysthenes is navigable. There, when their king dies, they dig a large square hole in the ground; and having prepared this, they take up the corpse, having the body covered with wax, the belly opened and cleaned, filled with bruised cypress, incense and parsley and aniseed, and then sown up again, and carry it in a chariot to another nation; those who receive the corpse brought to them, do the same as the Royal Scythians; they cut off part of their ear, shave off their hair, wound themselves on the arm, lacerate their forehead and nose, and drive arrows through their left hand. Thence they carry the corpse of the king to another nation whom they govern; and those to whom they first came accompany them. When they have carried the corpse round all the provinces, they arrive among the Gerrhi, who are the most remote of the nations they rule over, and at the sepulchres. Then, when they have placed the corpse in the grave on a bed of leaves, having fixed spears on each side of the dead body, they lay pieces of wood over it, and cover it over with mats. In the remaining space of the grave they bury one of the king's concubines, having strangled her, and his cup-bearer, a cook, a groom, a page, a courier, and horses, and firstlings of everything else, and golden goblets: they make no use of silver or brass. Having done this, they heap up a large mound, striving and vieing with each other to make it as large as possible.

"When a year has elapsed, then they do as follows: having taken the most fitting of his remaining servants, they are all native Scythians; for they serve him whomsoever the king may order, and they have no servants bought with money: when therefore they have strangled fifty of these servants, and fifty of the finest horses, having taken out their bowels and cleansed them, they fill them with chaff, and sew them up again. Then having placed the half of a wheel, with its concave side uppermost, on two pieces of wood, and the other half on two other pieces of wood, and having fixed any of these in the same manner, then having thrust thick pieces of wood through the horses lengthwise, up to the neck, they mount them on the half-wheels; and of these the foremost part of the half-wheels supports the shoulders of the horses, and the hinder part supports the belly near the thighs, but the legs on both sides are suspended in the air: then having put bridles and bits on the horses, they stretch them in front, and fasten them to a stake; they then mount upon a horse each one of the fifty young men that have been strangled, mounting them in the following manner: when they have driven a straight piece of wood along the spine as far as the neck, but a part of this wood projects from the bottom, they fix it into a hole bored into the other piece of wood that passes through the horse. They depart, having placed such horsemen round the monument."[95]

Those were the ancestors of the stone-watchers of the Orchon tombs.

None of the experts who devoted their activities to discovering these monuments engraved with runes managed to decipher the script: Wilhelm Radlov alone made a few general observations approaching the truth on the subject. But the decipherment, which has been termed in the history of philology as the most typical of "armchair decipherments" and is still quoted today as the brilliant *tour de force* of a single investigator, was realised by one of the leading lights of the group of Scandinavian scholars we have already mentioned.

Vilhelm Ludwig Peter Thomsen (1842–1927), son of a Randers postmaster, spent his early youth in that town, where he attended secondary school. Having begun his university career, like so many scholars of his generation, by studying theology, he soon renounced this subject in favour of languages. At the start he hesitated between philology or physics and natural science: botany and physics exercised a great attraction on him; but he was gradually carried away by his love of science. Outstanding university professors were not only able to win him for their faculty but also instilled in him an exemplary method and a vast knowledge which distinguished him among his colleagues. He continued to amass more knowledge during the course of his journeys. His teachers, among others, were Madvig, a star classical philologist, and N. M. Pedersen and his successor, K. J. Lyngby, who aroused in him an interest for Nordic philology; Westergaard, who collaborated in the decipherment of Elamite cuneiform, and the Slavonic languages expert, C. W. Smith. Thomsen became interested very early in the Finnish people and their language; the publication in 1869 of a work on this subject made him famous overnight. His travels took him to Berlin and Leipzig, thence to Prague, where he studied Czech; he continued his Slavonic studies at Vienna under Miklosich and took private lessons in Serbo-Croat, Polish and Hungarian, which he later perfected at Budapest. He then extended his studies to Arabic, Persian, Chinese and Tamil. He was also familiar with the Turkish language.

Although a well-known personality, on his return home, from 1871 to 1878 he became Professor of Latin and Greek, then for some years occupied a higher post in an Upper School, until in 1887 he was given a chair of comparative philology at Copenhagen University—a chair which he continued to hold until 1913.

Thomsen, who in 1877 published a sensational treatise on the relations between Ancient Russia and Scandinavia and the origin of the Russian State, had been particularly intrigued by the epigraphs from Siberia, the Yenisei, Mongolia and the Orchon, although they were outside his personal tastes and interests in the historical and philological field.

Having soon recognised the known Yenisei and Orchon signs as variants of the same "Siberian" script, as we say today, Thomsen concentrated on the largest and lengthiest inscriptions in the hope of achieving an early success. They were from the tombs of Kül-tigin and Bilge Kagan near Orchon. His first reflections on seeing these Siberian runes are reminiscent of the initial stages of all other decipherments.

He established at the outset (Grotefend, too, had begun in this way) the run of the writing, thus resolving the question as to how the inscriptions were to be read. Radlov had made an error on this score. Studying the layout and the position of whole passages and isolated lines, Thomsen was able to show that they were not to be read from left to right, as Radlov had believed, but from right to left, as in the vertical lines of Chinese.

The next step was the count of the letters: he gave the interesting number thirty-eight signs. A very instructive result, because it obviously indicated an intermediate system between a pure alphabet and a syllabary; hitherto known syllabaries usually possessed no fewer than fifty; alphabets, on the other hand, rarely had more than thirty signs. From this Thomsen came to a very important conclusion: the script in question must be an alphabet in which certain signs served to translate the same sound in specific conditions, according to the sound which preceded or followed it. He studied the alternation of several consonants subject to the influence of the preceding or following vowel.

Thomsen had started from a very simple premise: in a series of signs x y x—that is, a series composed of two similar signs separated by a different one—either the x's represented the consonants and y the vowel, or else y was the consonant between the two vowels x. The Danish expert carried out a series of careful comparisons, and by this method reached his first objections—the vowels he was looking for—and duly found them after a number of false starts and errors. He thus recognised the signs 𐰆 𐰃 and 𐰇 as vowels; far from determining them accurately at the start he first mistook the sign 𐰆 u/o for ö/ü and the real ö/ü i.e. 𐰇 for e. He spotted the i, 𐰃, at once, but it was only after a process of trial and error that he discovered the fourth vowel, 𐰀, a/ä.

Although convinced that his equations were correct, Thomsen had not proved them definitely. To obtain this proof he had recourse to one of the favourite and best-tried instruments of decipherment. He looked for proper names, of which the Chinese version offered a few examples.

It was reasonable to suppose that the proper names would appear as isolated groups of signs—the discoverers had already noticed the word separator in the form of a double dot—would recur with a particular frequency, or again would betray themselves by their position in the text: for example, at the beginning of a paragraph.

He did not have to search very long. He was struck in particular by the group 𐱅𐰭𐰼𐰃 frequently repeated on the two Orchon stones. The first fix was afforded by the fourth and ultimate sign (on the extreme left, the writing being sinistrograde), the 𐰃, which he had already established as an i. Its frequency and position in conjunction with the terminal sound i of this series of signs encouraged him to set a bold equation. He deduced an ornamental epithet for the prince's title, a familiar word in Mongolian and in all the Turkish dialects for "heaven" or "god". His previous observations and conclusions drawn from the number of signs of the alphabet encouraged him to presume the suppression of a vowel. He therefore identified the group 𐱅𐰭𐰼𐰃 (according to the run of the original script) as i-r-g͠n- ät, the word which we read as *tän͠gri*, "sky" or "god".

This equation was pure hypothesis. The search for proper names continued. Thomsen soon noticed that a second longer group of signs, 𐰚𐰇𐰠𐱅𐰃𐰏𐰤, repeated several times on stone I did not appear on stone II. This group must therefore represent the name of the prince to whom the first memorial was dedicated. In the Chinese text, as we have already said, it took the form Kiu-te(k)-ch'in, the second part of which was immediately recognised as the Turkish *tigin*, "prince"; the Dutch sinologist, Schlegel, and others after him had tried unsuccessfully various ways of explaining the first part of the word. Thomsen recalled that Chinese, which has no syllabic ending, frankly drops it when adopting foreign names and resolved the whole group 𐰚𐰇𐰠𐱅𐰃𐰏𐰤 as Kül-Tigin, "Prince Kül"; not only the Chinese tradition but also the two signs 𐱅 (= t before or after e, i, ä, ö, ü) and 𐰃 (i, y) which he had already discovered in *tän͠gri*, confirmed this reading. The same conclusion drawn from the absence of the l as a syllable ending led to his establishing the most frequently repeated group on stone II—the Chinese pi-chia coincided with 𐰋𐰃𐰠𐰏𐰀, Bilge, "the wise".

His theory seemed gradually to be proving correct; there was one doubtful point: *tän͠gri* had been built with the aid of combinations, the two names being based on comparison with the

Chinese. A fourth group now dispelled all the scholar's doubts: it was the word 𐰚 𐰼 𐰇 𐱅, often repeated on the two monuments from Orchon. Thomsen already knew three out of these four signs; they are (from right to left) 𐱅 = t (from *tängri* and Kül-tigin), 𐰇 = ü (from Kül-tigin) and 𐰼 = r (from *tängri*); this word t-ü-r could signify nothing else except *türk*. In this way he had discovered in the sign 𐰚 not only a second k, but also established without a shadow of doubt the language of the inscriptions. Historical evidence and the confirmation given by the proper names in the Chinese text established it as the language of the people whom the Chinese called Tu-kiu, a pure Turkish idiom far older than all the Turkish languages previously known.

Nine signs had now been determined, and although Thomsen, a remarkable expert on Turkish dialects, still had a number of details to work out, he had no major difficulty in applying the values discovered to other words, and ultimately to reconstruct it piecemeal and wrest the entire language from limbo. The crowning achievement of his efforts came three years later with his great work, *Inscriptions of Orchon Deciphered* (Helsingfors, 1896), in which he published not only the alphabet, but a complete translation of the inscriptions.

This major discovery for the history of writing was greeted by historians as a precious key to the history of Central Asia; they could now with relative certainty trace back the origin of the new writing to the Arsacid Pehlevi script (Middle Persian), itself derived from Aramaic—a valuable advance for the history of civilisation, since it could be tied up with the history of the Manichaean evangelical activities. Philology, too, owes to Thomsen an unexpected broadening of its knowledge: the new script with its rich vocabulary of thirty-eight letters was far purer in rendering faithfully the phonetic value of the sounds of Old Turkish than the twenty letters of the Uighur alphabet, which had completely ousted Old Turkish by A.D. 800.

The language of the Ancient Turkish monuments can still affect us. Bilge Kagan, the hardy sovereign addressing his people, mourning his brother or the old statesman, Tonjukuk, continuing to evoke on his tomb the misfortunes which might have befallen the Turkish people had Tonjukuk not been there —all these manifestations of a Turkish race which did not yet know Allah or his prophet, Mohammed, speak to us most eloquently.

Siberian script			Arsac. Pehlevi		Siberian script			Arsac. Pehlevi	
Yenisei	Orchon	Phonetic value	Symbol	Phonetic value	Yenisei	Orchon	Phonetic value	Symbol	Phonetic value
		a, *ä*		*a*			*l* (before or after e, i, ä, ö, ü)		
		b (before or after a, o, u, y)		*b*			*m*		*m*
		ṅg		*g*			*n* (before or after a, o, u, y)		*n*
		d (before or after a, o, u, y)		*d*			*n* (before or after e, i, ä, ö, ü)		
		g (before or after a, o, u, y)		*h*			*z*		*s*
		g (before or after e, i, ä, ö, ü)		*h*			*š*		
		o, *u*		*w*			*p*		*p*, *f*
		s (before or after e, i, ä, ö, ü)		*z*			*b* (before or after e, i, ä, ö, ü)		
		k (before or after a)		*ḥ*			*s* (before or after a, o, u, y)		*č*, *ǧ*
		t (before or after a, o, u, y)		*t*			*k* (before or after o, u)		*q*
		nd, *nt*					*k* (before or after y)		
		i, *y*		*j*			*r* (before or after a, o, u, y)		*r*
		j (before or after e, i, ä, ö, ü)					*r* (before or after e, i, ä, ö, ü)		
		j (before or after a, o, u, y)					*š*		*š*
		nasal *j*					*č*		
		ö, *ü*					*nč*		
		k (before or after e, i, ä)		*k*			*t* (before or after e, i, ä, ö, ü)		*t*
		k (before or after ö, ü)					*d* (before or after e, i, ä, ö, ü)		
		l (before or after a, o, u, y)		*l*, *r*			*ld*, *lt*		

FIG. 87.—Old Turkish runic alphabet.

"The whole earth obeys me," Turxanthos had cried to the Byzantine envoy; 160 years later Bilge Kagan would use the same language:

"I, the heaven born wise Turkish Kagan, now that I have ascended the throne. Hear my words, you who come after me, my younger brothers and sisters and you, men of my race . . .

"When the blue sky above and the brown earth beneath

were created, between them were created the sons of men. Over the sons of men rose my ancestors, Boumin Kagan and Istemi Kagan. When they came to power they inaugurated the rule and laws of the Turks. From the four corners of the earth their enemies rose against them, but they went to war and conquered the peoples of the four corners of the earth, making them bow their heads and bend the knee . . .

"Now my brother, Kül-Tigin, is dead. I mourn him. My eyes, which still see are now become blind, my thoughts, although alert, have become unconscious. I mourn for him. But the sons of men are all born to die at heaven's appointed hour . . ."[96]

"I, the wise Tonjukuk, was born a vassal to the Chinese realm, for the Turkish people were then in thrall to China . . . By the grace of heaven I have allowed no foe to wear the cuirass, no bridled horse to caracole among my Turkish folk. Without the actions of Elteriš Kagan and without my own deeds after him, there would be neither realm nor people. . . . Now I am . . . old . . . and bowed down with years. But if a people governed by a Kagan in some country of the world had at its head only good for nothings, what misfortunes would befall them! I, the wise Tonjukuk, have caused to be written these words for the subjects of Bilge Kagan, the Turk."[97]

The Old Turkish runes had a strange epilogue, still a subject for controversy today and far from satisfactory for the history of writing.

A little more than forty years ago the Würzburg Orientalist, Franz Babinger, sprang a great surprise on the public by a discovery he had made in the family archives of the Fuggers of Hamburg—a description of the journey of Hans Dernschwam of Hraditschin during the years 1553–55. This man was a German from Bohemia who had studied at Vienna and Leipzig and later for thirty-five years occupied the post of administrator of the Fugger mines at Neusohl. Dernschwam was a member of the famous Imperial delegation sent to the Court of Suleiman I, whose future leader, Aughier Ghislain de Busbecq, had introduced to Europe the famous tale of the mighty deeds of the Emperor Augustus, the *Monumentum Ancyranum*. Dernschwam, student at the University of Vienna, promoted "bachelor of arts" at Leipzig, followed his master's example, collecting and copying a great number of valuable Greek and Latin inscriptions which, without him, would have totally disappeared today. At the end of the Codex which contains the description of his travels he conscientiously records a certain number of Roman and Greek inscriptions copied at Constantinople. But among these Roman inscriptions one of a particular nature caught the eye of the explorer. Dernschwam copied it from the wall of a stable of the delegation building in Constantinople, later called the "Khan of the Tatars", formerly a caravanserai where the sovereign lodged all the envoys of European powers, keeping them under surveillance like prisoners. Busbecq also stayed in this building; it was completely demolished in a fire in the 19th century. After describing the "inn", Dernschwam continues as follows: "I copied the following inscription on a marble plaque set in the stable wall. It is quite legible." [98]

Franz Babinger sent a photograph of the runic inscription, the presence of which in Constantinople he could not explain, to the decipherer of the Old Turkish runes, Vilhelm Thomsen in Copenhagen.

Thomsen identified it as a so-called Hunno-Scythian inscription in Hungarian; he was able to decipher several words and the approximate meaning of the writing. Franz Babinger completed the decipherment and the reading in collaboration with the Hungarian scholar, J. Sebestyén. This inscription threw a decisive light on an historical event already known from the Hungarian chronicles: the fate of a delegation of five people sent to the Court of Sultan Selim I by Ladislas II, King of Bohemia, who also ruled Hungary from 1490 to 1516. This delegation, led by Barnabas von Bela, was held for two years on the Golden Horn with vain promises. The tablet on the stable wall in the city of the Sultan, written in *gjaur jazizi*, "the writing of the infidels", was no less than a cry of distress from these messengers of the King of Bohemia and Hungary, who were virtually prisoners in the "Khan of the Envoys".

We reproduce here the exact text transcribed and translated by Franz Babinger; [99] the suppression of the e is reminiscent of Old Turkish writing.

This Constantinople inscription copied by Dernschwam was not the only known document in runic writing. Others had been known for centuries, the most ancient having been

Der richtiggestellte Text der Kerbinschrift.

Tausend · fünfhundert · fünfzehn · Jahre im schrieb man dies · Ladislau · Königs · fünf · Gesandte · ließ man warten · hier

· Béla + von · Barnabas · zwei · Jahre · hier · gewesen · Nichts · tat · Kaiser ·

· Kelej + von · Székel Thomas · schrieb · von hier aus · Sel (im türki) sche · Kaiser · fiel · ein · hundert · Pferde + mit ·

FIG. 88.—Runic inscription in Old Hungarian from Constantinople.

discovered in Nagy Szent Miklos. But the message of the envoys of Ladislas differs from the others because it is written from left to right. In a book published in 1598 on the language of the Huns (*Rudimenta priscae Hunnorum linguae . . .*) the Hungarian historian, J. Thelegdi, also speaks of these signs, which he declared frankly to be the writing of the ancient Huns. His opinion was not so incorrect as it might appear. All the known vestiges of this script came from one single region—the land of the Szeklers in Transylvania, who have always been, and still are, considered as the descendants of the authentic Huns.

The exaggerated nationalism of the Hunno-Hungarians (still alive today) received a serious blow when it was maintained that the Szekler runes, which H. Dernschwam, although he lived in the land for more than fifty years, no longer understood and identified as entirely unknown letters, possibly dating back to the runes of Ancient Turkey.

The resemblance between the two writings, recognised from 1890 from more ancient documents, is so striking that it cannot be contested.

The Fig. 89 below shows that four letters have been borrowed from the Greek and two from Glagolitsa, an ancient Slav alphabet.

This situation, so clear to outward appearance, poses a difficult problem. This is not caused by the presence of two letters of ancient Slav origin, easily explained by neighbouring influences, nor by the adoption of four Greek characters, which merely proves that the original content had been completed in eastern Europe within the sphere of Greek civilisation; but the signs which give food for thought are rather those for which no prior model exists (see Fig. 89). The most difficult problem, which has not yet been satisfactorily solved, resides in the chronological lacunae which separates the Old Turkish inscriptions of the 8th century A.D. and the Szekler runes which appear for the first time at the beginning of the 16th century. Some investigators have tried to see in the Old Hungarian runes a secret writing of the Szeklers which remained a jealously guarded secret and unknown to the masses; but it is difficult to admit that the secret could have been preserved so perfectly for centuries.

On thing is quite certain: it is not a question of the writing of Attila the Hun and his warrior hordes—no one has seriously

Phonetic value	Old Hungarian	Siberian	Greek or Glagolitsa	Phonetic value	Old Hungarian	Siberian	Greek or Glagolitsa
a, á			gr.	*m*			
b				*n*			
cz = ts				*ny = ń*			
cs = č				*o, ó*			gl.
d				*ö, ő*	later:		
e, é			gl.	*p*			
f			= þ gr.	*r*			
g				*s = š*			
gy = d'				*sz = s*			
h			= χ gr.	*t*			
i, í				*ty = t'*			
j				*u, ú*			
-k-				*ü, ű*	later:		
k(a-),(-a)k				*v*			
l			gr.	*z*			
ly = l'				*zs = ž*		(č)	

Fig. 89.—Old Hungarian compared with Old Turkish runes and Greek and Glagolitsa characters.

envisaged this possibility. Among the more recent theories, both of them highly controversial, the first maintains that the Szeklers are the descendants of the Chazar Turks, a race of whom the Magyars were slaves at the critical date for a possible adoption of writing, i.e. in the 9th century A.D.; the second, upheld by the Hungarian scholar B. Munkacsi, maintains that the literate intermediaries between the Ancient Turks and the Ancient Hungarians were the Comans, the nearest neighbours of the Szeklers, in the 12th and 13th centuries A.D.—a race descended from the Oghuses, themselves divided into tribes and frequently quoted as "Nine Oghuses", "Six Oghuses" and "Three Oghuses" in the Old Turkish inscriptions, either as subjects or enemies of the Kagan.

Whichever is the case, the epigraphic discoveries and decipherment work such as that of Vilhelm Thomsen have brought to light facts completely new to us Europeans; they have unveiled the mysterious threads stretching between the East and the West, the connections and undercurrents which play a hidden but often essential role in the common life of races —today, as in the age when Boumin Kagan and Istemi Kagan subjected to their yoke, "the peoples of the four corners of the earth, between the blue sky above and the brown earth below".

CHAPTER X

DECIPHERMENTS OF TOMORROW

ETRUSCAN, THE SCRIPTS OF THE INDUS VALLEY AND OF EASTER ISLAND

"*Gewöhnlich glaubt der Mensch, wenn er nur worte hört,*
Es musse sich dabei doch auch was denken lassen."—Goethe: Faust I.

"*The problem which arose on the Indus is . . . to all intents fruitless, at least as far as the text is concerned.*"—Piero Meriggi.[100]

"*And then they prayed to the God of Rangitea.*"—Tablet from Easter Island after Thomas Barthel.

To conclude the succinct choice of "voices in stone" that this book has endeavoured to present, let us take a look at three of the latest problems which so far have put up a stubborn resistance to all investigations. Two of them—Etruscan and the writing of Easter Island—are as bastions already breached: the outposts and battlements have fallen, but the citadel resists all attacks. The third, the Indus Valley script, is a fortress against which all assaults have been repulsed, whether in mass or single attacks. Today still riddles and labyrinths, these writings may well be deciphered tomorrow, to further enrich man's knowledge.

One of the riddles differs from the others inasmuch as it stubbornly resists all attempts at interpretation and has preserved its secret, although for two millennia it has lain at the very heart of the ancient civilised world. This is the "enigma of all Italic enigmas"—the language of the Etruscans.

It is not a question of the script; we have long since known how to read this. It needed Humanism and the Renaissance to wrest from the past the graphic characters of this race who taught and bequeathed so much to her nearest neighbours, the Romans—probably more than we believe today. Slowly and progressively their mystery was unveiled until Richard Lepsius was able to add to the new-found alphabet one of its last and most important letters. This decipherment has, therefore, taken centuries.

A discovery made in 1944 aroused the interests of students of the epigraphic problems of Ancient Italy. At Gubbio, the Ancient Umbrian Iguvium, were found by chance in a vaulted cave seven bronze tablets partly engraved on both sides, which were subsequently preserved in the local town hall. Five of these tablets were incised in the Umbrian script and language; the writing, like the other Italic alphabets bequeathed by the Etruscans, is of Greek origin and does not deny this affiliation; the language is closely akin to Latin. Despite these encouraging fixes, the decipherment of the Umbrian script, and even more the interpretation of the language which won for Lepsius at the age of twenty-two not only his doctorate but his spurs as a decipherer, remain a remarkable performance.

In the 15th century, and even later, it was believed that in the Iguvine Tables could be recognised not the Umbrian language but that of the Ancient Etruscans. This was to cause a serious delay to the decipherment. Notable progress was made by Teseo Ambrogio of Pavia, the Orientalist and *famoso autore*, in his *Introduction to Chaldaean, Syrian, Armenian and Ten Other Languages*, printed in 1539. The author of this imposing work in Latin discovered a correct value, extremely valuable for a knowledge of Etruscan, the sign 8 = f. This identification was rejected only to be readopted later.* Two centuries later Anton Francesco Gori published at Florence a *Museum Etruscum*, containing an Etruscan alphabet in which he gave the precise values of fifteen letters. Abbot Luigi Lanzi, in a once famous three-volume work published in 1789, established the true reading of the sign M = s. Richard Lepsius then proved that the letter ⵜ should read as z and not x, for the name of Ulysses transliterates in Etruscan in the form Utuze, very near to the Greek original, and not to the Latin form Uluxe, as it had been incorrectly read. When, after further knowledge acquired in the interval on the archaic forms of the different Greek alphabets, it was possible to identify the γ with the Greek χ (ch) and to discover at last in the inscriptions the long-sought-for q (1880), the decipherment of Etruscan writing was ended to the extent that we can talk of a decipherment here. The task of the 19th and 20th centuries was merely to collect the texts and

* In 1733 by Ludovic Bourget (cf. *Février Histoire de l'écriture*, p. 438).

Normal forms	Early forms 7th–5th centuries B.C.	Late forms 4th–1st centuries B.C.	Phonetic value	Normal forms	Early forms 7th–5th centuries B.C.	Late forms 4th–1st centuries B.C.	Phonetic value
𐌀	𐌀	𐌀	a	⊞			(s)
𐌁			(b)	O			(o)
𐌂	𐌂	𐌂	c(k)	𐌐	𐌐	𐌐	p
𐌃			(d)	𐌑	𐌑	𐌑	ś
𐌄	𐌄	𐌄	e	𐌒	𐌒		q
𐌅	𐌅	𐌅	v	𐌓	𐌓	𐌓	r
𐌆	𐌆	𐌆	z	𐌔	𐌔	𐌔	s
𐌇	𐌇	𐌇	h	𐌕	𐌕	𐌕	t
𐌈	𐌈	⊙	θ(th)	𐌖	𐌖	V	u
𐌉	𐌉	𐌉	i	𐌗	𐌗, +		ṡ
𐌊	𐌊		k	𐌘		𐌘	φ (ph)
𐌋	𐌋	𐌋	l	↓		↓	χ (ch)
𐌌	𐌌	𐌌	m		8	8	f
𐌍	𐌍	𐌍	n				

FIG. 90.—The Etruscan alphabet.

wait for them to be interpreted. But in this domain we can only signal a series of essays and isolated observations. The language in the main remains as before, a mystery.

The Etruscan alphabet displays a series of special characteristics; the most striking is the sign 8 = f, already known to have the same significance in the Lydian alphabet of Asia Minor—one of the many grounds in support of the ancient tradition dating from Herodotus, according to which the Etruscans migrated from Asia Minor, and were not autochthonous in Italy. The Etruscan alphabet abandoned the old signs O, X and F (o, ks and v) and always writes the "h" in its old closed form: 𐌇. Nor does it possess signs corresponding to the explosive sounds b, d and g. The script uses the letters 𐌈, 𐌘 and 𐌙 (th, ph and ch) without distinction for t, p and k. And finally the method of writing—almost always from right to left—shows that the Etruscan alphabet was borrowed at an early date, probably in the 8th century B.C., from the original Greek alphabet which was written for preference from right to left.

How can it be explained, then, that, knowing how to read Etruscan word for word for a long time now, we still understand nothing or practically nothing of the language?

It is fashionable to shift the responsibility for this state of affairs on the insufficiency of documents preserved. We possess about 9,000 Etruscan inscriptions, four-fifths of which are very short funeral inscriptions giving the bare names and indications of ancestry. Among the fuller documents we must quote the clay tablet of Santa Maria di Capua dating from the 5th century B.C. containing about 300 words, the earlier *Cippus Perusinus*, a 200-word epigraph in the Perugia Museum, two tablets of curses, two with the numbers 1–6 written in letters, an interesting leaden tablet from Magliano (6th century B.C.) the text of which (at least seventy words) is arranged in a spiral, and finally the famous bronze liver from Piacenza which served to teach apprentice augurers and has often been compared to certain similar objects of Babylonian and Hittite origin. All the inscriptions are engraved on stone, clay or metal.

By way of manuscripts we possess a unique example of incomparable value: the famous Agram mummy bandages, which are of great interest not only for Etruscology but for the history of writing in general, because they are the only extant examples of the *liber linteus*, the book written by hand on linen.

This linen manuscript was originally in the form of a roll, later cut into strips and used to swathe the mummy of an Egyptian woman; it probably dates from the 1st century B.C.; found in Egypt it was sent by a Croatian traveller to the Zagreb Museum,

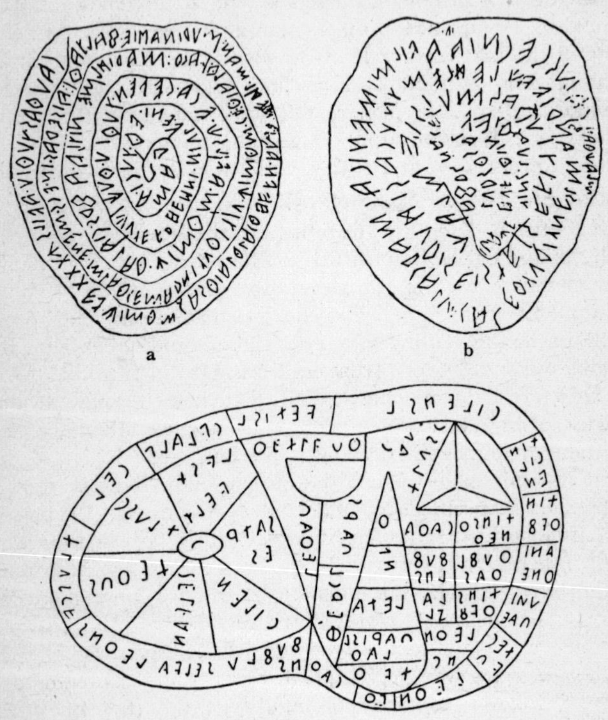

FIG. 91.

Above: Leaden tablet from Magliano with text written in spiral form (a = recto, b = verso).
Below: Bronze liver from Piacenza.

where, in 1872, J. Krall discovered the writing on the bandages. This Etruscan text of more than 5,000 words is the longest we possess.

As we see, then, there exists a considerable documentation, including a text of more than 5,000 words! Decipherments have succeeded with a far more restricted material—for example, the Gublitic script. One is, therefore, justified in asking why in these circumstances the language cannot be interpreted, and even more so since, in 1932, it was found possible to read the most-effaced, formerly illegible passages on the Zagreb mummy bandages by submitting them to infra-red rays.

The reasons are many. First, all the longer texts are monolingual—Latino-Etruscan bilingual texts exist only in the very short burial inscriptions, which are of little linguistic interest: proper names, names of parents and kin, official titles, indications of dates and the oft-repeated words "died" or "deceased". That is all that can be extracted. The absence of a lengthy Latino-Etruscan bilingual text is one of the main reasons for the delay in decipherment, despite the work on the mummy bandages that seemed so full of promise.

Investigators have applied and are still applying on the one hand a method of decipherment of the actual inscriptions based on combinations (a method which proved itself in the initial stages of a series of successful decipherments) and, on the other hand, the etymological method of comparison with languages that are obviously akin to it. And this is the main obstacle.

According to the meagre knowledge so far acquired, the Etruscan language is in fact completely unique, not only in Italy but in general (certain scholars believe it to be related to Lydian, which itself is too little known to be of much help). This is why there exists no master key which in one form or another helped in all the great decipherments to reveal the secret of the language—the conviction or even the bare supposition that such and such a language was related to the one about to be "broken". Thus Champollion was helped by Coptic, Grotefend by Avestan, Hans Bauer and Edouard Dhorme by Semitic. But even in the case where the discovery of the language brought certain surprises to the decipherers—let us recall Hrozný recognising the Indo-European character of Hittite cuneiform, Smith the Greek origin of Cypriote, Ventris that of Creto-Mycenaean—the language, once recognised, was of decisive help in the continuation and completion of the task.

This is the obstacle which has so far faced all attempts at deciphering Etruscan despite the names of Gods and persons, official titles, designations of parents and the other meagre vocabulary discovered mainly by combinations, and recently by the bilingual path, i.e. by a thorough comparison of Etruscan inscriptions with Greek and Latin examples analogous in their content, purpose and according to sundry archaeological conditions.

The Romans, whose empire and people absorbed the Etruscans so completely, and who preserved with such loving care and pride their own antiquities, the memorials of an ancient past, also preserved the precious cultural patrimony of their first teachers, almost to the decline of the Western Empire in the 5th century A.D.; 400 years after Christ the Etruscan language was still being used in the Roman camps. Although Etruscan is lost to us, the fault lies with the copyists of the Middle Ages, who in principle only copied and perpetuated mainly Latin, seldom Greek and never the other languages. Had Maecenas, the wealthy friend of the Emperor Augustus, proverbial patron of the great Roman poets (he traced his descent to the Etruscan kings) with only a trace of his usual generosity in favouring verse and the *ars latina*—protected the language of his ancestors, his influence might have safeguarded to posterity at least a superficial knowledge of this language. In fact the bilingual document, the long, pithy, Latino-Etruscan document, remains the nostalgic dream of the Etruscologist. In 1956 Massimo Pallottino, the leading expert on this subject, at Rome University said: "The discovery of such an inscription would revolutionise the entire course of Etruscan investigation by providing basic external elements for the interpretation of the texts and resolving once and for all the greater part of this age old problem."[101]

It is not surprising, therefore, to find with what keenness the Italians have sought for these inscriptions. In February 1957 the Press announced that the ancient Etruscan town of Vulci on the slope of Monte Amiata, the extinct Tuscan volcano, might, in the opinion of Italian archaeologists, provide the key to the mystery. Excavations continue. The hope of the specialists, still very much alive according to Pallottino, is based on the fact that the purpose of these excavations is no longer the finding of tombs which would bring no important revelation on the writing and the language, but for a forum, the centre of the political, economic and cultural life of the ancient city.

But for the moment to approach nearer to this mysterious race, to sound its true nature, we must be content with the documents afforded by the characteristic art preserved in their tombs, and above all by the incomparable frescoes—these visions of a serenity already obscured by the shadow of sadness, "the message of farewell" of the former powerful masters of Central Italy.[102]

Let us now consider the riddle of another writing. One of its great charms is that the documents which have survived—seals and steatite amulets—are usually little masterpieces. Let us cross the seas—in one enormous bound from Central Italy to north-west India. Let us go back in time to the middle of the 1st as far as the middle of the 3rd century B.C. Twenty-five years of excavation, investigation and study have won for us 2,000 years of Indian history, and this achievement can be considered one of the most remarkable in the history of archaeology.[103]

During this very short period a new civilisation had been discovered: the so-called Indus Valley cultures of Harappa and Mohenjo-Daro.

The massive hill of ancient ruins on which stands the small town of Harappa in the Punjab had already been observed in 1820 and studied more closely in 1853. For several score of years new seals were discovered, and some of them were published from 1875 onwards. The seals, mostly bearing pictures of animals and symbolic signs, aroused considerable interest in scientific circles as soon as they appeared, and their origin gave rise to many bold theories, one of the first being that the newly discovered writing was the ancestor of Indian Brahmi. This somewhat dubious hypothesis found partisans until very recently.

Unfortunately during the first years Harappa did not turn out to be for archaeology as fruitful a region as had been hoped; in common with nearly all classical ruins it had long served as a quarry for the nearby towns and villages. When the British built the Karachi–Lahore railway in 1856 they also took a mass of material from these ruins. It was not until January 1921, under the direction of Rai Bahadur Daya Ram Sahni, that excavations according to modern scientific methods were undertaken and successfully pursued from 1926 to 1934 by Madhu Sarup Vats.

Chance led to the discovery of a second ruined site, the name of which has been given to this lost civilisation. In 1922 the Indian archaeologist, Rakhal Das Banerjee, dug up a stupa (a Buddhist shrine in the form of a tower) dating from the 1st century B.C. and the monastery to which it belonged, and discovered that the ancient buildings had themselves been built on foundations formed by far more ancient "prehistoric" rubble. Sir John Marshall, at the time Director of Archaeological Works in India, immediately recognised the importance of the new site, Mohenjo-Daro, or "the place of the dead", some 400 miles south-west of Harappa and about 20 miles from Larkana in Central Sind. He supervised the excavations in person from 1922 to 1927; his work was continued by E. J. H. Mackay from 1927 to 1931; among the sites of lesser importance was that of Chanhu-Daro, south of Mohenjo-Daro. The activity of these two investigators was the basis of Sir John Marshall's monumental works: *Mohenjo-Daro and the Indus Civilisation*, 3 vols., London, 1931, and of E. J. H. Mackay's, *The Indus Civilisation*, London, 1935, and *Further Excavations at Mohenjo-Daro*, Delhi, 1937–38, to which was soon added the important monograph by G. R. Hunter: *The Script of Harappa and Mohenjo-Daro and its Connection with other Scripts*, London, 1954.

For readers who wish to study in greater detail this proto-Indian civilisation the above works are of great instructive interest. We shall confine ourselves here to casting a rapid glance at this script which has not yet been deciphered.

The characters, as we have already mentioned, were found exclusively engraved on seals (or amulets, as Mackay thought, because the seals are pierced in various ways, so that it could not be determined whether they were worn or attached to some merchandise, sack or utensil), either in the form of texts accompanying pictures of animals or as simple autonomous inscriptions.

This accounts for the various setbacks in the decipherment of this script; the brevity of the known inscriptions presents a serious obstacle; moreover, the signs are so numerous and varied that scholars have not yet been able to agree on their final total. While certain experts distinguish 400, and G. R. Hunter considers a great number of them to be simple variants and arrives at a total of 150 basic signs, we prefer to take the middle course, and to follow Piero Meriggi, who gives the number as approximately 200 signs.

A quick glance will show us that a part of these signs consist of stylised images, while others are of a linear nature. This fact, combined with the number of signs—too large for a

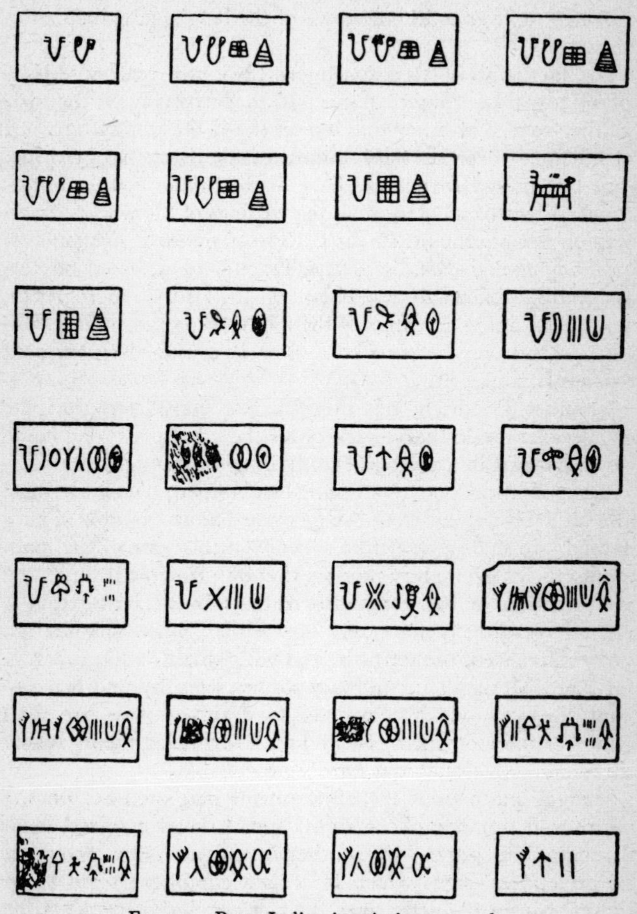

FIG. 92.—Proto-Indian inscriptions on seals.

syllabary but too small for a purely ideographic script—allows us to conclude that it is a mixture of ideograms and phonetic signs.

But the toughest obstacle to decipherment and to a credible reading does not essentially reside either in the constricted number of surviving documents or in the brevity of the texts. Another difficulty became apparent, and one far more difficult to overcome: our total ignorance of the language embodied in this script.

The fact that isolated specimens obviously reached Mesopotamia by trade routes has given birth to extravagant theories. Another source of untenable hypothesis is the purely outward resemblance of certain signs to those of other systems of writing. Thus Friedrich Hrozný—we have already described the attack launched by this scholar on all the writings of the world—in an essay on decipherment, *On the Earliest Migration of Races and the Problem of Proto-Indian Civilisation*, Prague, 1939, based on certain purely external resemblances to Hittite hieroglyphs, applied the phonetic values of these in reading the Indian symbols. In this way he reached a most surprising decipherment of proto-Indian writing.

Johannes Friedrich, not unjustifiably, considered that the only serious preliminary work of all the attempts so far made was to be read in a profound study by Piero Meriggi.[104]

Apart from the concrete results he obtained, which are most difficult to refute, this work can be quoted as an example of pure method; we shall give a brief account of this: one of the main reasons for its exemplary merit is that on principle it limits the interpretation of the actual inscriptions by declaring that a phonetic reading is absolutely impossible. Since this has not yet been realised, the script is, and will remain, undeciphered. But Piero Meriggi's preliminary studies seem by and large to point the way which may lead to decipherment—we shall ignore for the moment a new and most surprising theory which still seems provisional and hardly practicable.

Meriggi starts from the above-mentioned premises on the nature and number of the signs, and deduces a mixed ideo-phonographic system. With other investigators, he recognises the presence of signs which in certain conditions seem to be simultaneously phonetic signs, and in conclusion presents the results which he considers established in the following form: first, the knowledge of certain secondary signs (word separators and recognition ideograms); secondly, the signs for the three most frequent nominal endings of the unknown language, and thirdly, the transliteration (but naturally not the reading) of a series of individual signs.

From this sum total we shall deal with the second and third points, which are particularly instructive.

On the principle adopted by Alice Kober when compiling her first grid for Creto-Mycenaean Linear B, Meriggi compares groups of signs, distinguished from each other by their terminations, which allows him to fix three particularly frequent nominal terminations, the signs [sign] [sign] and [sign], which for technical reasons he transcribes as A, U and Y (ψ) (this, we must repeat, does not mean that he attributes to them phonetic values, a, u and y, i.e. ps). Now, considering the majority of the seals as administrative hand stamps with no indication as to proper names, he already expects to find in the texts three cases: the nominative as the case denoting the object described, the genitive to indicate the ownership or the complementary partitive, and finally a dative to denote the goal or destination of the objects in question. He recognised these three cases in the three above-mentioned signs (A = nominative, U = genitive, Y/ψ = dative).

We have indicated broadly the objective considerations which led Meriggi to admit these relations grammatically expressed by the nominative, genitive and dative cases. Another factor gives support and illustrates his reasoning, viz. the interpretation of the signs themselves, which we mentioned above as the third point. Professor Meriggi held in principle to the symbolical significance closest to the signs and subsequently tried to relate them to each other, objectively and grammatically.

The examples given below allow us to understand Meriggi's interpretation of the graphic signs. His most important equivalents are as follows:

Seal [sign]
Mortar (with corn pestle) [sign]
Load, load to carry [sign]
Quadruple load to carry [sign]
Horse [sign]
Mattock [sign]
Scythe ("to scythe" "harvest") [sign]
Reaper, harvester [sign]

Man with the mortar, pounder, miller 

Genitive ending!

Corn

Seed, sowing

Fruit with pods

Couch

House

Temple

Table

Man

Archer, soldier

Inspector

Officer, employee

Thanks to these equations, very revealing readings were achieved. Thus the series of signs , which recurs twice in Meriggi's transcription: CORN–OFFICER–LOZENGE–TABLE reads: "Corn (for) the Officer's (?) mess."

But parallel to these eminently feasible deductions drawn by Meriggi from the symbolical nature of the signs, another fact speaks even more clearly in favour of his interpretation: certain translations once admitted were confirmed when applied to other inscriptions, giving them plausibility; all the texts translated in this manner point to one and the same order of ideas, to an expressly agricultural terminology, from the corn, the seeds and the podded fruits to the scythes, mattocks, mills and mortars.

The main criticism that can be levelled at this conception lies in the fact that the images, from the moment they become stylised, naturally give place to all kinds of interpretations; Hrozný, for example, explained that Meriggi's "podded fruits" could be a bucket and cord!

As we have already said, one of the main difficulties of this decipherment is that we do not know the language we are investigating. The most ancient Indo-European language known in India, Vedic Sanskrit, is eliminated *a priori* because the vestiges of the Indus valley scripts date from a period long before the Aryan migrations. To evoke the language of the nearby island of Brahui—Dravidian, therefore pre-Aryan—as Sir John Marshall did, gives no better results, because between this language and that of the Harappa and Mohenjo-Daro texts some 500 years have elapsed—an unbridgeable gap which would no longer allow us to make any correlation even had one existed, particularly since Brahui is strongly marked with foreign influence.

The year 1934 saw one of the boldest hypotheses known in Orientalism, which has always been so rich in hypotheses. Let us state categorically that most modern investigators reject it as a pure figment of the imagination: this the layman will find hard to admit. This audacious theory consists in affirming the parenthood of the two scripts compared in Fig. 93—and who could deny it on examining the table?

At first glance the resemblance between the Indus script and that of Easter Island seems undeniable. In order to understand why experts, in the face of this evidence, reject, at least provisionally, this convincing comparison let us study more closely the writing of Easter Island.

We owe the exceptional documents of this strange script to a stroke of good fortune. The *kohau rongo rongo*, "the speaking woods", of Easter Island had for the most part been destroyed by the fanatical zeal of the natives during the last few decades, when the population of this small island was decimated and reduced to less than 200 souls, and when the French and Belgian missionaries began to proselytize the survivors. A small number of these tablets, however, came into the possession of Bishop Jaussen of Tahiti, who, recognising their historical importance, tried to decipher and preserve for posterity these vestiges of a lost civilisation. Since none of the natives who knew the writing had survived, his task was exceedingly difficult. The Bishop finally learnt that a well-born native was living as a refugee in Tahiti; he summoned him and gave him a text to read. A knowing smile appeared on the face of young Metoro; he took the proffered tablet and started a monotonous chant. Following each line with his finger, he then turned and read it from the other direction. The Bishop noted down what the islander was singing. He could, however, neither understand nor translate it into French; having been able to draw no rational conclusion from his Polynesian version, he jotted down what he had heard to the best of his ability, completing and adding here and there,

FIG. 93.—Comparison between the Indus Valley and Easter Island scripts (I, III, V, VII: Indus script; II, IV, VI, VIII: Easter Island script).

transcribed the poem and produced an intelligible French translation. Doubtless the good Metoro, proud of his half-forgotten knowledge, did his best with this honorary task, but cheated because he was ignorant of what he was uttering.

It is obvious that the glossary compiled by the Bishop based on such data could not fail to lead the experts into error. Moreover, the original text compiled from Metoro's audition had disappeared.

The desire to recover this document, to examine its content and to see whether or not it could be used, encouraged the young Hamburg ethnologist, Thomas Barthel, in 1954 to search in Rome the archives of the Order to which Bishop Jaussen had belonged. To his joy, he discovered in an old dusty tome an insignificant but precious bilingual document—Metoro's chant in Polynesian and the Bishop's French version.

Barthel, too, was forced to admit what had raised so many difficulties for his predecessors: it was not a genuine bilingual; it did, however, offer certain fixes, and we shall now give a brief account of how the young investigator obtained the first tangible results. The Easter Island script—it comprises about 500 signs, which Barthel took some years to assemble, compare and study—is manifestly based on a familiar principle: that of the phonetic rebus. We find, for example, in the middle of a text which both the French and Polynesian versions revealed to be of religious tenor the stylised image of an open shell. Now, the word for shell in Polynesian is *pure*, and *pure* also means prayer!

After a detailed study, which consisted in patiently and progressively comparing the two linguistic versions with the symbolical text of the "speaking woods", Thomas Barthel established with certainty, at the beginning of 1955, a small series of basic signs. Fig. 94 shows the first phrase which he succeeded in translating (see page 310).

But the most sensational result of Barthel's decipherment was the reading of an oft-repeated refrain: "Then they addressed their prayers to the god of Rangitea." Rangitea, "bright field", is the name of one of the Friendly Islands, 1,500 miles from Easter Island. Were we to see in this the first concrete solution to the problem of the origin of the islanders, a hotly discussed problem which for many years had employed archaeologists, ethnologists and historians—apart from the subsidiary

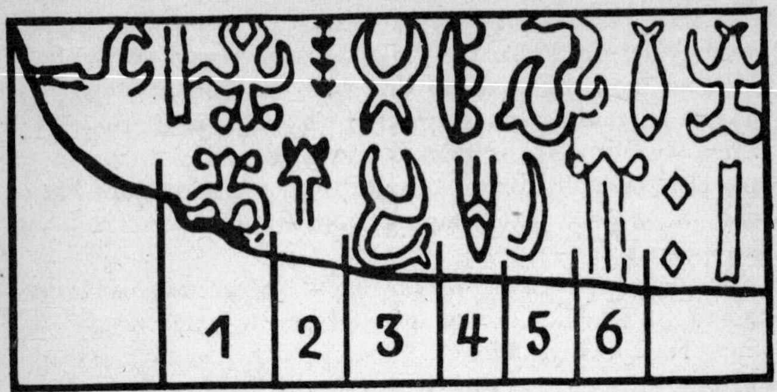

FIG. 94.—"Rongo, Lord of the sky and the earth, who created light." The incipit of a tablet from Easter Island after Thomas Barthel: (1) the lord, (2) of the sky, (3) Rongo (name of the god), (4) of the earth, (5) made, (6) light.

questions of Polynesian colonisation and the relations of Easter Island with that other eastern land from which, according to another tradition, came the ancestors of the present-day natives: Peru of the Incas? Specialist judgment on Doctor Barthel's decipherment is by no means unanimous.

We shall confine ourselves here to casting a swift glance at these problems within the framework of the history of writing. The really astounding resemblance between certain Indus Valley signs and those of Easter Island remains to be explained.

But almost insuperable obstacles oppose a direct or even indirect correlation between the two scripts. "Anyone who disbelieves miraculous intervention will best consider the outward resemblance of the two scripts as a matter of pure chance."[105]

As a start, we must "unmask" the apparently convincing proof afforded by Fig. 93. This compares forty-eight characters of each language, and even the hundred or so signs which the propounder of this theory of kinship, W. von Hevesy,[106] uses in this figure represent only a small proportion of the total number of Easter Island signs—i.e. about a fifth. Moreover, in this table all the signs were especially apposite, and this procedure cannot be allowed to pass without some scientific doubt being raised, because the selection was made without reference to the frequency or the typical form of certain signs: when it is necessary to have recourse to rare variants, or possibly unique items, this type of comparison loses much of its powers of persuasion.

Even if we are prepared to admit without reservation the outward resemblance, this in itself proves nothing at all about the meaning and value of the signs. Especially a symbolical sign as world-wide, as clear and as obvious as that representing "man" cannot serve as proof, because the more stylised it becomes, the less chance there is for other possible representations. "Two legs, two arms and a head on top"—the image is finally valid from the North Pole to the Equator; it will invariably be: or something approaching it!

But this correlation becomes unlikely when we consider the enormous distance which separates the two writings both in space and time. It was in the middle of the 19th century A.D. that the use and knowledge of Easter Island script disappeared; the Indus script, on the other hand, flourished *circa* 2500 B.C. The gap is almost 4,000 years; and even if we credit the most recent as yet unconfirmed theories, according to which we must add 1,000 years to the age of Easter Island writing, there still remains a gap of 3,500 years. As to the geographical distance involved—the second great obstacle to the correlation—attempts have been made to bridge this gap by means of various theories which will not convince the impartial observer.

Should the decipherment of Indus script never be accomplished, we may in the near future obtain a tolerably accurate reading of all the characters of the "speaking woods". For months, Thomas Barthel has been wrestling with the riddles of this small Pacific Island—all the secrets which the "speaking woods", caves, petroglyphs and the well-known colossal statues, the "arikis" and "mohais" may conceal.

A long journey, a pilgrimage rich in surprise, has led us from the banks of the Nile to the shores of Easter Island, from the Sumerians, Babylonians and Assyrians to the Ancient Turks, the Island of Minos and the tombs of Etruria to the Valley of the Indus—a path with a host of detours through epochs and continents. But how many subjects have we left untouched? East Turkestan, for example, with its astounding epigraphic discoveries; the Far East, the cradle and homeland of an incomparable civilised script and literature; Ancient America and its hieroglyphs; the sinister grimaces of pre-Columbian civilisations; North and Central Africa and southern Arabia, whose burning sands take their toll of the investigators in search for inscriptions, in search of the "mother of all scripts which speak" and the "father of the wise", as a Sumerian saying proclaims.

We were obliged to curb our ambition. *Non multa, sed multum*, said the Romans—we did not wish to present a sketchy outline of too many subjects, but to recreate by a few well-chosen examples, significant for the civilisation of the West, the miracle of signs, and to delve deeply into the recesses where the human mind has deposited its most precious possessions, upon which it eternally feeds. Language distinguishes man from the beast and raises him above all creatures. Language is the very essence of the mind—it is the sound and the echo, designed to disappear with no possibility of recapture, until the noble vessel of writing has assured its preservation and its survival down the ages.

As old as man is the conflict between mind and matter, the principle of his existence. Now dedicated to the spirit in ecstasy, now subjected wholly to matter, he continues his struggle to reach the perfect balance, and often crashes against this duality, against the inexorable and perpetual exigencies of reconciling contrasts. In writing, man has achieved one of the happiest marriages of mind and matter. It is also the power and the glory, the plenitude and beauty, the imperishable charm, of this marvellous alliance that we have tried to evoke in this book, by unveiling a realm where man, made in the image of his Creator, has in turn become a creator.

NOTES

CHAPTER I

[1] Franz Miltner, "Wesen und Geburt der Schrift", *Historia Mundi*, Vol. III (Berne, 1954), p. 27.

[2] Arnold Toynbee, *An Historian's Approach to Religion* (Oxford University Press, 1956), p. 3.

[3] Franz Miltner, op. cit.

[4] Hans Jensen, *Die Schrift in Vergangenheit und Gegenwart* (Glückstadt, 1935), p. 16.

[5] Ibid., p. 16 et seq.

[6] Translated by H. F. Cary.

[7] Hans Jensen, op. cit., p. 24.

[8] Jan Tschichold, *Geschichte der Schrift in Bildern* (Basel O.J.), 2nd ed., p. 1.

[9] *Quick*, No. 42, Jg. 9 (Munich, October 2nd, 1956), p. 38.

CHAPTER II

[10] Herodotus II, 125, translated by H. F. Cary. The figure is far too low as a result of Herodotus making a miscalculation in converting Egyptian into Greek (Attic) currency.

[11] This version and the quotations from Horapollo are according to A. Wiedemann.

[12] To what extent Horapollo's symbolical and allegorical interpretations appealed to the taste of the age, and how enduring was his influence, can probably be traced to the fact that no less an artist than Albrecht Dürer made a series of drawings based on hieroglyphs. These drawings (particularly those for the Emperor Maximilian's triumphal arches) are of great artistic merit, both in concept and execution, but their effect is un-Egyptian (Vienna, Kunsthistorisches Museum).

[13] This and other quotations referring to the life and works of Champollion have been taken from Hermine Hartleben's excellent biography, *Champollion* (Berlin (Weidmann), 1906), 2 vols.

[14] The Copts (Egyptian Christians) were partly united to Rome thanks to the efforts of the previously mentioned Propaganda Congregation which actively favoured the revival of Coptic.

[15] Hans Jensen, op. cit., p. 38.

[16] Max Pieper, *Die ägyptische Literatur* (Wildpark-Potsdam, 1927), p. 67.

CHAPTER III

[17] The Danish assyriologist, Scend Aage Pallis, in his all-embracing work *The Antiquity of Iraq* (Copenhagen, 1956), p. 63, points out that the British orientalist, Thomas Hyde, in his *Historia religionis veterum Persarum*, 1700, calls Persian writing *dactuli pyramidales seu cuneiformes*, thus speaking of "cuneiform" twelve years before the appearance of Kämpfer's book. He is indignant that the whole of the specialised literature credits Kämpfer with the discovery of this term. In spite of Pallis's objection the author has followed the majority of scholars, first because Hyde uses the term "cuneiform" only as an alternative to "pyramidal", and secondly because Kämpfer, as the history of decipherment proves, has found a more lasting echo with his designation *litterae cuneatae*. This fact should be established, although we do not dispute Hyde's priority in time.

[18] K. Meier-Lemgo, *Engelbert Kämpfer* (Stuttgart, 1937), p. 26.

[19] Ibid., p. 67.
[20] Ibid.
[21] Translated by H. F. Cary.
[22] Not 1815, as most learned works maintain.
[23] Ernst Diez, *Iranische Kunst* (Vienna (Andermann), 1944), p. 114.
[24] *Archaeolgia*, Vol. XXXIV (London, 1852), p. 75.
[25] Ibid., pp. 75 et seq.
[26] Translated by H. F. Cary.
[27] Translated by F. W. König, *Relief und Inschrift des Königs Dareios I. am Felsen von Bagistan* (Leyden (Brill), 1938), p. 36.
[28] Ibid., p. 38.

CHAPTER IV

[29] Cf. J. Friedrich.
[30] Carl Bezold, "Julius Oppert", *Zeitschrift für Assyriologie*, Vol. 19, 1905/6, pp. 169–73.
[31] Ibid.
[32] Bruno Meissner, *Die babylonisch-assyrische Literatur* (Wildpark–Potsdam, 1930), p. 80.
[33] Ibid., pp. 81–2.

CHAPTER V

[34] Dr. A. D. Mordtmann, "Entzifferung und Erklärung der armenischen Keilschriften von Van und der Umgegend", *Zeitschrift der Deutschen Morgenländischen Gesellschaft*, XXVI, 1872, p. 625.
[35] Ibid., p. 626.
[36] Ibid., p. 627.
[37] Translated by H. F. Cary.
[38] Mordtmann, op. cit., p. 628.
[39] Ibid.
[40] Johannes Friedrich: *Entzifferungsgeschichte der hethitischen Hieroglyphenschrift* (Stuttgart, 1939), p. 17.
[41] Gustav Herbig, *Wege und Ziele der hethitischen Sprachforschung* (Breslau, 1922), p. 5.
[42] Hugo Winckler, "Nach Boghasköi!" *Der Alte Orient*, Jg. 14, pp. 17 et seq.
[43] Ibid., pp. 27 et seq.
[44] Ibid., pp. 29 et seq.
[45] Not in Poland, as Kurt Marek-Ceram maintains in *Enge Schlucht und Schwarzer Berg* (Hamburg, 1955), p. 73, but in the Austro-Hungarian Monarchy, today C.S.R.
[46] *Mitteilungen der Deutschen Orientgesellschaft*, 56, December 1915, p. 25.
[47] Johannes Friedrich, "Entzifferung verschollener Schriften und Sprachen", *Verstandl. Wissensch.*, vol. 51 (Berlin–Göttingen–Heidelberg), 1954.
[48] Ibid., pp. 60 et seq.
[49] J. Friedrich (cf. note 40), p. 25.
[50] Piero Meriggi, "Die hethitische Hieroglyphenschrift", *Zeitschrift für Assyriologie*, N.F.V., XXXIX, 1930, p. 199.
[51] Ibid., p. 201.
[52] Letter to the author from Professor Gelb dated August 14th, 1957.
[53] Emil Forrer, *Die Entzifferung der hethitischen Bilderschrift*, *Forschungen und Fortschritte*, 1932, VIII, p. 4.
[54] J. Kohler and F. E. Peiser, *Hammurabi's Gesetz*, Vol. I (Leipzig, 1904), XXVI, 15–40.
[55] J. Friedrich (cf. note 40), p. 83.

[56] Letter to the author from Professor Gelb dated August 14th, 1957.
[57] J. Friedrich, op. cit., pp. 37 et seq.
[58] Ibid., p. 38.
[59] J. Friedrich (cf. note 47), p. 83.
[60] For the different variants of the characters see above all the reproduction of Meriggi's decipherment (Fig. 58).
[61] Dr. Margarete Riemschneider, "Die Welt der Hethiter", *Grosse Kulturen der Frühzeit* (Stuttgart, 1954), pp. 93 et seq.
[62] From a relief at Marash showing Prince Tarhumpias on the lap of the queen or of a nurse.
[63] Riemschneider, op. cit., p. 93.
[64] Ibid., p. 110.
[65] Ibid., pp. 37 et seq.

CHAPTER VI

[66] "Die Entzifferung des Keilschriftalphabets von Ras Schamra," *Forschungen und Fortschritte*, VI, 1930, 306–8.
[67] With respect for the truth, and to show to what point errors can arise in such combinations elaborated by great experience, remarkable insight and with all the means at the disposal of science, we must mention that Bauer in this instance made a mistake which was soon to be corrected by Dhorme: Bauer's "k" was really an "m" and his "m" was an "s". Bauer had not observed (this was inevitable at this initial stage) that the scribe had not put the word separator before a certain word and that what he had taken for a suffix was in reality a monosyllabic word. This error resulted in a number of further inaccuracies. In our explanation we have followed Bauer's arguments because his method, accurate in principle, led him to his goal.
[68] The most meagre documents at times have their uses. One of the most surprising confirmations of this fact was in the decipherment of Ugaritic, the subsequent discovery of a list in Ugaritic cuneiform enumerating localities with their deliveries of wine, the number of jars expressed in Ugaritic numbers, written phonetically. The sum total of these numbers amounted to 148 jars, and at the foot of this list, in Akkadian and in numbers, gave the number "148 jars of wine". Cf. Johannes Friedrich, *Entzifferung verschollener Schriften und Sprachen* (Berlin–Göttingen–Heidelberg), 1954, pp. 71 et seq.
[69] *Syria*, XII, pp. 15–23 and 193–224; also on p. 194 the table of the alphabet in its new form.
[70] Pascal continues: "It is of the greatest importance for the whole of life to know whether the soul is mortal or immortal." This duality which Pascal thought to discern in the spiritual state of his period was resolutely opposed by Virolleaud: a scholar of the 20th century, he pursued the "Copernican" way of indefatigable search for truth, even in the domains of history and religion.
[71] Johannes Friedrich, "Ras Schamra. Ein Uberblick, über Funde und Forschungen": *Der Alte Orient*, Vol. 33, Heft 1/2 (Leipsig 1933), pp. 32 et seq.
[72] In a letter to the author dated March 11th, 1957.
[73] Ibid.
[74] *Syria*, XXV, pp. 1–35.
[75] A. Jirku, "Wortschatz und Grammatik der gublitschen Inschriften", *Zeitschrift der Deutschen Morgenländischen Gesellschaft*, 1952, pp. 102/206 et seq. For readers who are more closely acquainted with the material we must mention that the author is well aware of the close connection of the two newly deciphered scripts in this chapter with the problem of the Sinai script and the origin of the alphabet. Since the latter does not come within the scope of this book and the former is still a matter of controversy, he has renounced any elaboration.

CHAPTER VII

76 He tried to see in this tablet from Dali (Edalion) a decree of the Egyptian Pharaoh Amasis (568–525 B.C.). The Duke was of the same opinion.
77 *Entzifferung verschollener Schriften und Sprachen* (Berlin–Göttingen–Heidelberg), 1954, p. 104.
78 Actually written "ka—se", since the Cypriote script which Brandis had not yet seen consists only of syllables (some consisting of a single vowel) and never of single consonants.

CHAPTER VIII

79 Sir Arthur J. Evans, *Scripta Minoa I* (Oxford, 1909), p. 16.
80 Michael Ventris/John Chadwick, *Documents in Mycenaean Greek* (Cambridge, 1956), p. 11.
81 Ibid.
82 Ibid., p. 15.
83 Letter to the author from John Chadwick dated February 22nd, 1957.
84 Ibid.
85 Ibid.
86 H(ugo) M(ühlestein), *Basler Nachrichten*, September 20th, 1956, supplement No. 400.
87 Ventris/Chadwick, op. cit., p. 25.
88 Dr. W. Merlingen, "Die kretische Schrift entziffert", *Der Mittelschullehrer und die Mittelschule*, Nr. 9 (Vienna, 1954), p. 12.
89 Ibid., p. 13.

CHAPTER IX

90 In this connection may I mention the collection published by my teacher, Professor E. von Ivanka, *Byzantinische Geschichtsschreiber* (*Styria*, Graz–Vienna–Cologne 1954), in which he has aimed at revealing the wealth of Byzantine historical sources, hitherto available only to professional historians, not merely as scientific sources but as literary documents of general interest to the history of civilisation? This collection, warmly acclaimed by international critics, is a companion volume to *Osmanische Geschichtsschreiber* by Richard Kreutel issued by the same publishing house.
91 Ernst Doblhofer, "Byzantinische Diplomaten und östliche Barbaren", *Byzantinische Geschichtsschreiber*, edited by E. von Ivanka, Vol. IV (Graz–Vienna–Cologne, 1955), pp. 136 et seq.
92 Ibid., pp. 137 et seq.
93 Ibid., pp. 170–2.
94 Ibid., p. 173.
95 Translated by H. F. Cary.
96 Vilhelm Thomsen, *Inscriptions de l'Orkhon dechiffrées* (Helsingfors, 1896), pp. 114 et seq., 97 and 113.
97 Vilhelm Thomsen, "Alttürkische Inschriften aus der Mongolei", *Zeitschrift der Deutschen Morgenländischen Gesellschaft*, Vol. 78 (N.F.3, 1924), pp. 121–75.
98 Franz Babinger, "Eine neuentdeckte ungarische Kerbschrift aus Konstantinopel vom Jahre 1515", *Ungarische Rundschau für historische und soziale Wissenschaften*, III (Jg. 1914), p. 44.
99 Ibid., p. 51.

[100] "Zur Indusschrift", *Zeitschrift der Deutschen Morgenländischen Gesellschaft*, 87 (N.F. 12, 1934), p. 198.

[101] Massimo Pallottino, *The Etruscans*, Pelican Book, A 310, 1956, p. 241.

[102] *Tarquinia. Wandmalereien aus etruskischen Grabern.* Photos by Walter Dräyer, introduction by Massimo Pallottino (Munich (Piper), 1955), p. 48.

[103] David Diringer, *The Alphabet* (London (Hutchinson), 1949), p. 81.

[104] Johannes Friedrich, *Entzifferung verschollener Schriften und Sprachen* (Berlin–Göttingen–Heidelberg, 1954), p. 137; Piero Meriggi, *Zur Indusschrift*, cf. note 100, and "Uber wichtige Indussiegel aus Vorderasien", *Orientalistische Literatur-Zeitung*, 1937.

[105] J. Friedrich, op. cit., cf. note 104, p. 140.

[106] "Österinselschrift und Indusschrift," *Orientalistische Literatur-Zeitung*, 1934.

BIBLIOGRAPHY

The literature on the decipherment and interpretation of unknown scripts and languages has become monumental, and the student of the individual subjects in this field will find his task bewildering since, as I have mentioned in my introduction, it is impossible to describe a decipherment or interpretation without to a certain extent being familiar with the script or language in question. A complete bibliography comprising a mere fraction of the existing scientific literature I have consulted for this work would fill many pages. As a result I have compiled a list of suggested reading which I hope will serve two purposes: to elucidate the first steps for those who wish to probe more deeply into the subject and at the same time to give a glimpse into the paths followed by the author himself. I have not included in this bibliography the hitherto unpublished, scholarly, autobiographical and biographical data for which I have to thank many of the scholars referred to in my text.

I suggest the following main informative works on all problems of language:

David Diringer: *The Alphabet. A key to the History of Mankind* (London–New York–Melbourne–Sydney–Cape Town, 1949[2]).

James G. Février: *Histoire de l'écriture* (Paris, 1948).

Hans Jensen: *Die Schrift in Vergangenheit und Gegenwart* (Glückstadt, 1935).

A sound and compact picture of the decipherment of most of the languages dealt with in this work will be found in the exhaustive work by Johannes Friedrich: *Entzifferung verschollener Schriften und Sprachen* (Berlin–Göttingen–Heidelberg, 1954) (*Verständliche Wissenschaft*, Vol. 51).

The four above-mentioned works form the basis of the author's work. Diringer, Février and Jensen contain a wealth of literary excerpts. The older literature is catalogued in the main by Paul Sattler/Götz von Selle: "Bibliographie zur Geschichte der Schrift," *Archiv für Bibliographie*, Supplement 17, Linz/Donau, 1935. H. Jensen's book is announced in a new and revised edition in Berlin for 1957.

The following are a few works dealing with the individual chapters:

CHAPTER I

Miltner, F., "Wesen und Geburt der Schrift", *Historia Mundi*, Vol. III (Berne, 1954).

Tschichold, J., *Geschichte der Schrift in Bildern* (Basel o.J.), 2nd edition.

Weule, K., *Vom Kerbstock zum Alphabet* (Stuttgart, 1915).

CHAPTER II

Brischar, K., "Athanasius Kircher. Ein Lebensbild", *Katholische Studien*, III, 1877, Heft 5.

Ebers, G., *Richard Lepsius. Ein Lebensbild* (Leipzig, 1885).

Erman, A., *Die Entzifferung der Hieroglyphen*, *Sitz.-Ber. d. Berliner Akad. d. Wissenschaften*, 1922, XXVII–XLIII.

Hartleben, H., *Champollion. Sein Leben und sein Werk.*, 2 vols. (Berlin, 1906).

Wiedemann, A., *Die Entzifferung der Hieroglyphen*, *Neue Jahrb. f. d. klass. Altertum*, 51, 1923, 1–15.

CHAPTERS III AND IV

Budge, Sir E. A. W., *The Rise and Progress of Assyriology* (London, 1925).

König, F. W., *Relief und Inschrift des Konigs Dareios I. am Felsen von Bagistan* (Leyden, 1938).

Meier-Lemgo, K., *Engelbert Kämpfer, Stuttgart*, 1937.

Meissner, Br., *Die babylonisch–assyrische Literatur* (Wildpark–Potsdam, 1930).

Pallis, S. A., *The Antiquity of Iraq* (Copenhagen, 1956).

CHAPTER V

Barnett, R. D., "Karatepe, the Key to the Hittite Hieroglyphs", *Anatolian Studies*, III, 1953, 53–95.

Bossert, H. Th., "Šantaš und Kupapa", *Mitteilungen d. Altorient.* Ges. VI/3 (Leipzig, 1932).

Ein hethitisches Königssiegel (Berlin, 1944).

Forrer, E., "Die acht Sprachen der Boghazköi–Inschriften", *Sitz.-Ber. d. preuss. Akad. d. Wiss.*, LIII, 1919, 1029–41.

"Die Entzifferung der hethitischen Bilderschrift", *Forschungen und Fortschritte*, VIII, 1932, pp. 3 et seq.

Die hethitische Bilderschrift (Chicago, 1932).

Frank, C., "Die sogenannten hettitischen Hieroglypheninschriften", *Abh. f. d. Kde. a. Morgenlandes*, XVI/3 (Leipzig, 1923).

Friedrich, J., *Entzifferungsgeschichte der hethitischen Hieroglyphenschrift* (Stuttgart, 1939).

Gelb, I. J., *Hittite Hieroglyphs*, I–III (Chicago, 1931–42).

Hrozný, F. *Die Sprache der Hethiter I* (Leipzig, 1917).

"Die Lösung dez hethitischen Problems," *Mittlgn. d. Dt. Orientges.*, LVI, 1915.

Meriggi, P., "Die hethitische Hieroglyphenschrift. Eine Vorstudie zur Entzifferung", *Zeitschrift f. Assyriologie*, 39, 1930, 165–212.

"Die Entzifferung unbekannter Schriften," *Wiener Vortrag*, Mai 1957.

Remschneider, M., *Die Welt der Hethiter* (Stuttgart, 1954).

Winckler, H., "Nach Boghasköi!" *Der Alte Orient*, Jg. 14, Heft 3 (Leipzig, 1912).

CHAPTER VI

Bauer, H., *Die Entzifferung der Keilschrifttafeln von Ras Schamra* (Halle, 1930).

"Zur Entzifferung der Keilschrift von Ras Schamra," *Forschungen und Fortschritte*, VI, 1930, 306–8.

Dhorme, E., "Déchiffrement des inscriptions pseudo-hiéroglyphiques de Byblos", *Syria*, XXV, 1946–48, I, et seq; "Sur l'ecriture ougaritique," *Revue Biblique*, 1930, 571 et seq., and 1931, 1 et seq.

Driver, G. R., *Semitic Writing from Pictograph to Alphabet* (London, 1954).

Dunand, M., *Byblia Grammata* (Beirut, 1945).

Eissfeldt, O., *Ras Schamra und Sanchunjaton* (Halle, 1939).

Friedrich, J., "Ras Schamra. Ein Uberblick uber Funde und Forschungen", *Der Alte Orient*, 33, Heft 1/2 (Leipzig, 1933).

Jirku, A., *Die Ausgrabugen in Palästina und Syrien* (Halle, 1956).

"Wortschatz und Grammatik der gublitischen Inschriften," *Zeitschrift d. Dt. Morgenland.*, Ges. 102/1952, 201–14.

Schaeffer, C. F. A., *Ugaritica*, 2 vols. (Paris 1939–49).

Virolleaud, Ch. "Les inscriptions cunéiformes de Ras-Shamra", *C.R. de l'Academie des Inscript. et Belles-Lettres*, p. 265, and *Syria*, X, 245–55.

"Le déchiffrement des tablettes alphabétiques de Ras-Shamra," *Syria*, XII, 15–23.

CHAPTER VII

Brandis, J., "Versuch zur Entzifferung der kyprischen Schrift", *Mon.-Ber, d. Preuss. Akad. d. Wiss.*, 1873, 643–71.

Breal, M., "Le déchiffrement des inscriptions cypriotes", *Journal des Savants*, 1877.

Koetschau, P., "Moritz Schmidt", *Bursians Jb. 61, Jb., 12 Jg.* 1889, 83–130.

CHAPTER VIII

Beattie, A. J., "Mr. Ventris' Decipherment of the Minoan Linear B Script", *Journal of Hellenic Studies*, LXXVI, 1956, 1–17.

Eilers, W., "Kretisch–Kretisches." *Betrachtungen zur angeblichen Entzifferung der minoischen Strichschrift B: Forschungen u. Fortschville*, Bd. 31, Heft 11, Nov. 1957, 326–332.

Evans, Sir A. J., *Scripta Minoa I* (Oxford, 1909).

Gordon, Cyrus H., "Notes on Minoan Linear A", *Antiquity*, Sept. 1957, and "Akkadian Tablets in Minoan Dress", ibid., December 1957.

Grumach, E., Bemerkungen zu M. Ventris–J. Chadwick: "Evidence for Greek Dialect in the Mycenaean Archives", *Orientalist. Lit. Zeitung L11*, 7/8.

Merlingen, W., "Die kretische Schrift entziffert", *Der Mittelschullehrer und die Mittelschule 9* (Vienna 1954), 11–13.

Ventris, M., and Chadwick J., "Evidence for Greek Dialect in the Mycenaean Archives", *Journal of Hellenic Studies*, LXXIII, 1953, 84–103.

Documents in Mycenaean Greek (Cambridge, 1956).

CHAPTER IX

Babinger, F., "Eine neuentdeckte ungarische Kerbschrift aus Konstantinopel vom Jahre 1515", *Ungarische Rundschau f. hist. u. soz. Wissenschaften*, III, Jg., 1914, 41–52.

Doblhofer, E., *Byzantinische Diplomaten und östliche Barbaren* (Graz–Vienna–Cologne, 1955).

Thomsen, V., "Déchiffrement des inscriptions de l'Orkhon et de l'Iénisséi", *Bulletin de l'Academie Royale des Sciences et des Lettres de Danemark* (Copenhagen, 1893), 285–99.

"Inscriptions de l'Orkhon déchiffrées", *Mémoires de la Société Finno-Ougrienne V* (Helsingfors, 1896).

CHAPTER X

Buonamici, G., *Epigrafia Etrusca* (Florence, 1932).

Hevesi, M. G. de., "Osterinselschrift und Indusschrift", *Orientalist.* Lit.-Zeitung 1934, Nr. 11.

Meriggi, P., "Zur Indusschrift", *Zeitschr. d. Dt. Morgenl. Ges.*, 87 N.F. 12, 1934, 198–241.

Pallottino, M., *The Etruscans*, Pelican Book, A 310, 1956.

INDEX

Acrology, theory of, 73
Acrophony, 33
Åkerblad, David, 50, 51, 52, 53
Alkim, Dr. Bahadir, 194
Alphabets:
  Armenian, 14
  Egyptian, *vide* Egyptian Scripts
  Etruscan, 299–301
  Genealogy of, 37
  Greek, 34
  Meroitic, 80
  Old Hungarian, 292
  Old Persian cuneiform, 119
  Old Turkish, 287
  Old Semitic, 34
  Phoenician, 15
  Ugaritic, 201–6
"Alpine" script, 15
Altamira, 22
Alvand inscriptions, 115, 117
Ambrogio, Teseo, 295
America, pre-Columbian, 312
Anatolian script, 15
Anquetil-Duperron, Abraham H., 95, 96, 107
Arabic script, 15
"Aroko", 19
Arzawa Letters, 164, 167, 174
Assyrian script, *vide* Cuneiform

Babinger, Franz, 288–90
Babylonian language, 121
Babylonian script, *vide* Cuneiform
Banerjee, R. D., 302
Bankes, William J., 66–9
Barbaro, Giosofat, 87, 88
Barnett, R. D., 179, 258
Barthel, Dr. Thomas, 309–11
Barthélemy, Abbé, 45, 60, 124
Bauer, Hans, 206–16, 299
Beauchamps, Abbe, 124
Beer, E. E. F., 117
Behistun, inscriptions, 85, 110–14, 116–19, 123–7
Belzoni, Giambattista, 64–6
Bennett, Emmett J., 246, 250–3
Bezold, Carl, 133, 142–5
Bilge Kagan, 271, 279–83
Birch, Samuel, 77, 230
Bittel, Kurt, 191
Blegen, Karl W., 245, 259–60
Boghaz-Keui, 155, 165–9
Bor, inscription, 160
Bossert, Helmuth Th., 179, 185–93, 259
Botta, Paul Emile, 97, 232
Brandis, Johannes, 228, 232 f.
Brugsch, Heinrich, 77
Bruyn, Cornelius van, 93–5
Bugge, Sophus, 164
Bumin Kagan, 271, 288, 293
Bunsen, Karl Josias von, 74
Burckhardt, Johann Ludwig, 151 f.
Burnouf, Eugène, 107, 115
Burton, Captain P., 152
Byblos, *vide* Gubla, 221–46

"Cape Fennel", *vide* Râs Shamra
Carchemish, 163 f., 173 f., 188
Cartwright, John, 88, 252, 255 f.
Castren, M. A., 278
Caylus, Count, 96
Cave paintings, 22
Cesnola, Palma di, 229
Chadwick, John, 242, 258 ff.
Champollion, Jean-François, 24, 50–75
Champollion-Figeac, J. J., 62
Chardin, Jean, 90
Chenet, G., 204
Chinese script, 31, 32
Churrian, *vide* Hurrian
Coptic language, 43, 46, 63, 71
Coptic script, 50, 51

Cowley, A. E., 244
Cuneiform:
  Akkadian, *vide* Babylonian, 139 ff.
  Assyrian, *vide* Babylonian, 139 ff.
  Babylonian, 139
  Elamite, 139 ff.
  Hittite, 149 ff.
  Mesopotamian, *vide* Babylonian and Elamite
Curtius, Ernst, 232
Cretan scripts, *vide* Linear "A", 241–5, *and* "B", 241–5
Cryptanalysis, 175, 220
Cyril, Saint, 14
Cyrillic script, 15
Cypriote syllabary, 135, 236, 242
Cypro-Minoan script, 237
Cyprus, 227 ff.
Cyrus II The Great (Kurush), 86
  tomb of, 87

Dacier, Bon Joseph, 72
Dananiyim-Danaans, 196
Darius I (Daryavush), 20, 85
Deecke, Wilhelm, 235
Delitzch, F., 169
Deluge Saga, *vide* Gilgamesh Epic
Demotic, *vide* Egyptian script
Dernschwam, Hans, 288 ff., 291
Determinatives:
  Babylonian, 128
  Egyptian, 82
  Elamite, 125
  Hittite hieroglyphic, 157
Dhorme, Edouard, 213 ff., 219 f.
"Divine" writing, 15
Dunand, Maurice, 203, 221
Dussaud, René, 213

Easter Island inscriptions, 307 ff.
Ebers, Geog, 49
Eckhardt, André, 26, 44
Egyptian:
  Books of the Dead, 66
  scripts, 66–84
  uniconsonantal phonetic signs, 33
Ehelolf, H., 173, 178
Eilers, W., 263
Elamite language, 125
Elteris Kagan, 276
Etruscan script, 297
Evans, Sir Arthur J., 238 ff., 268

Figulla, H. H., 168
Forrer, Emil, 173, 174, 181 f.
Fourier, Jean Baptiste, 58–60
Fox Talbot, William Henry, 131, 133
Frank, Carl, 175
Friedrich, Johannes, 29, 173, 182, 231

Garstang, John, 165
Gelb, Ignace J., 179 f., 192
Gilgamesh Epic, 135–137
Glagolitsa script, 291
Goetze, A., 173
Gordon, Cyrus H., 266
Gori, Francesco, 295
Gouvea, Antonio de, 88
Grotefend, Georg Friedrich, 100–8
Gubla, *vide* Byblos, 221–46
Gublitic script, 221
Guignes, Joseph de, 45, 54, 60
Güterbock, H., 191

Hama, 150 f.
Hama Stones, 151 ff.
Hamath, *vide* Hama
Hammer-Purgstall, Joseph, Baron von, 73
Hammurabi Code, 184
Harappa, 301 f.
Hatti, land of, 149
Hattic, 174
Hebrew script, 15
Heeren, Arnold Hermann, 101
Heikel, A., 278 f.
Herodotus, 20, 38, 103, 116, 281
Hesychius, 233
Hevesy, W. von, 310
Heyne, Christian Gottlob, 100
Hieratic, *vide* Egyptian script
Hieroglyphs:
  Cretan, 265–70
  Egyptian, 66–84
  Hittite, 161–202

Hincks, Edward, 77
Hittite cuneiform, 157 ff.
hieroglyphic, 161–202
royal seal, 156
Horapollo, 39
Hrozný, Friedrich (Bedřich), 168 ff., 242, 304
Humboldt, Alexander von, 74
Humboldt, Wilhelm von, 73
"Human" writing, 15
Hunter, G. R., 302
Hurrian cuneiform, 139, 175, 217
Hystaspes (Vištaspa), 117 f.

Ibrahim, Sheik, *vide* Burckhardt, J. L.
Ideograms, *vide* Ideography, 15, 26
Iguvine tablets, 75, 295
Indians:
Crow, 22
North American, 18
Indus script, 302
Incas, 17
Istemi Kagan, 272, 293

Janson, Karel, 26, 44
Japanese writing, 31
Jaussen, Bishop, 307 f.
Jensen, Hans, 21, 28
Jensen, Peter, 157, 162 f., 176
Jessup, Dr., 152
Jirku, Anton, 221
Johnson, Augustus, 152 f.
Justinian II, Emperor, 273

Kämpfer, Engelbert, 90–3
Kapagan Kagan, 276
Karatepe ("Black Mountain"), 193 f.
Katakana, Syllabary, 32
Kircher, Father Athanasius, S. J., 41, 44
Klaproth, Julius, 73, 278
Knossos Tablets, 241 f., 243–5
Knot writing, *vide* Quipus
Knudtzon, J. A., 164 f.
Kober, Dr. Alice E., 245 ff.
Koch, Councillor, 45
Kohelet the Babylonian, 147
Krall, J., 298
Kristopoulos, K. D., 252

Lang, R. H., 229, 232
Lanzi, Luigi, 295
Lassen, Christian, 116
Layard, Austen Henry, 97, 232
Leibniz, Gottfried Wilhelm, 47
Lepsius, Richard, 74, 76, 82, 259, 295
Letronne, Jean Antoine, 68
Linear "A", *vide* Cretan script
Lone Dog's winter count, 23
Löwenstern, 126 f.
Luvian, 175
Luynes, Duc de, 228

Mackay, E. J. H., 302
Madhu Sarup Vats, 301
Marash, 160
Marash lion, 160
Marshall, Sir John, 307
Mahomet Ali, 66
Menander the Protector, 273
Menant, J., 161
Meriggi, Piero, 176 f., 302, 305
Meroitic script, 216
Mesrop, Saint, 14
Messenger's batons, 16
Messerschmidt, Daniel Gottlieb Leopold, 161, 175, 277
Methodius, Saint, 14
Minet-el-Beida, 203, 205
Mnemonic devices, 16, 19
Mohenjodaro, 301 ff.
Mohl, Julius, 125
Mopsus, 195 f.
Mopsuhestia, 197
Mordtmann, A. D., 156 f.
Müller, D. H., 168
Münter, Friedrich Christian, 98, 99
Murshilish's Plague prayer, 201
Myres, Sir John, 242, 254

Naksh-i-Rustam, 95 ff.
Napoleon, 47, 48, 49
Nesic, *vide* Hittite cuneiform
Niebuhr, Carsten, 46, 48, 93–5

Norris, Edwin, 118, 131
Nsibidi writing, 28

Old Iberian writing, 15
Oppert, Julius, 132 ff.
Orchon inscriptions, 271 ff.
Oshcabawi Petition, 23

Palaic, 175
Palin, Count, 45
Pallottino, Massimo, 300
Parsees, 96
Pasiega Cave, 21
Pehlevi writing, 50, 286
Peiser, F. E., 161
Pernier, L., 267
Persepolis, 95
Petroglyphs, 22, 195 ff.
Phaistos Disc, 267
Picto, *vide* Universal languages, 26, 27
Pictograms, *vide* Picto, 26
Pictography, 21
Pictorial chronicle of the Crow Indians, 22
Pictorial writing, *vide* Pictography
Hittite, *vide* Hittite hieroglyphic
Polyphony of Babylonian cuneiform, 130
Proto-Hattic, *vide* Hattic
Pylos Tablets, 246
Phonetic rebus, 19
Phonetic signs, 31
Phonetic writing, 29–31

Quipus, *vide* Knot writing, 16, 17

Radlov, Wilhelm, 280, 282
Rai Bahadur Daya Ram Sahni, 301
Râs Shamra, 203 ff., 216 ff.
Rask, Rasmus Christian, 106
Rassam, Hormuzd, 135
Rawlinson, Sir Henry C., 108–15, 229
Rich, Claudius James, 97
Rock inscriptions, *vide* Petroglyphs
Roeth, E., 228
Rosellini, Ippolito, 76
Rosetta Stone, 45, 47, 50, 53, 62, 66
Runic writing, 288

Sacy, Sylvestre de, 50, 51, 52, 53, 61, 74
Safo, *vide* Universal languages, 27
Sahak, Katholikos, 14
Salt, Henry, 73
Sandeš, *vide* Santaš
Santaš, 188, 189
Sayce, Archibald Henry, 153 f., 190, 238
Schaeffer, C. A. F., 204
Shamans, Old Turkish, 273
Schliemann, Heinrich, 165, 240
Schmidt, Moritz, 228
Schulz, F. E., 108
Scythians, 281–83
Seyffarth, Gustav, 73
Shorthand systems, 26
Siegismund, Justus, 235
Single letter words, 33
Silva Figueroa, Don Garcia, 88, 89
Sittig, Ernst, 236
Smith, George, 134 ff.
Sommer, F., 152
"Speaking woods", *vide* Easter Island inscriptions
Steinherr, Franz, 195
St. Jacquet, E. V., 117
Street traffic signs, 26
Sturtevant, E. H., 173
Subhi Pasha, 152
Sumerian, 28
Sundwall, Johannes, 242
Syllabary Katakana, 31
Syllabic writing, *vide also* Gublitic; Hittite hieroglyphic; Japanese writing; Babylonian and Elamite; Cretan Linear "A" and "B"; Cypriote syllabary; Katakana syllabary

Tallies, 16, 17
Tarkumuwa Boss, 156 ff.
Tarkondemos Boss, *vide* Tarkumuwa Boss

Texier, Charles, 155
Thlegedi, J., 291
Thompson, R. C., 173
Thomsen, Vilhelm, 280, 282 ff.
Tonjukuk, 271, 288 f.
Torp, A., 164
Turxanthros, 274 f., 281
Tychsen, Oluf Gerhard, 45, 97

Ugaritic script, *vide* Râs Shamra
Uigur script, 283–5
Umbrian script and language, 295
Universal languages, 26, 27

Valle, Pietro della, 98
Vater, Johann Severin, 53
Ventris, Michael, 242, 251 ff.
Virolleaud, Charles, 203, 208 f., 219 f.
Vocalization of the alphabet, 34–7

Wace, A. J., 244
Wampum belt, 18, 19
Warburton, William, 44
Ward, Hayes, 153
Weidner, Ernst, 171
"White Huns", 272
"White Harbour", *vide* Minet-el-Beida
Westergaard, Niels Ludwig, 122
Winckler, Hugo, 165, 166
Wright, William, 153, 160
Writing:
- definition of, 15, 16
- forerunners of, 15, 22
- nature of, 15, 16
- normalisation of, 26 f.
- origins of, 15
- phonetisation of, 29
- types of, 15–29, 31
- value of, 13, 14

Writing materials, 36
Wulfila, 14

Xerxes, 87

Yazilikaya, 155–7
Yebu, 19
Yoruba, 19
Young, Thomas, 50, 52, 53, 54, 63, 68
Yukagirian love letters, 24, 25

Zoëga, Johann Georg, 45, 54